BATTLE ROYALE

KOUSHUN TAKAMI & MASAYUKI TAGUCHI

SHIRO IWA Junior High School - Grade 9/Class B - Student Roster

Boys: 21 - Girls: 21 - Total: 42

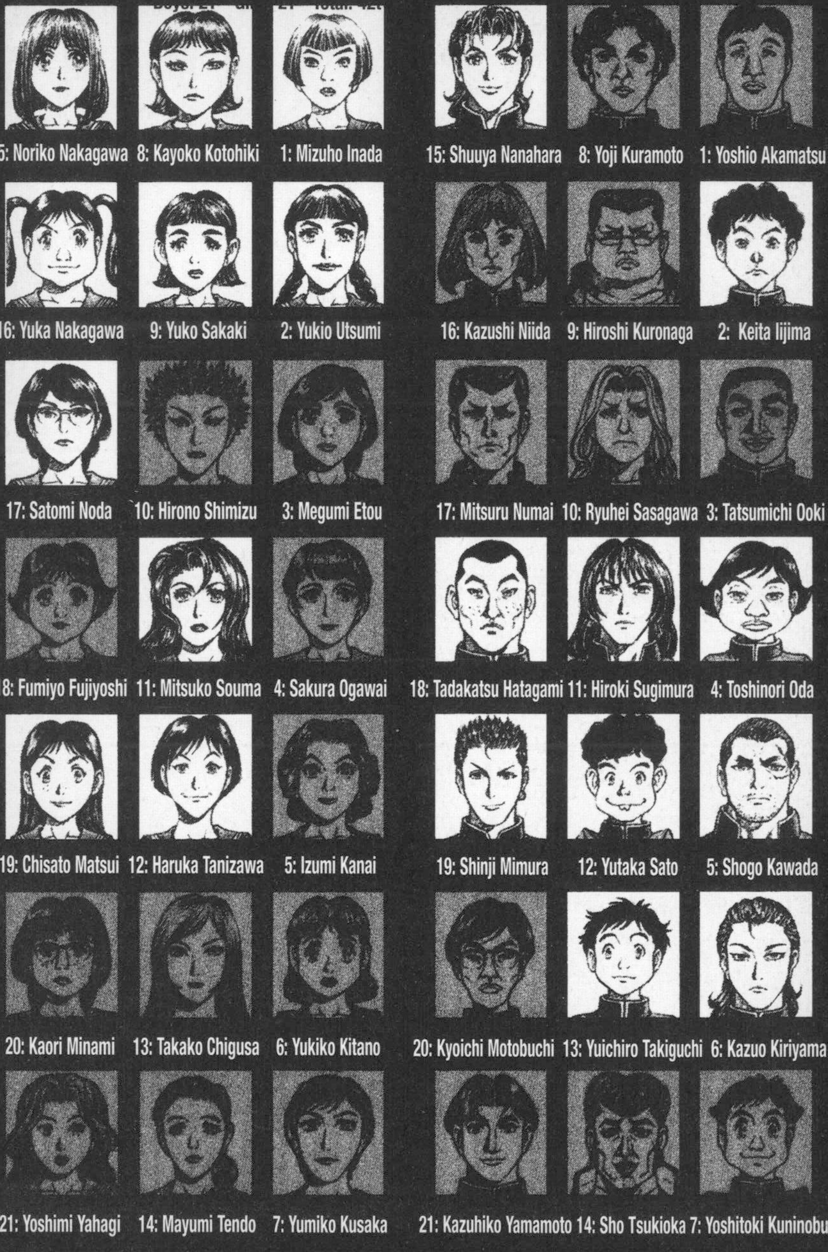

15: Noriko Nakagawa	8: Kayoko Kotohiki	1: Mizuho Inada	15: Shuuya Nanahara	8: Yoji Kuramoto	1: Yoshio Akamatsu
16: Yuka Nakagawa	9: Yuko Sakaki	2: Yukio Utsumi	16: Kazushi Niida	9: Hiroshi Kuronaga	2: Keita Iijima
17: Satomi Noda	10: Hirono Shimizu	3: Megumi Etou	17: Mitsuru Numai	10: Ryuhei Sasagawa	3: Tatsumichi Ooki
18: Fumiyo Fujiyoshi	11: Mitsuko Souma	4: Sakura Ogawai	18: Tadakatsu Hatagami	11: Hiroki Sugimura	4: Toshinori Oda
19: Chisato Matsui	12: Haruka Tanizawa	5: Izumi Kanai	19: Shinji Mimura	12: Yutaka Sato	5: Shogo Kawada
20: Kaori Minami	13: Takako Chigusa	6: Yukiko Kitano	20: Kyoichi Motobuchi	13: Yuichiro Takiguchi	6: Kazuo Kiriyama
21: Yoshimi Yahagi	14: Mayumi Tendo	7: Yumiko Kusaka	21: Kazuhiko Yamamoto	14: Sho Tsukioka	7: Yoshitoki Kuninobu

BATTLE ROYALE

BY
Koushun Takami & Masayuki Taguchi

VOL. 7

LOS ANGELES • TOKYO • LONDON • HAMBURG

Translator - Tomo Iwo
English Adaptation - Keith Giffen
Associate Editor - Tim Beedle
Retouch & Lettering - Joseph Mariano
Cover Layout & Design - Gary Shum

Editor - Rob Tokar
Digital Imaging Manager - Chris Buford
Pre-Press Manager - Antonio DePietro
Production Managers - Jennifer Miller, Mutsumi Miyazaki
Art Director - Matt Alford
Managing Editor - Jill Freshney
VP of Production - Ron Klamert
President & C.O.O. - John Parker
Publisher & C.E.O. - Stuart Levy

E-mail: info@TOKYOPOP.com
Come visit us online at www.TOKYOPOP.com

A  Manga

TOKYOPOP Inc.
5900 Wilshire Blvd. Suite 2000
Los Angeles, CA 90036

Battle Royale Vol. 7

BATTLE ROYALE vol. 7 ©2002 Koushun Takami/Masayuki Taguchi. All rights reserved.
First published in Japan in 2002 by Akita Publishing Co., Ltd. Tokyo
English translation rights arranged through Akita Publishing Co., Ltd.

English text copyright © 2004 TOKYOPOP Inc.

ISBN: 1-59182-419-2

First TOKYOPOP® printing: June 2004

10 9 8 7 6 5 4 3 2

Printed in the USA

BATTLE ROYALE
STORY THUS FAR

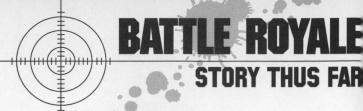

In the near future, a random class of 9th graders has been kidnapped, marooned on an island, and forced to compete on The Program, a popular reality show that requires its contestants to battle to the death.

Shuuya Nanahara, Shogo Kawada and Noriko Nakagawa have banded together, forming an alliance that's united in their determination to get off the island. Since waking to the nightmare of The Program, they've weathered challenge after unthinkable challenge, but even they weren't prepared for a showdown with the relentless Kazuo Kiriyama, a cold, uncaring, heavily armed student determined to win the game. Finding themselves in an open field with very little cover, Shuuya made a break from the group, drew Kiriyama's fire and gave his teammates a chance to escape. However, it was a sacrifice that came at a great cost. Taking a shot in the back, Shuuya nearly became Kazuo's latest kill, a tragedy prevented by a last-minute save by Hiroki Sugimura, who escaped with Shuuya off a cliff...into the hands of a mysterious--and very well-armed--group of young ladies.

Meanwhile, Shinji and Yutaka are on the verge of completing their plan to take out the Program command center. Under a cloak of secrecy, using objects found on the island and a special "gift" from Shinji's uncle, they've assembled a bomb. All they need do now is deliver it...

BATTLE ROYALE
KOUSHUN TAKAMI & MASAYUKI TAGUCHI

TABLE OF CONTENTS

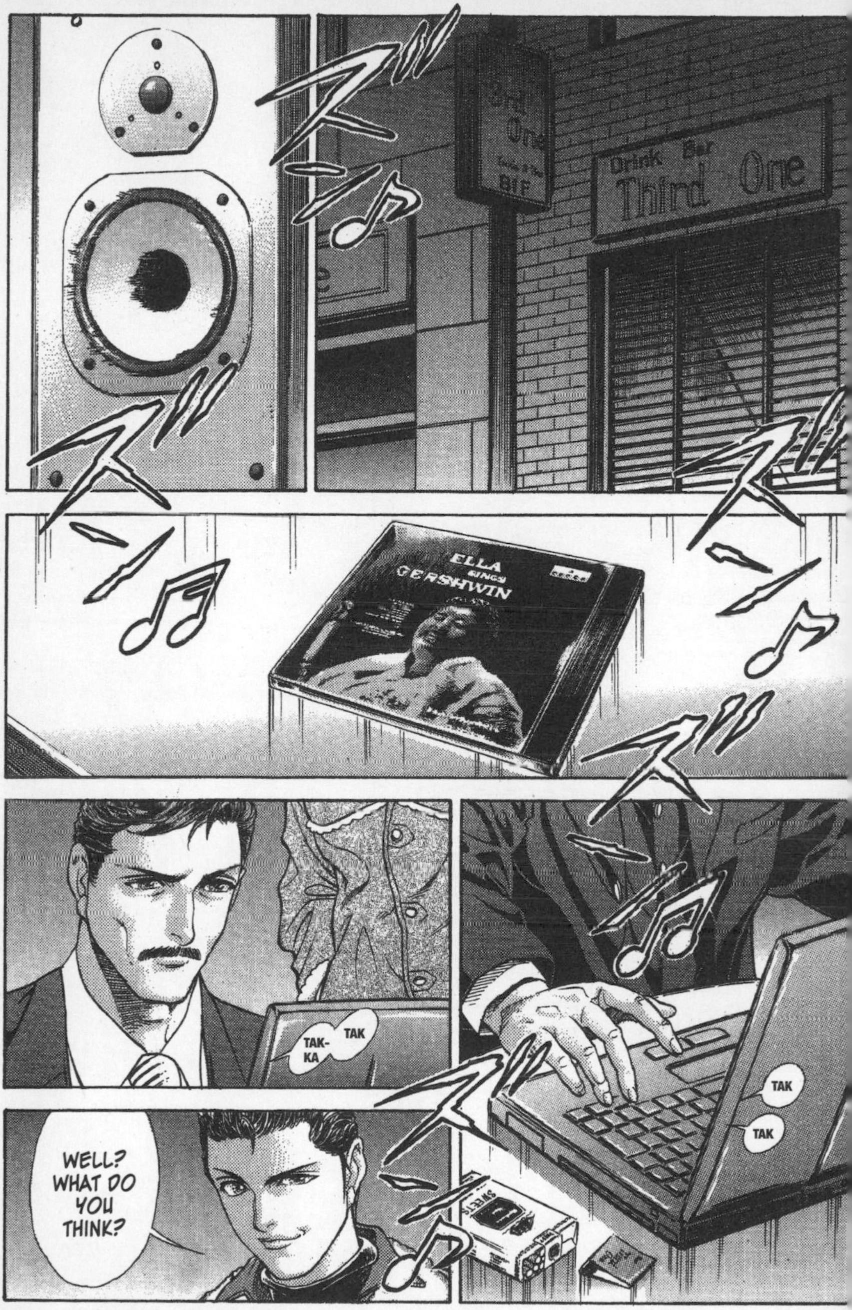
Drink Bar Third One
ELLA sings GERSHWIN
TAK
TAK
TAK-KA TAK
WELL? WHAT DO YOU THINK?

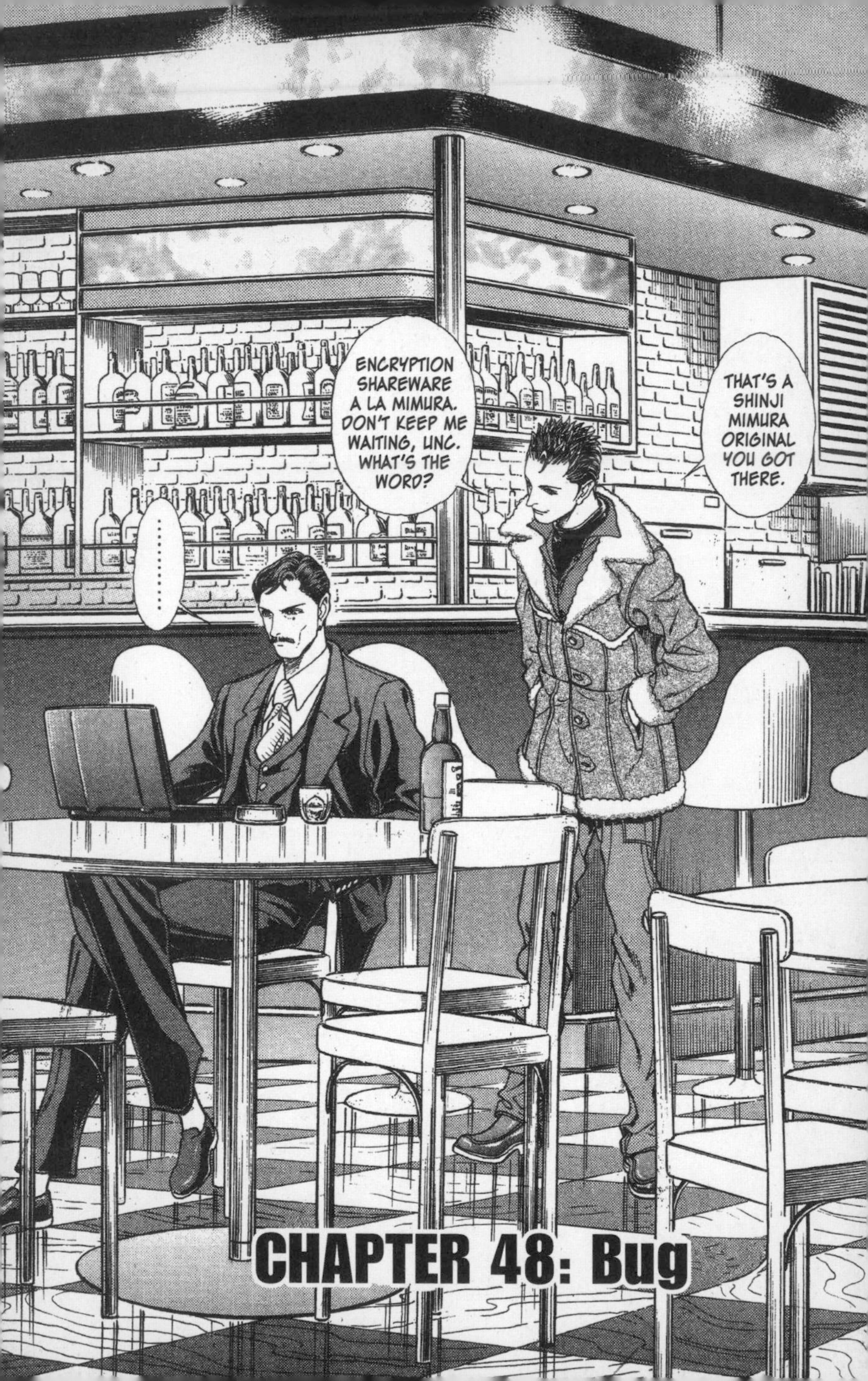
THAT'S A SHINJI MIMURA ORIGINAL YOU GOT THERE.
ENCRYPTION SHAREWARE A LA MIMURA. DON'T KEEP ME WAITING, UNC. WHAT'S THE WORD?
......
CHAPTER 48: Bug

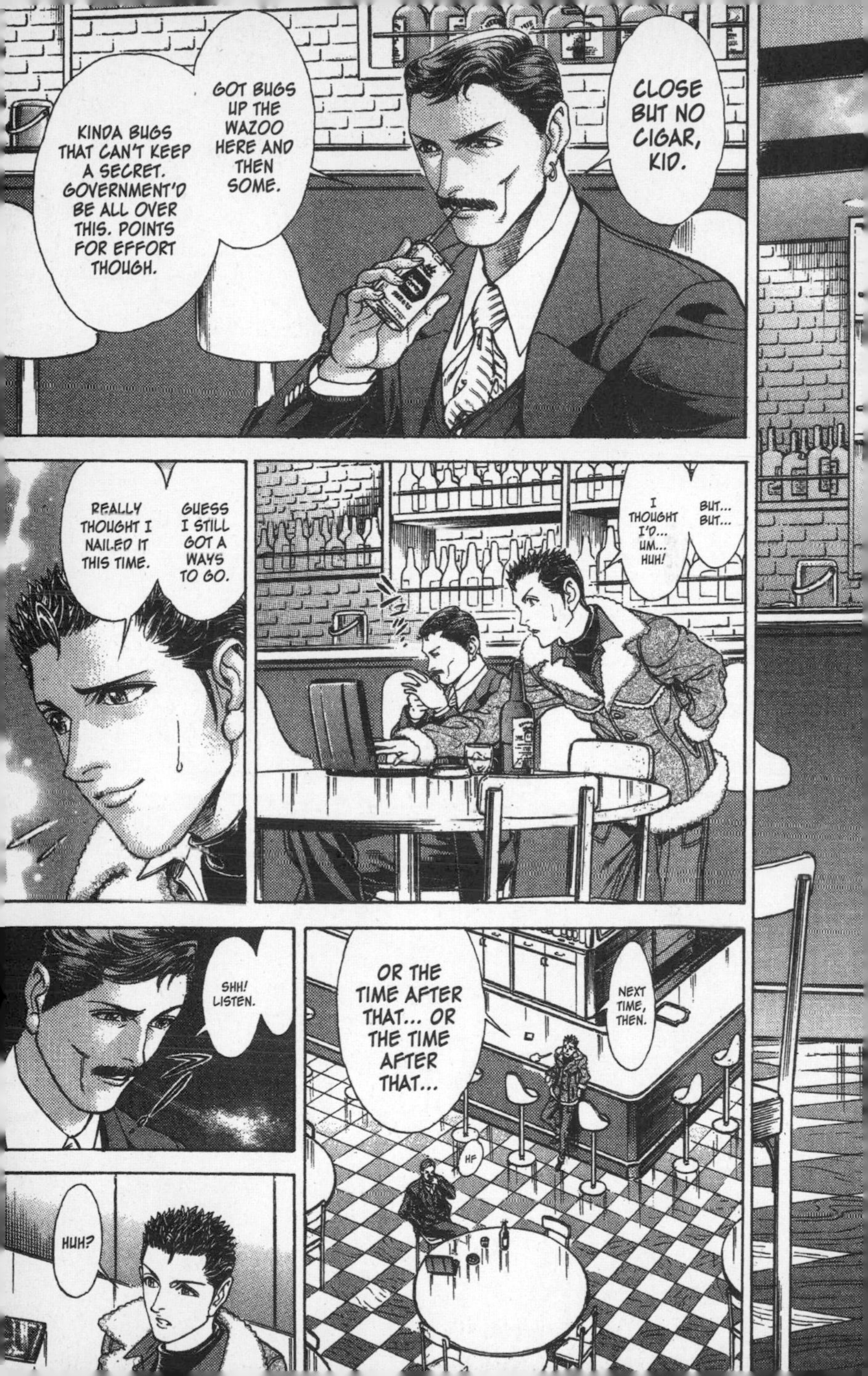
CLOSE BUT NO CIGAR, KID.
GOT BUGS UP THE WAZOO HERE AND THEN SOME.
KINDA BUGS THAT CAN'T KEEP A SECRET. GOVERNMENT'D BE ALL OVER THIS. POINTS FOR EFFORT THOUGH.
BUT... BUT...
I THOUGHT I'D... UM... HUH!
GUESS I STILL GOT A WAYS TO GO.
REALLY THOUGHT I NAILED IT THIS TIME.
NEXT TIME, THEN.
OR THE TIME AFTER THAT... OR THE TIME AFTER THAT...
HF
SHH! LISTEN.
HUH?

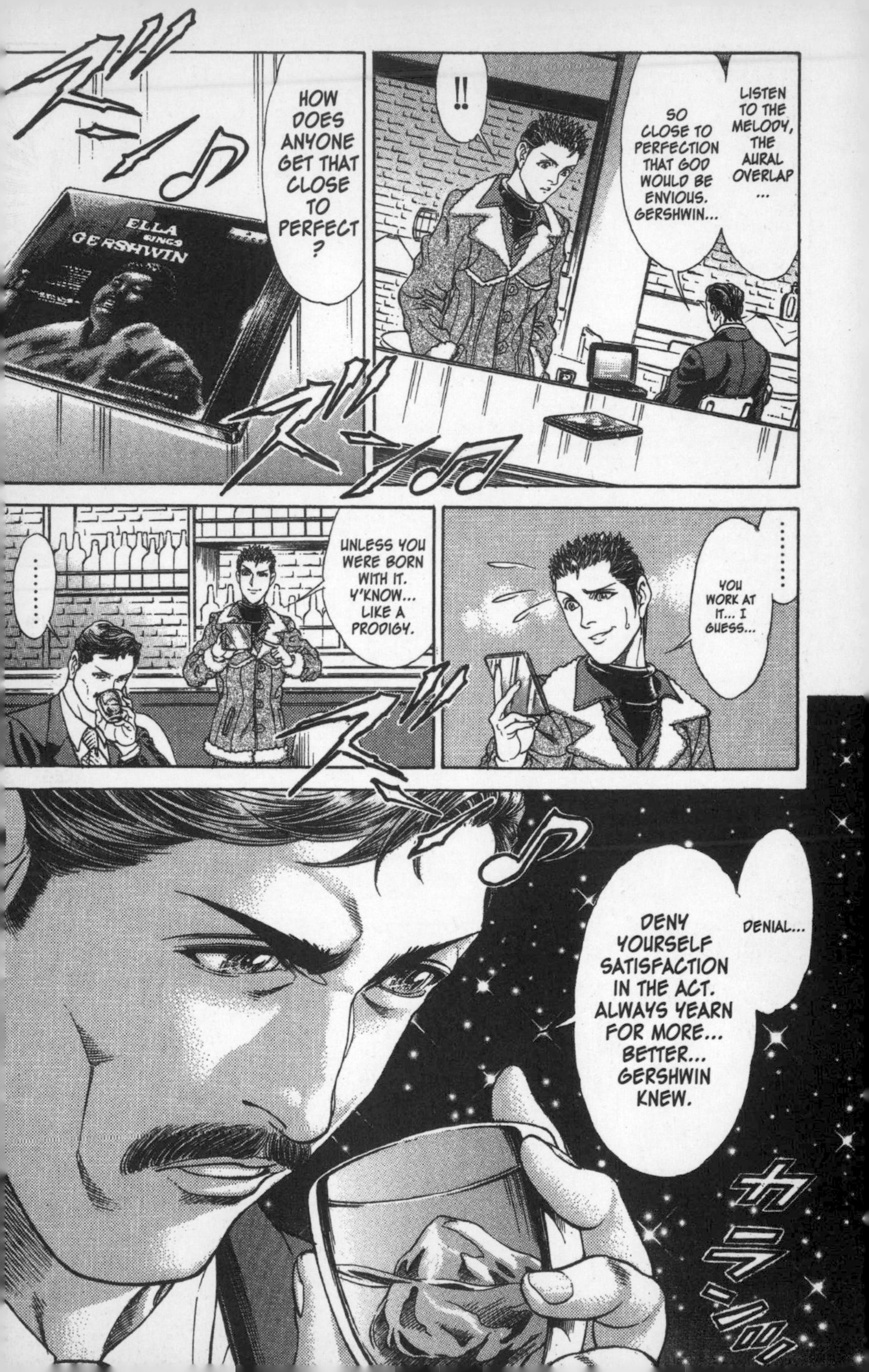
LISTEN TO THE MELODY, THE AURAL OVERLAP ...
SO CLOSE TO PERFECTION THAT GOD WOULD BE ENVIOUS. GERSHWIN...
!!
ELLA SINGS GERSHWIN
HOW DOES ANYONE GET THAT CLOSE TO PERFECT?
......
YOU WORK AT IT... I GUESS...
UNLESS YOU WERE BORN WITH IT. Y'KNOW... LIKE A PRODIGY.
......
DENIAL...
DENY YOURSELF SATISFACTION IN THE ACT. ALWAYS YEARN FOR MORE... BETTER... GERSHWIN KNEW.

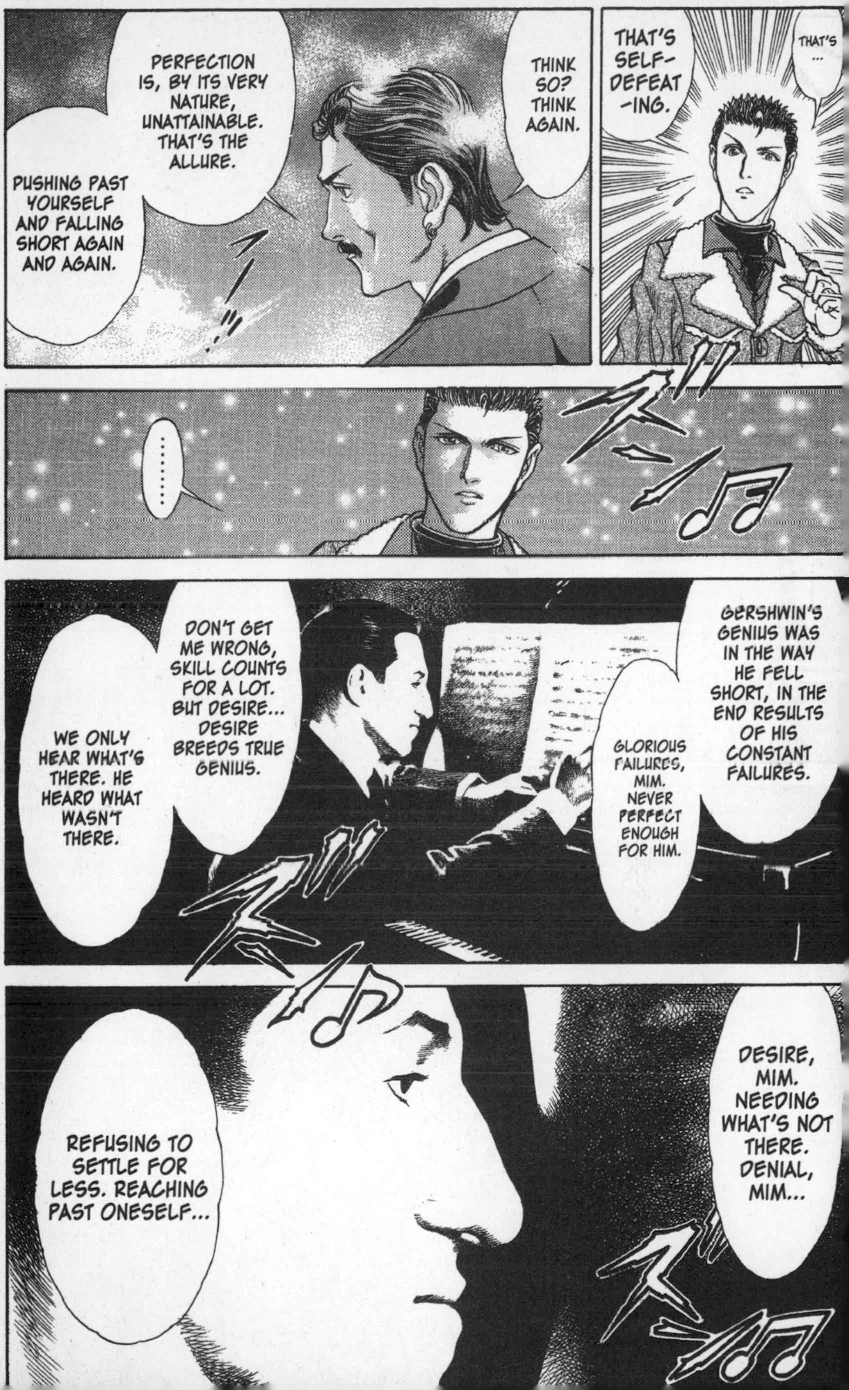
THAT'S ...
THAT'S SELF-DEFEAT-ING.
THINK SO? THINK AGAIN.
PERFECTION IS, BY ITS VERY NATURE, UNATTAINABLE. THAT'S THE ALLURE.
PUSHING PAST YOURSELF AND FALLING SHORT AGAIN AND AGAIN.
....
GERSHWIN'S GENIUS WAS IN THE WAY HE FELL SHORT, IN THE END RESULTS OF HIS CONSTANT FAILURES.
GLORIOUS FAILURES, MIM. NEVER PERFECT ENOUGH FOR HIM.
DON'T GET ME WRONG, SKILL COUNTS FOR A LOT. BUT DESIRE... DESIRE BREEDS TRUE GENIUS.
WE ONLY HEAR WHAT'S THERE. HE HEARD WHAT WASN'T THERE.
DESIRE, MIM. NEEDING WHAT'S NOT THERE. DENIAL, MIM...
REFUSING TO SETTLE FOR LESS. REACHING PAST ONESELF...

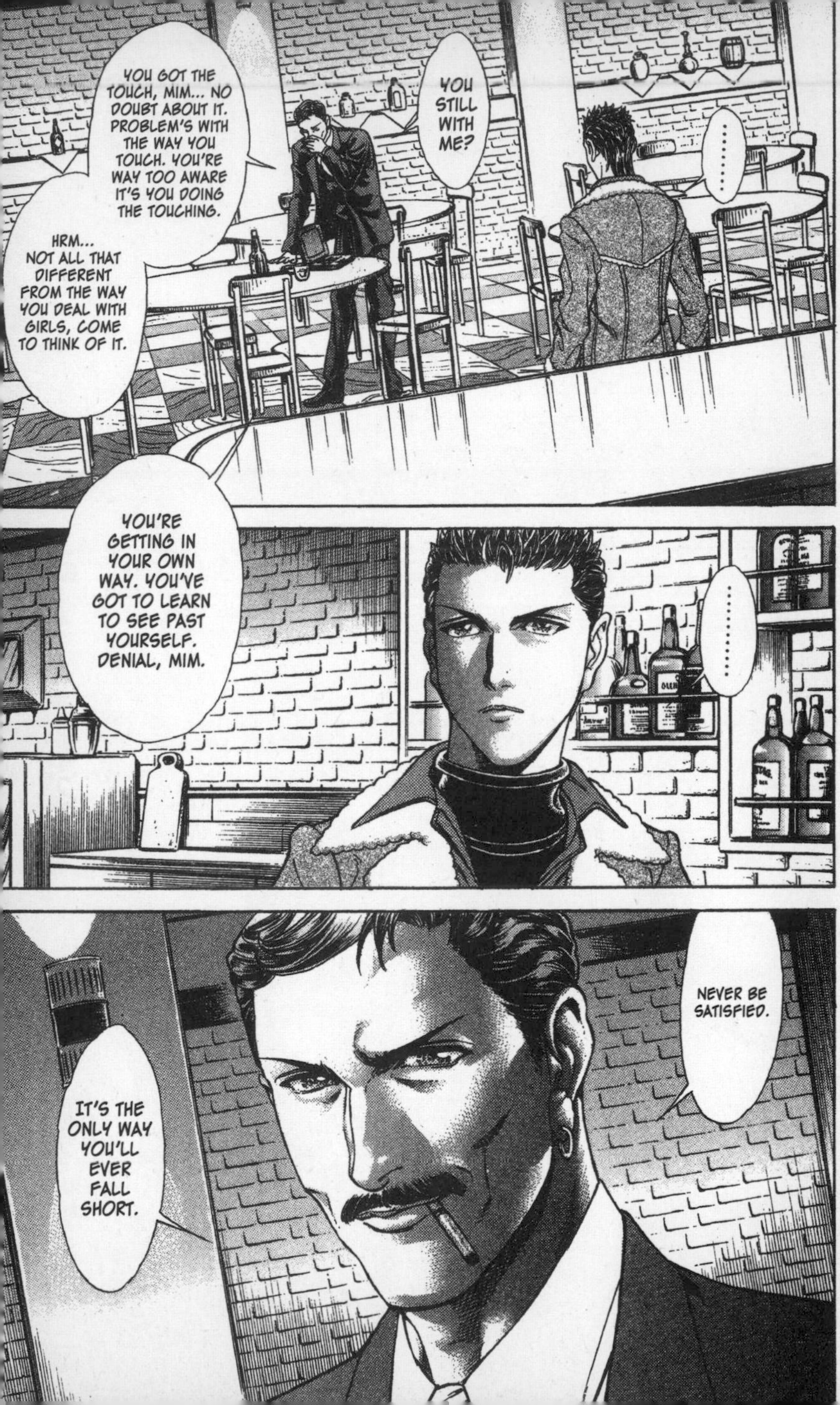
YOU GOT THE TOUCH, MIM... NO DOUBT ABOUT IT. PROBLEM'S WITH THE WAY YOU TOUCH. YOU'RE WAY TOO AWARE IT'S YOU DOING THE TOUCHING.
HRM... NOT ALL THAT DIFFERENT FROM THE WAY YOU DEAL WITH GIRLS, COME TO THINK OF IT.
YOU STILL WITH ME?
......
YOU'RE GETTING IN YOUR OWN WAY. YOU'VE GOT TO LEARN TO SEE PAST YOURSELF. DENIAL, MIM.
......
NEVER BE SATISFIED.
IT'S THE ONLY WAY YOU'LL EVER FALL SHORT.

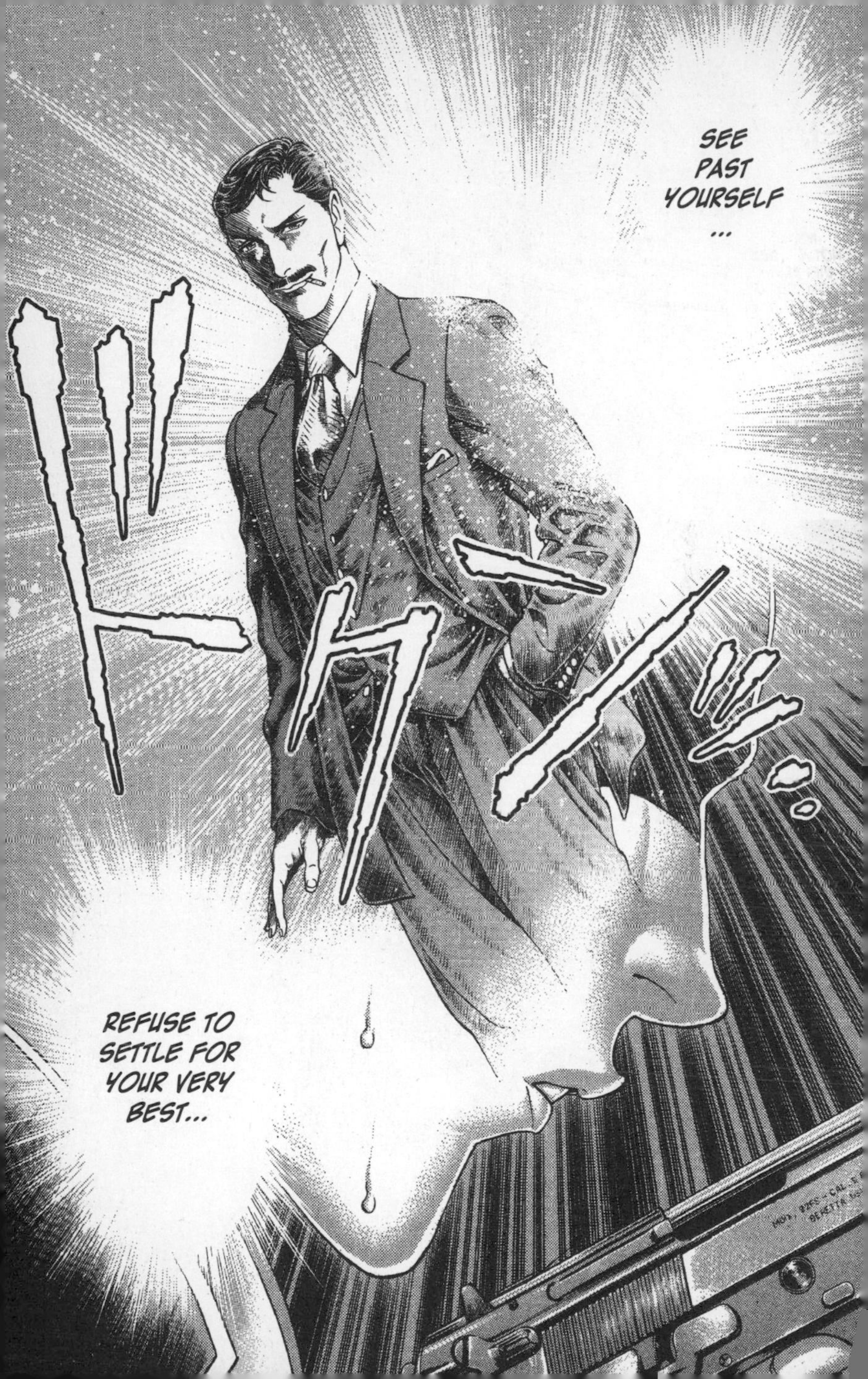
SEE PAST YOURSELF ...
REFUSE TO SETTLE FOR YOUR VERY BEST...

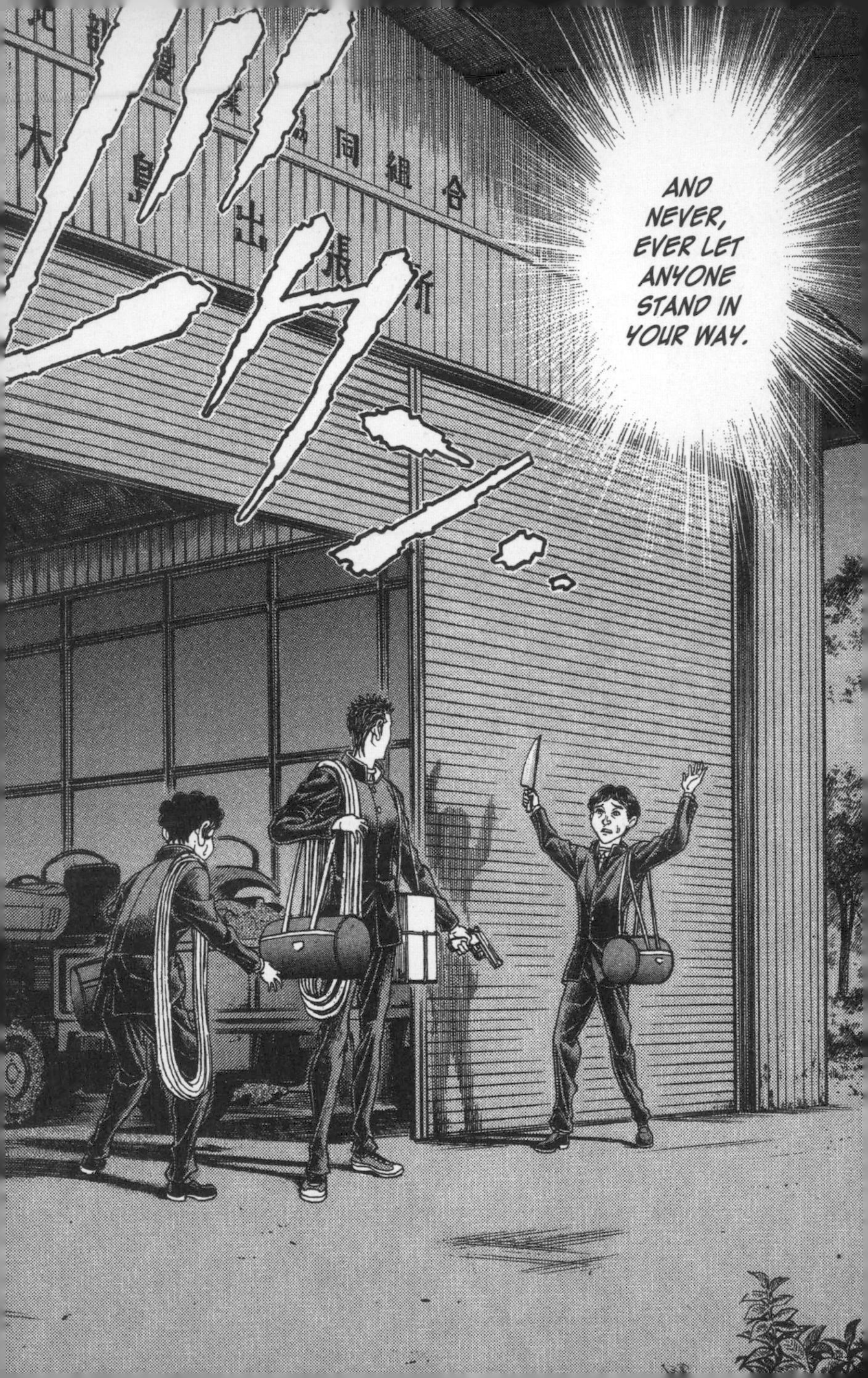
AND NEVER, EVER LET ANYONE STAND IN YOUR WAY.

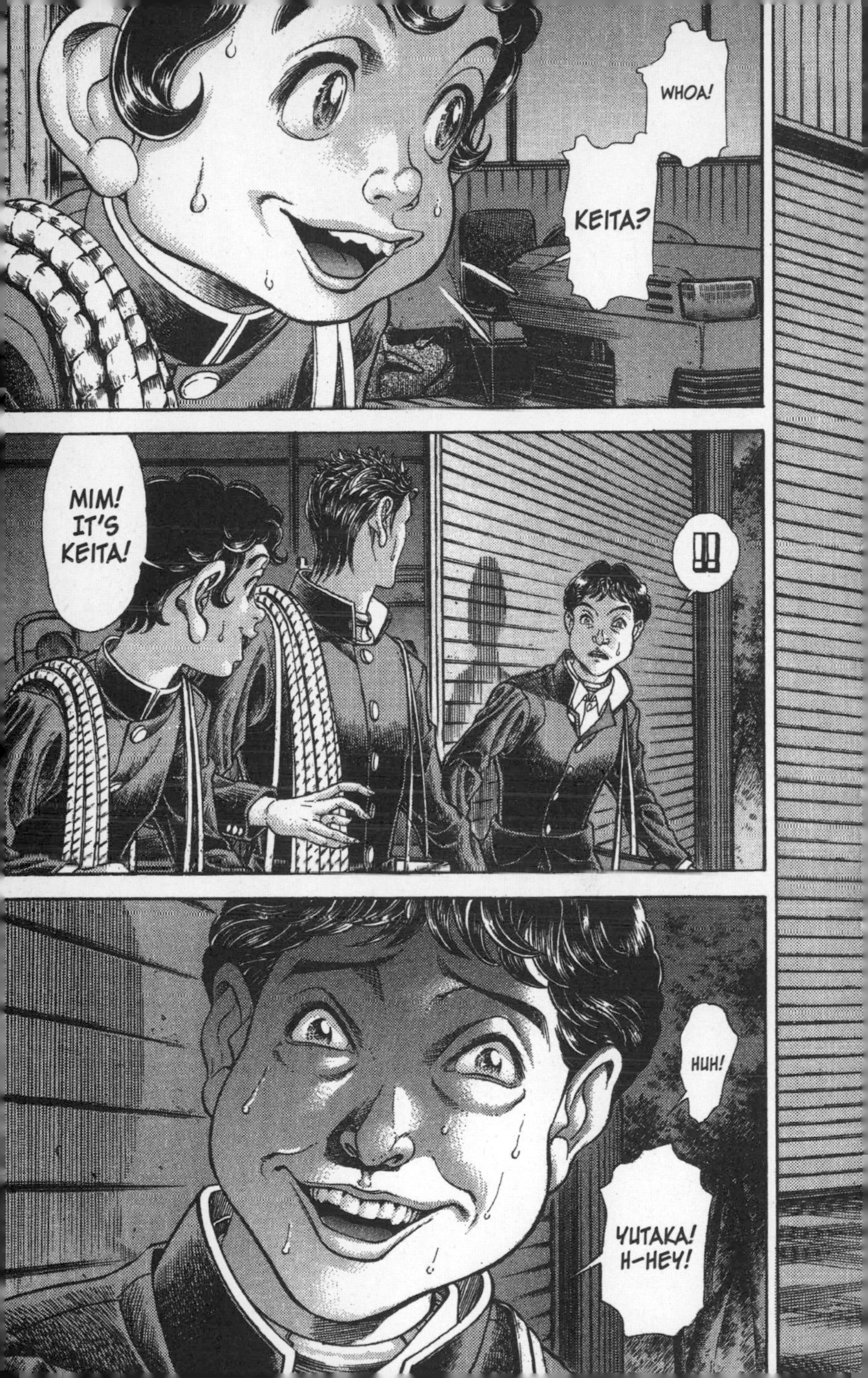
WHOA!
KEITA?
!!
MIM! IT'S KEITA!
HUH!
YUTAKA! H-HEY!

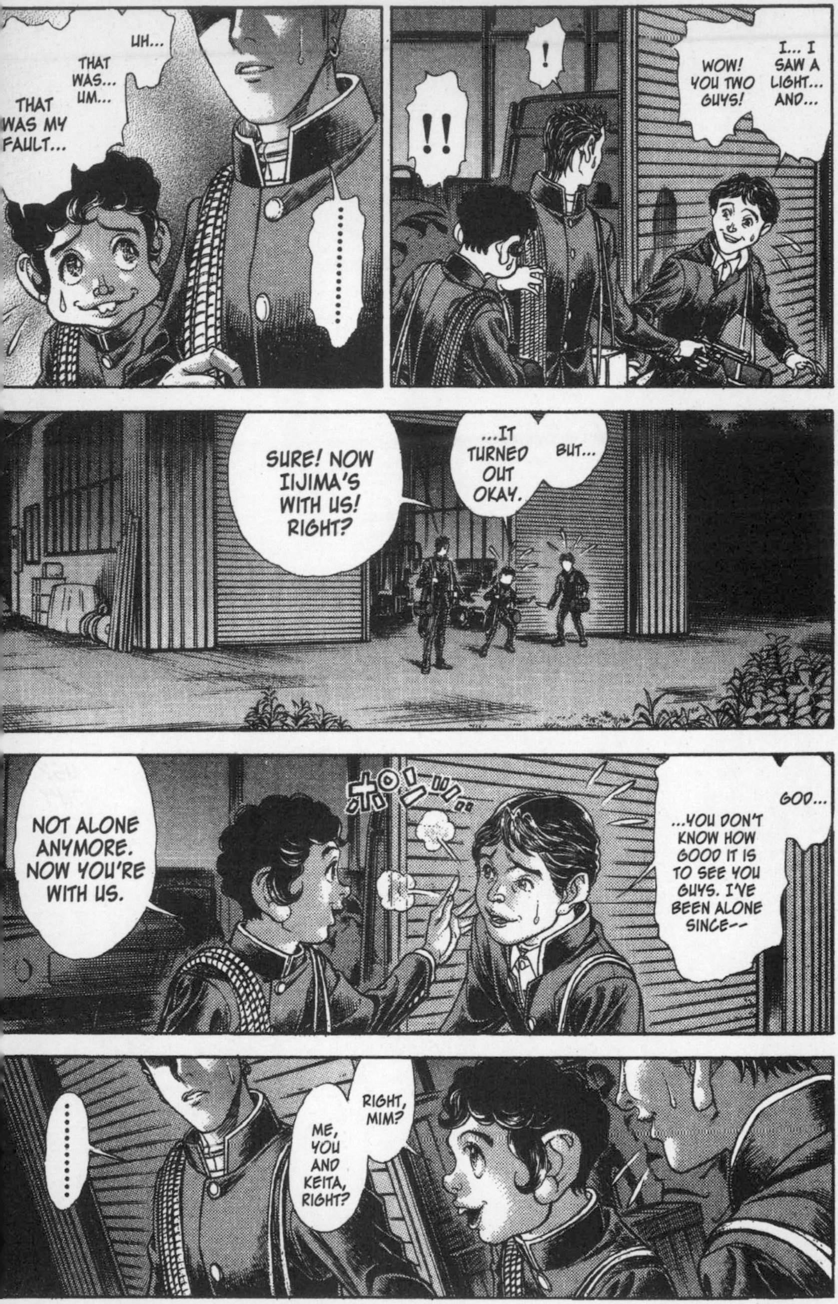
I... I SAW A LIGHT... AND...
WOW! YOU TWO GUYS!
!
!!
UH...
THAT WAS... UM...
THAT WAS MY FAULT...
......
BUT...
...IT TURNED OUT OKAY.
SURE! NOW IIJIMA'S WITH US! RIGHT?
GOD...
...YOU DON'T KNOW HOW GOOD IT IS TO SEE YOU GUYS. I'VE BEEN ALONE SINCE--
NOT ALONE ANYMORE. NOW YOU'RE WITH US.
RIGHT, MIM?
ME, YOU AND KEITA, RIGHT?
......

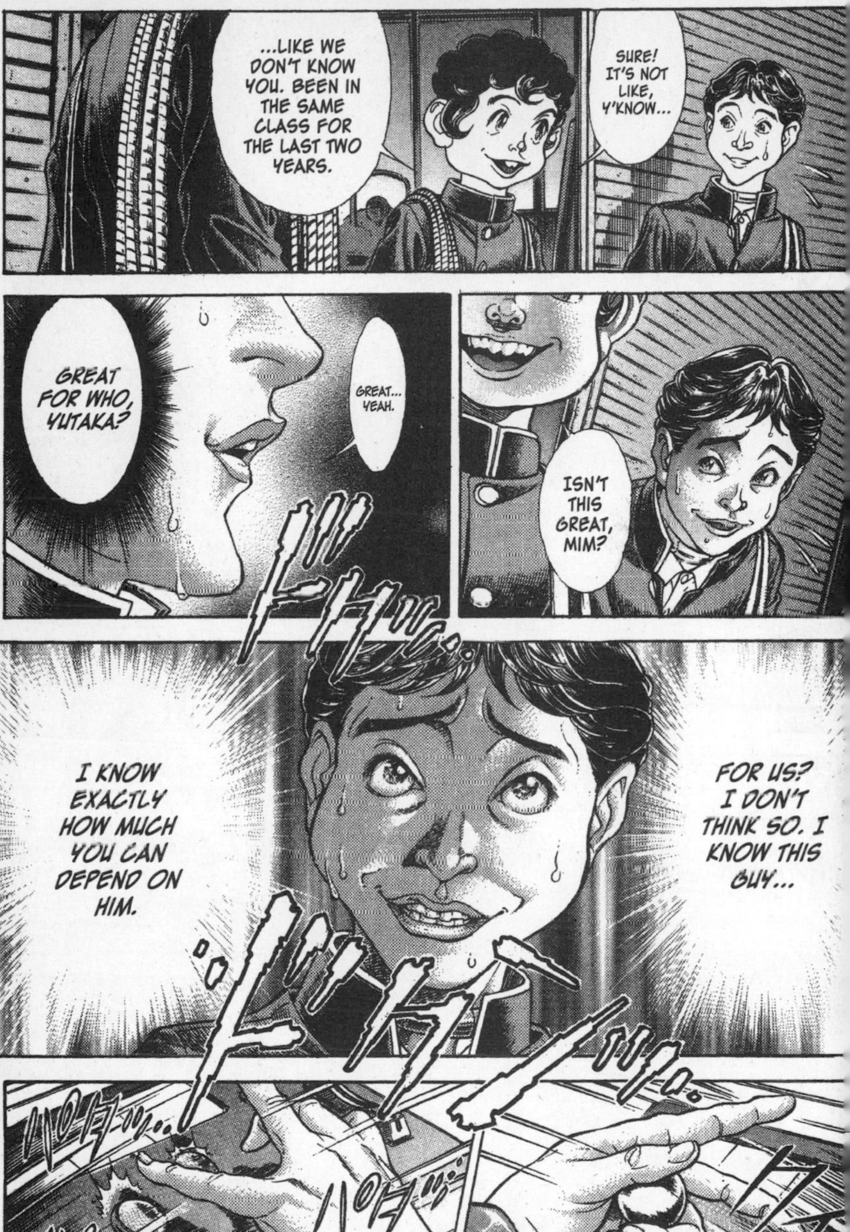
SURE! IT'S NOT LIKE, Y'KNOW...
...LIKE WE DON'T KNOW YOU. BEEN IN THE SAME CLASS FOR THE LAST TWO YEARS.
ISN'T THIS GREAT, MIM?
GREAT... YEAH.
GREAT FOR WHO, YUTAKA?
FOR US? I DON'T THINK SO. I KNOW THIS GUY...
I KNOW EXACTLY HOW MUCH YOU CAN DEPEND ON HIM.

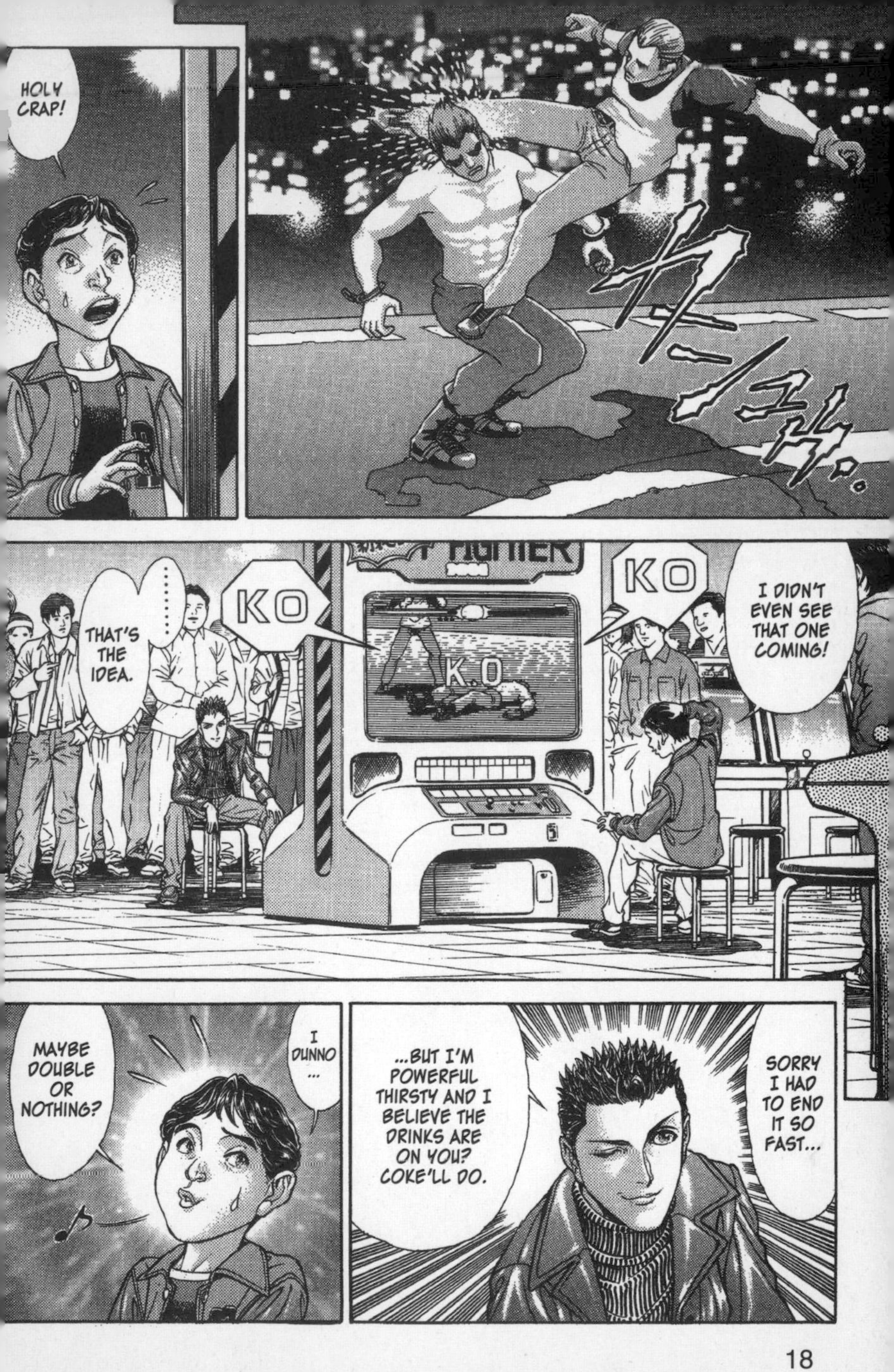

HOLY CRAP!
I DIDN'T EVEN SEE THAT ONE COMING!
KO
KO
......
THAT'S THE IDEA.
SORRY I HAD TO END IT SO FAST...
...BUT I'M POWERFUL THIRSTY AND I BELIEVE THE DRINKS ARE ON YOU? COKE'LL DO.
I DUNNO...
MAYBE DOUBLE OR NOTHING?

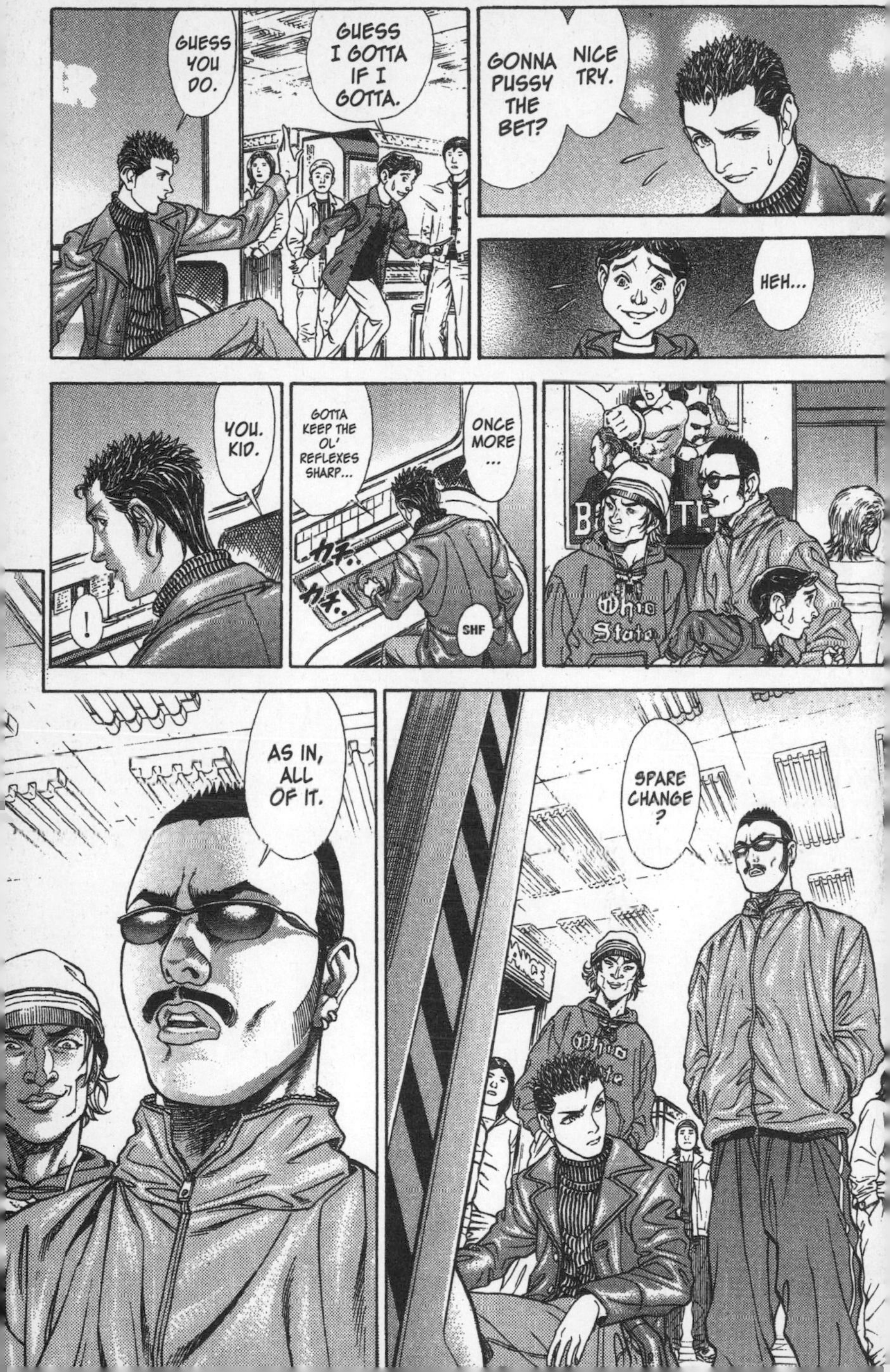
NICE TRY.
GONNA PUSSY THE BET?
HEH...
GUESS I GOTTA IF I GOTTA.
GUESS YOU DO.
ONCE MORE ...
GOTTA KEEP THE OL' REFLEXES SHARP...
カチ
カチ
SHF
YOU. KID.
!
SPARE CHANGE ?
AS IN, ALL OF IT.

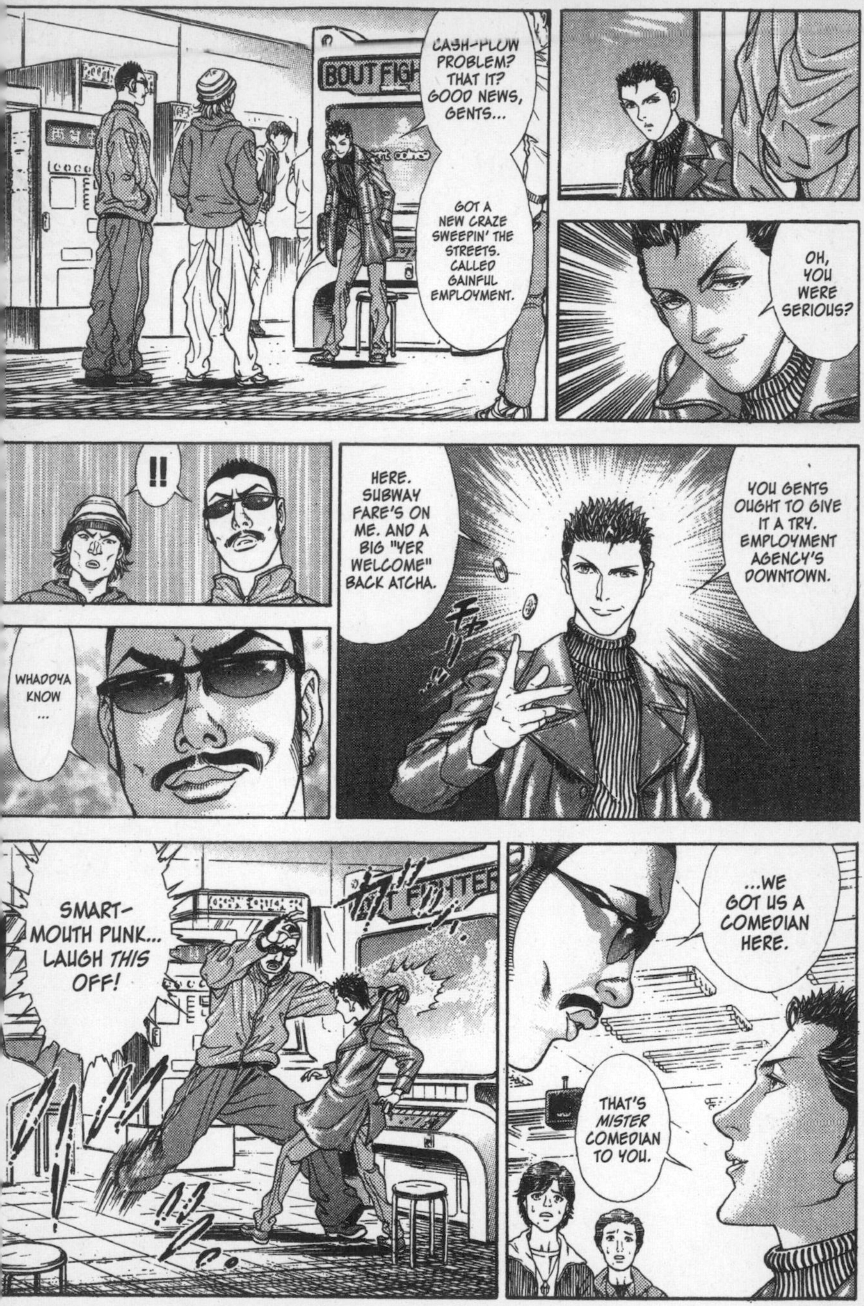
OH, YOU WERE SERIOUS?
CASH-FLOW PROBLEM? THAT IT? GOOD NEWS, GENTS...
GOT A NEW CRAZE SWEEPIN' THE STREETS. CALLED GAINFUL EMPLOYMENT.
BOUT FIGH
YOU GENTS OUGHT TO GIVE IT A TRY. EMPLOYMENT AGENCY'S DOWNTOWN.
HERE. SUBWAY FARE'S ON ME. AND A BIG "YER WELCOME" BACK ATCHA.
!!
WHADDOYA KNOW ...
...WE GOT US A COMEDIAN HERE.
THAT'S *MISTER* COMEDIAN TO YOU.
SMART-MOUTH PUNK... LAUGH *THIS* OFF!

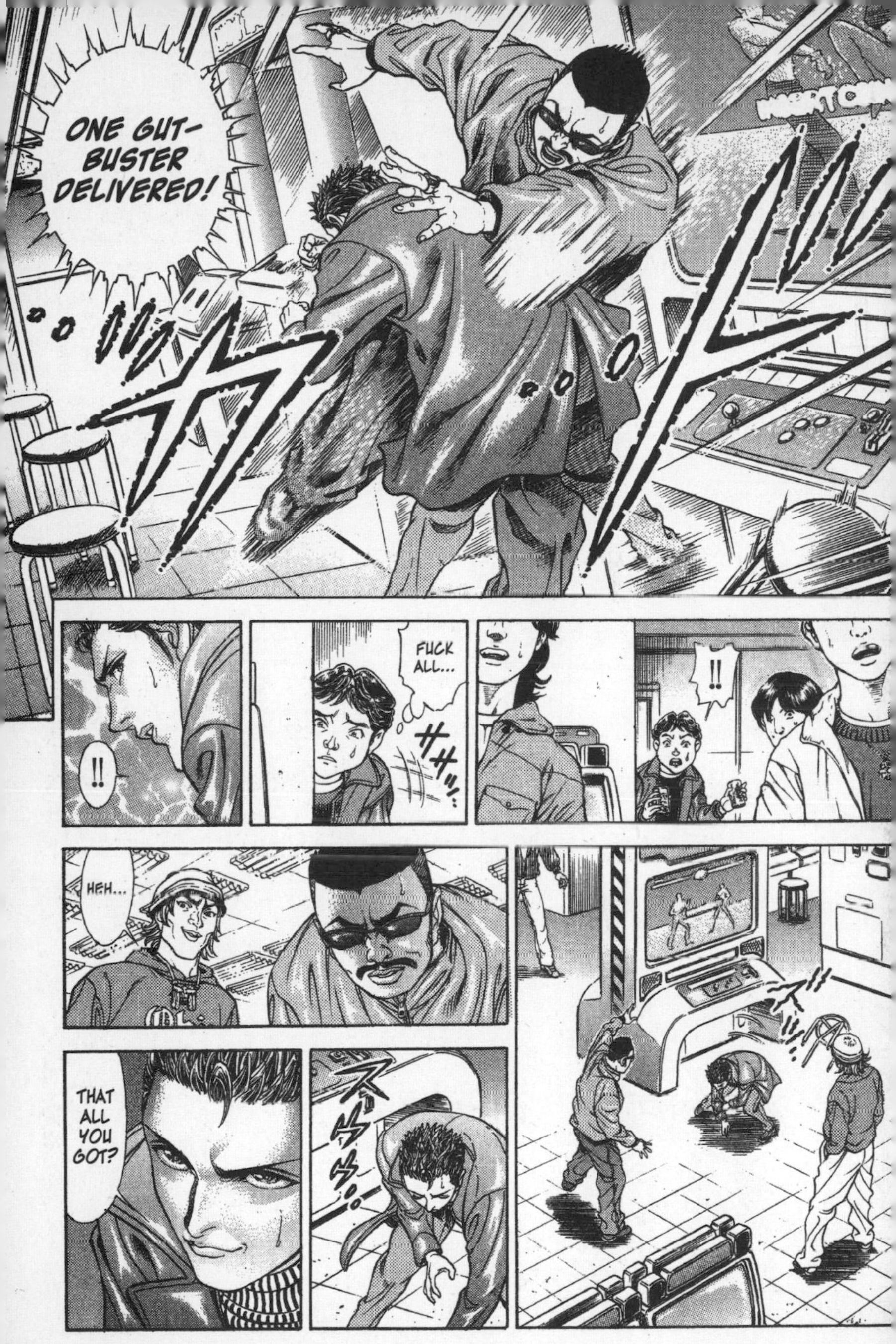
ONE GUT-BUSTER DELIVERED!
!!
FUCK ALL...
!!
HEH...
THAT ALL YOU GOT?

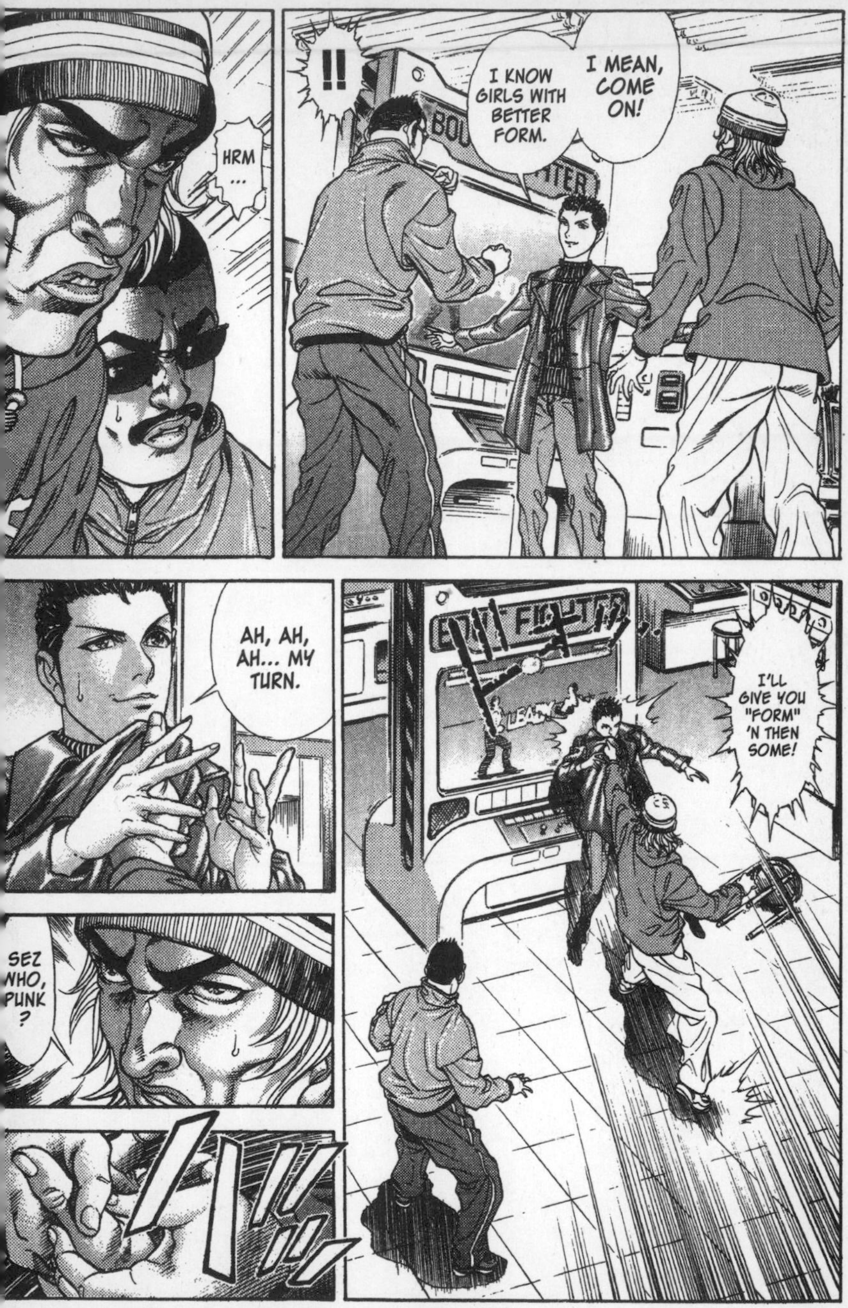
I MEAN, COME ON!
I KNOW GIRLS WITH BETTER FORM.
!!
HRM ...
I'LL GIVE YOU "FORM" 'N THEN SOME!
AH, AH, AH... MY TURN.
SEZ WHO, PUNK ?

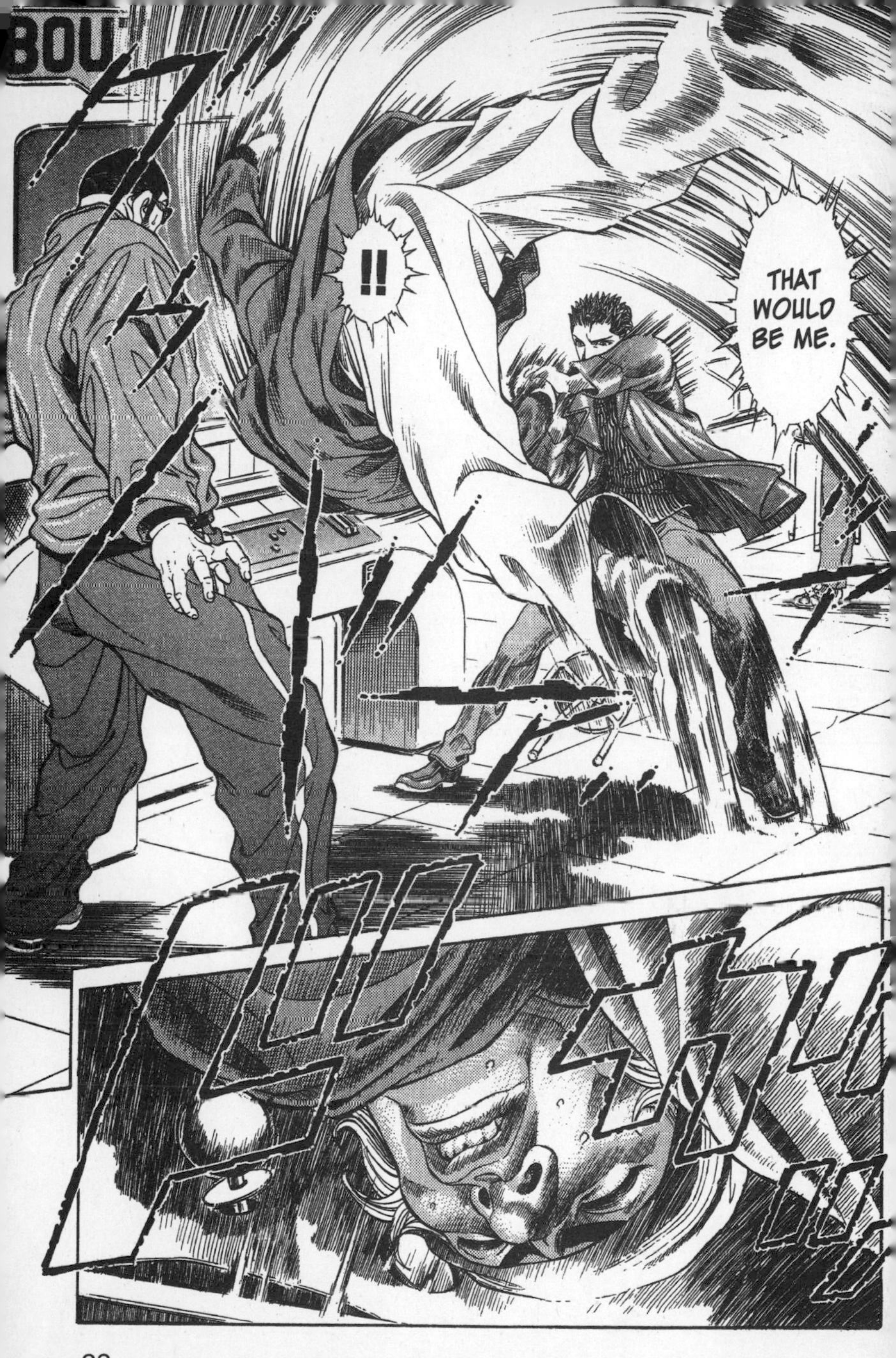
THAT WOULD BE ME.
!!

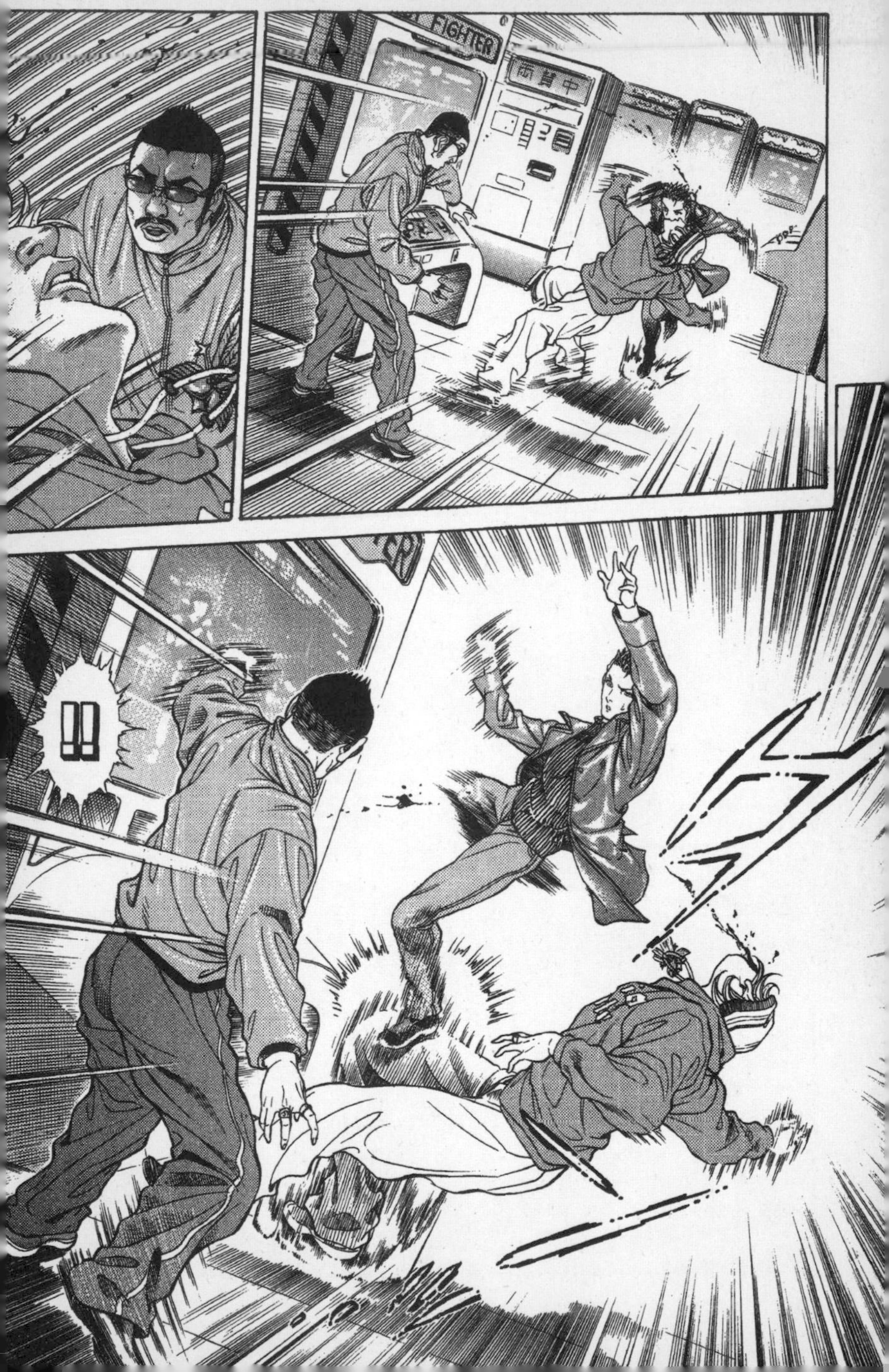
FIGHTER
!!

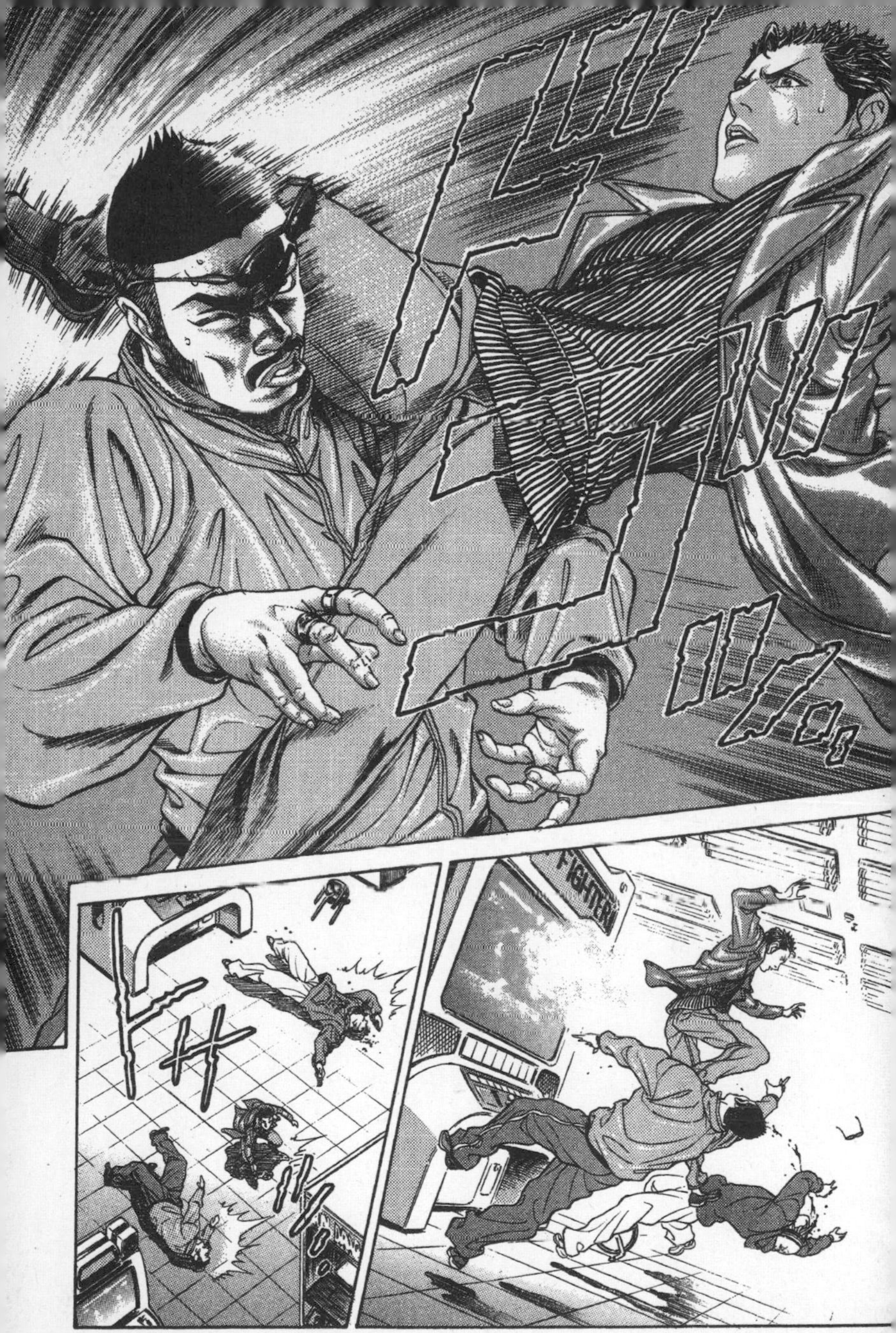
FIGHTER

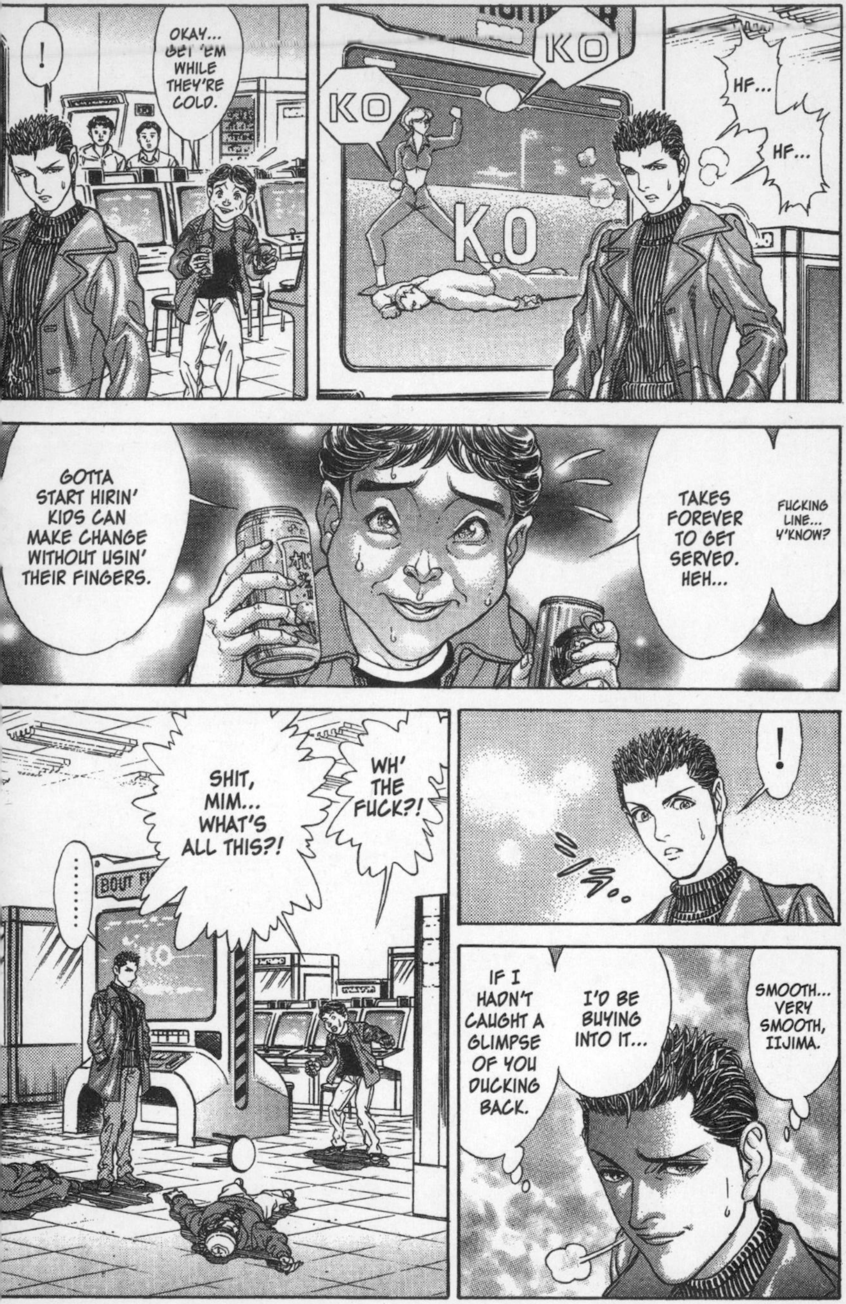
KO
KO
K.O
HF...
HF...
OKAY... GET 'EM WHILE THEY'RE COLD.
!
TAKES FOREVER TO GET SERVED. HEH...
FUCKING LINE... Y'KNOW?
GOTTA START HIRIN' KIDS CAN MAKE CHANGE WITHOUT USIN' THEIR FINGERS.
!
SMOOTH... VERY SMOOTH, IIJIMA.
I'D BE BUYING INTO IT...
IF I HADN'T CAUGHT A GLIMPSE OF YOU DUCKING BACK.
WH' THE FUCK?!
SHIT, MIM... WHAT'S ALL THIS?!
....
K.O

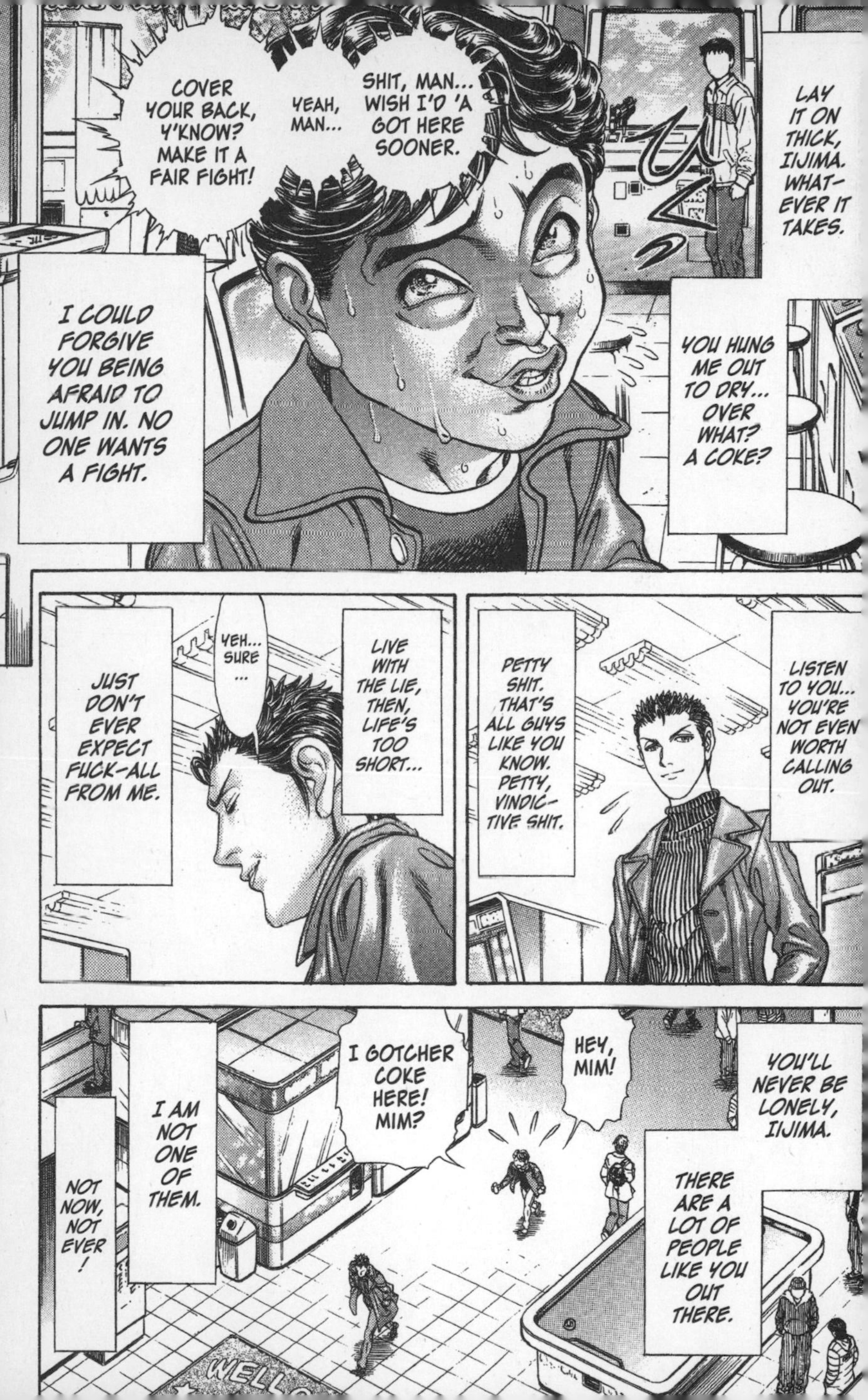
LAY IT ON THICK, IIJIMA. WHATEVER IT TAKES.
SHIT, MAN... WISH I'D 'A GOT HERE SOONER.
YEAH, MAN...
COVER YOUR BACK, Y'KNOW? MAKE IT A FAIR FIGHT!
YOU HUNG ME OUT TO DRY... OVER WHAT? A COKE?
I COULD FORGIVE YOU BEING AFRAID TO JUMP IN. NO ONE WANTS A FIGHT.
LISTEN TO YOU... YOU'RE NOT EVEN WORTH CALLING OUT.
PETTY SHIT. THAT'S ALL GUYS LIKE YOU KNOW. PETTY, VINDICTIVE SHIT.
LIVE WITH THE LIE, THEN, LIFE'S TOO SHORT...
YEH... SURE...
JUST DON'T EVER EXPECT FUCK-ALL FROM ME.
YOU'LL NEVER BE LONELY, IIJIMA.
THERE ARE A LOT OF PEOPLE LIKE YOU OUT THERE.
HEY, MIM!
I GOTCHER COKE HERE! MIM?
I AM NOT ONE OF THEM.
NOT NOW, NOT EVER!

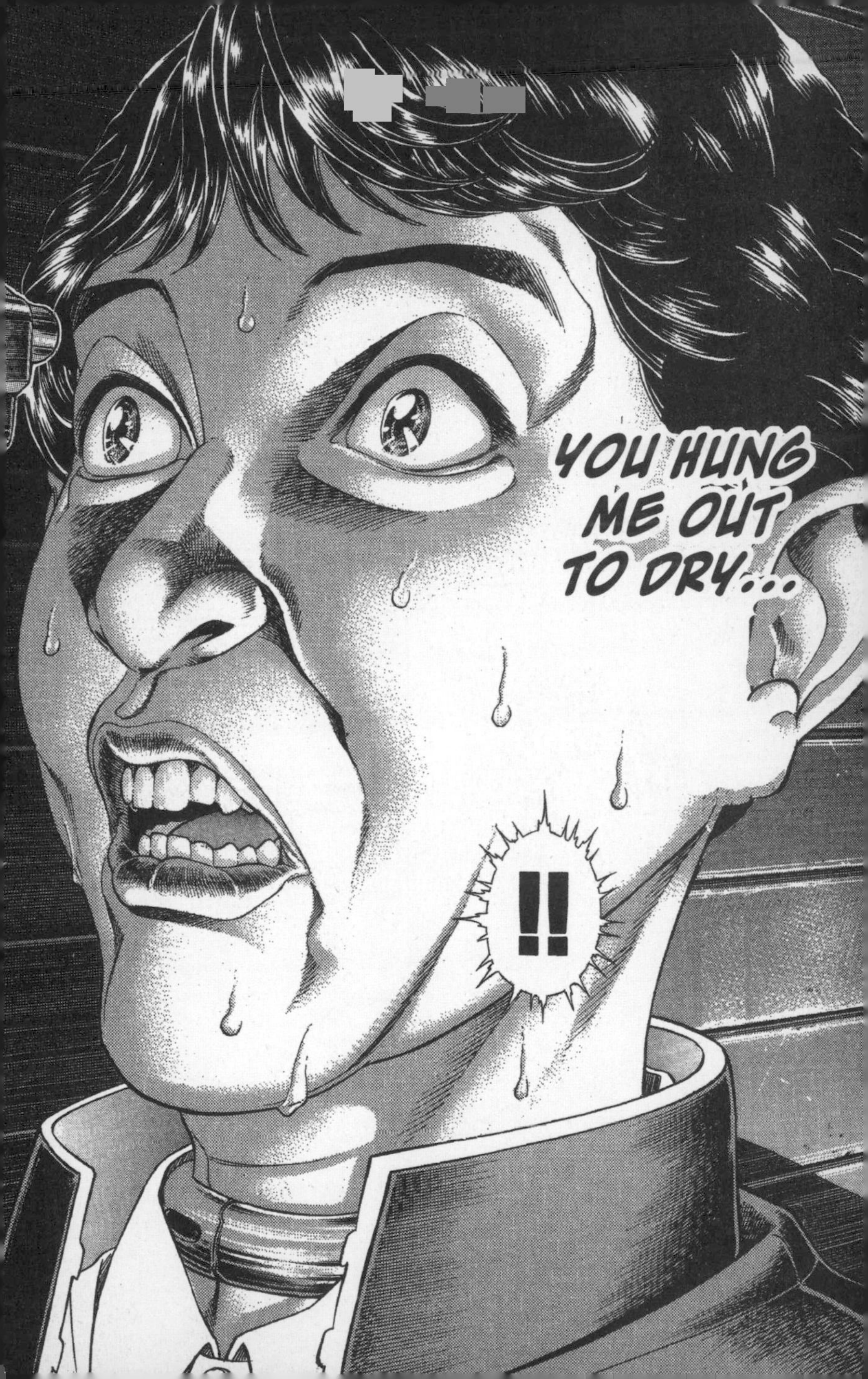
YOU HUNG ME OUT TO DRY...
!!

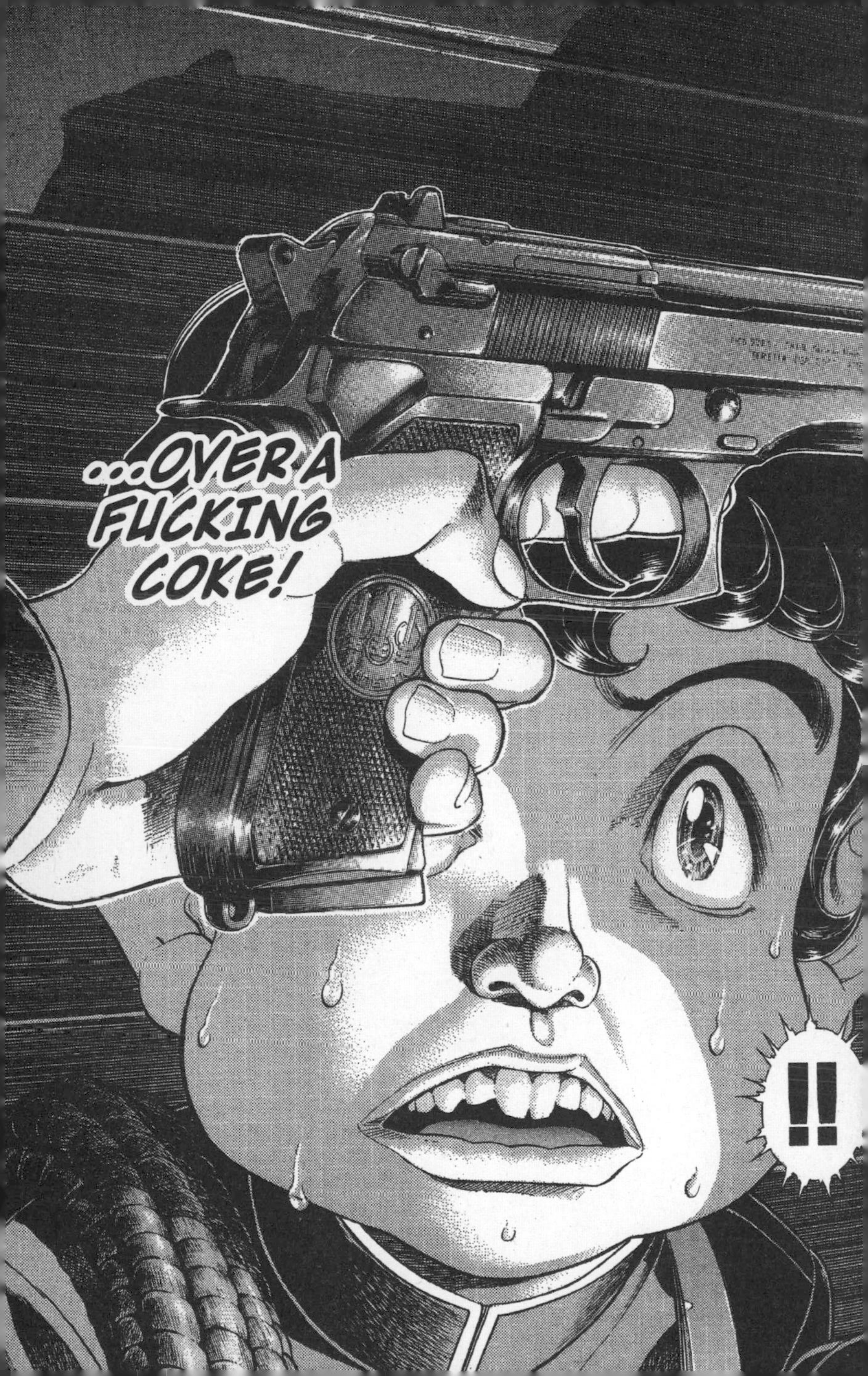
...OVER A FUCKING COKE!
!!

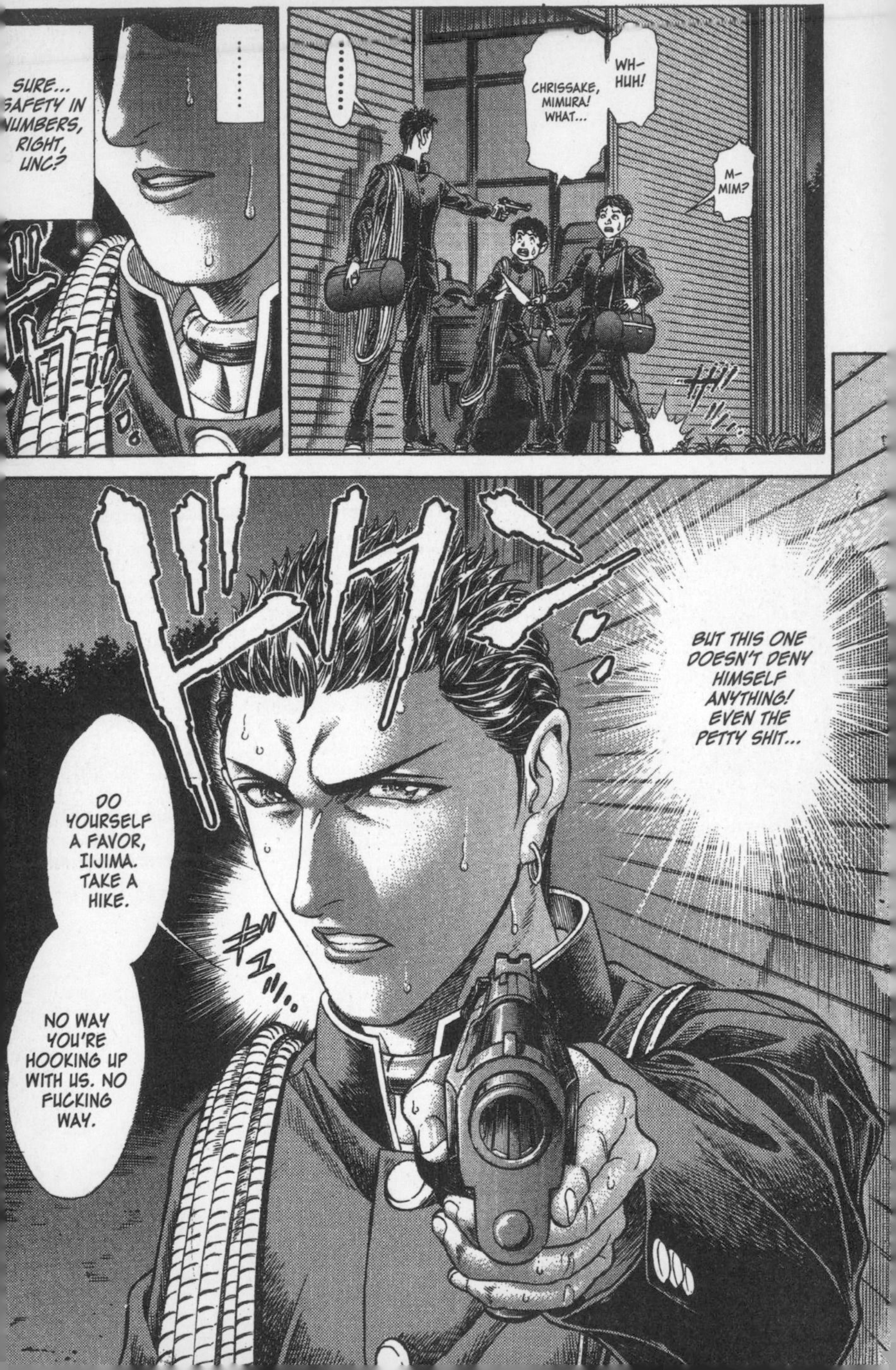

SURE... SAFETY IN NUMBERS, RIGHT, UNC?
......
......
WH-HUH!
CHRISSAKE, MIMURA! WHAT...
M-MIM?
BUT THIS ONE DOESN'T DENY HIMSELF ANYTHING! EVEN THE PETTY SHIT...
DO YOURSELF A FAVOR, IIJIMA. TAKE A HIKE.
NO WAY YOU'RE HOOKING UP WITH US. NO FUCKING WAY.

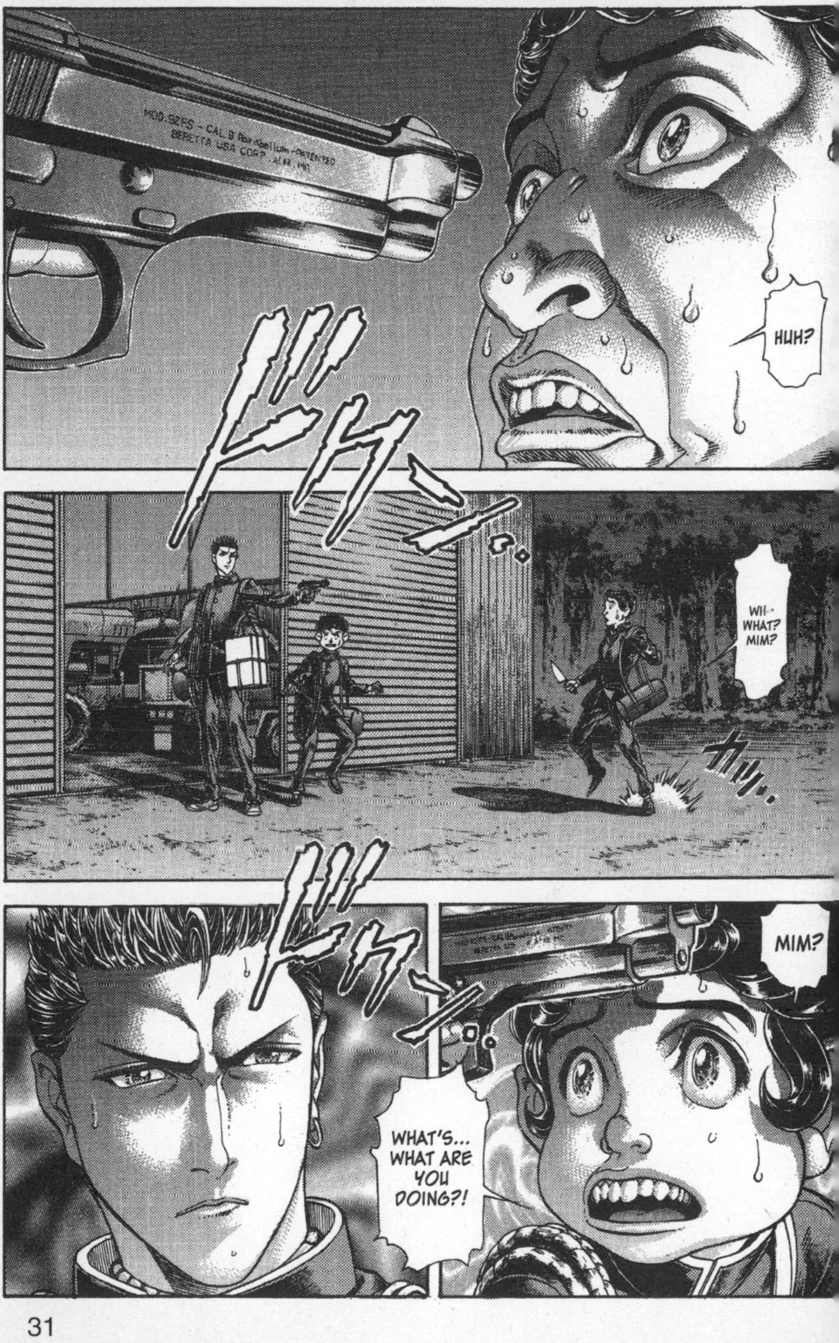
HUH?
ドガン
WH-- WHAT? MIM?
カッ
ドガン
MIM?
WHAT'S... WHAT ARE YOU DOING?!

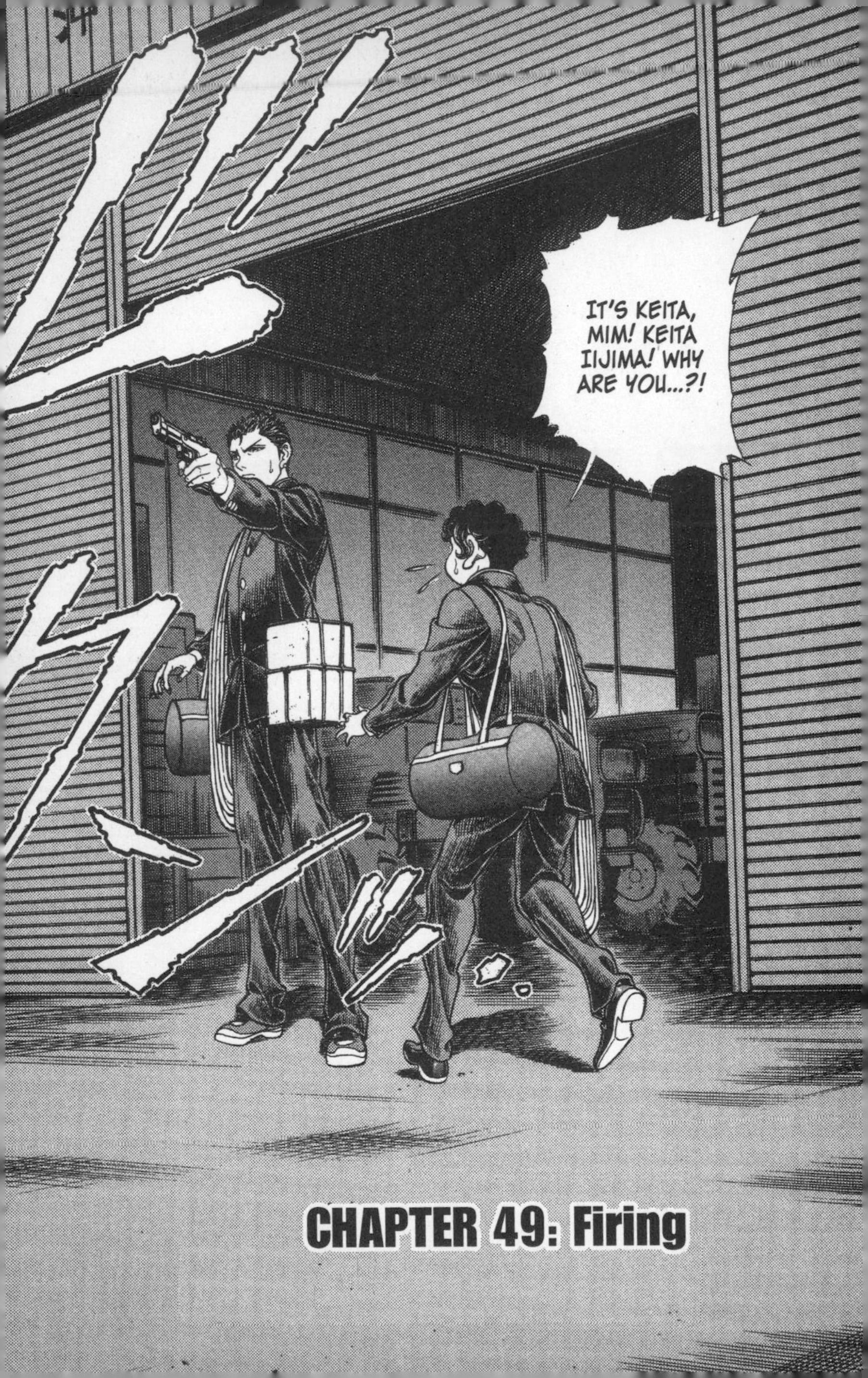
IT'S KEITA, MIM! KEITA IIJIMA! WHY ARE YOU...?!

CHAPTER 49: Firing

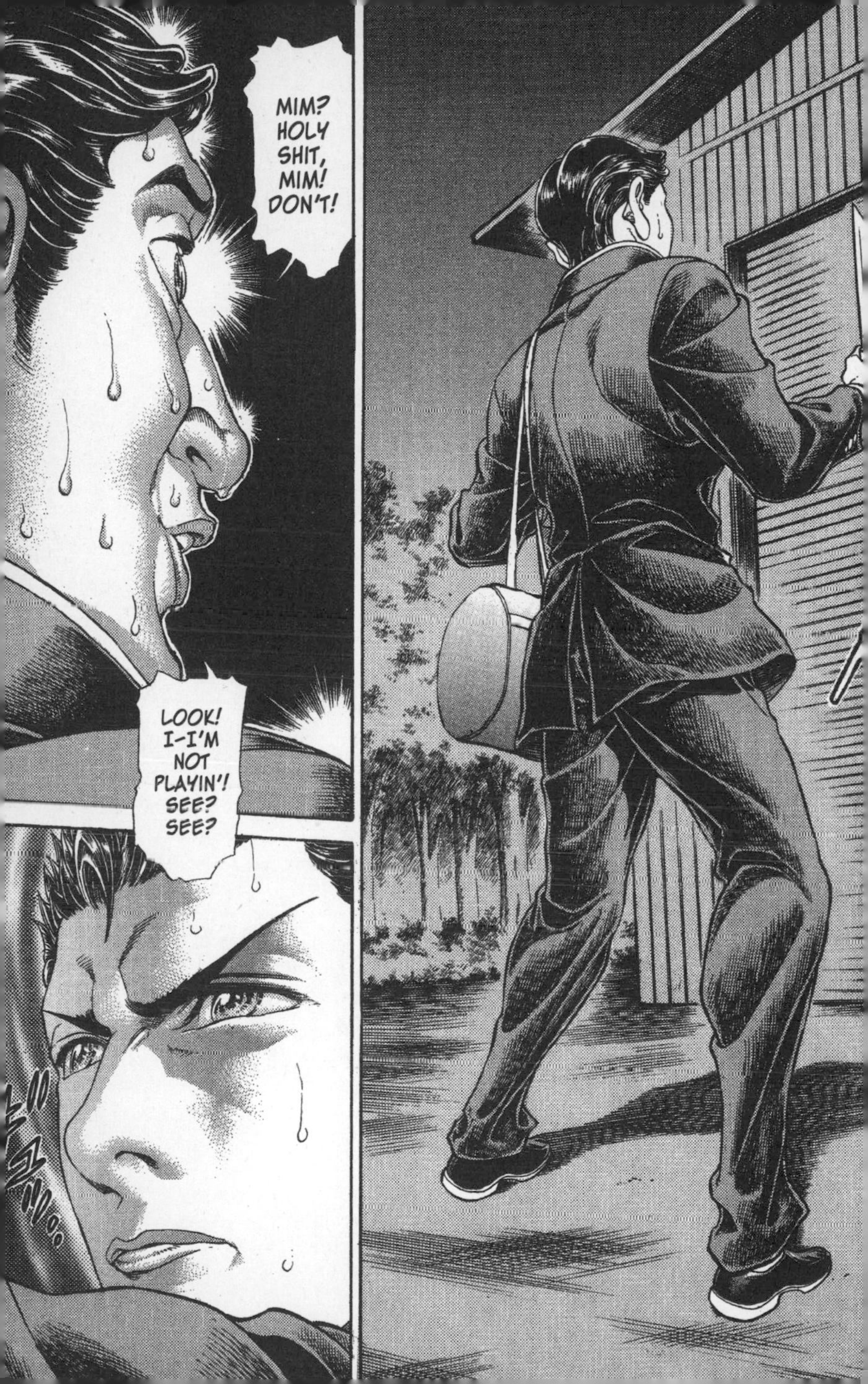
MIM? HOLY SHIT, MIM! DON'T!
LOOK! I-I'M NOT PLAYIN'! SEE? SEE?

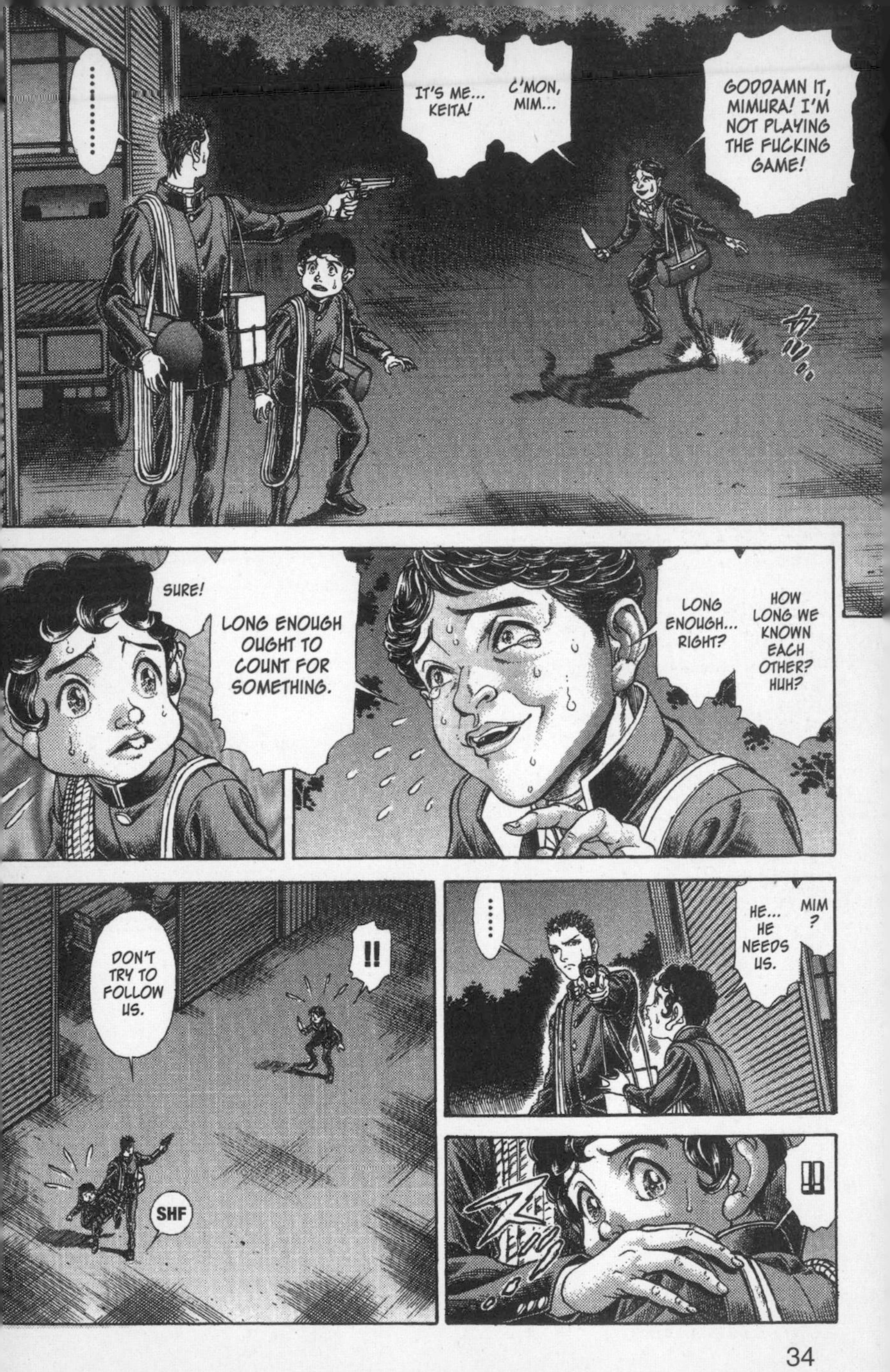
GODDAMN IT, MIMURA! I'M NOT PLAYING THE FUCKING GAME!
C'MON, MIM...
IT'S ME... KEITA!
......
HOW LONG WE KNOWN EACH OTHER? HUH?
LONG ENOUGH... RIGHT?
SURE!
LONG ENOUGH OUGHT TO COUNT FOR SOMETHING.
MIM?
HE... HE NEEDS US.
......
!!
!!
DON'T TRY TO FOLLOW US.
SHF

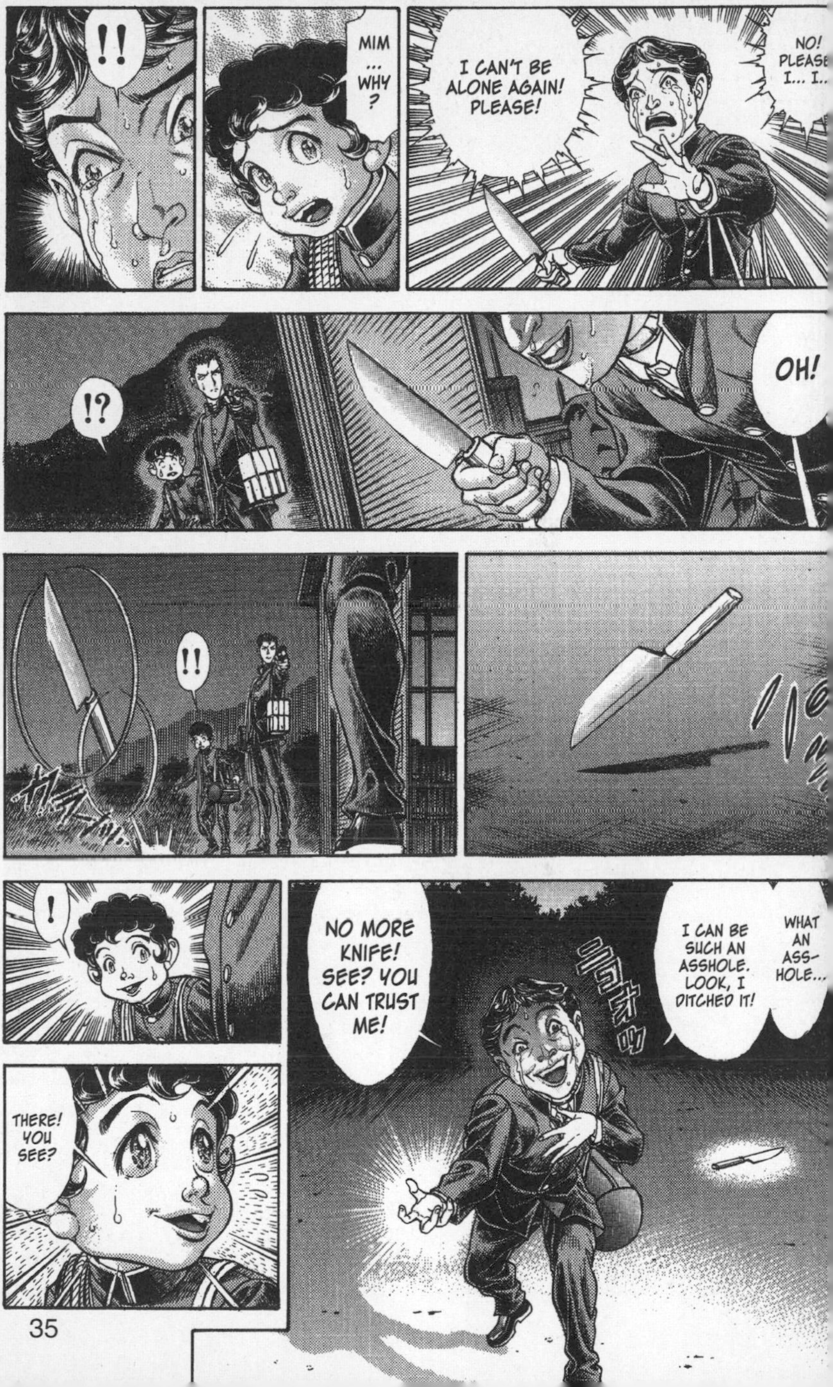
NO! PLEASE I... I...
I CAN'T BE ALONE AGAIN! PLEASE!
MIM ... WHY ?
!!
OH!
!?
!!
WHAT AN ASS-HOLE...
I CAN BE SUCH AN ASSHOLE. LOOK, I DITCHED IT!
NO MORE KNIFE! SEE? YOU CAN TRUST ME!
!
THERE! YOU SEE?

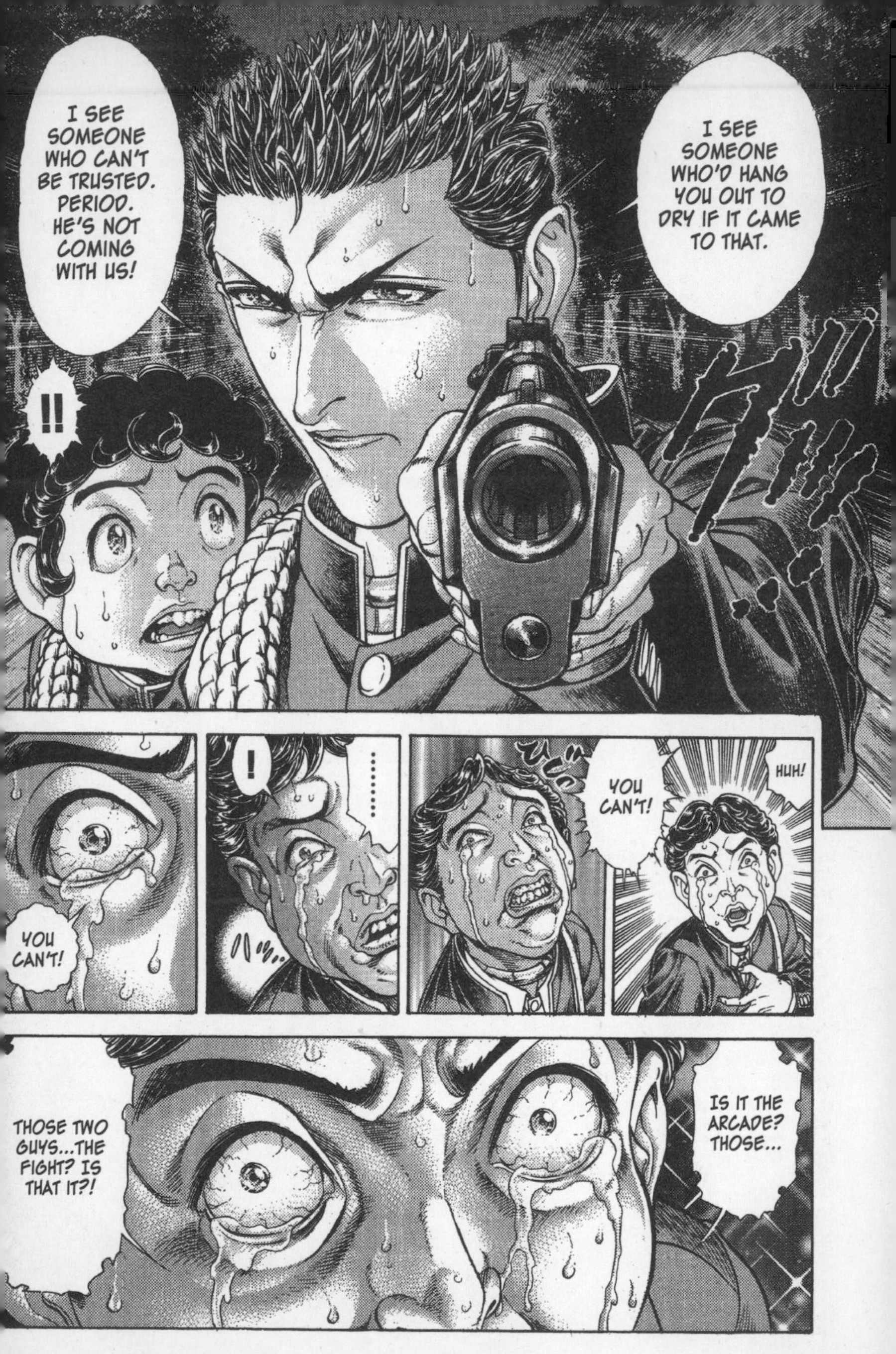
I SEE SOMEONE WHO'D HANG YOU OUT TO DRY IF IT CAME TO THAT.
I SEE SOMEONE WHO CAN'T BE TRUSTED. PERIOD. HE'S NOT COMING WITH US!
!!
HUH!
YOU CAN'T!
!
......
YOU CAN'T!
IS IT THE ARCADE? THOSE...
THOSE TWO GUYS...THE FIGHT? IS THAT IT?!

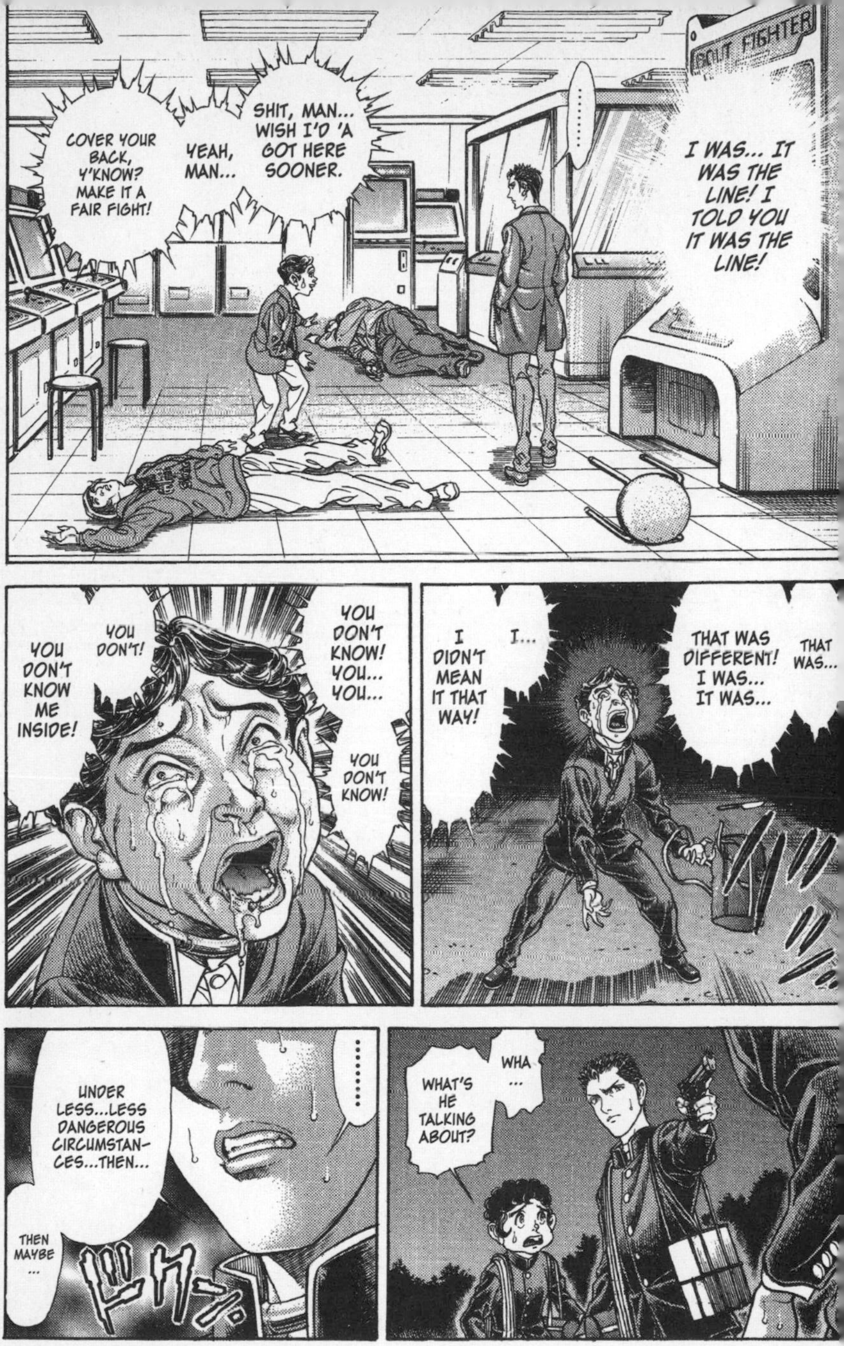
BOUT FIGHTER
I WAS... IT WAS THE LINE! I TOLD YOU IT WAS THE LINE!
......
SHIT, MAN... WISH I'D 'A GOT HERE SOONER.
YEAH, MAN...
COVER YOUR BACK, Y'KNOW? MAKE IT A FAIR FIGHT!
THAT WAS...
THAT WAS DIFFERENT! I WAS... IT WAS...
I...
I DIDN'T MEAN IT THAT WAY!
YOU DON'T KNOW! YOU... YOU...
YOU DON'T!
YOU DON'T KNOW ME INSIDE!
YOU DON'T KNOW!
WHA ...
WHAT'S HE TALKING ABOUT?
......
UNDER LESS...LESS DANGEROUS CIRCUMSTAN-CES...THEN...
THEN MAYBE ...

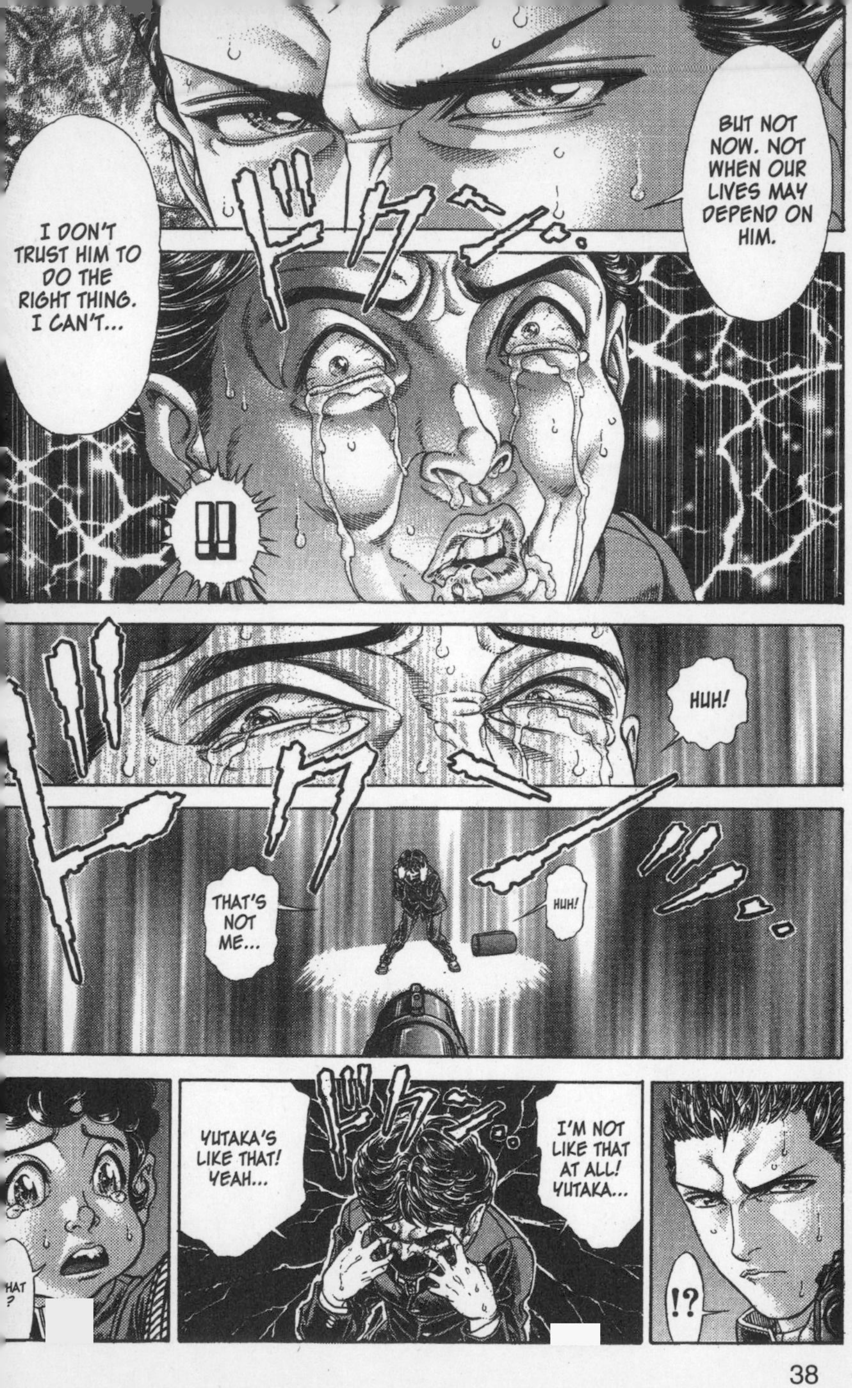
BUT NOT NOW. NOT WHEN OUR LIVES MAY DEPEND ON HIM.
I DON'T TRUST HIM TO DO THE RIGHT THING. I CAN'T...
!!
HUH!
HUH!
THAT'S NOT ME...
!?
I'M NOT LIKE THAT AT ALL! YUTAKA...
YUTAKA'S LIKE THAT! YEAH...

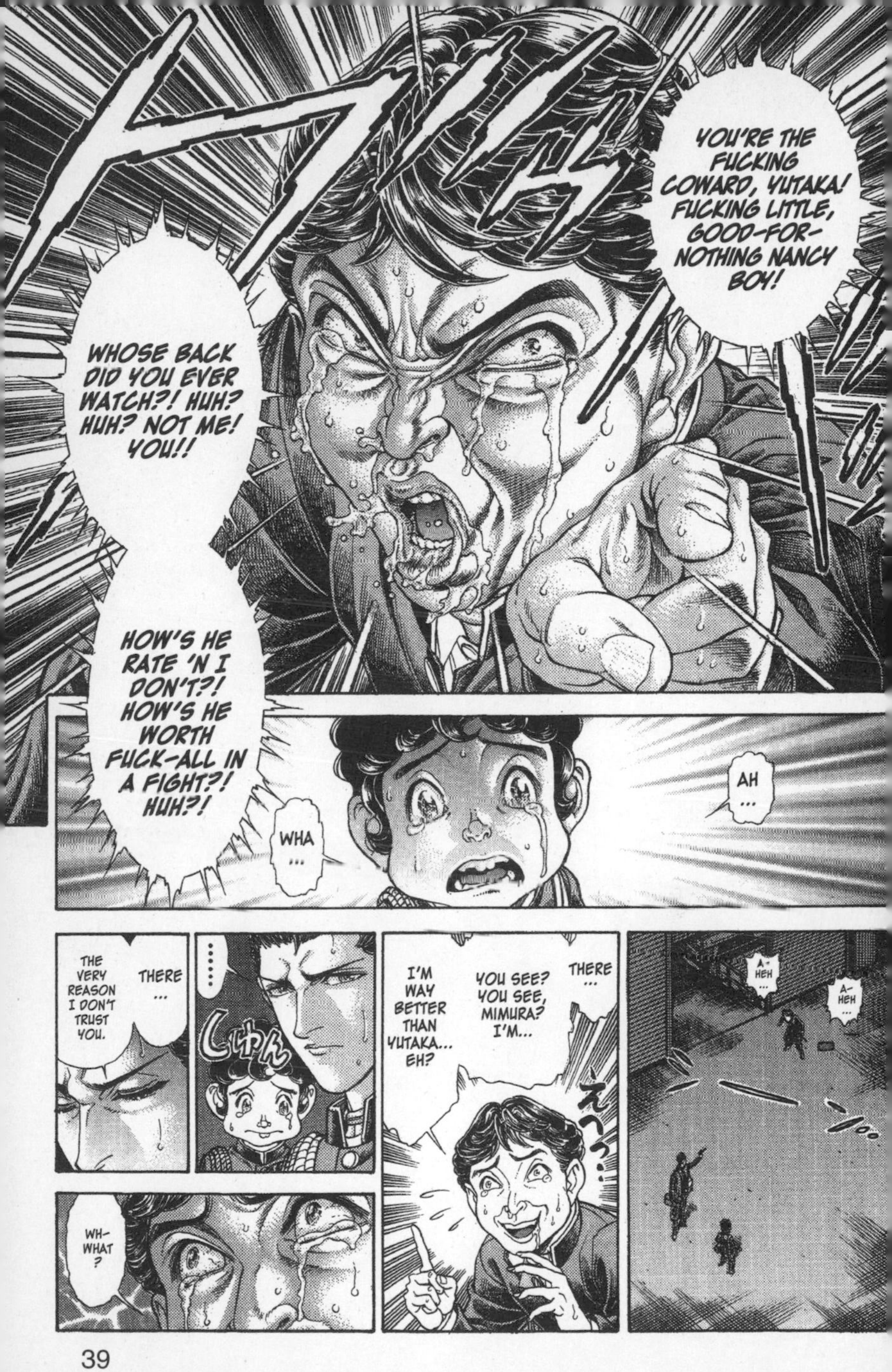
YOU'RE THE FUCKING COWARD, YUTAKA! FUCKING LITTLE, GOOD-FOR-NOTHING NANCY BOY!
WHOSE BACK DID YOU EVER WATCH?! HUH? HUH? NOT ME! YOU!!
HOW'S HE RATE 'N I DON'T?! HOW'S HE WORTH FUCK-ALL IN A FIGHT?! HUH?!
AH ...
WHA ...
A-HEH ...
A-HEH ...
THERE ...
YOU SEE? YOU SEE, MIMURA? I'M...
I'M WAY BETTER THAN YUTAKA... EH?
えっ
......
しゅん
THERE ...
THE VERY REASON I DON'T TRUST YOU.
WH-WHAT ?

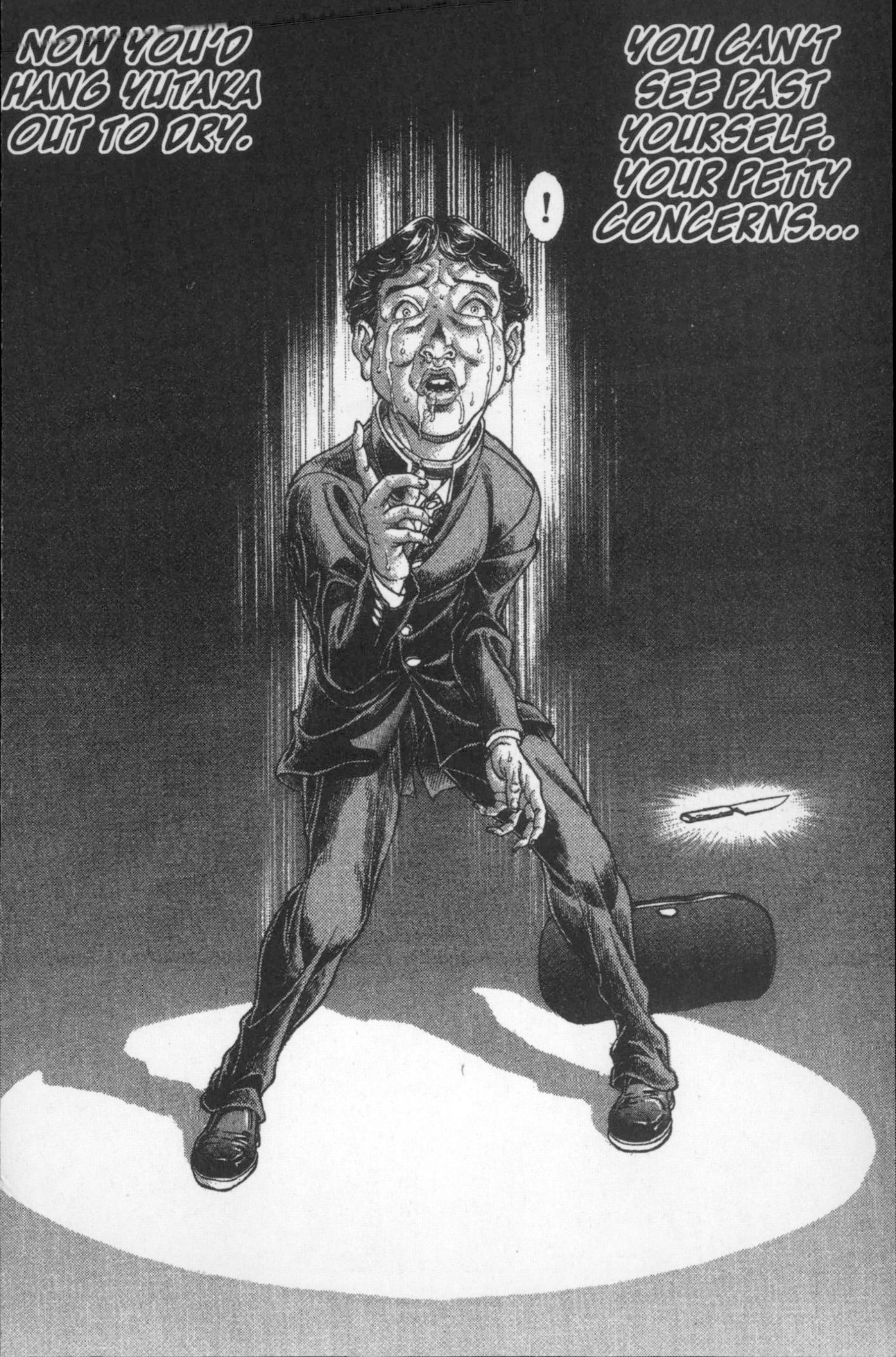
YOU CAN'T SEE PAST YOURSELF. YOUR PETTY CONCERNS...
!
NOW YOU'D HANG YUTAKA OUT TO DRY.

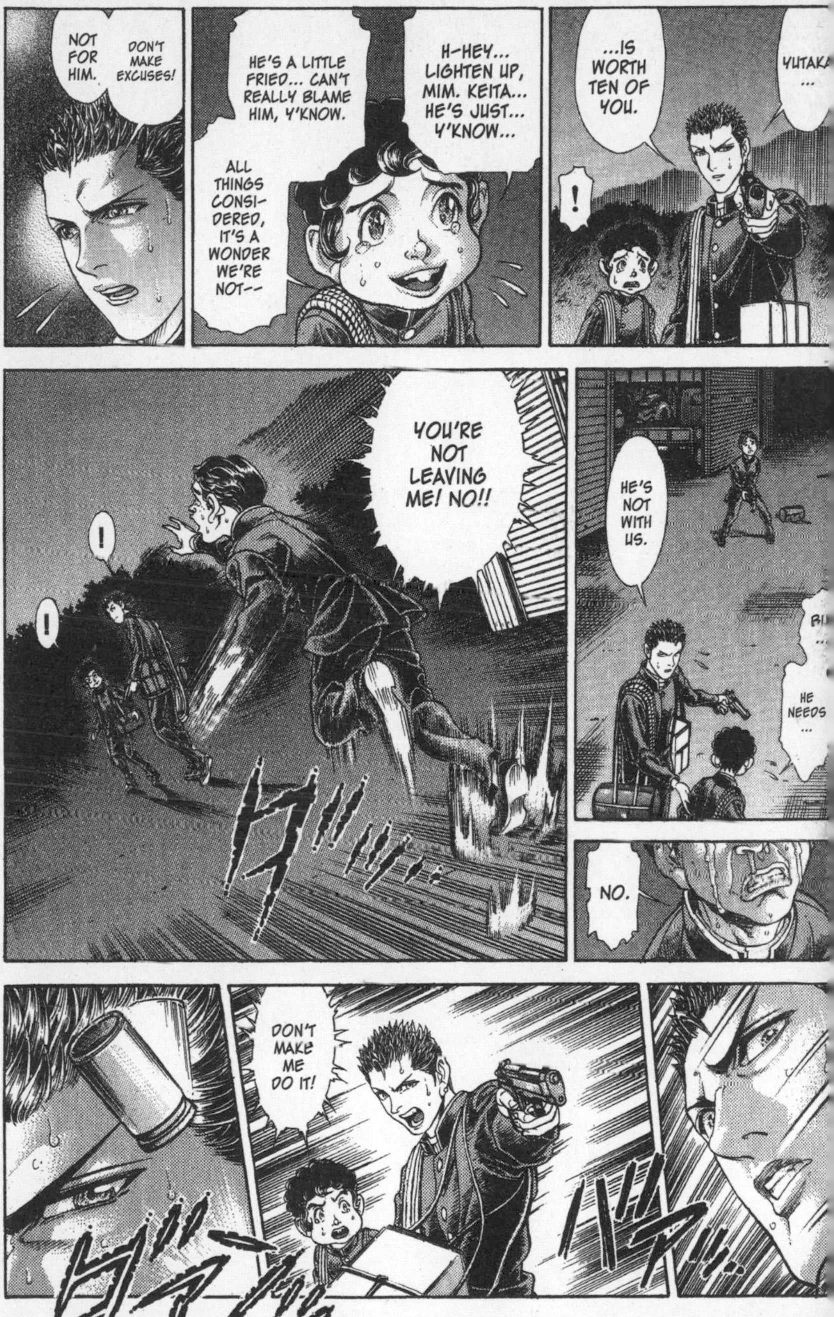
YUTAKA ...
...IS WORTH TEN OF YOU.
!
H-HEY... LIGHTEN UP, MIM. KEITA... HE'S JUST... Y'KNOW...
HE'S A LITTLE FRIED... CAN'T REALLY BLAME HIM, Y'KNOW.
ALL THINGS CONSIDERED, IT'S A WONDER WE'RE NOT--
DON'T MAKE EXCUSES!
NOT FOR HIM.
HE'S NOT WITH US.
HE NEEDS ...
NO.
YOU'RE NOT LEAVING ME! NO!!
!
!
DON'T MAKE ME DO IT!

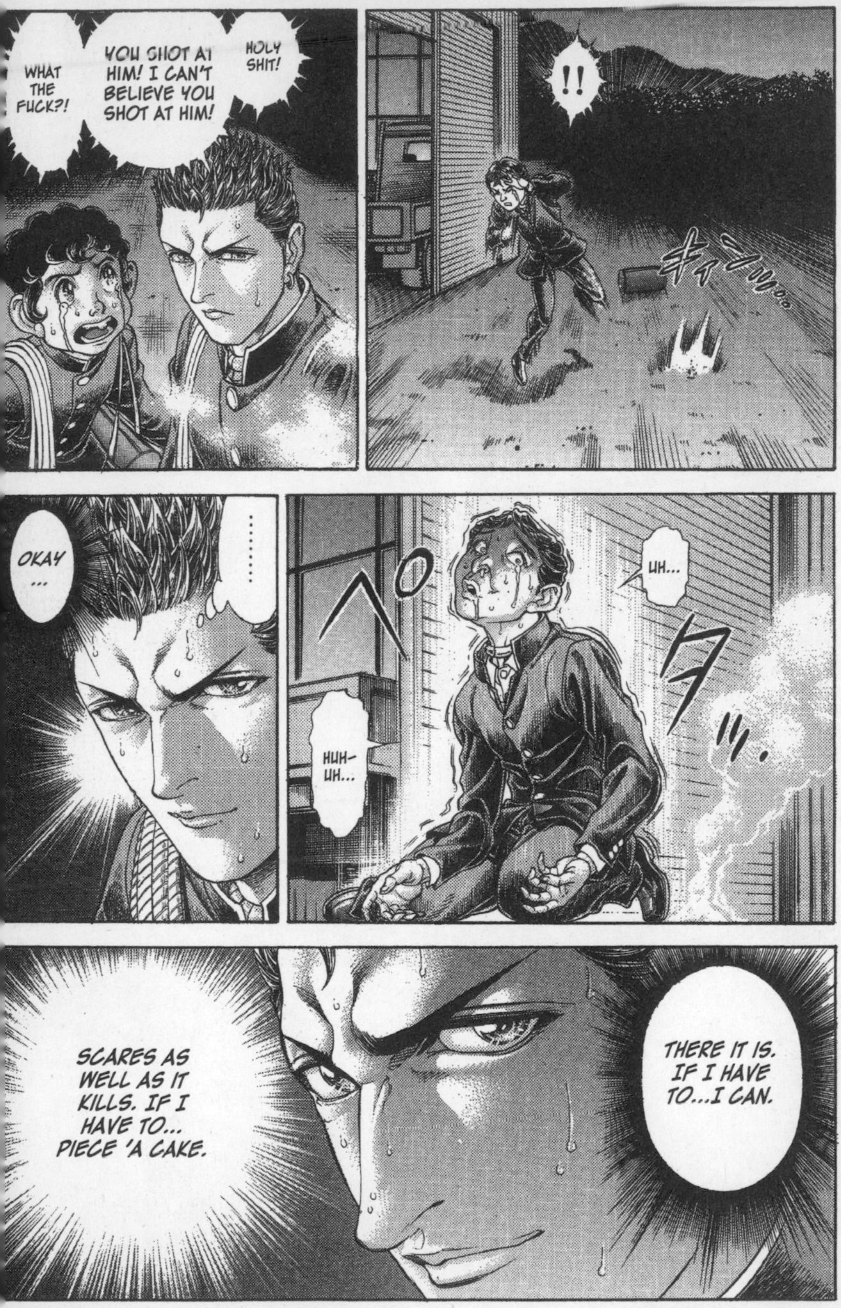
!!
HOLY SHIT!
YOU SHOT AT HIM! I CAN'T BELIEVE YOU SHOT AT HIM!
WHAT THE FUCK?!
UH...
HUH-UH...
......
OKAY ...
THERE IT IS. IF I HAVE TO...I CAN.
SCARES AS WELL AS IT KILLS. IF I HAVE TO... PIECE 'A CAKE.

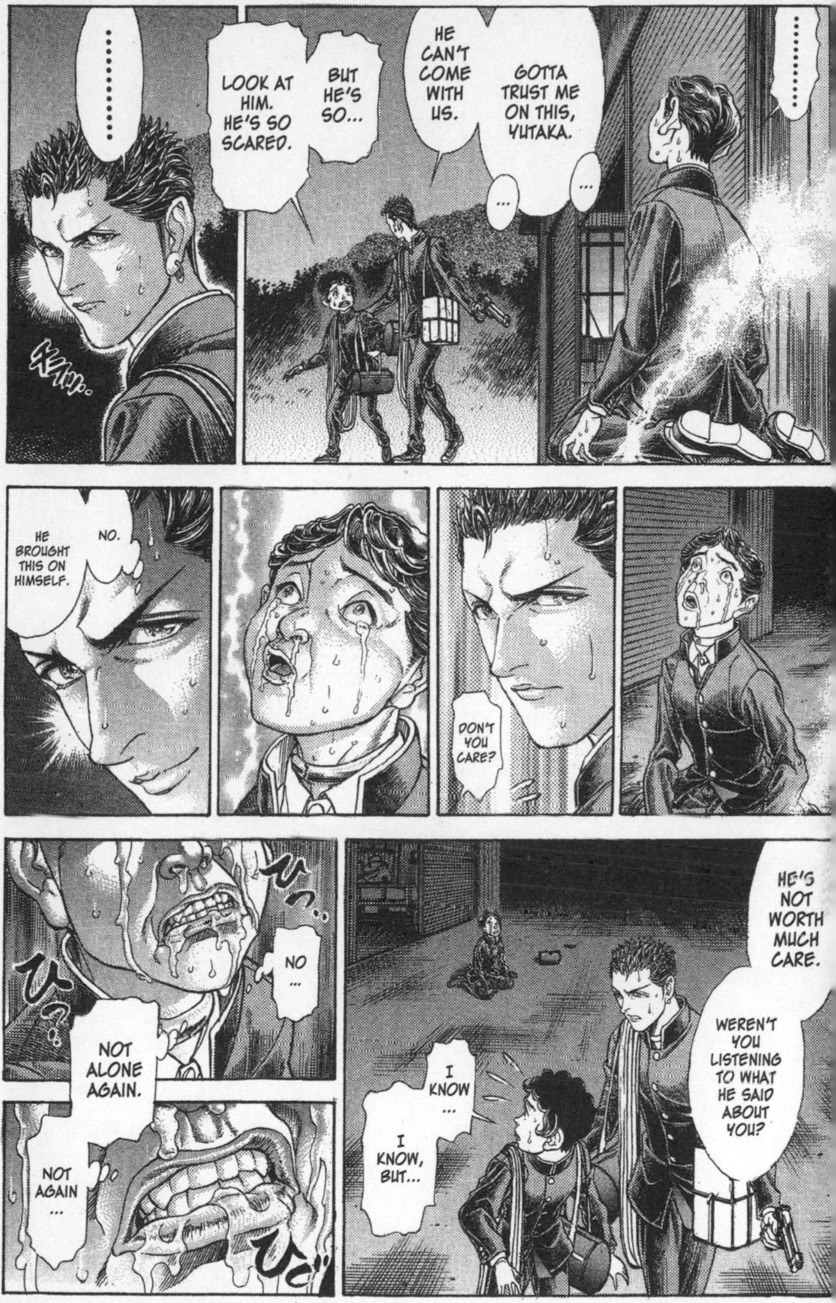
....
HE CAN'T COME WITH US.
GOTTA TRUST ME ON THIS, YUTAKA.
...
...
BUT HE'S SO...
LOOK AT HIM. HE'S SO SCARED.
....
DON'T YOU CARE?
NO.
HE BROUGHT THIS ON HIMSELF.
HE'S NOT WORTH MUCH CARE.
WEREN'T YOU LISTENING TO WHAT HE SAID ABOUT YOU?
I KNOW...
I KNOW, BUT...
NO...
NOT ALONE AGAIN.
NOT AGAIN...

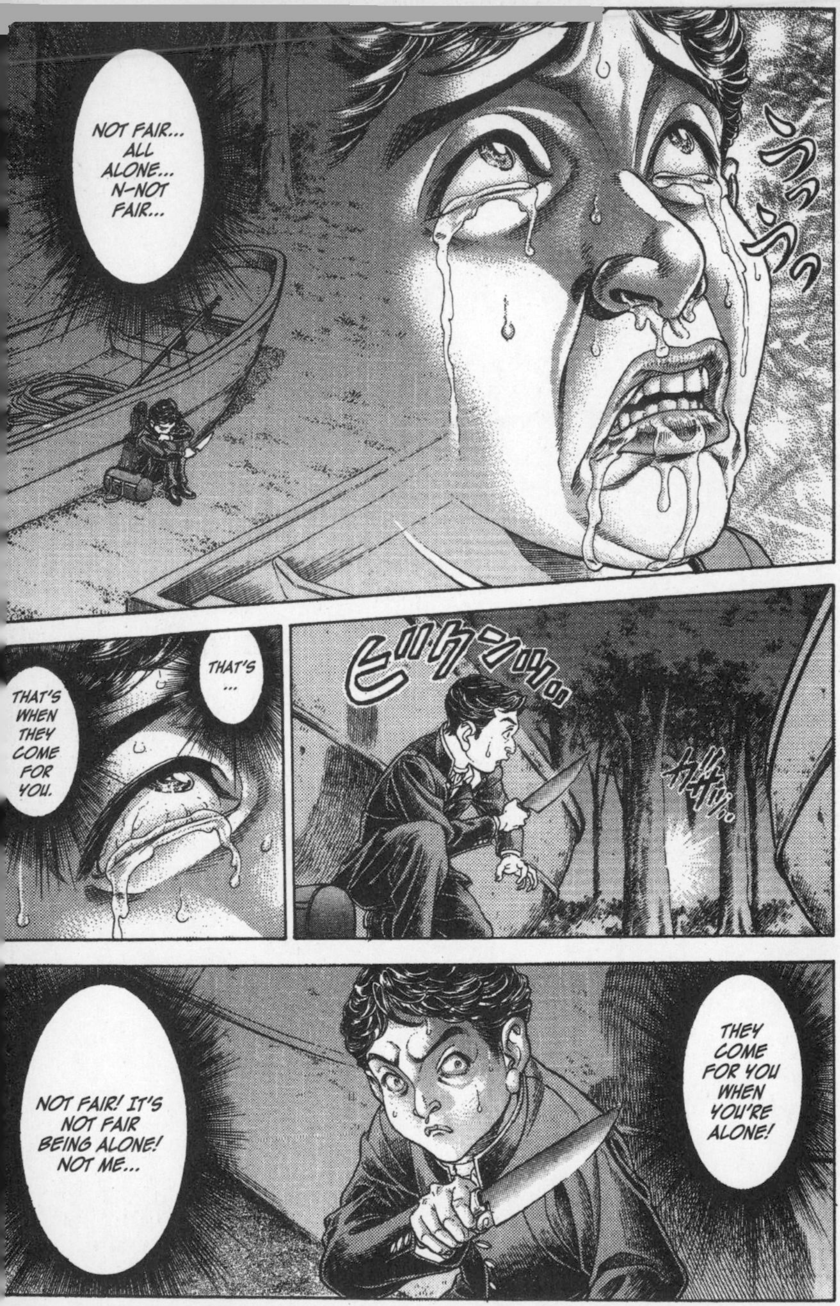
NOT FAIR... ALL ALONE... N-NOT FAIR...
THAT'S...
THAT'S WHEN THEY COME FOR YOU.
THEY COME FOR YOU WHEN YOU'RE ALONE!
NOT FAIR! IT'S NOT FAIR BEING ALONE! NOT ME...

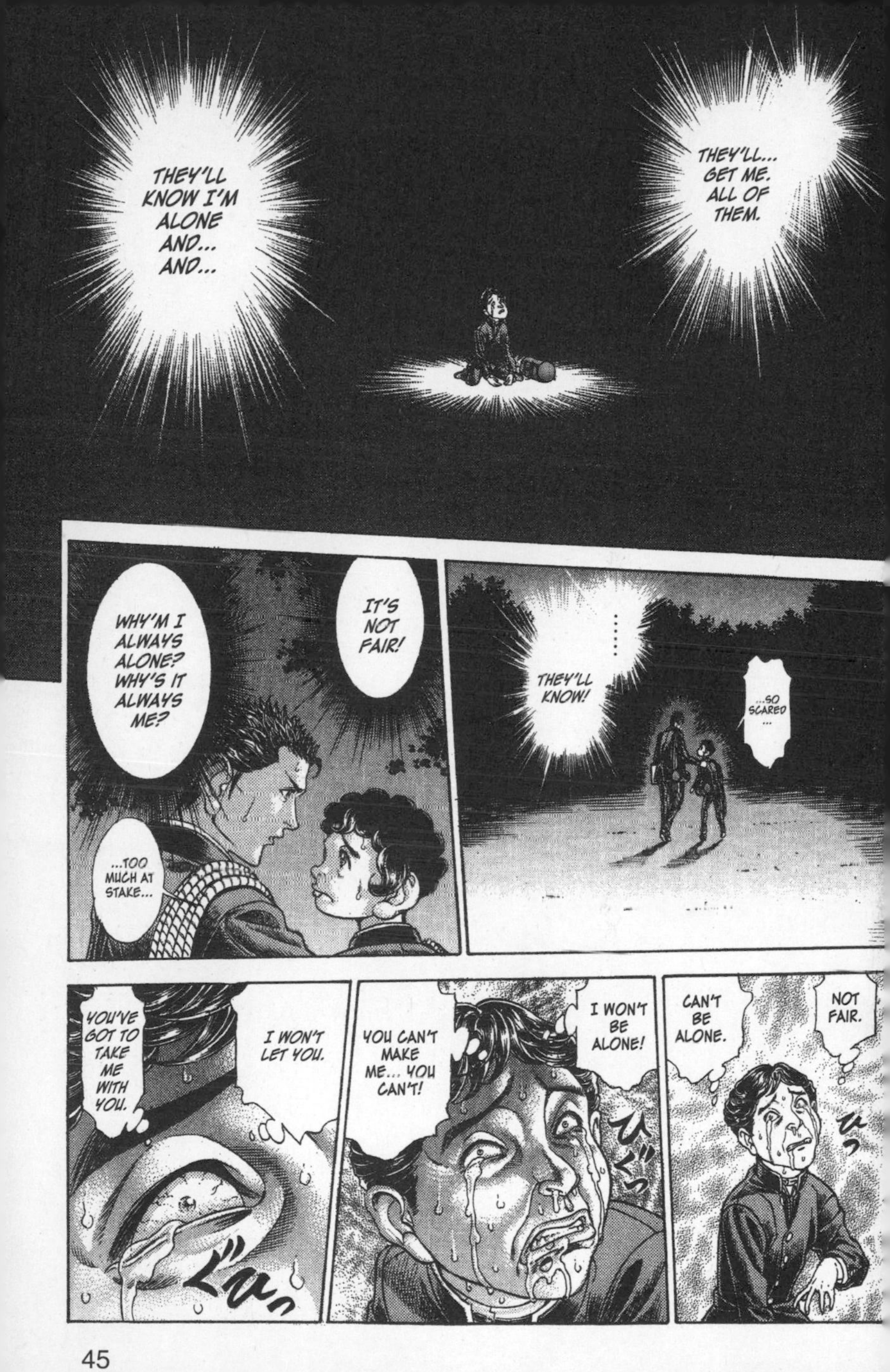
THEY'LL... GET ME. ALL OF THEM.
THEY'LL KNOW I'M ALONE AND... AND...
......
...SO SCARED...
THEY'LL KNOW!
IT'S NOT FAIR!
WHY'M I ALWAYS ALONE? WHY'S IT ALWAYS ME?
...TOO MUCH AT STAKE...
NOT FAIR.
CAN'T BE ALONE.
I WON'T BE ALONE!
YOU CAN'T MAKE ME... YOU CAN'T!
I WON'T LET YOU.
YOU'VE GOT TO TAKE ME WITH YOU.

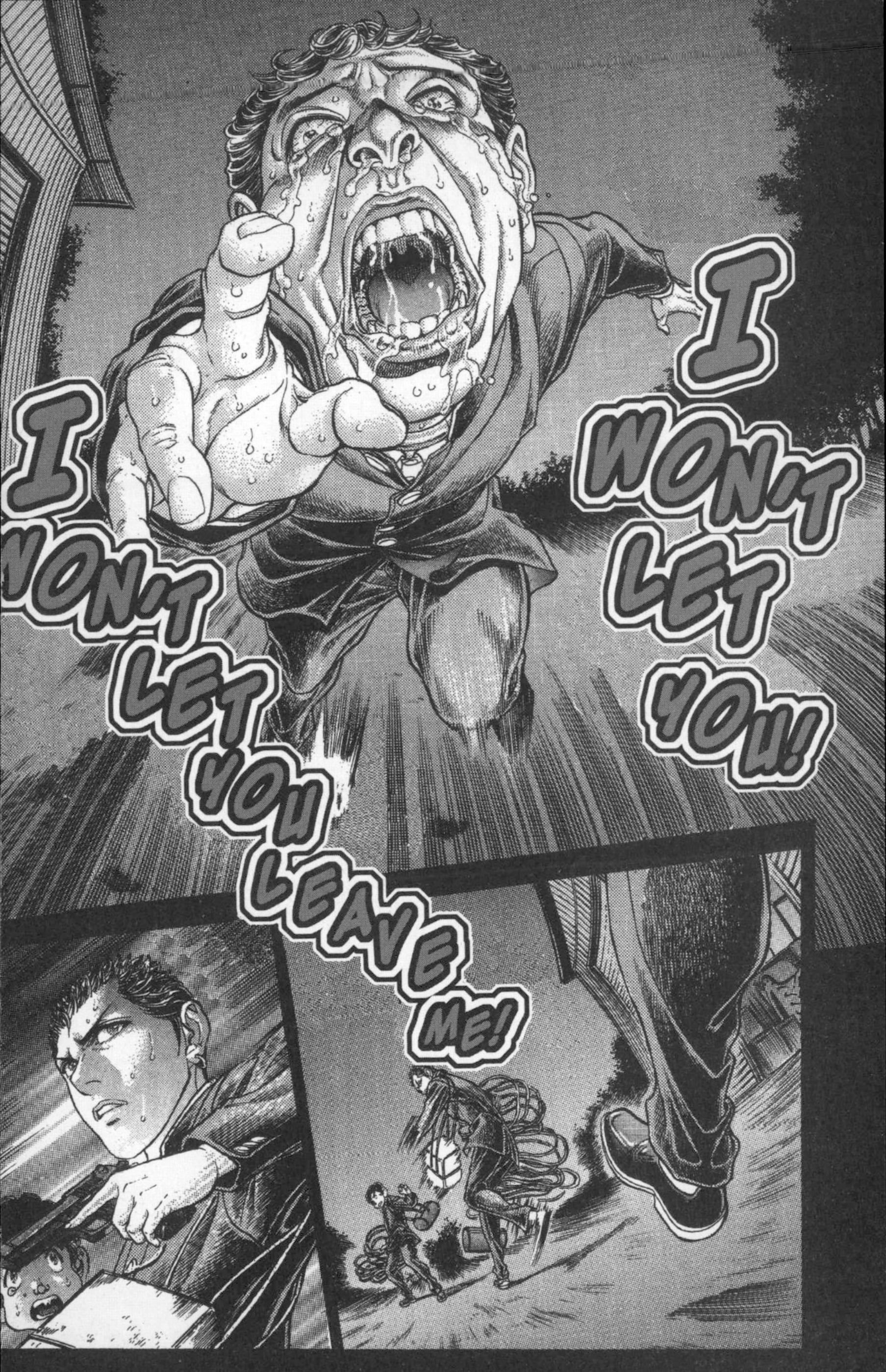
I WON'T LET YOU!
I WON'T LET YOU LEAVE ME!

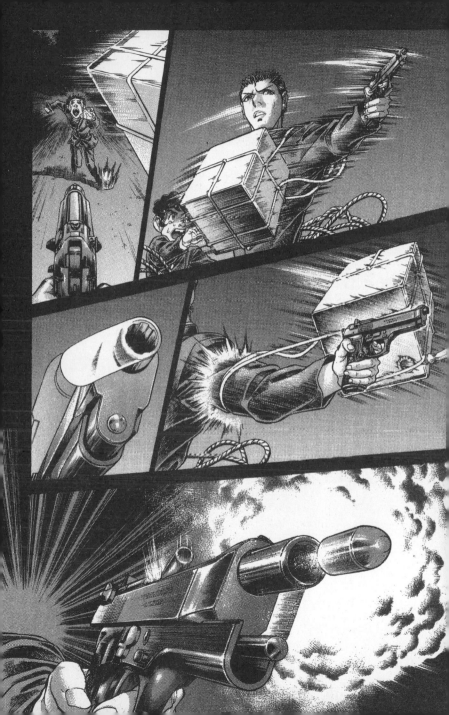

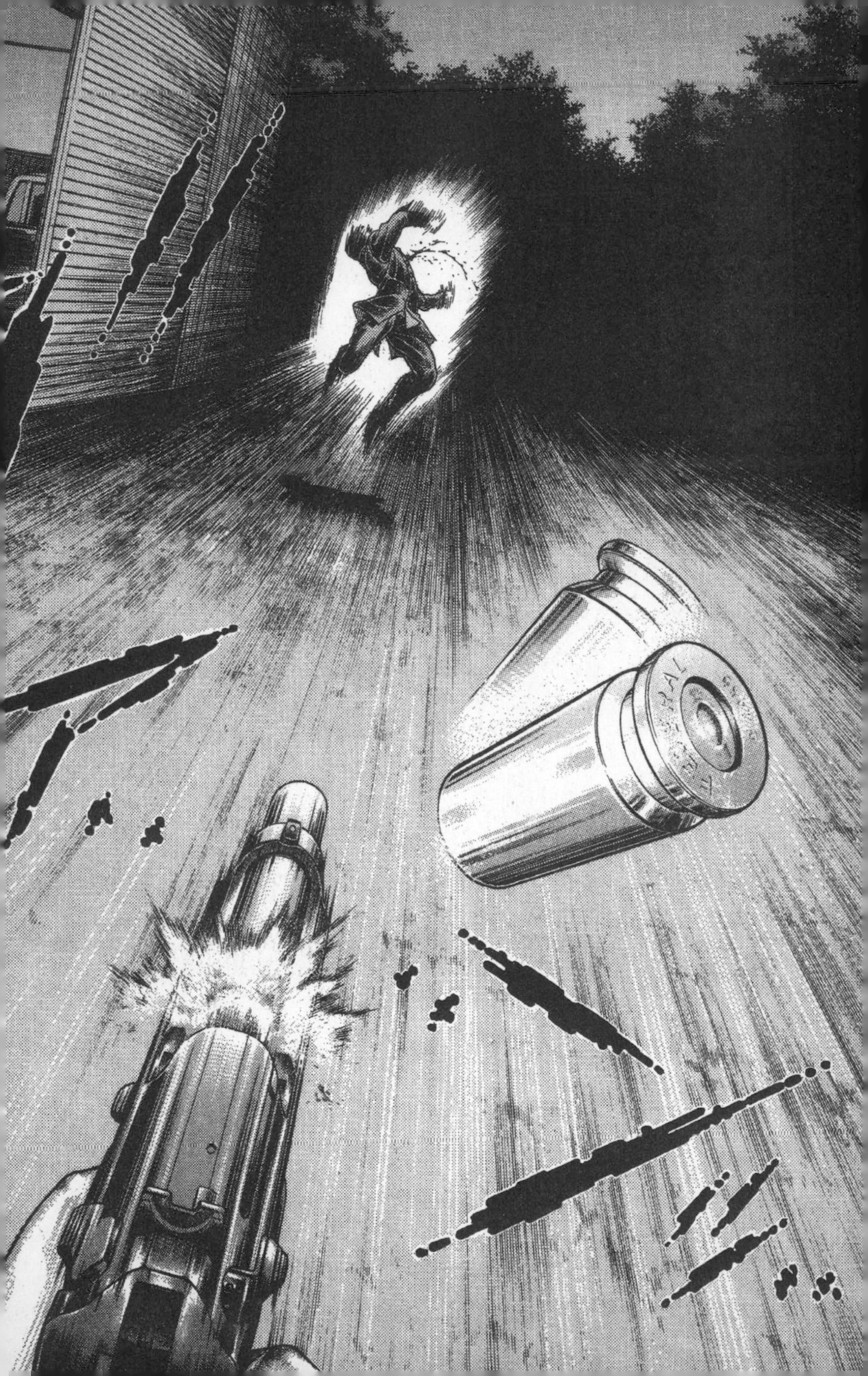

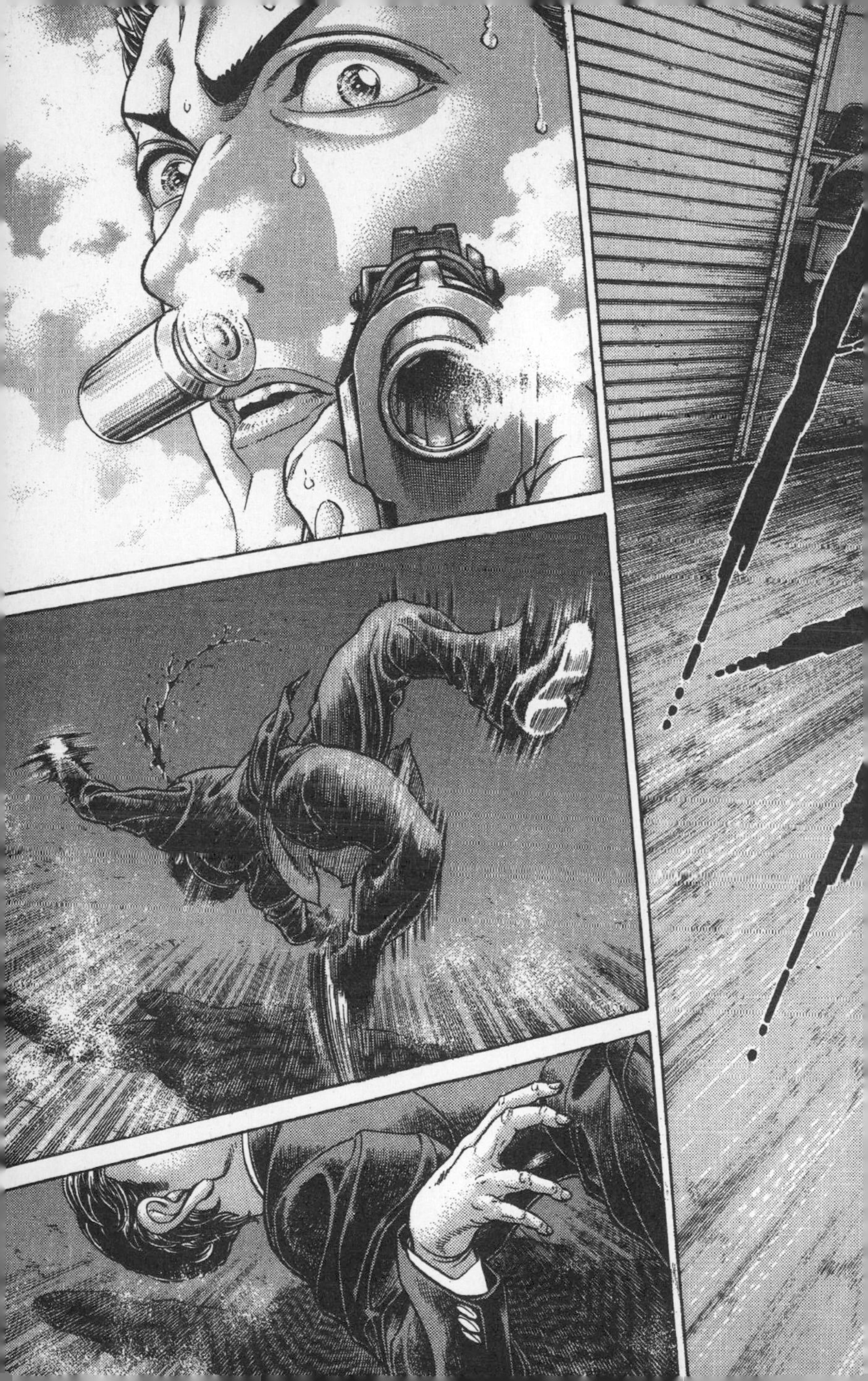

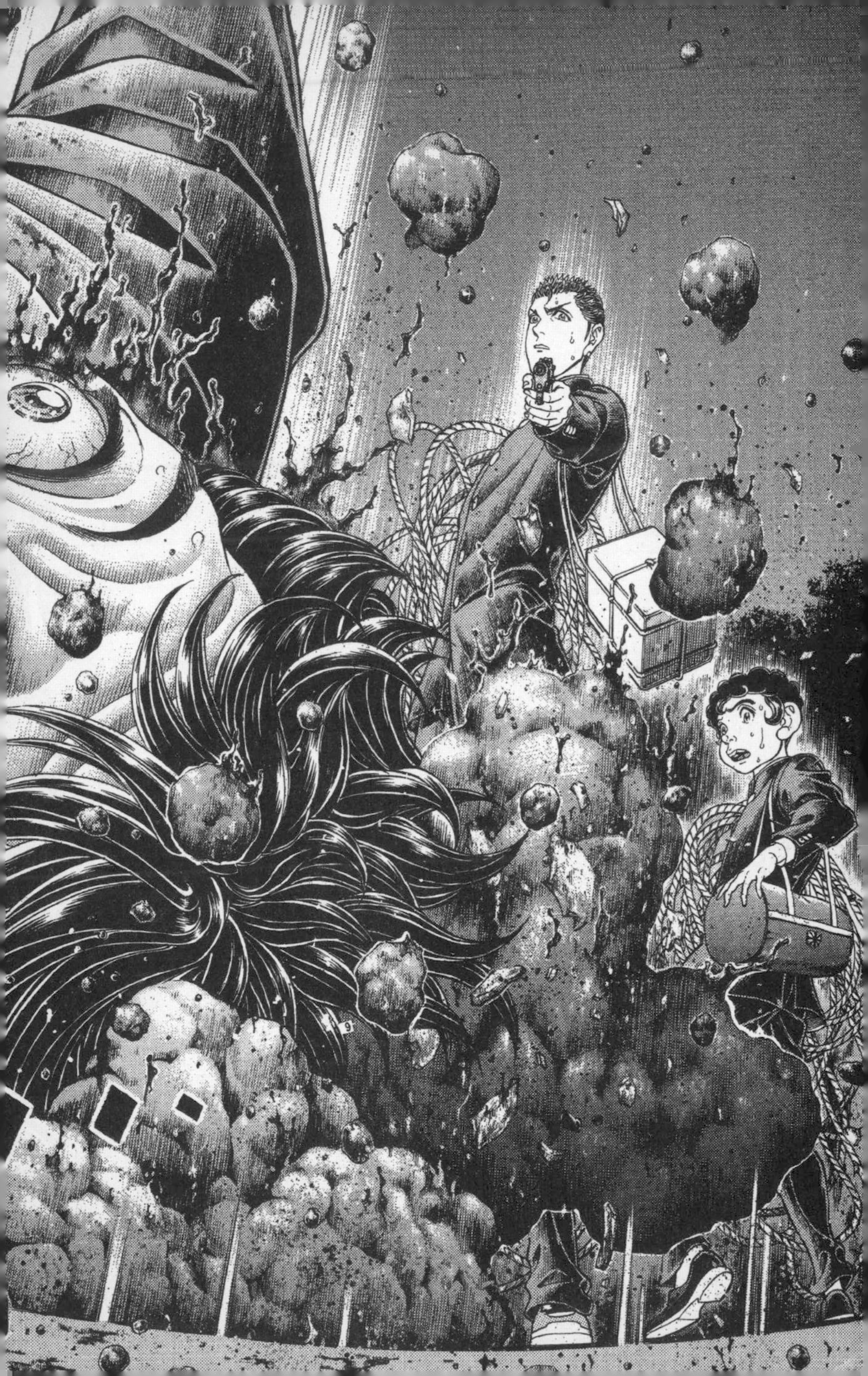

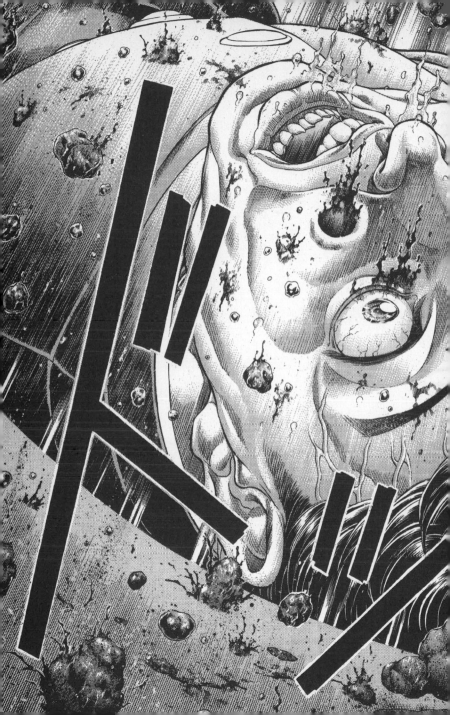

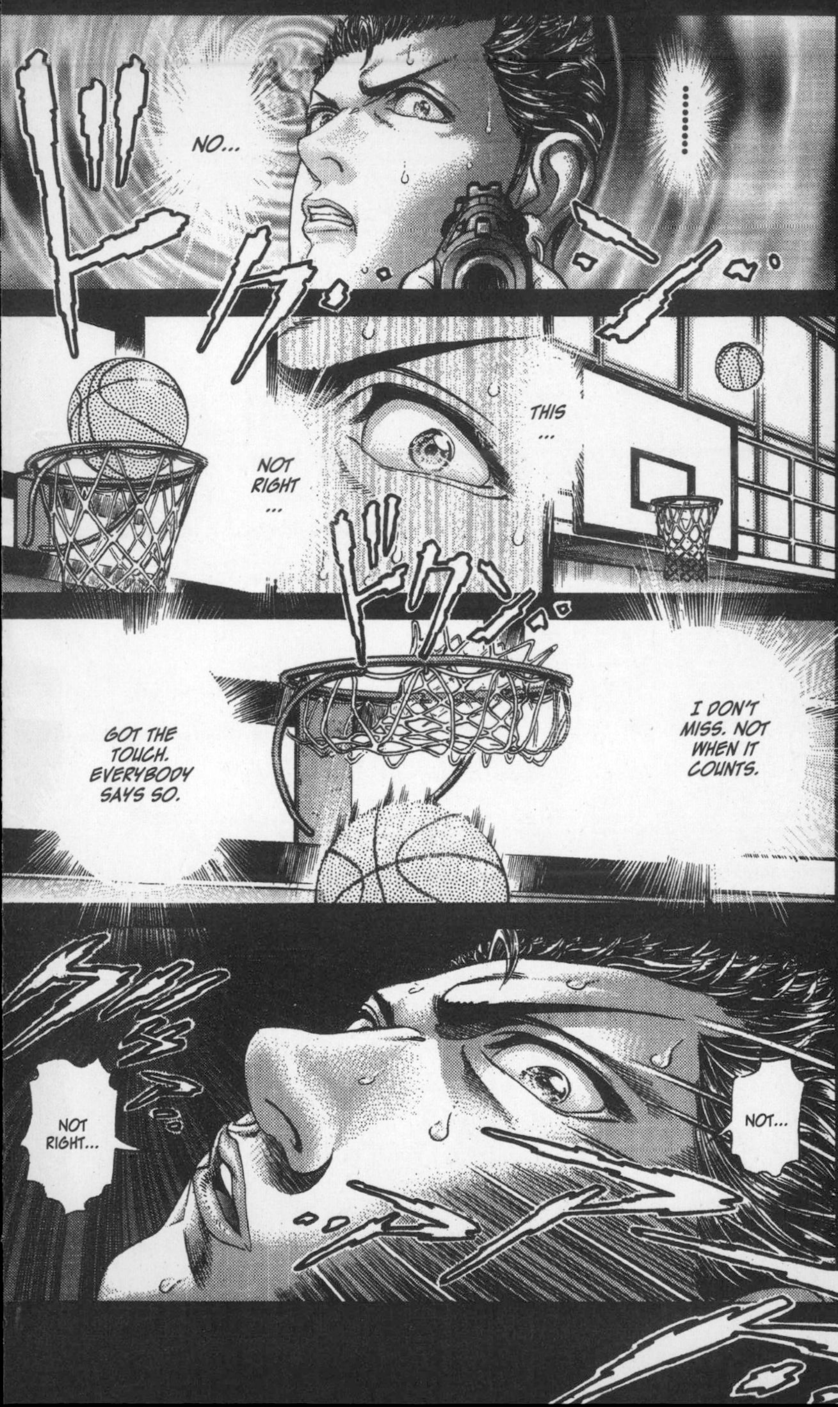
......
NO...
THIS ...
NOT RIGHT ...
I DON'T MISS. NOT WHEN IT COUNTS.
GOT THE TOUCH. EVERYBODY SAYS SO.
NOT...
NOT RIGHT...

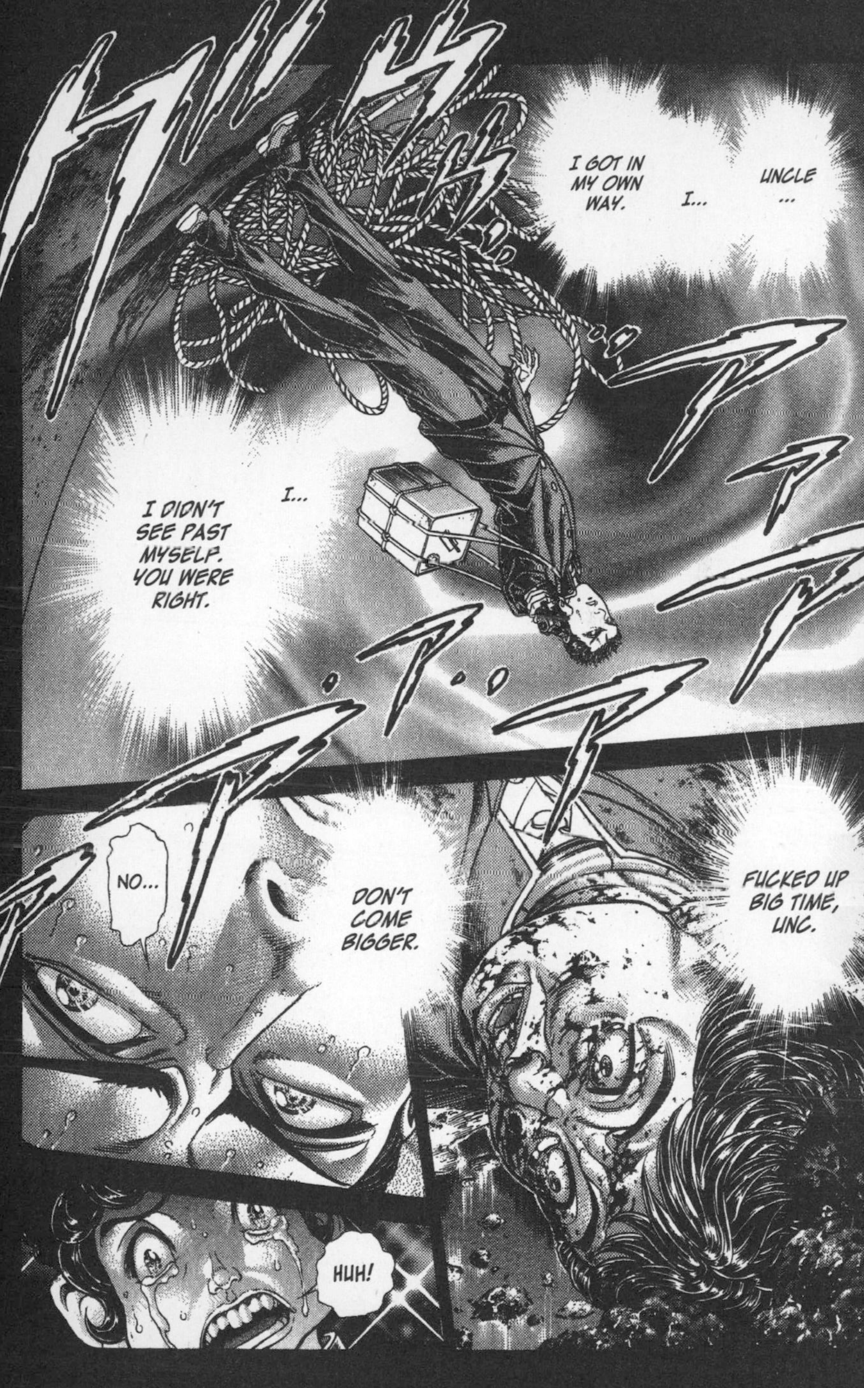
UNCLE ...
I...
I GOT IN MY OWN WAY.
I...
I DIDN'T SEE PAST MYSELF. YOU WERE RIGHT.
FUCKED UP BIG TIME, UNC.
DON'T COME BIGGER.
NO...
HUH!

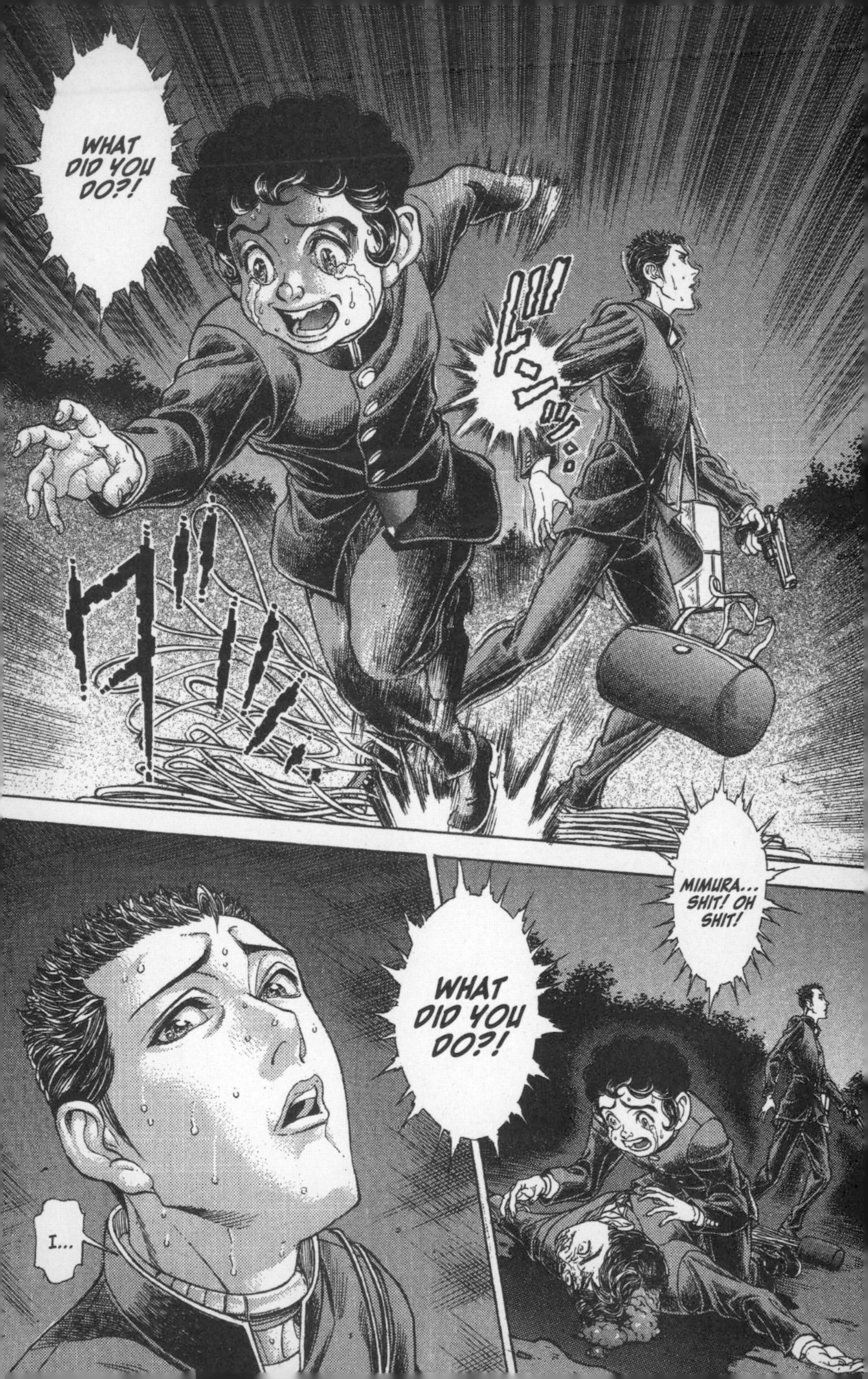
WHAT DID YOU DO?!
MIMURA... SHIT! OH SHIT!
WHAT DID YOU DO?!
I...

BATTLE ROYALE CONTESTANTS

number thirteen in a series
COLLECT THEM ALL!

Yutaka Sato

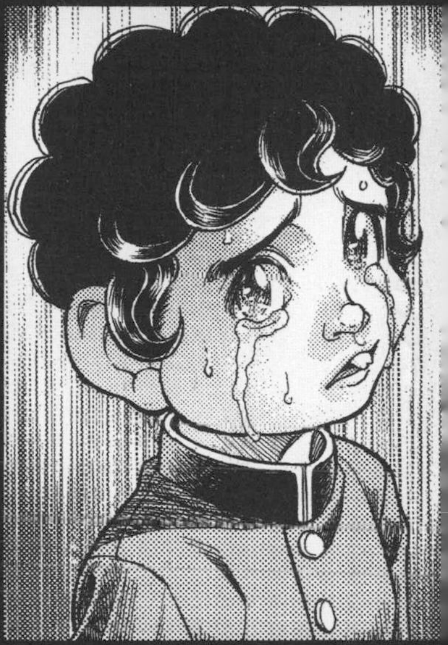

HEIGHT: 154 cm (5 ft. 1 in.)

WEIGHT: 50 kg (110 lb.)

DESIGNATED WEAPON: fork

SUMMARY: Class clown, more through necessity than choice (ref: personal dossier / sub-ref: interpersonal relationships). Decidedly non-physical, verging on frail. Sweet-natured and sentimental, which makes his close friendship with Shinji Mimura (ref: boy #19) that much more puzzling.

CONCLUSION(S): An early elimination, barring unforeseen alliance(s).

Yoshitoki Kuninobu

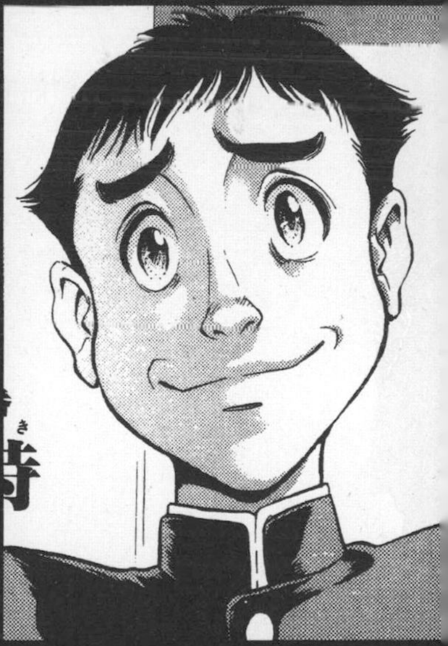

HEIGHT: 172 cm (5 ft. 8 in.)

WEIGHT: 55 kg (121 lb.)

DESIGNATED WEAPON: N/A

SUMMARY: File purged. Subject eliminated prior to game time.

CONCLUSION(S): N/A

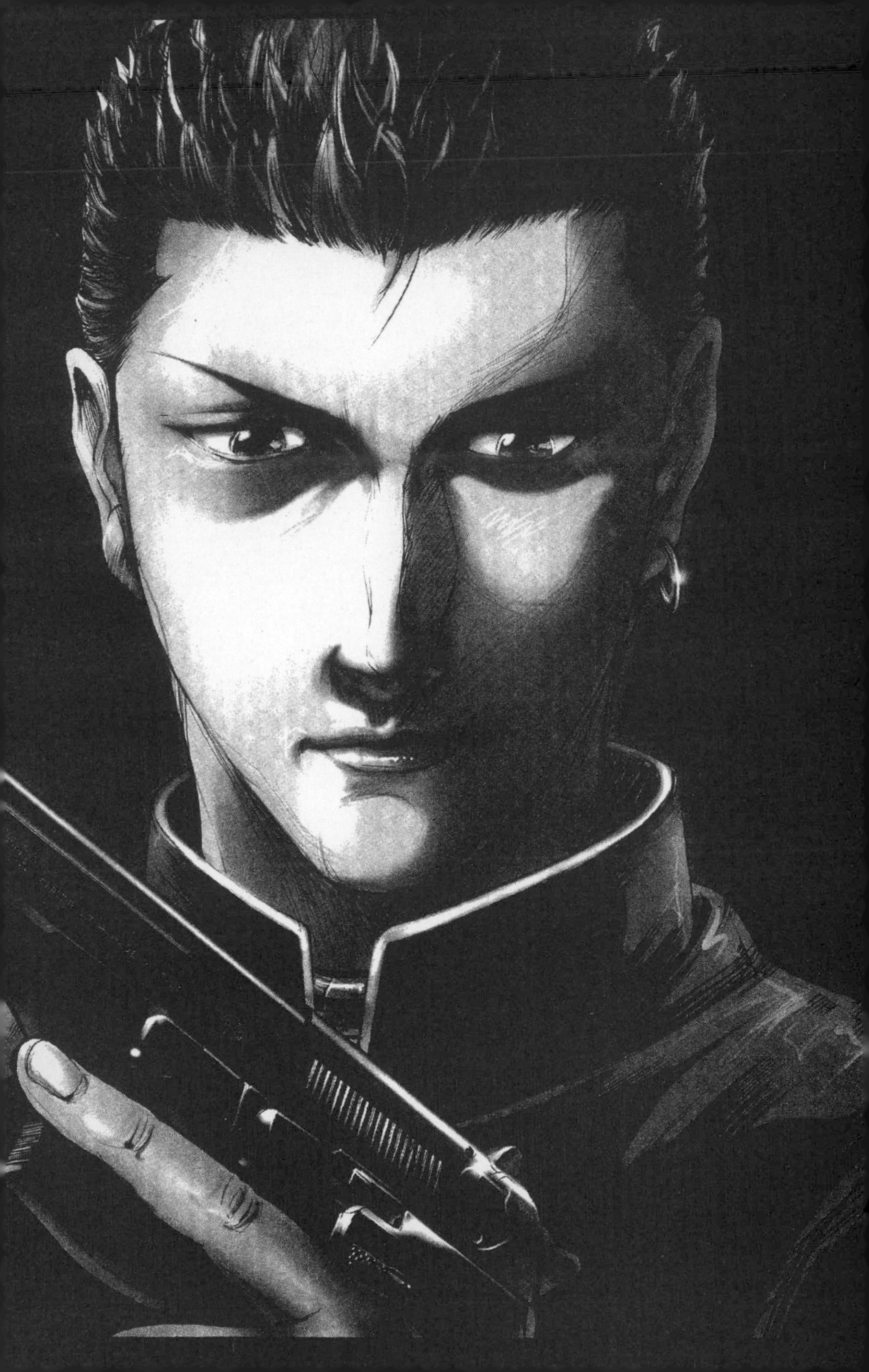

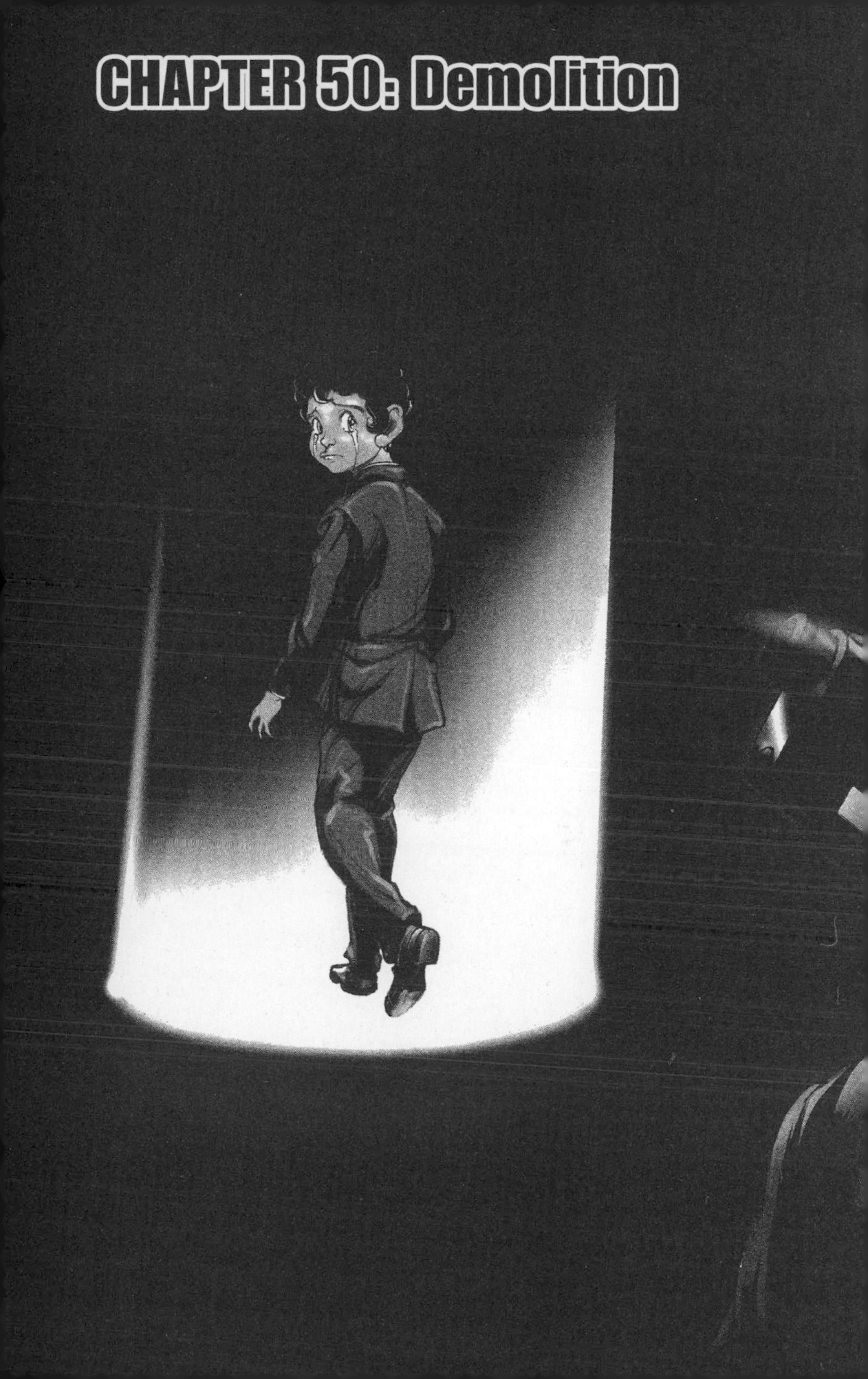
CHAPTER 50: Demolition

BATTLE ROYALE

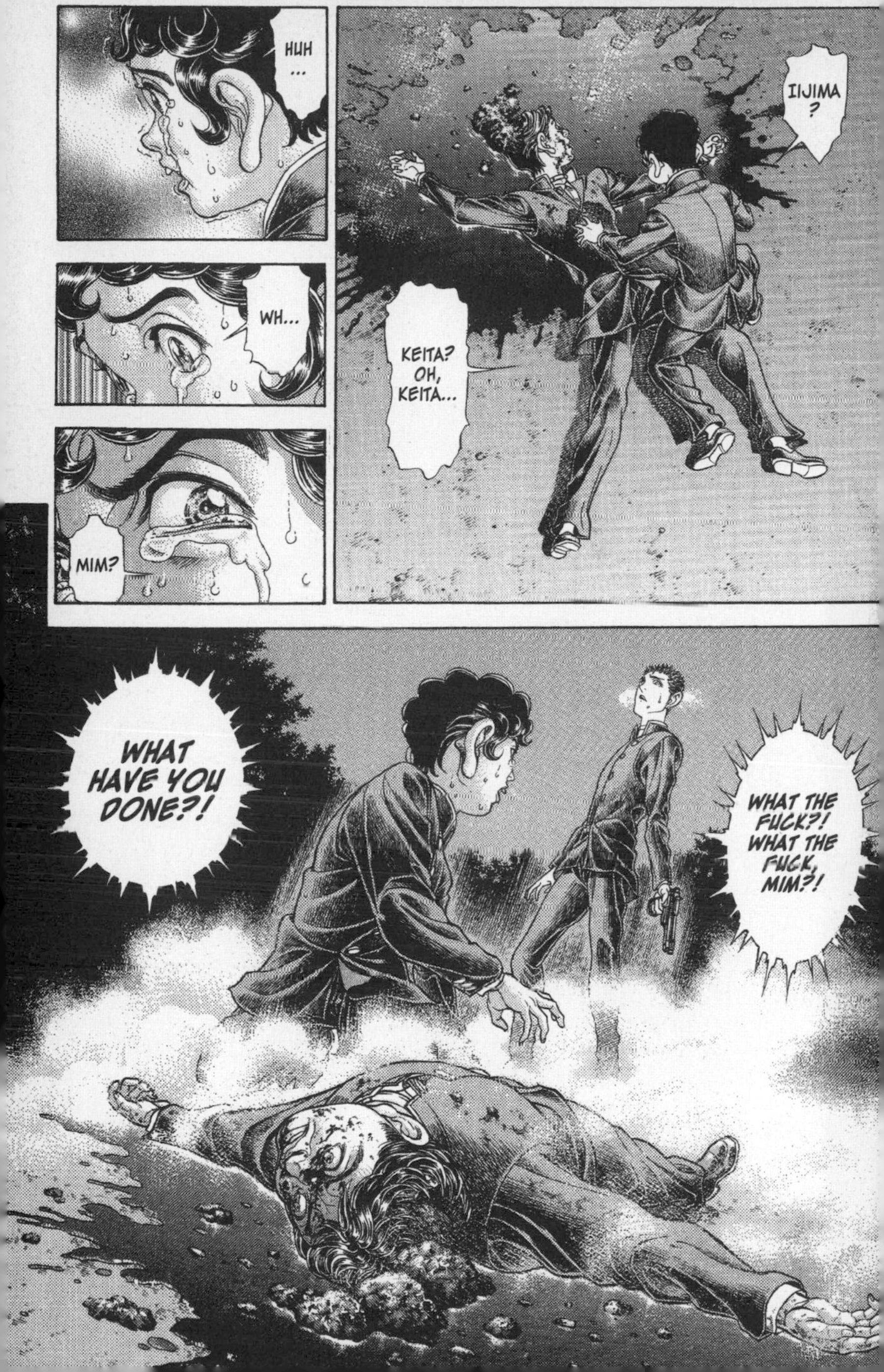
IIJIMA?
KEITA? OH, KEITA...
HUH...
WH...
MIM?
WHAT THE FUCK?! WHAT THE FUCK, MIM?!
WHAT HAVE YOU DONE?!

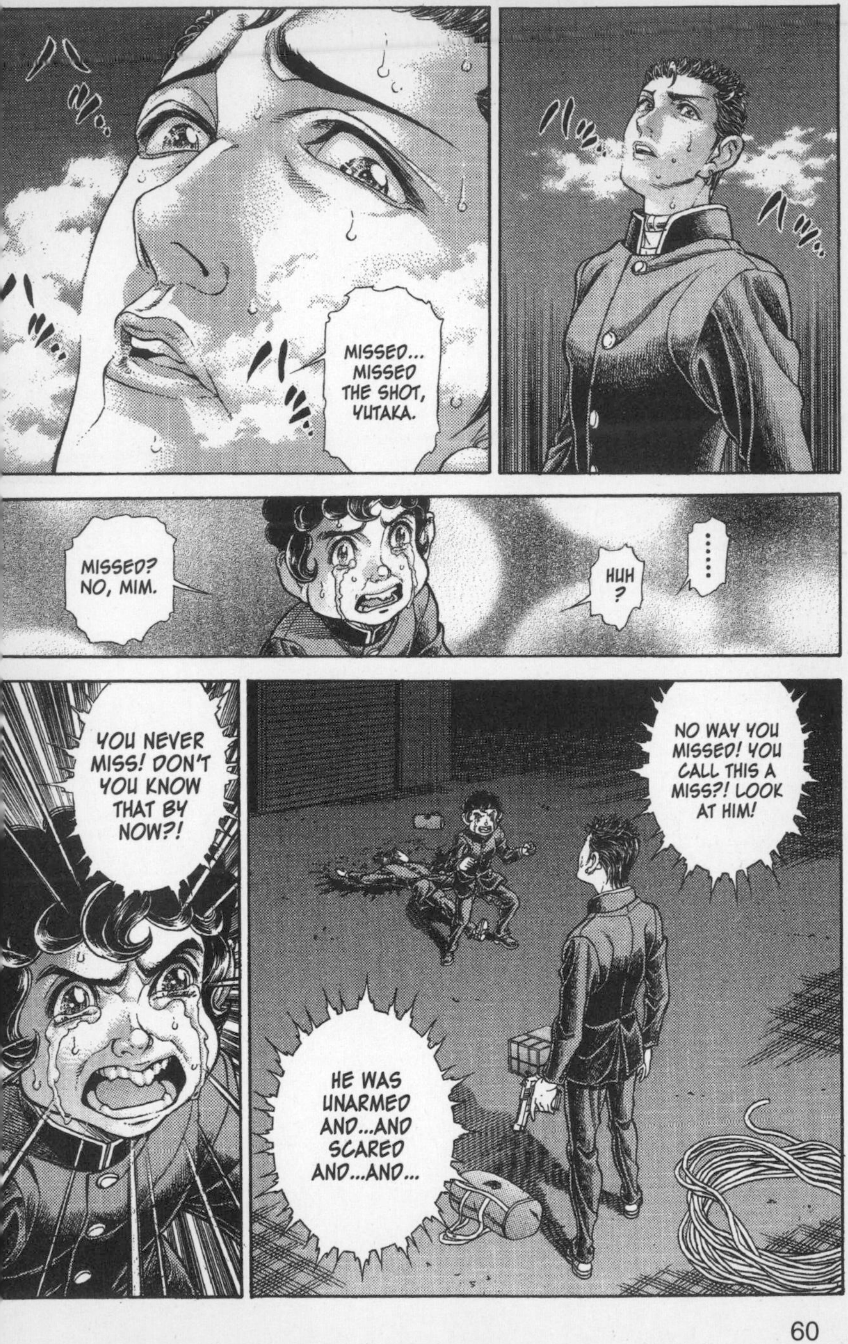
MISSED... MISSED THE SHOT, YUTAKA.
......
HUH?
MISSED? NO, MIM.
NO WAY YOU MISSED! YOU CALL THIS A MISS?! LOOK AT HIM!
HE WAS UNARMED AND...AND SCARED AND...AND...
YOU NEVER MISS! DON'T YOU KNOW THAT BY NOW?!

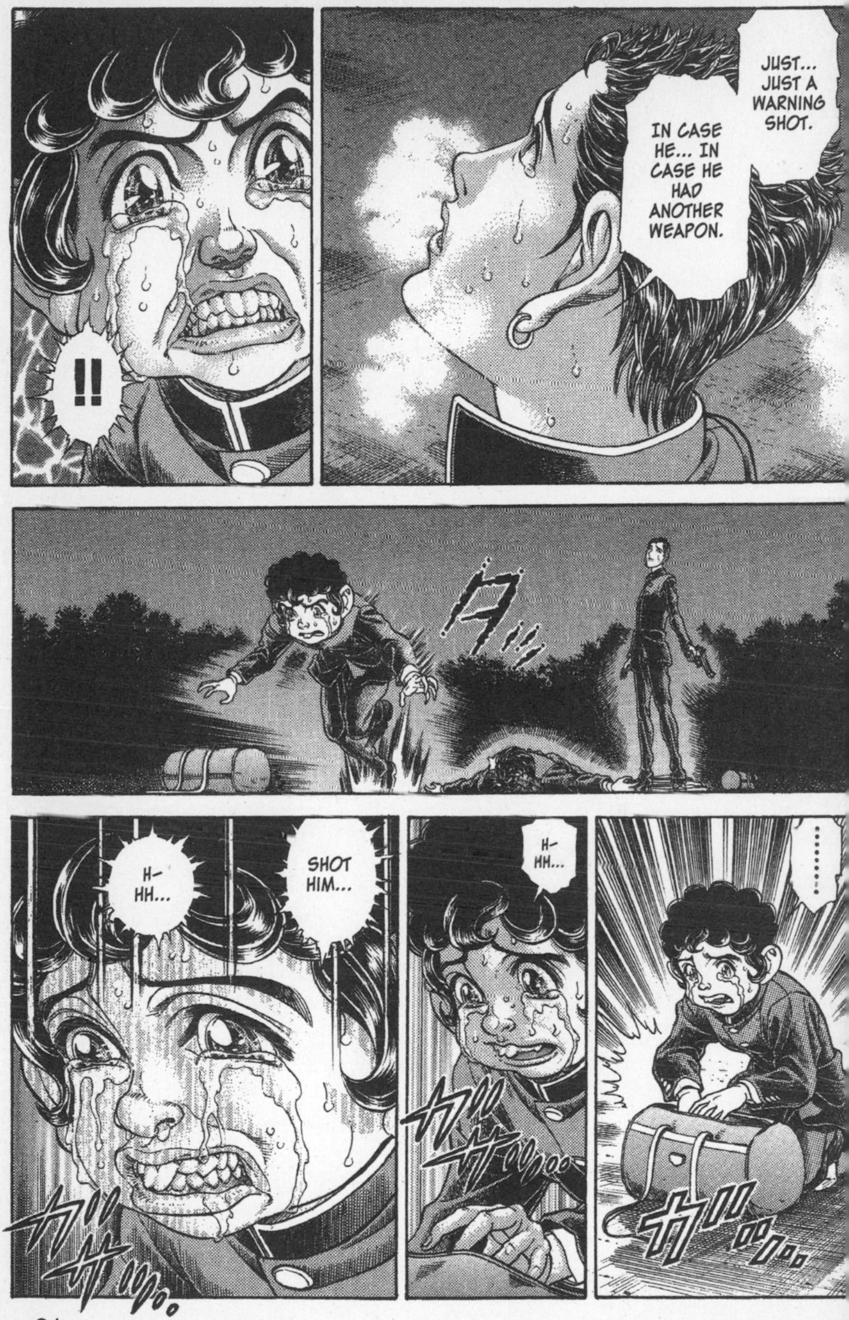
JUST... JUST A WARNING SHOT.
IN CASE HE... IN CASE HE HAD ANOTHER WEAPON.
!!
......
H- HH...
SHOT HIM...
H- HH...

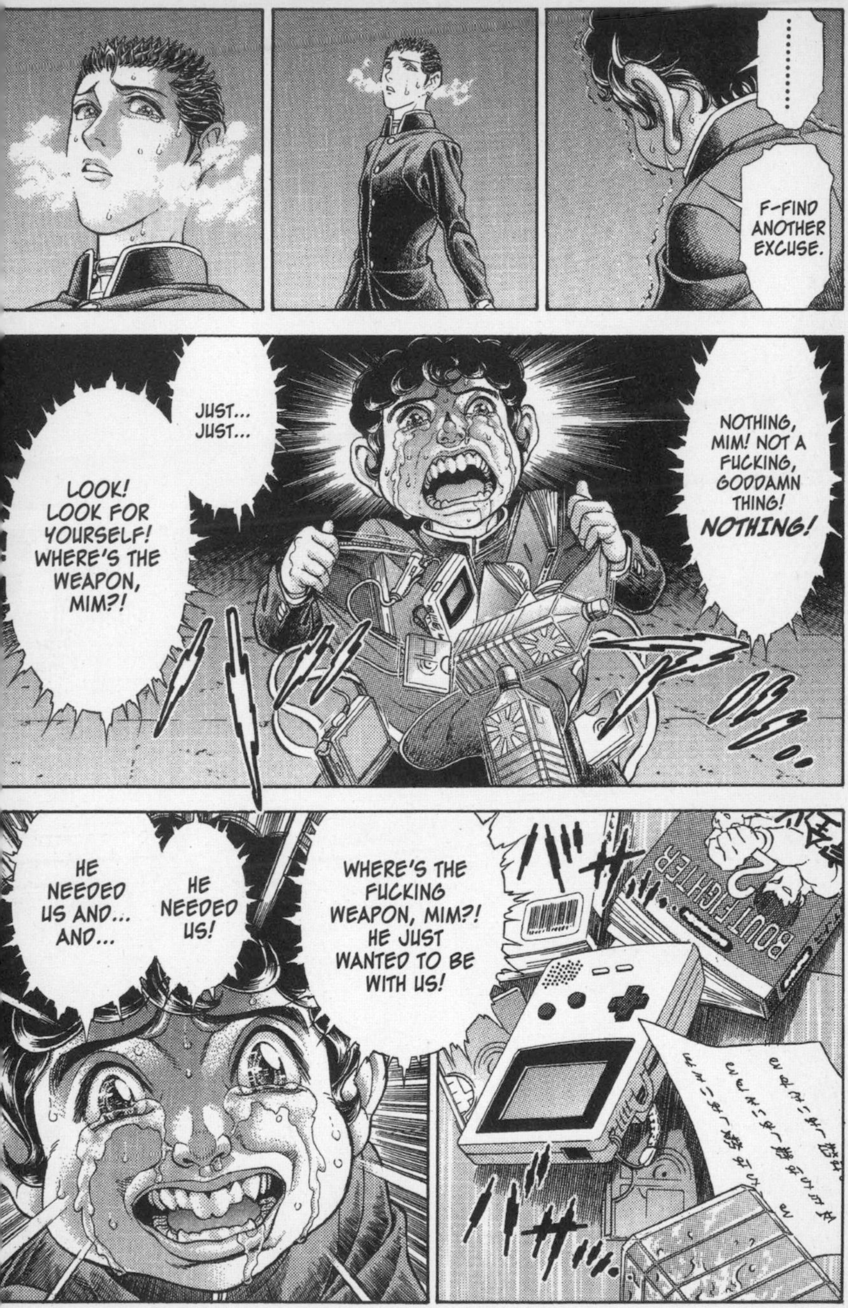
......
F-FIND ANOTHER EXCUSE.
NOTHING, MIM! NOT A FUCKING, GODDAMN THING! NOTHING!
JUST... JUST...
LOOK! LOOK FOR YOURSELF! WHERE'S THE WEAPON, MIM?!
WHERE'S THE FUCKING WEAPON, MIM?! HE JUST WANTED TO BE WITH US!
HE NEEDED US!
HE NEEDED US AND... AND...

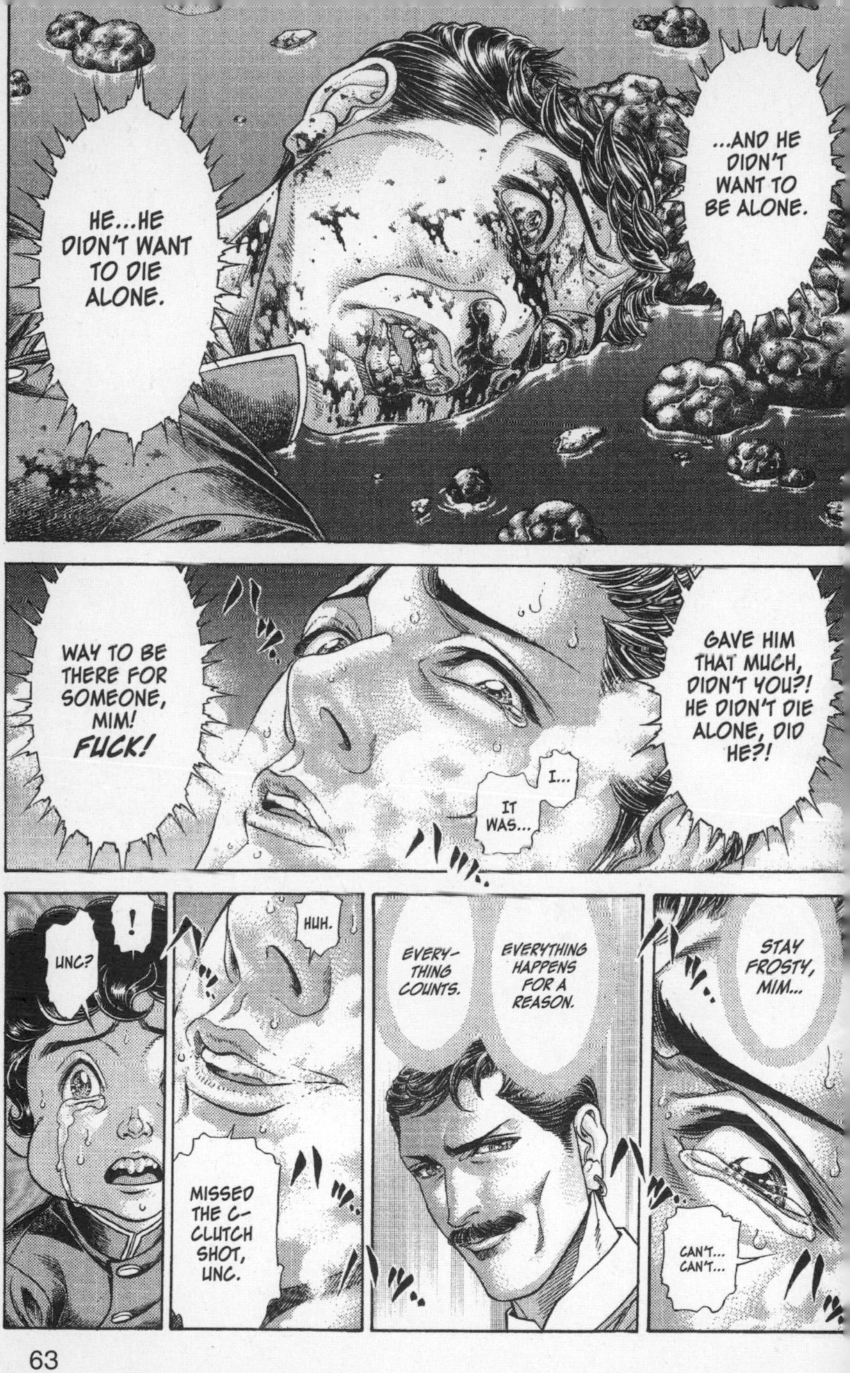
...AND HE DIDN'T WANT TO BE ALONE.
HE...HE DIDN'T WANT TO DIE ALONE.
GAVE HIM THAT MUCH, DIDN'T YOU?! HE DIDN'T DIE ALONE, DID HE?!
I...
IT WAS...
WAY TO BE THERE FOR SOMEONE, MIM! FUCK!
STAY FROSTY, MIM...
CAN'T... CAN'T...
EVERYTHING HAPPENS FOR A REASON.
EVERY-THING COUNTS.
HUH.
MISSED THE C-CLUTCH SHOT, UNC.
!
UNC?

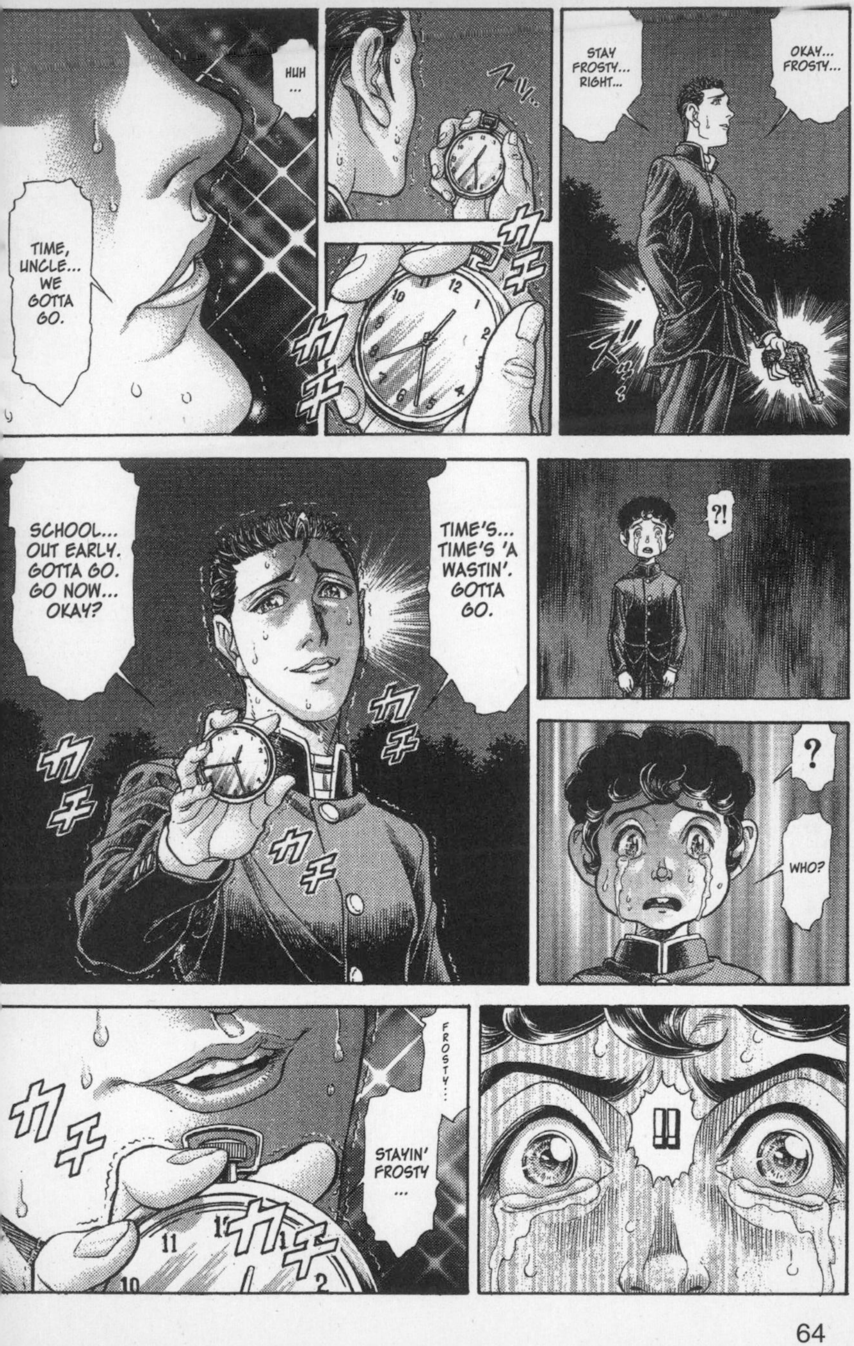
OKAY... FROSTY...
STAY FROSTY... RIGHT...
HUH ...
TIME, UNCLE... WE GOTTA GO.
?!
?
WHO?
TIME'S... TIME'S 'A WASTIN'. GOTTA GO.
SCHOOL... OUT EARLY. GOTTA GO. GO NOW... OKAY?
!!
FROSTY...
STAYIN' FROSTY ...

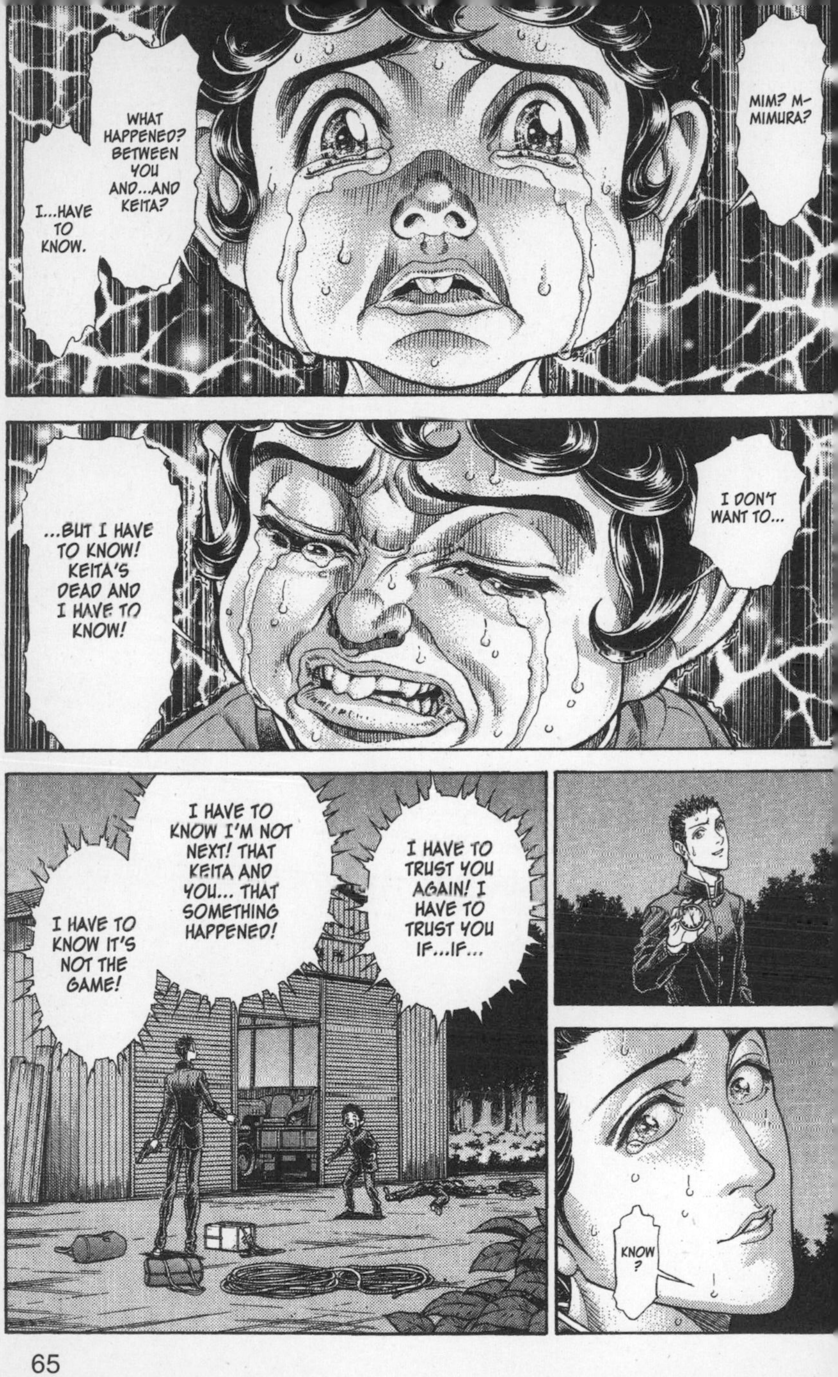
MIM? M-MIMURA?
WHAT HAPPENED? BETWEEN YOU AND...AND KEITA?
I...HAVE TO KNOW.
I DON'T WANT TO...
...BUT I HAVE TO KNOW! KEITA'S DEAD AND I HAVE TO KNOW!
KNOW?
I HAVE TO TRUST YOU AGAIN! I HAVE TO TRUST YOU IF...IF...
I HAVE TO KNOW I'M NOT NEXT! THAT KEITA AND YOU... THAT SOMETHING HAPPENED!
I HAVE TO KNOW IT'S NOT THE GAME!

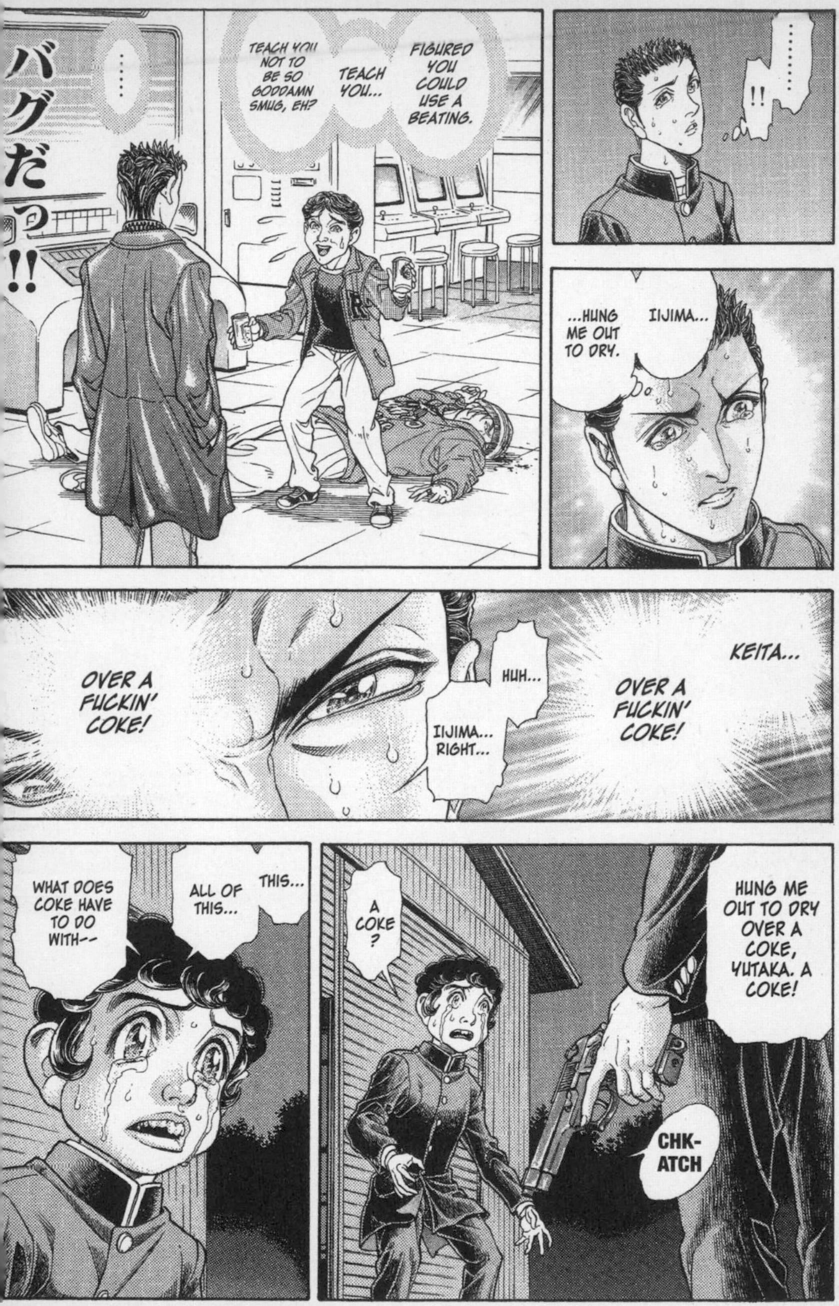
......
!!
IIJIMA...
...HUNG ME OUT TO DRY.
FIGURED YOU COULD USE A BEATING.
TEACH YOU...
TEACH YOU NOT TO BE SO GODDAMN SMUG, EH?
......
バグだっ!!
KEITA...
OVER A FUCKIN' COKE!
HUH...
IIJIMA... RIGHT...
OVER A FUCKIN' COKE!
HUNG ME OUT TO DRY OVER A COKE, YUTAKA. A COKE!
CHK-ATCH
A COKE?
THIS...
ALL OF THIS...
WHAT DOES COKE HAVE TO DO WITH--

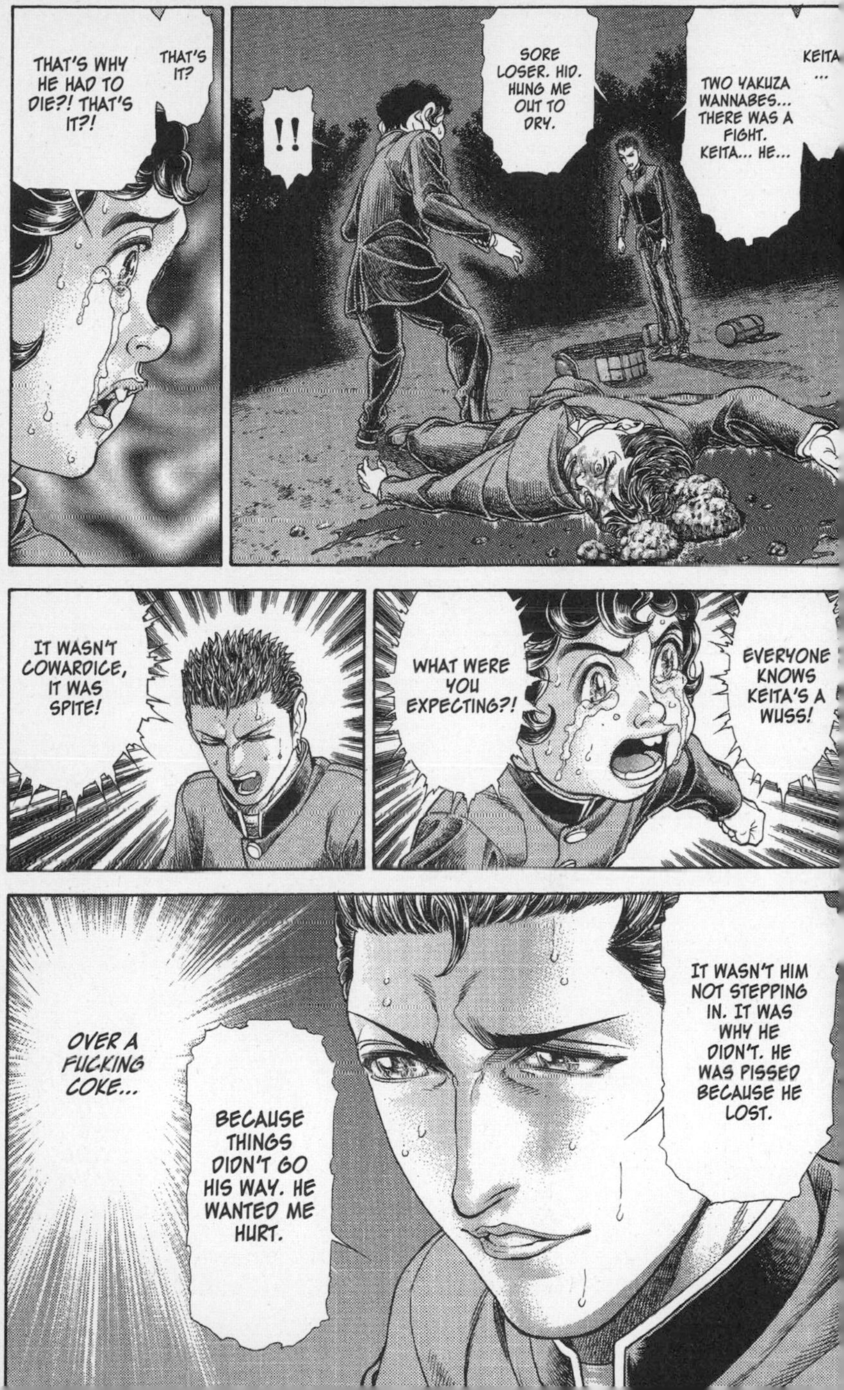
KEITA...
TWO YAKUZA WANNABES... THERE WAS A FIGHT. KEITA... HE...
SORE LOSER. HID. HUNG ME OUT TO DRY.
!!
THAT'S IT?
THAT'S WHY HE HAD TO DIE?! THAT'S IT?!
EVERYONE KNOWS KEITA'S A WUSS!
WHAT WERE YOU EXPECTING?!
IT WASN'T COWARDICE, IT WAS SPITE!
IT WASN'T HIM NOT STEPPING IN. IT WAS WHY HE DIDN'T. HE WAS PISSED BECAUSE HE LOST.
BECAUSE THINGS DIDN'T GO HIS WAY. HE WANTED ME HURT.
OVER A FUCKING COKE...

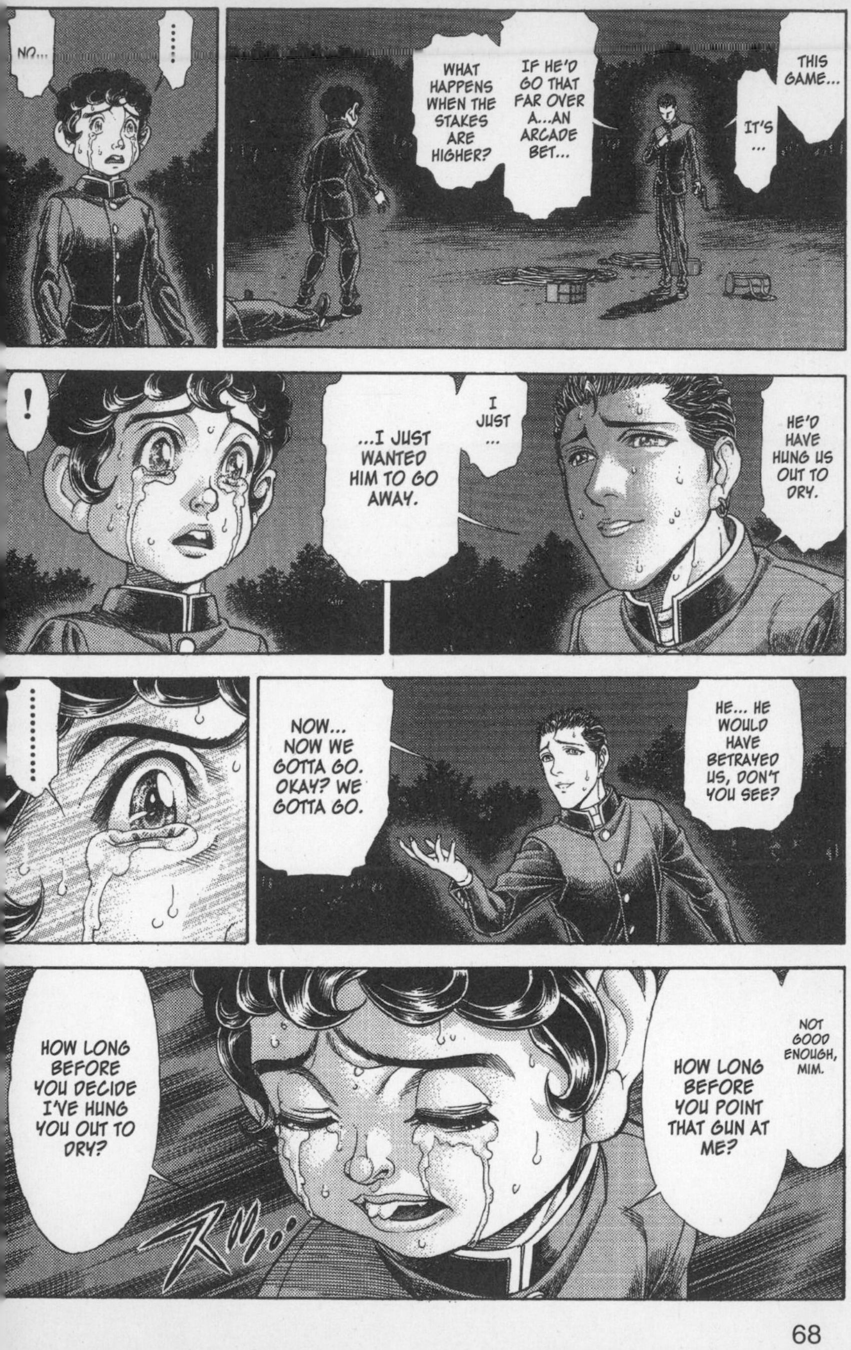
THIS GAME...
IT'S ...
IF HE'D GO THAT FAR OVER A...AN ARCADE BET...
WHAT HAPPENS WHEN THE STAKES ARE HIGHER?
......
NO...
HE'D HAVE HUNG US OUT TO DRY.
I JUST ...
...I JUST WANTED HIM TO GO AWAY.
!
HE... HE WOULD HAVE BETRAYED US, DON'T YOU SEE?
NOW... NOW WE GOTTA GO. OKAY? WE GOTTA GO.
......
NOT GOOD ENOUGH, MIM.
HOW LONG BEFORE YOU POINT THAT GUN AT ME?
HOW LONG BEFORE YOU DECIDE I'VE HUNG YOU OUT TO DRY?

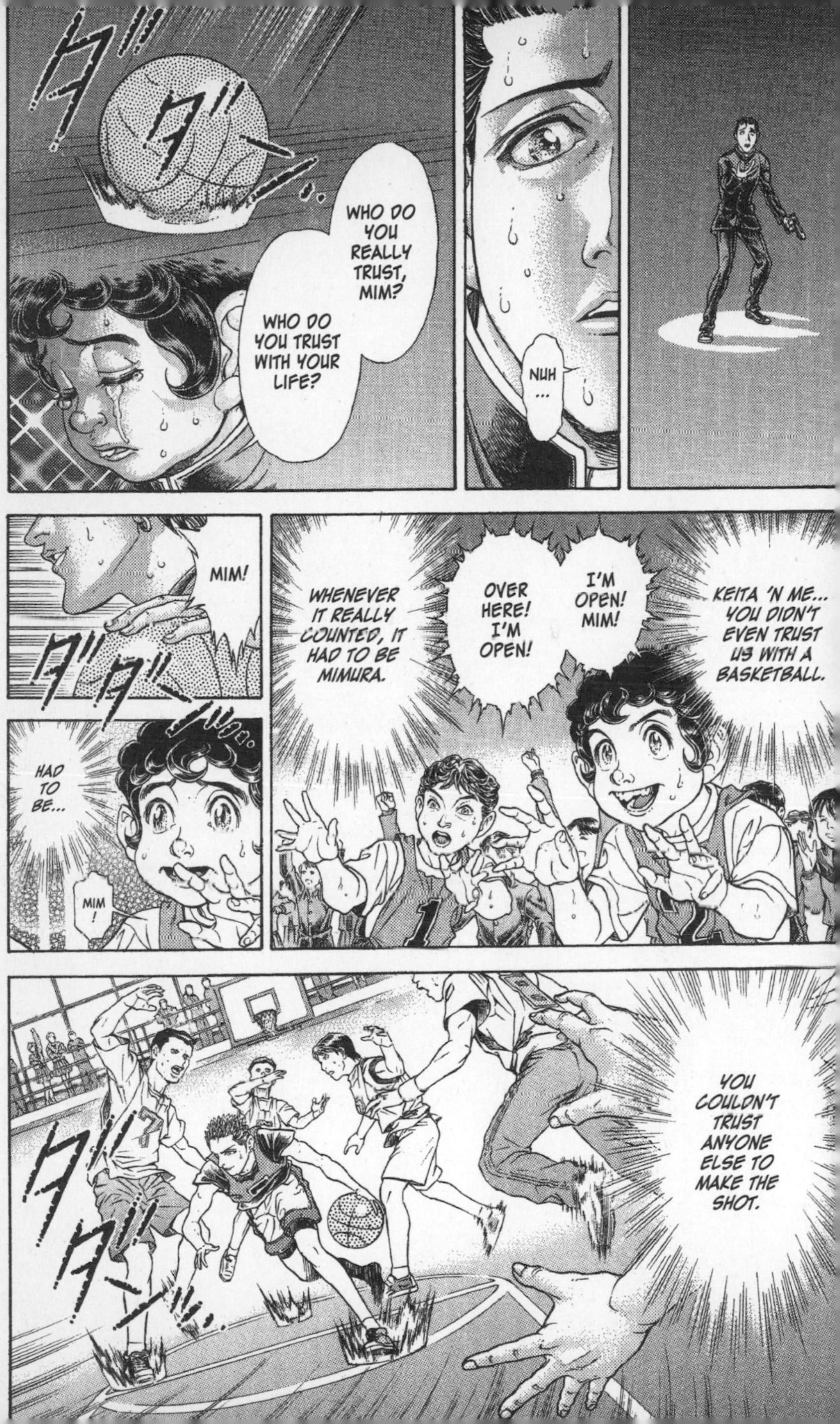
NUH ...
WHO DO YOU REALLY TRUST, MIM?
WHO DO YOU TRUST WITH YOUR LIFE?
KEITA 'N ME... YOU DIDN'T EVEN TRUST US WITH A BASKETBALL.
I'M OPEN! MIM!
OVER HERE! I'M OPEN!
WHENEVER IT REALLY COUNTED, IT HAD TO BE MIMURA.
MIM!
HAD TO BE...
MIM!
YOU COULDN'T TRUST ANYONE ELSE TO MAKE THE SHOT.

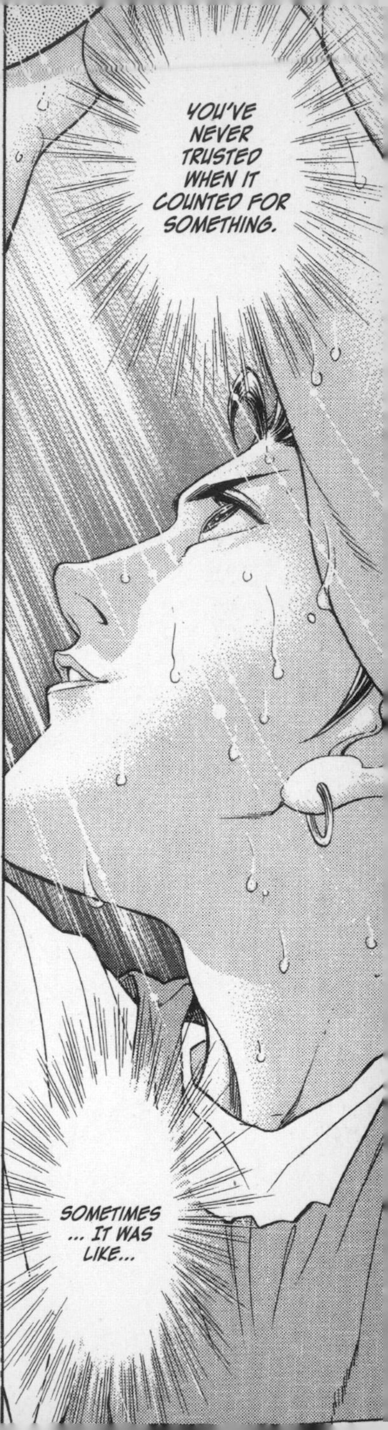
YOU'VE NEVER TRUSTED WHEN IT COUNTED FOR SOMETHING.
SOMETIMES ... IT WAS LIKE...
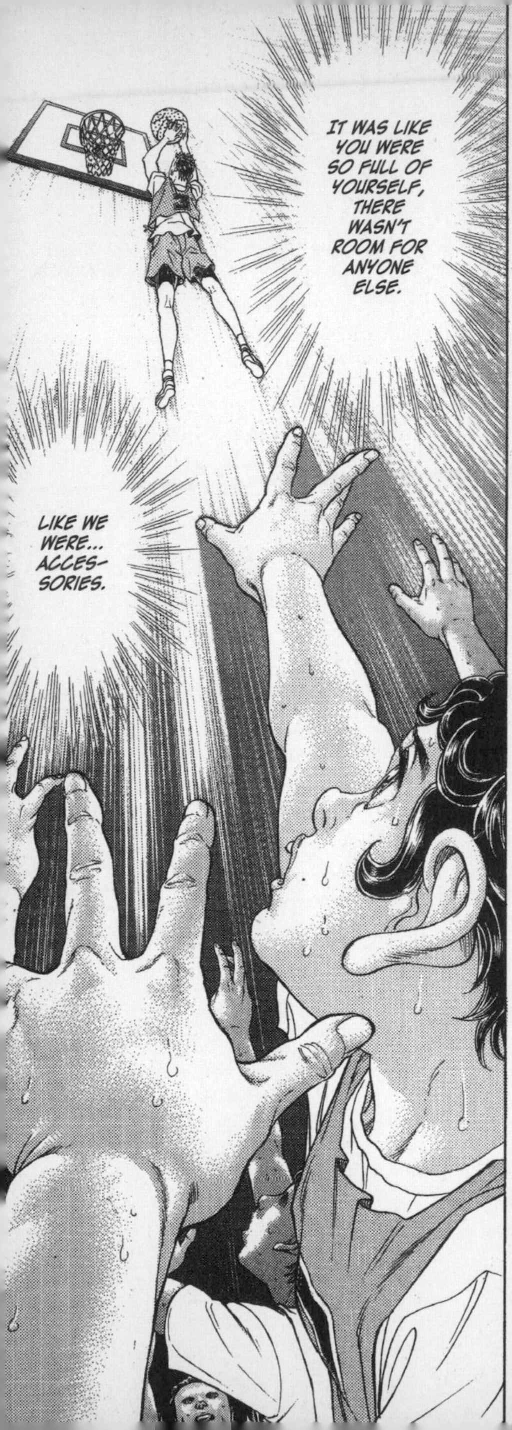
IT WAS LIKE YOU WERE SO FULL OF YOURSELF, THERE WASN'T ROOM FOR ANYONE ELSE.
LIKE WE WERE... ACCES-SORIES.

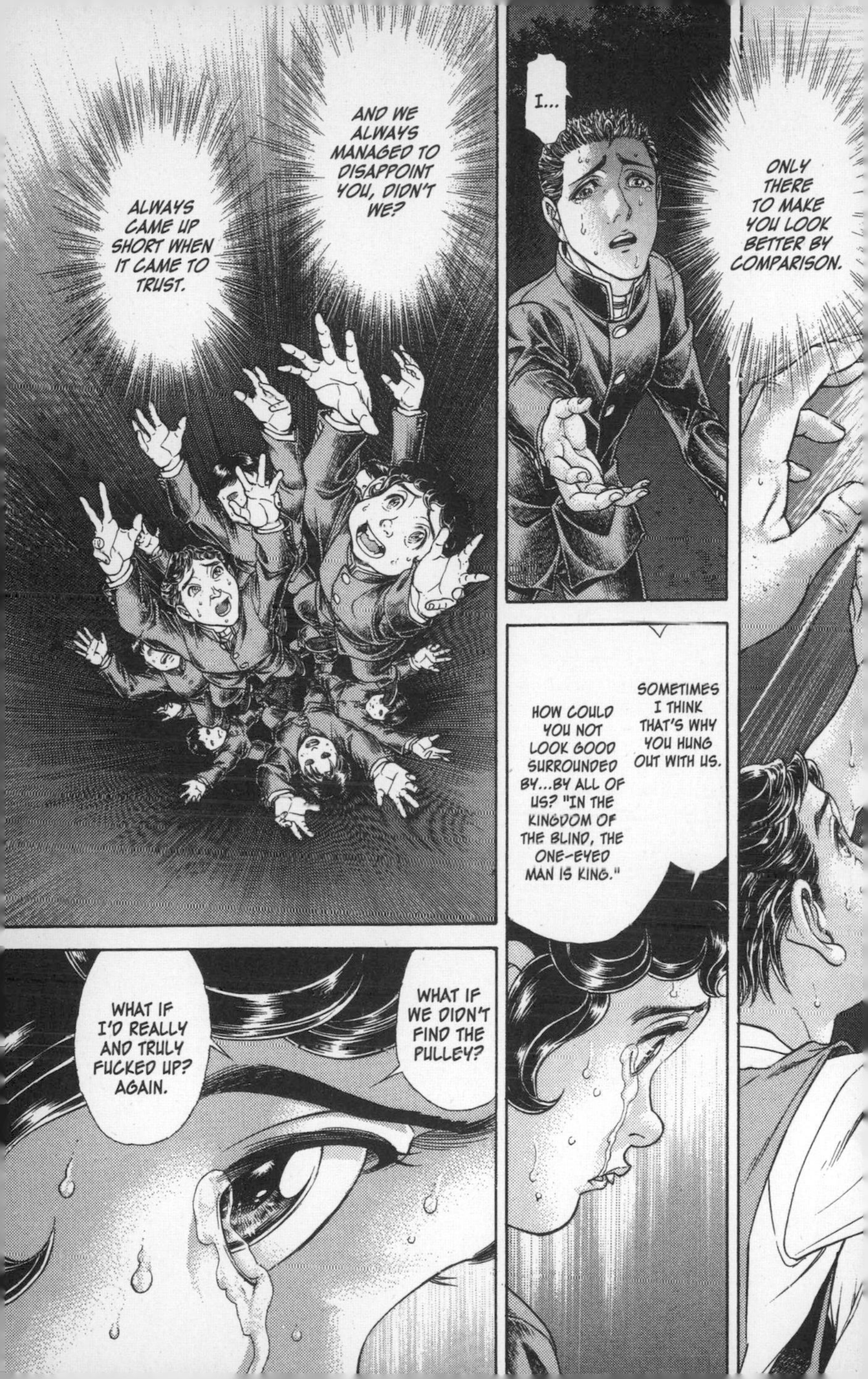
ONLY THERE TO MAKE YOU LOOK BETTER BY COMPARISON.
I...
AND WE ALWAYS MANAGED TO DISAPPOINT YOU, DIDN'T WE?
ALWAYS CAME UP SHORT WHEN IT CAME TO TRUST.
SOMETIMES I THINK THAT'S WHY YOU HUNG OUT WITH US.
HOW COULD YOU NOT LOOK GOOD SURROUNDED BY...BY ALL OF US? "IN THE KINGDOM OF THE BLIND, THE ONE-EYED MAN IS KING."
WHAT IF WE DIDN'T FIND THE PULLEY?
WHAT IF I'D REALLY AND TRULY FUCKED UP? AGAIN.

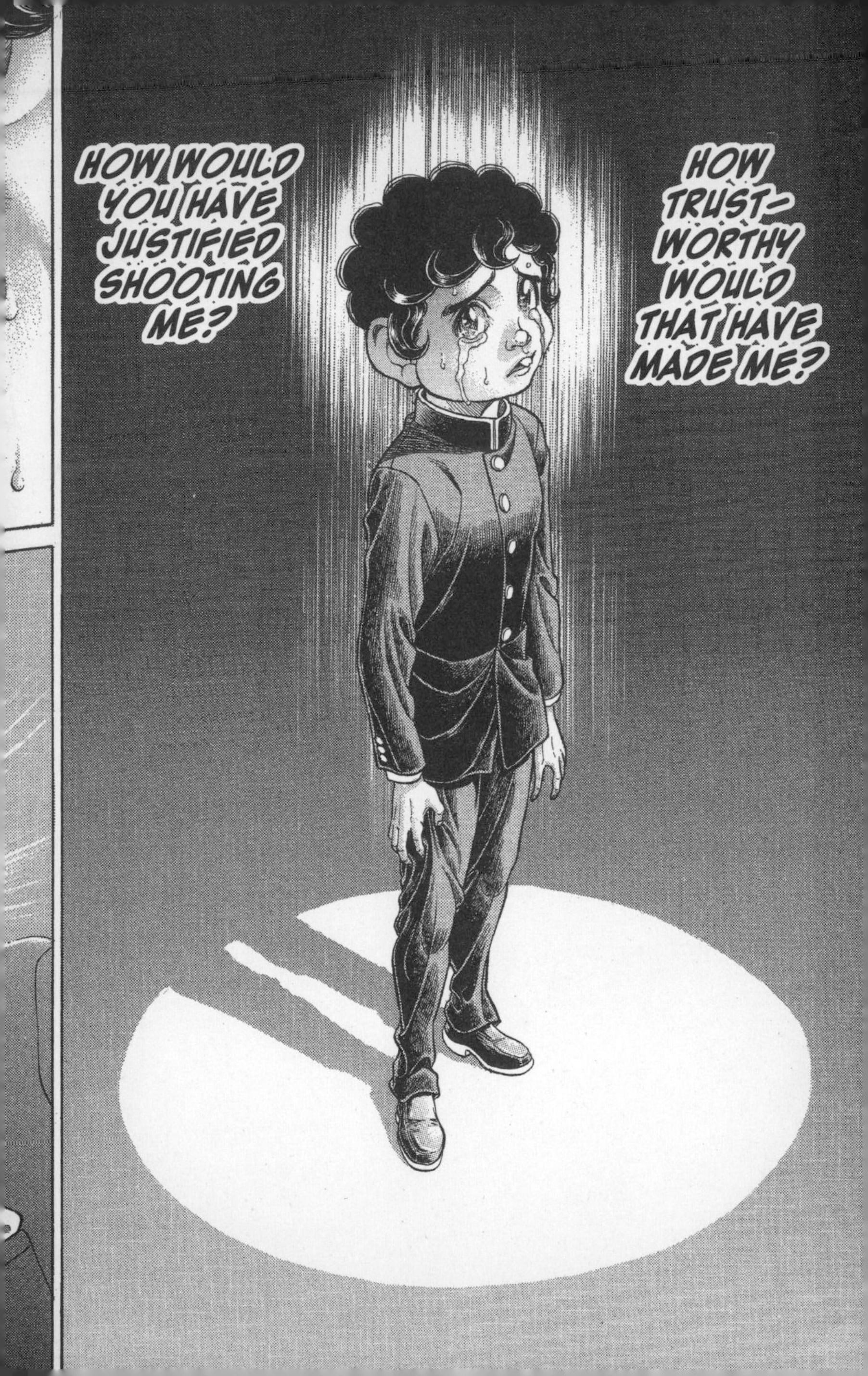
HOW TRUST-WORTHY WOULD THAT HAVE MADE ME?
HOW WOULD YOU HAVE JUSTIFIED SHOOTING ME?

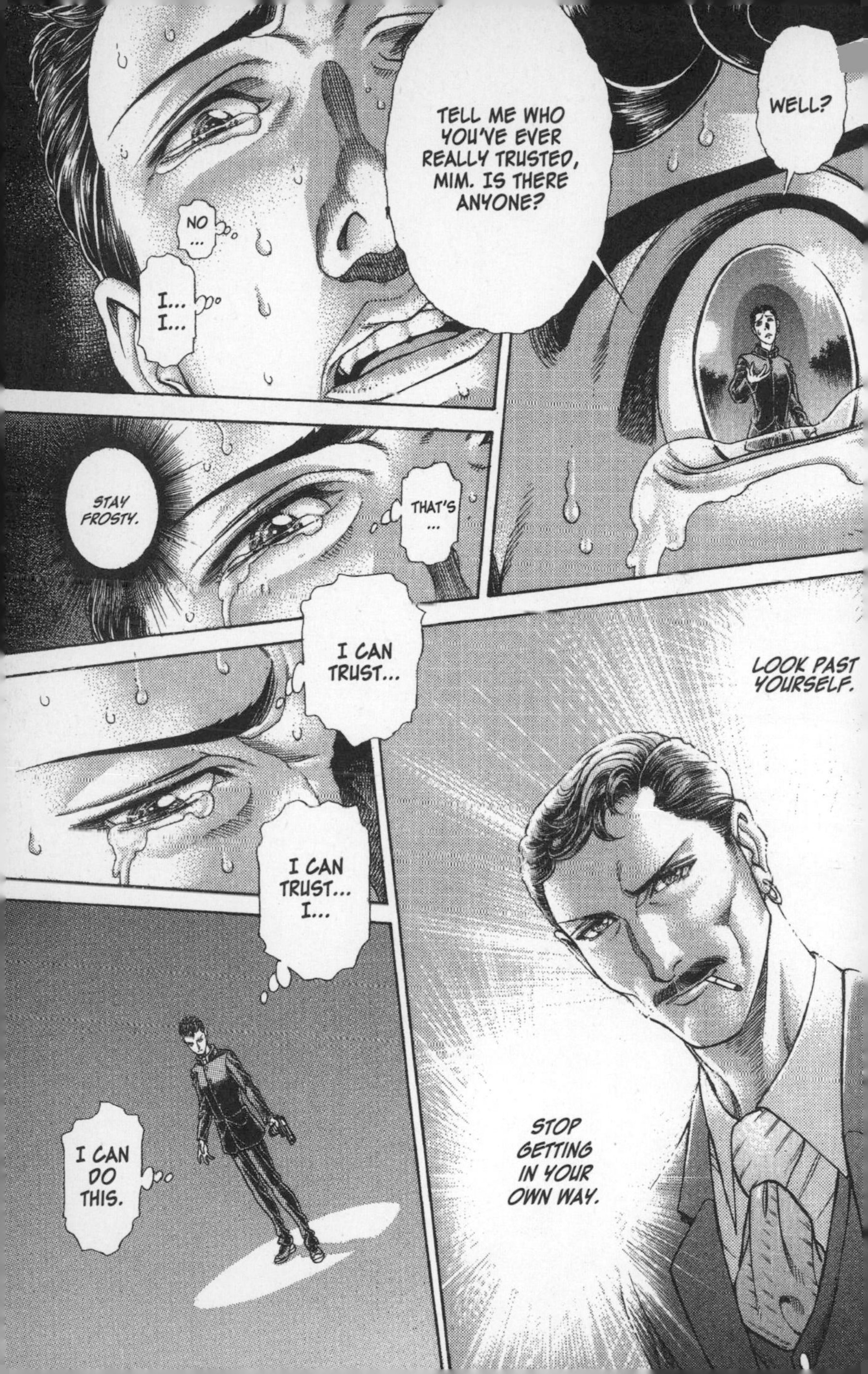
TELL ME WHO YOU'VE EVER REALLY TRUSTED, MIM. IS THERE ANYONE?
WELL?
NO ...
I... I...
THAT'S ...
STAY FROSTY.
I CAN TRUST...
LOOK PAST YOURSELF.
STOP GETTING IN YOUR OWN WAY.
I CAN TRUST... I...
I CAN DO THIS.

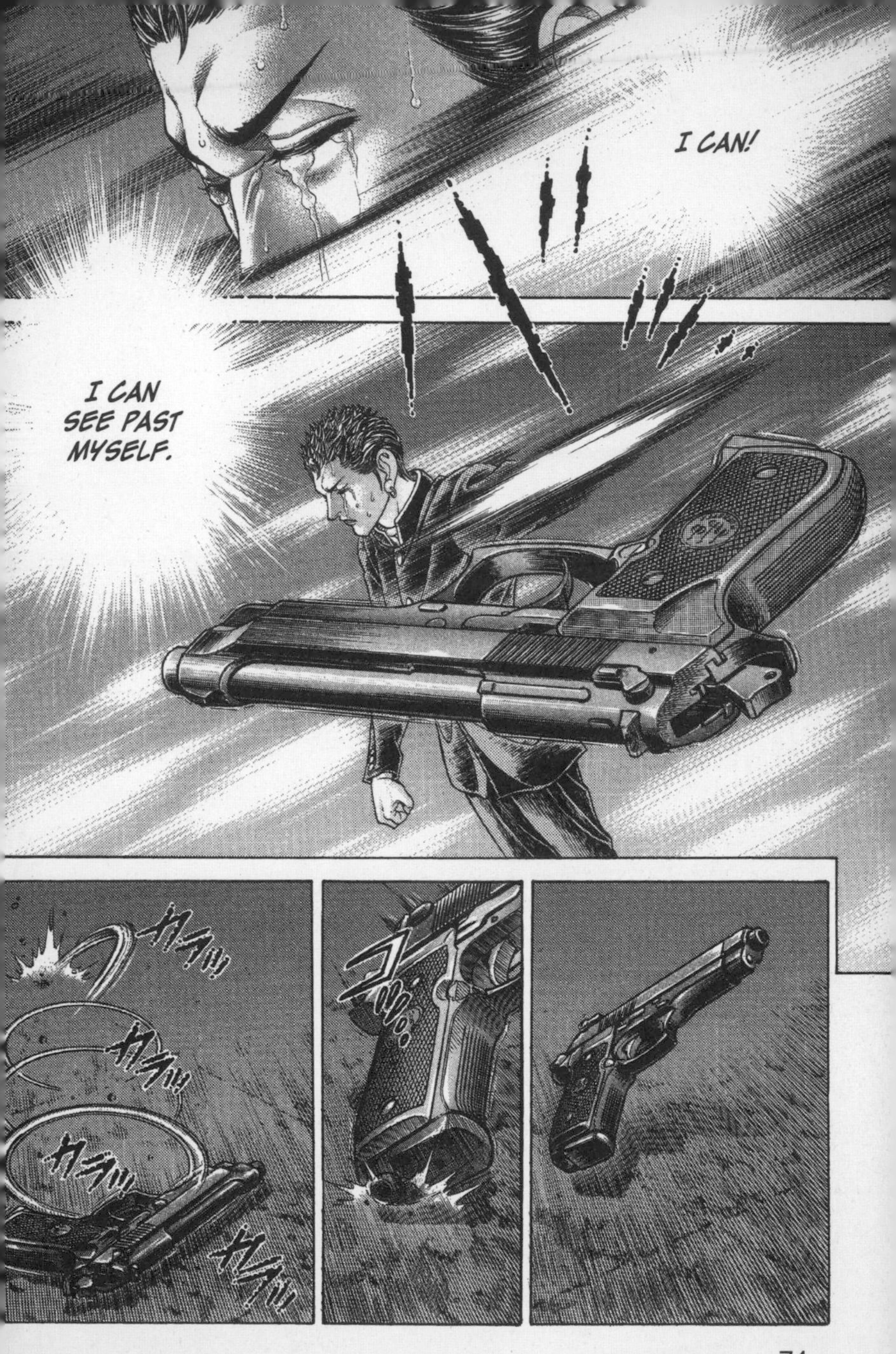
I CAN!
I CAN SEE PAST MYSELF.

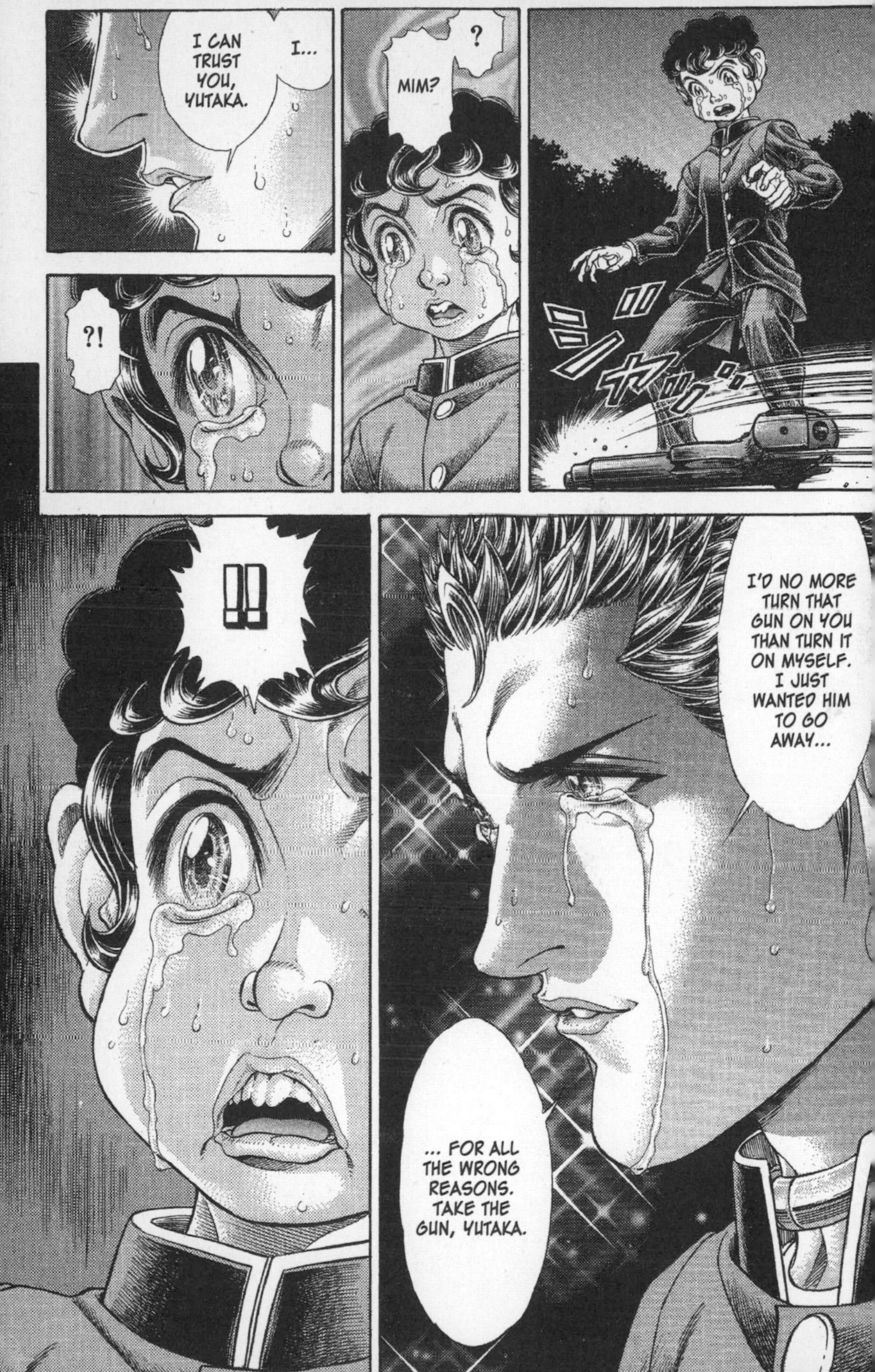
?
MIM?
I...
I CAN TRUST YOU, YUTAKA.
?!
I'D NO MORE TURN THAT GUN ON YOU THAN TURN IT ON MYSELF. I JUST WANTED HIM TO GO AWAY...
... FOR ALL THE WRONG REASONS. TAKE THE GUN, YUTAKA.
!!

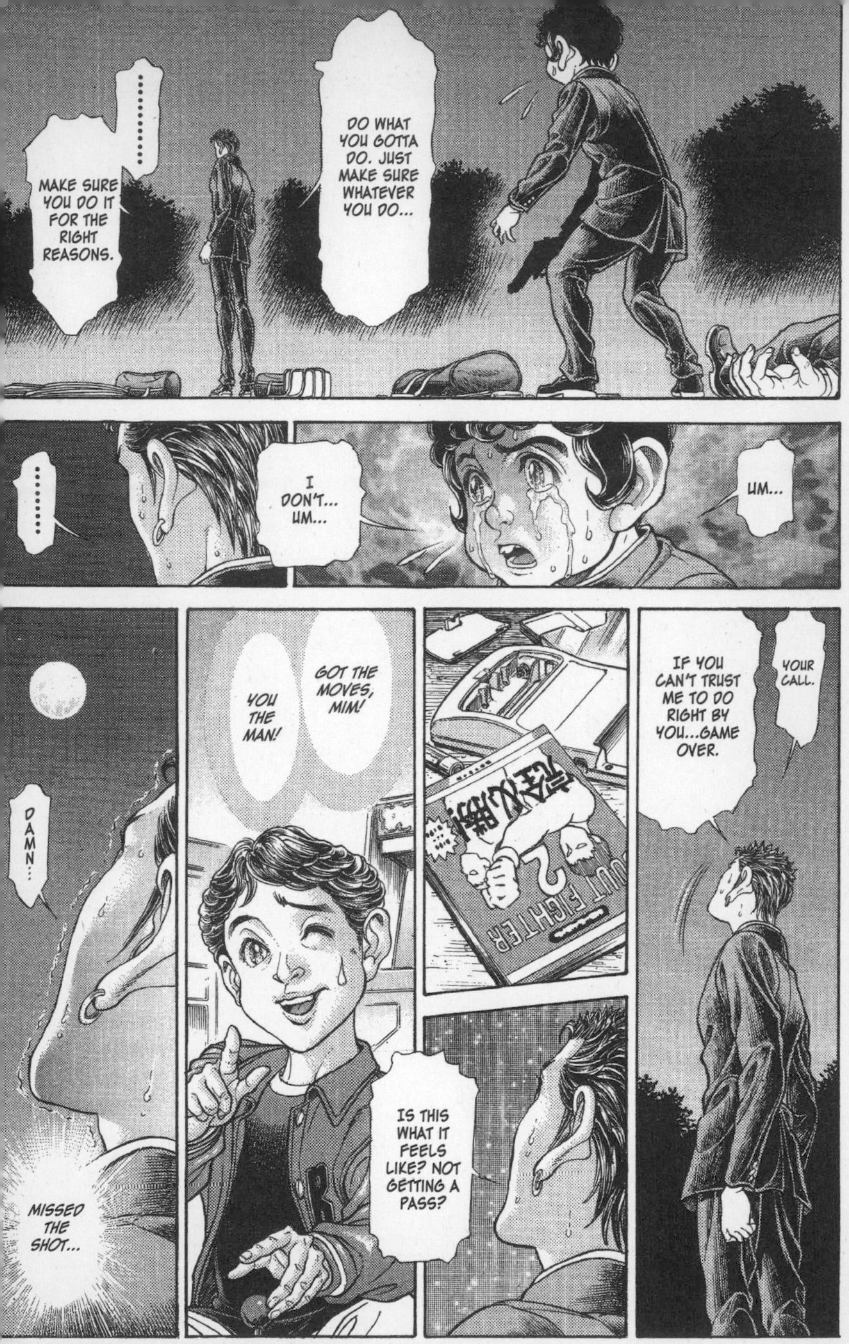
DO WHAT YOU GOTTA DO. JUST MAKE SURE WHATEVER YOU DO...
......
MAKE SURE YOU DO IT FOR THE RIGHT REASONS.
UM...
I DON'T... UM...
......
YOUR CALL.
IF YOU CAN'T TRUST ME TO DO RIGHT BY YOU...GAME OVER.
IS THIS WHAT IT FEELS LIKE? NOT GETTING A PASS?
GOT THE MOVES, MIM!
YOU THE MAN!
DAMN...
MISSED THE SHOT...

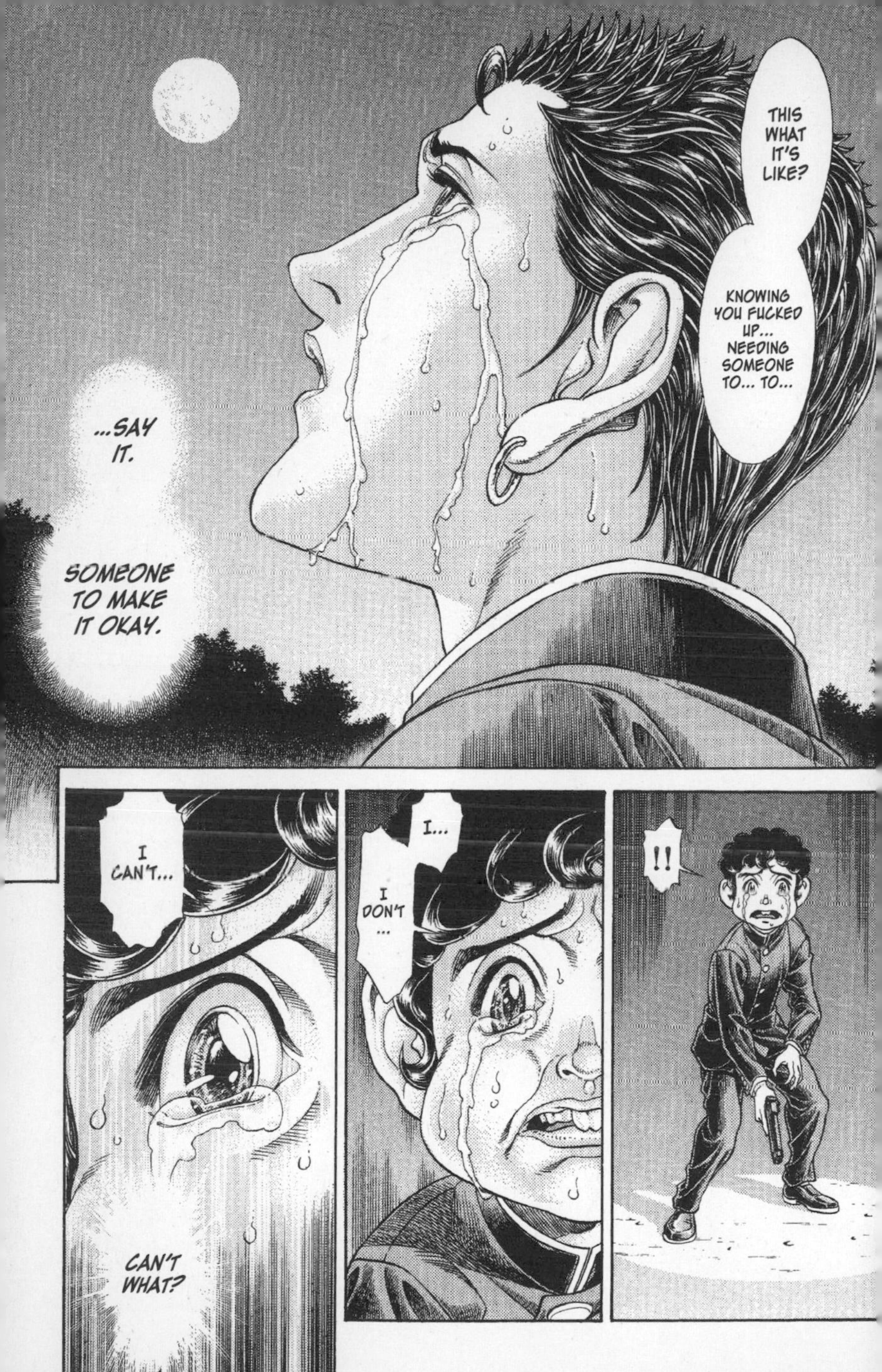
THIS WHAT IT'S LIKE?
KNOWING YOU FUCKED UP... NEEDING SOMEONE TO... TO...
...SAY IT.
SOMEONE TO MAKE IT OKAY.
!!
I...
I DON'T ...
I CAN'T...
CAN'T WHAT?

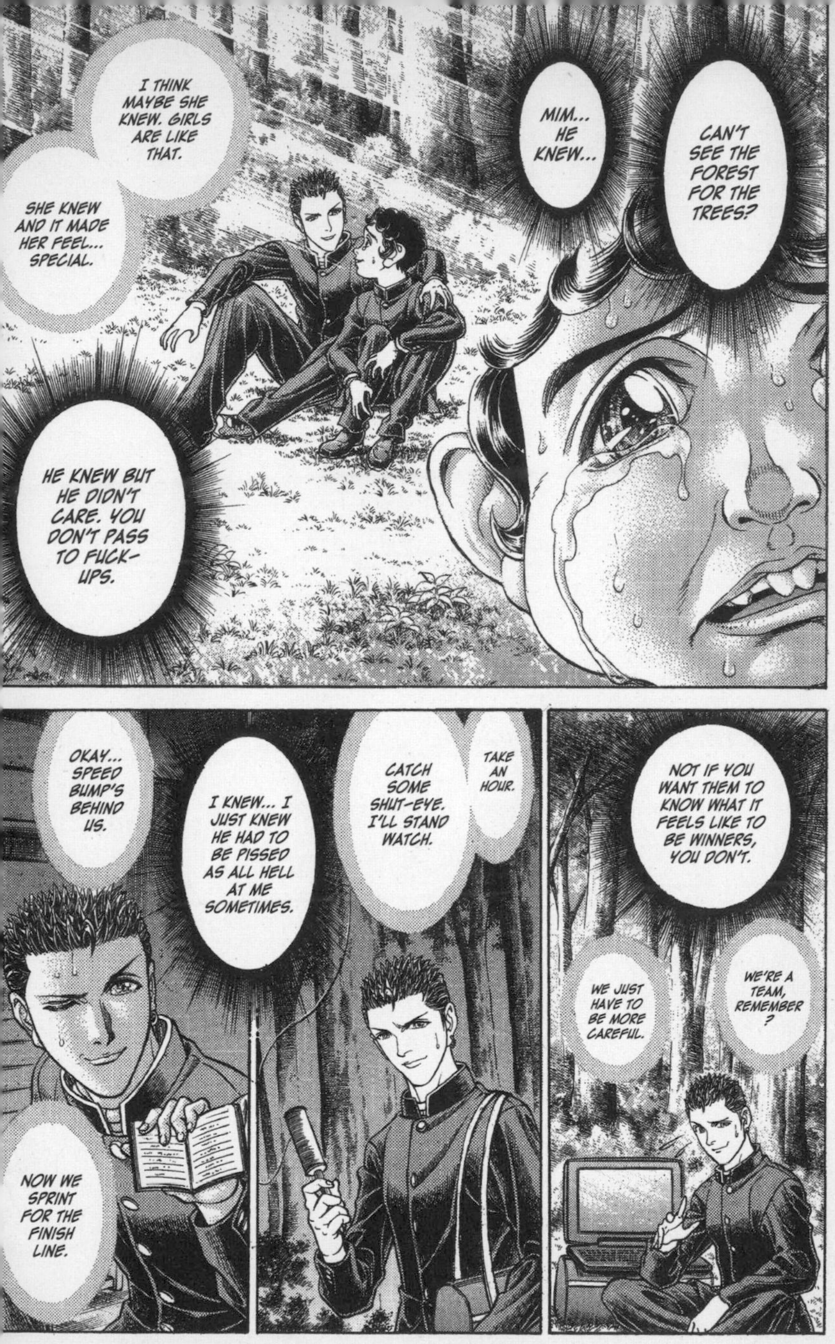
CAN'T SEE THE FOREST FOR THE TREES?
MIM... HE KNEW...
I THINK MAYBE SHE KNEW. GIRLS ARE LIKE THAT.
SHE KNEW AND IT MADE HER FEEL... SPECIAL.
HE KNEW BUT HE DIDN'T CARE. YOU DON'T PASS TO FUCK-UPS.
NOT IF YOU WANT THEM TO KNOW WHAT IT FEELS LIKE TO BE WINNERS, YOU DON'T.
WE'RE A TEAM, REMEMBER?
WE JUST HAVE TO BE MORE CAREFUL.
TAKE AN HOUR.
CATCH SOME SHUT-EYE. I'LL STAND WATCH.
I KNEW... I JUST KNEW HE HAD TO BE PISSED AS ALL HELL AT ME SOMETIMES.
OKAY... SPEED BUMP'S BEHIND US.
NOW WE SPRINT FOR THE FINISH LINE.

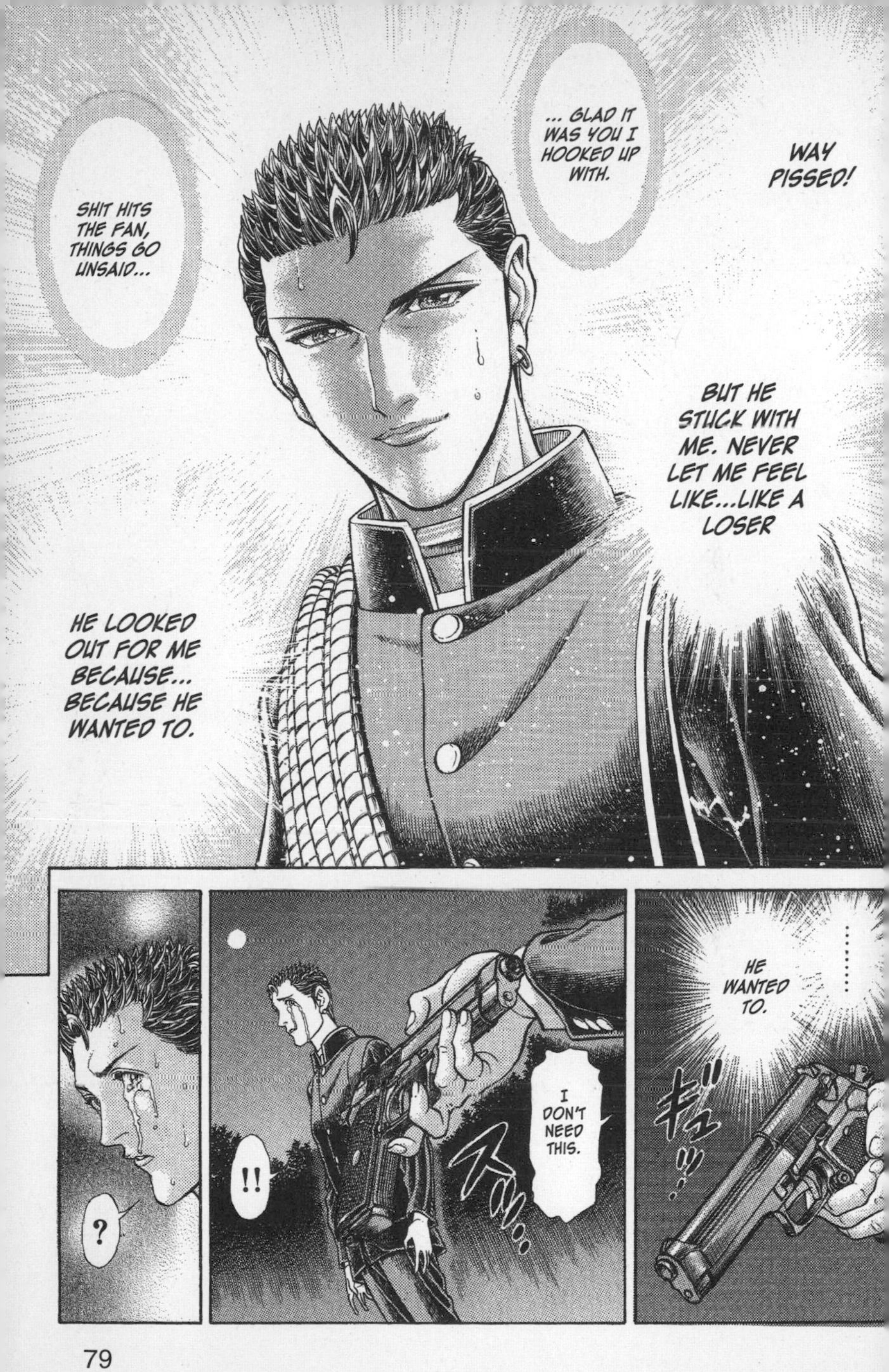
WAY PISSED!
... GLAD IT WAS YOU I HOOKED UP WITH.
SHIT HITS THE FAN, THINGS GO UNSAID...
BUT HE STUCK WITH ME. NEVER LET ME FEEL LIKE...LIKE A LOSER
HE LOOKED OUT FOR ME BECAUSE... BECAUSE HE WANTED TO.
......
HE WANTED TO.
I DON'T NEED THIS.
!!
?

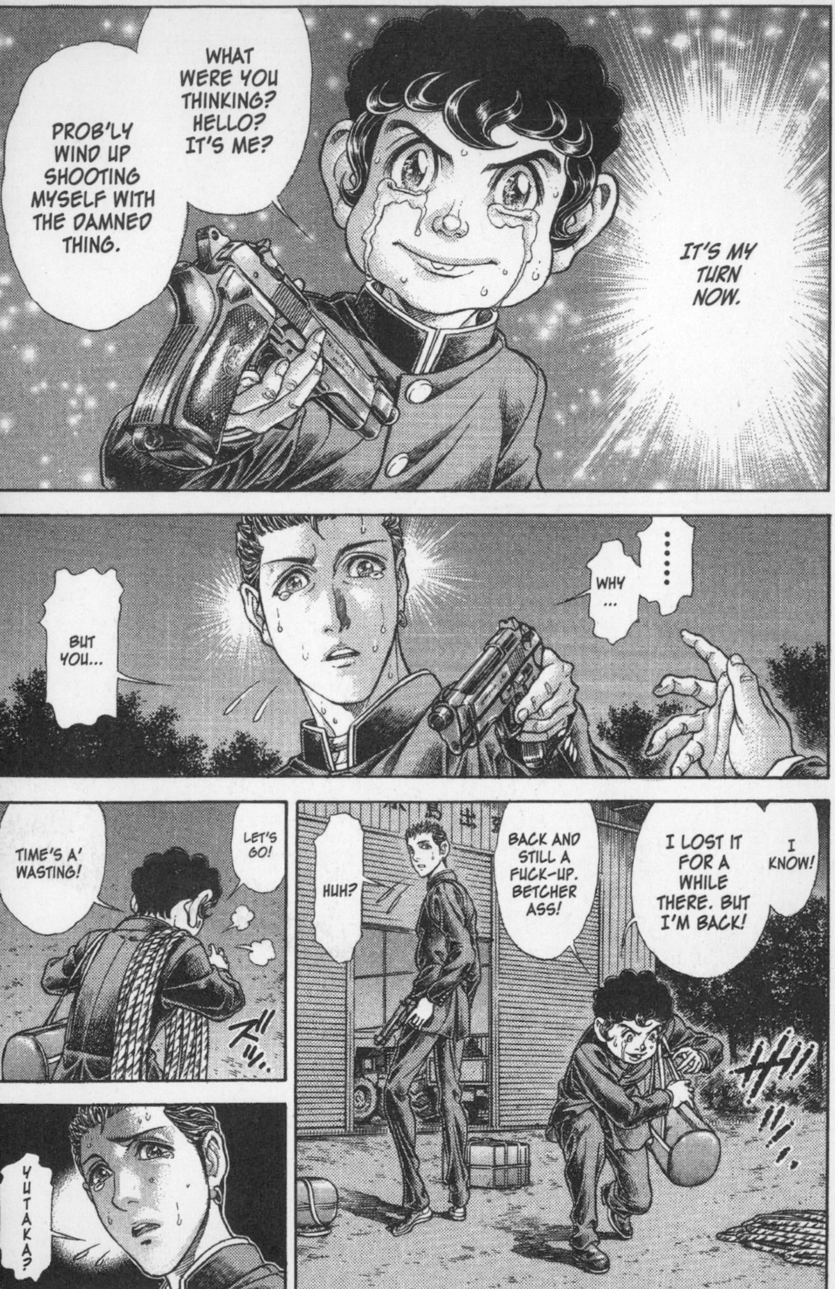
IT'S MY TURN NOW.
WHAT WERE YOU THINKING? HELLO? IT'S ME?
PROB'LY WIND UP SHOOTING MYSELF WITH THE DAMNED THING.
......
WHY ...
BUT YOU...
I KNOW!
I LOST IT FOR A WHILE THERE. BUT I'M BACK!
BACK AND STILL A FUCK-UP. BETCHER ASS!
HUH?
LET'S GO!
TIME'S A' WASTING!
YUTAKA?

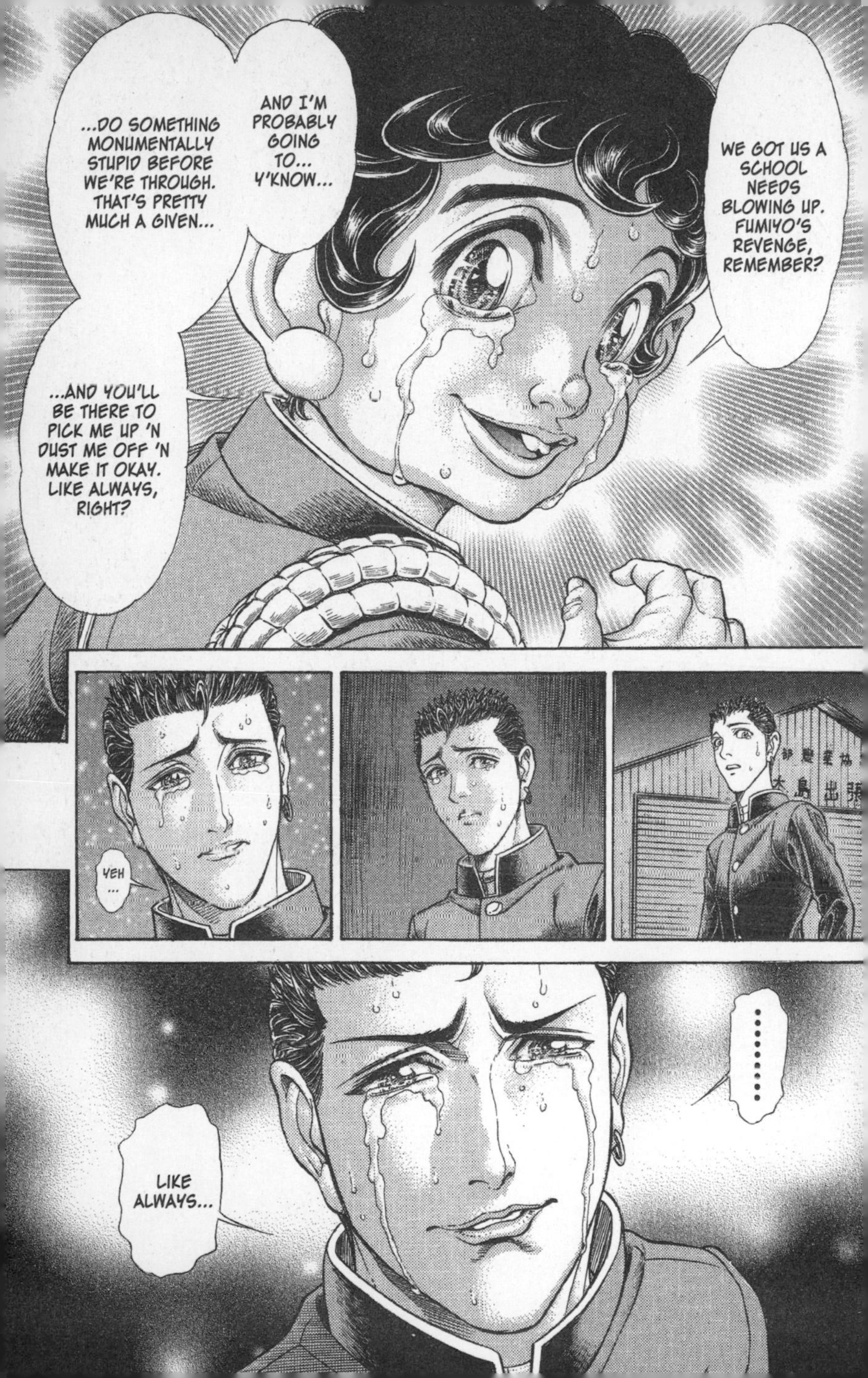
WE GOT US A SCHOOL NEEDS BLOWING UP. FUMIYO'S REVENGE, REMEMBER?
AND I'M PROBABLY GOING TO... Y'KNOW...
...DO SOMETHING MONUMENTALLY STUPID BEFORE WE'RE THROUGH. THAT'S PRETTY MUCH A GIVEN...
...AND YOU'LL BE THERE TO PICK ME UP 'N DUST ME OFF 'N MAKE IT OKAY. LIKE ALWAYS, RIGHT?
YEH...
....
LIKE ALWAYS...

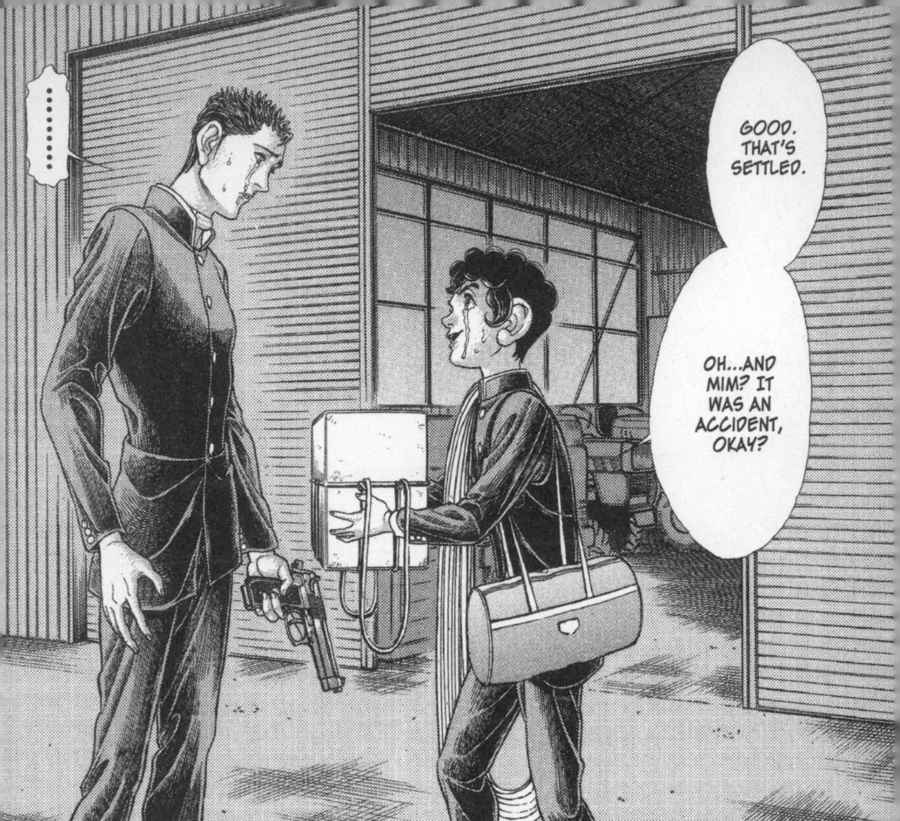
GOOD. THAT'S SETTLED.
OH...AND MIM? IT WAS AN ACCIDENT, OKAY?
......
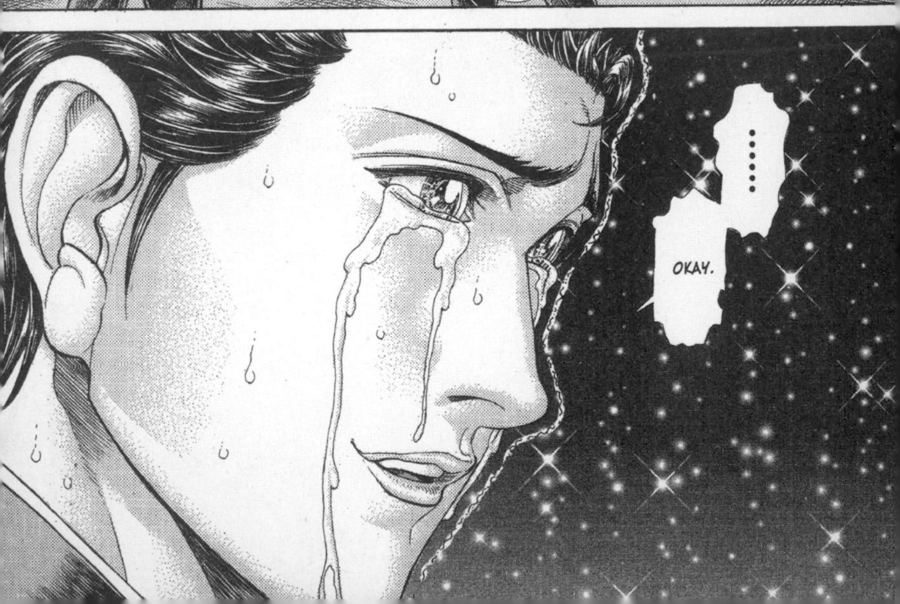
......
OKAY.

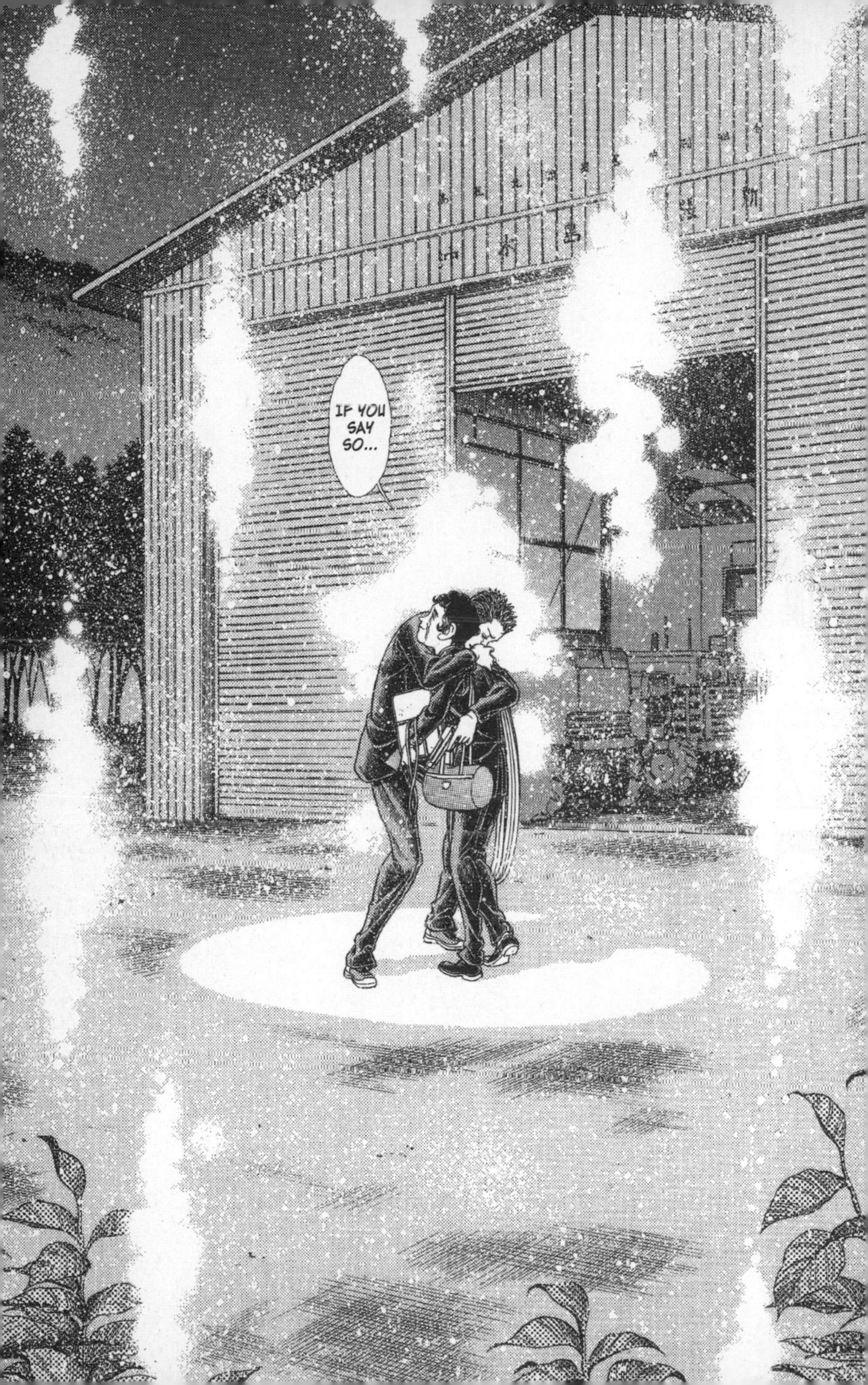
IF YOU SAY SO...

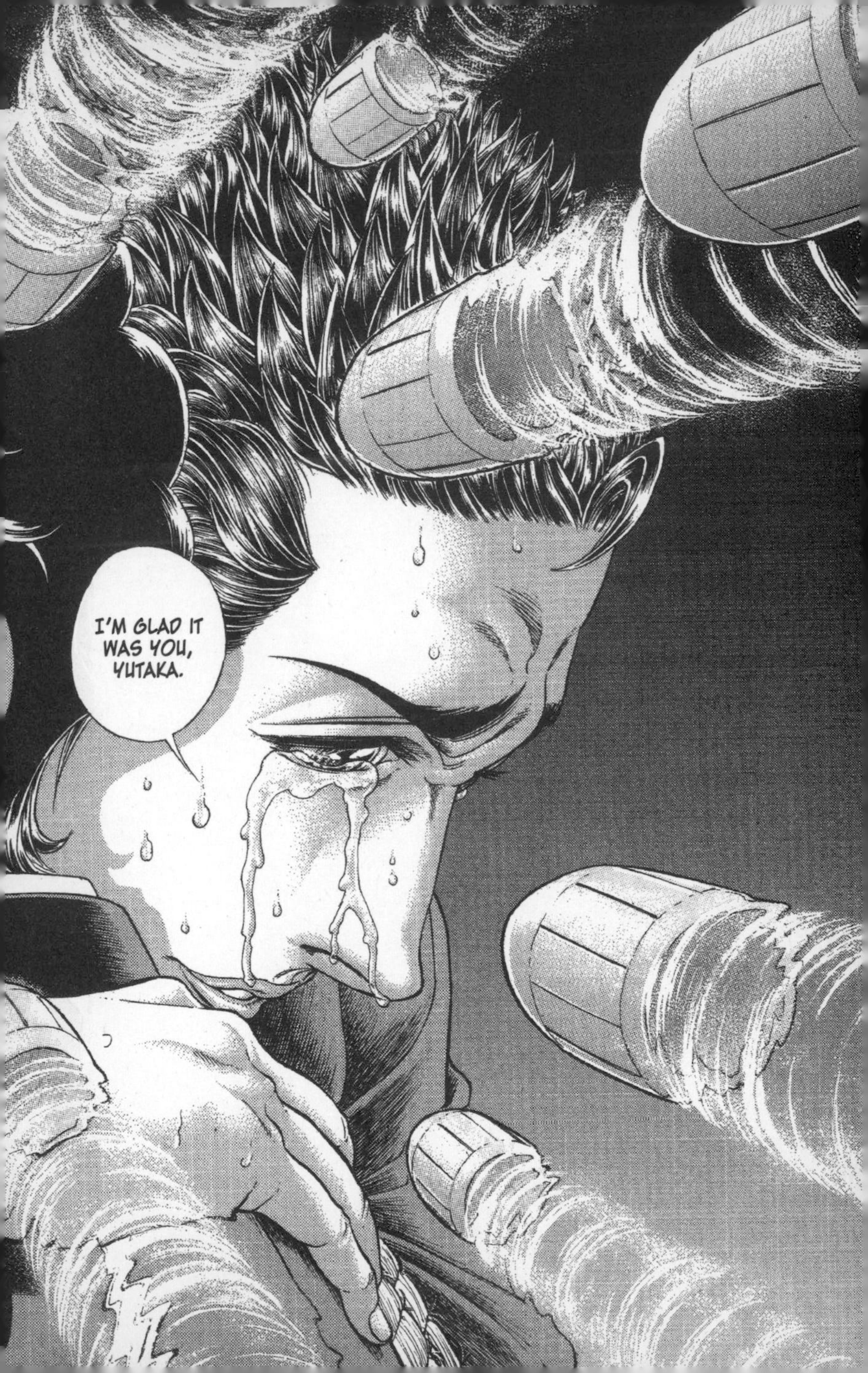
I'M GLAD IT WAS YOU, YUTAKA.

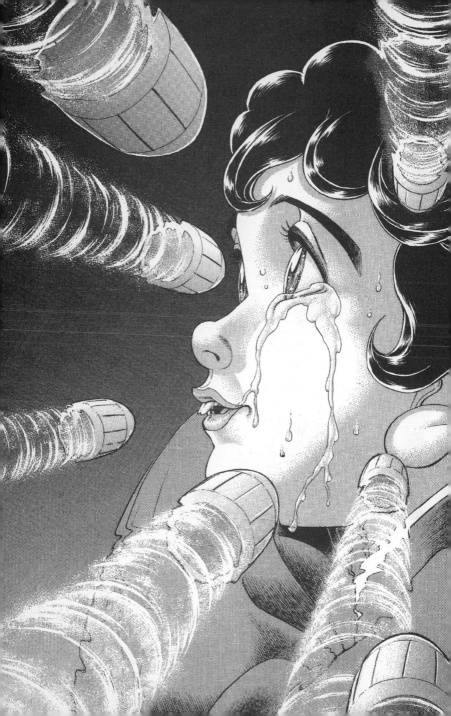

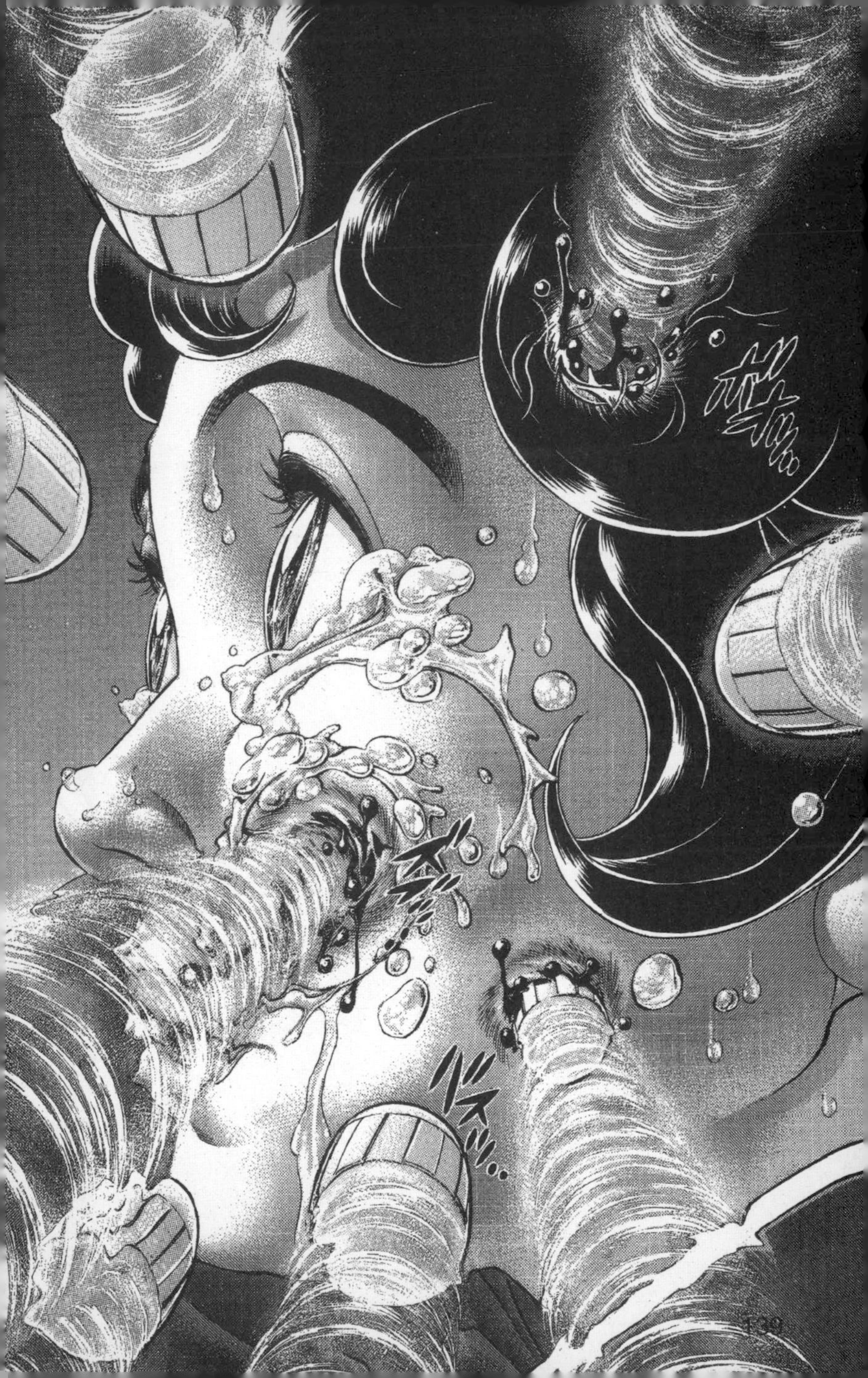
ブスッ..

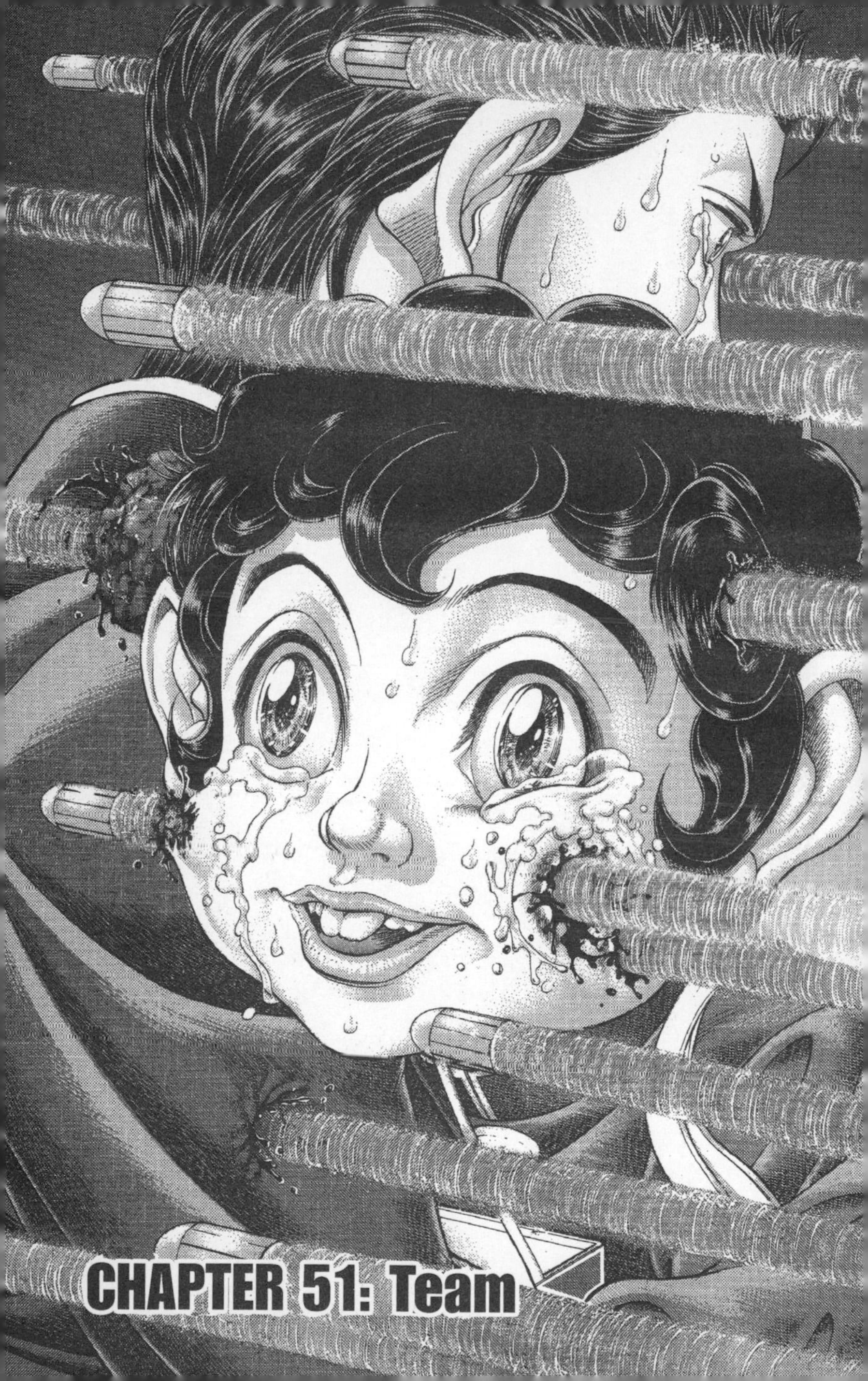
CHAPTER 51: Team

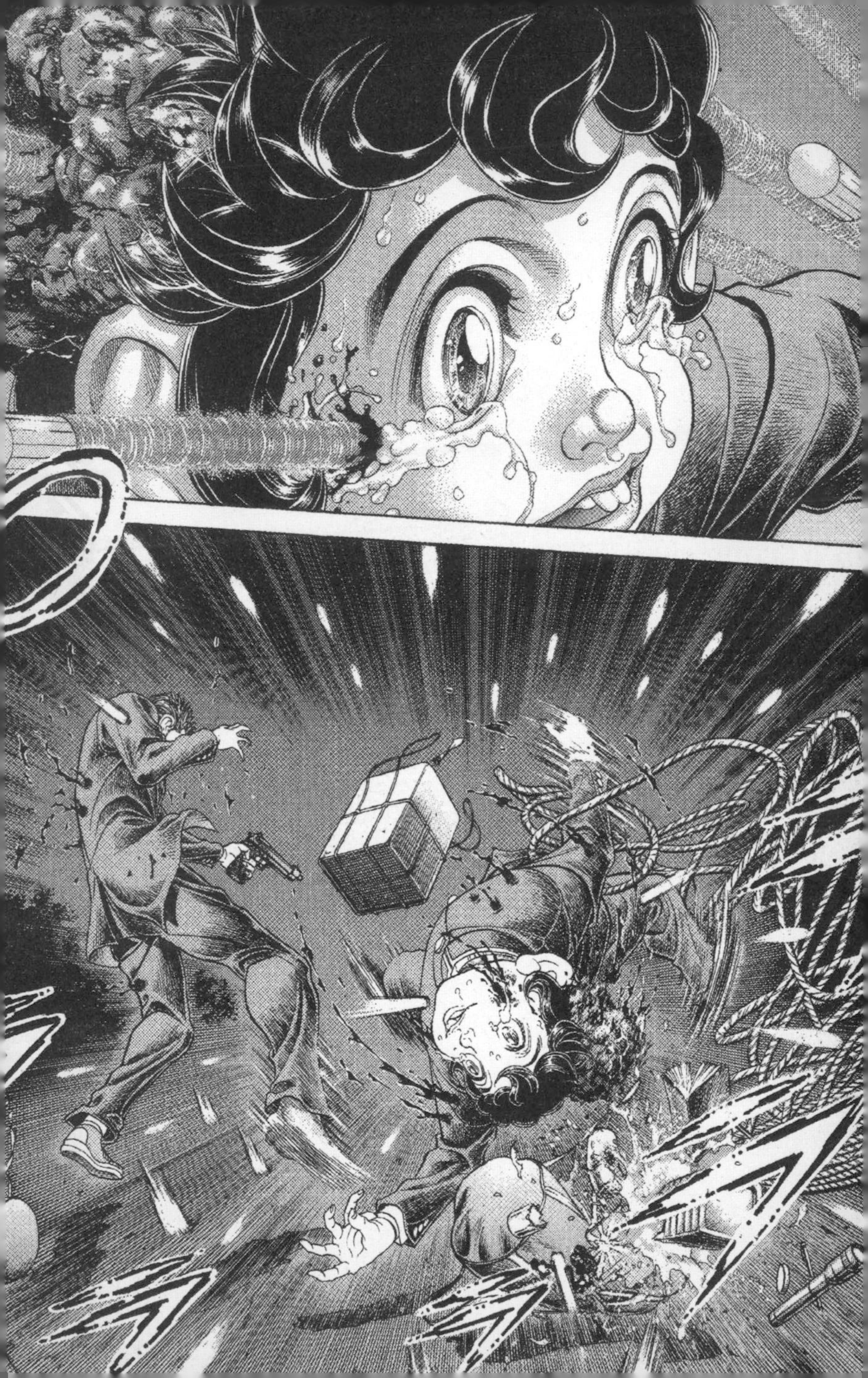

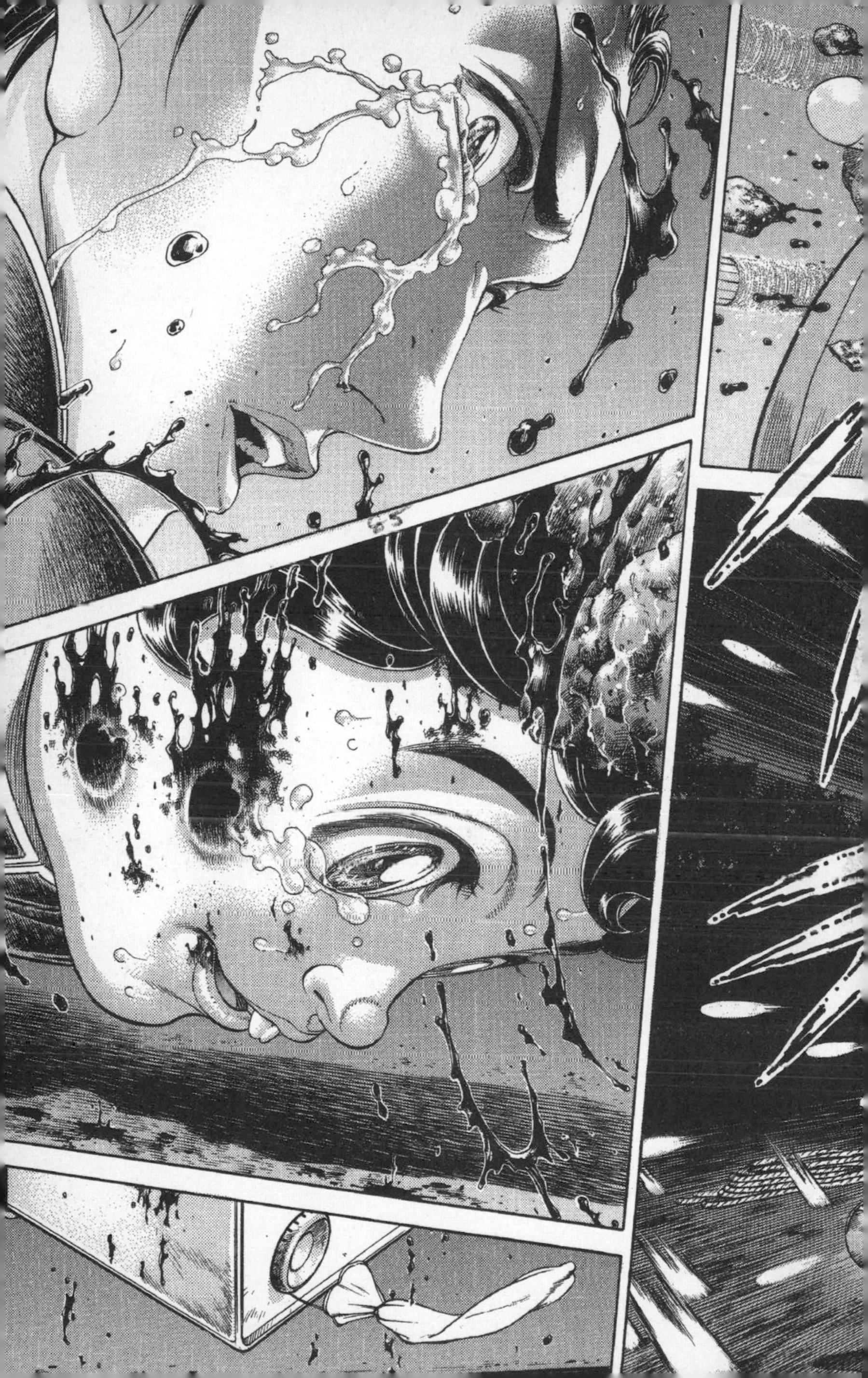

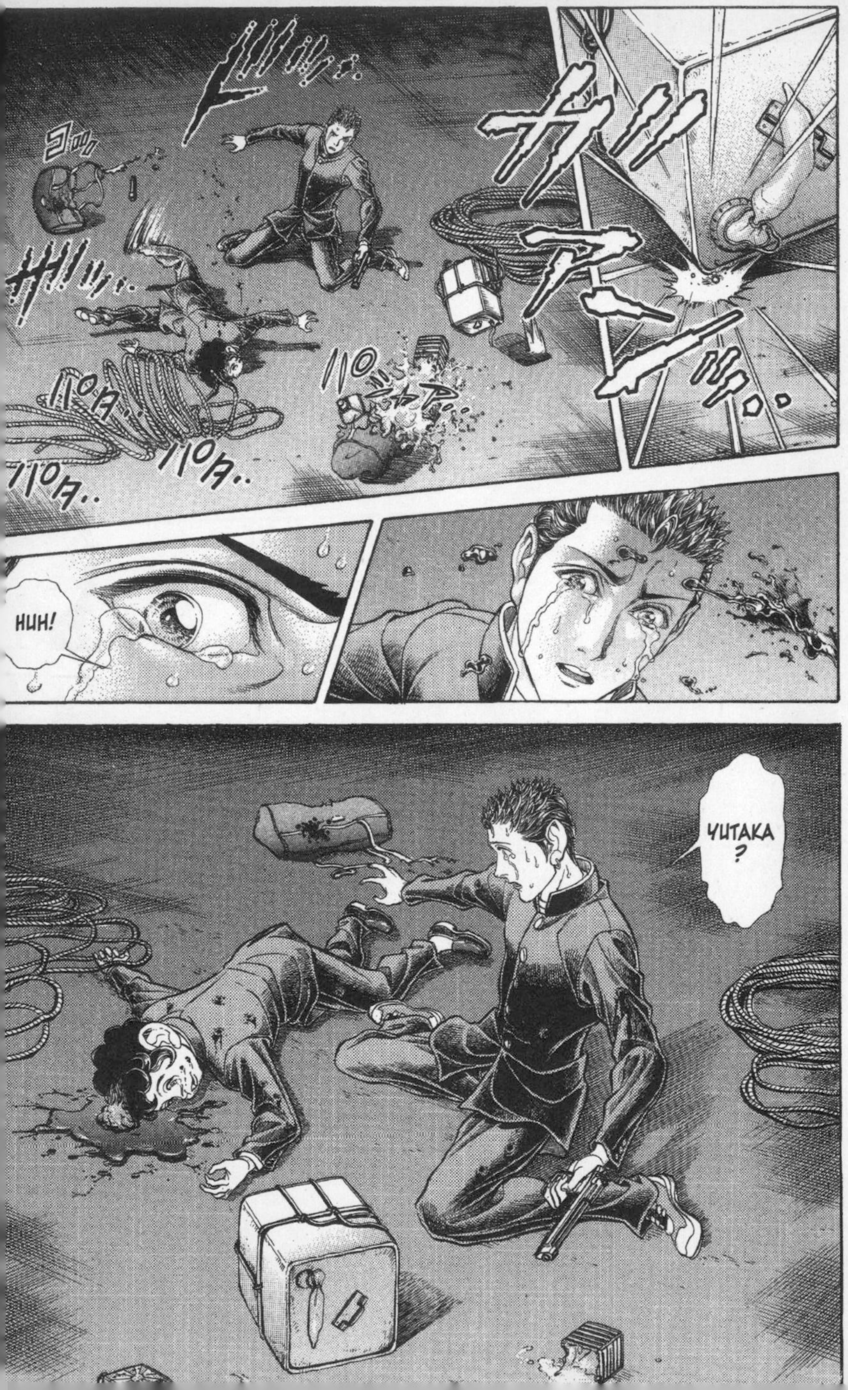
HUH!
YUTAKA ?

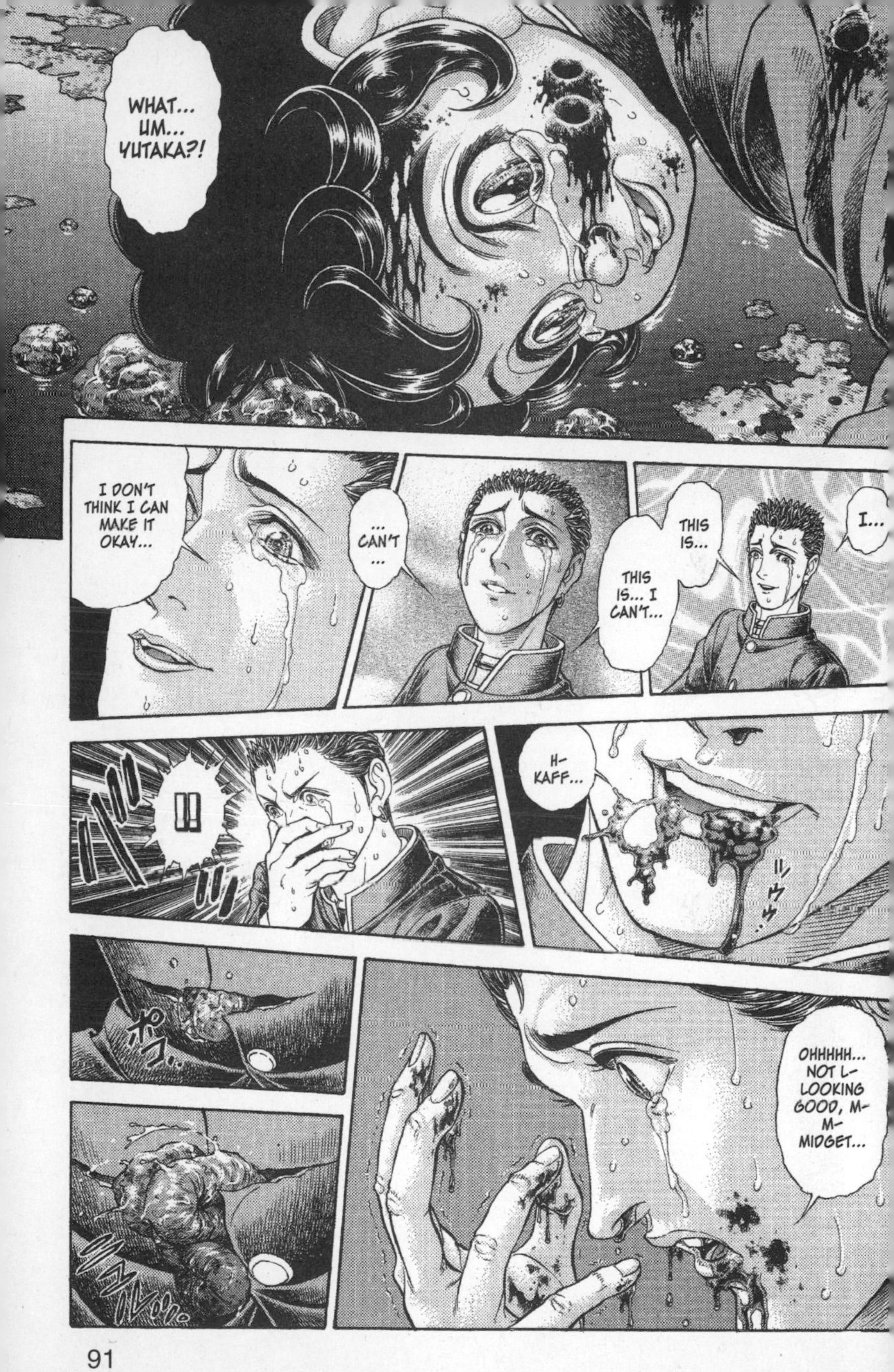
WHAT... UM... YUTAKA?!
I...
THIS IS...
THIS IS... I CAN'T...
... CAN'T ...
I DON'T THINK I CAN MAKE IT OKAY...
H-KAFF...
!!
OHHHHH... NOT L-LOOKING GOOD, M-M-MIDGET...

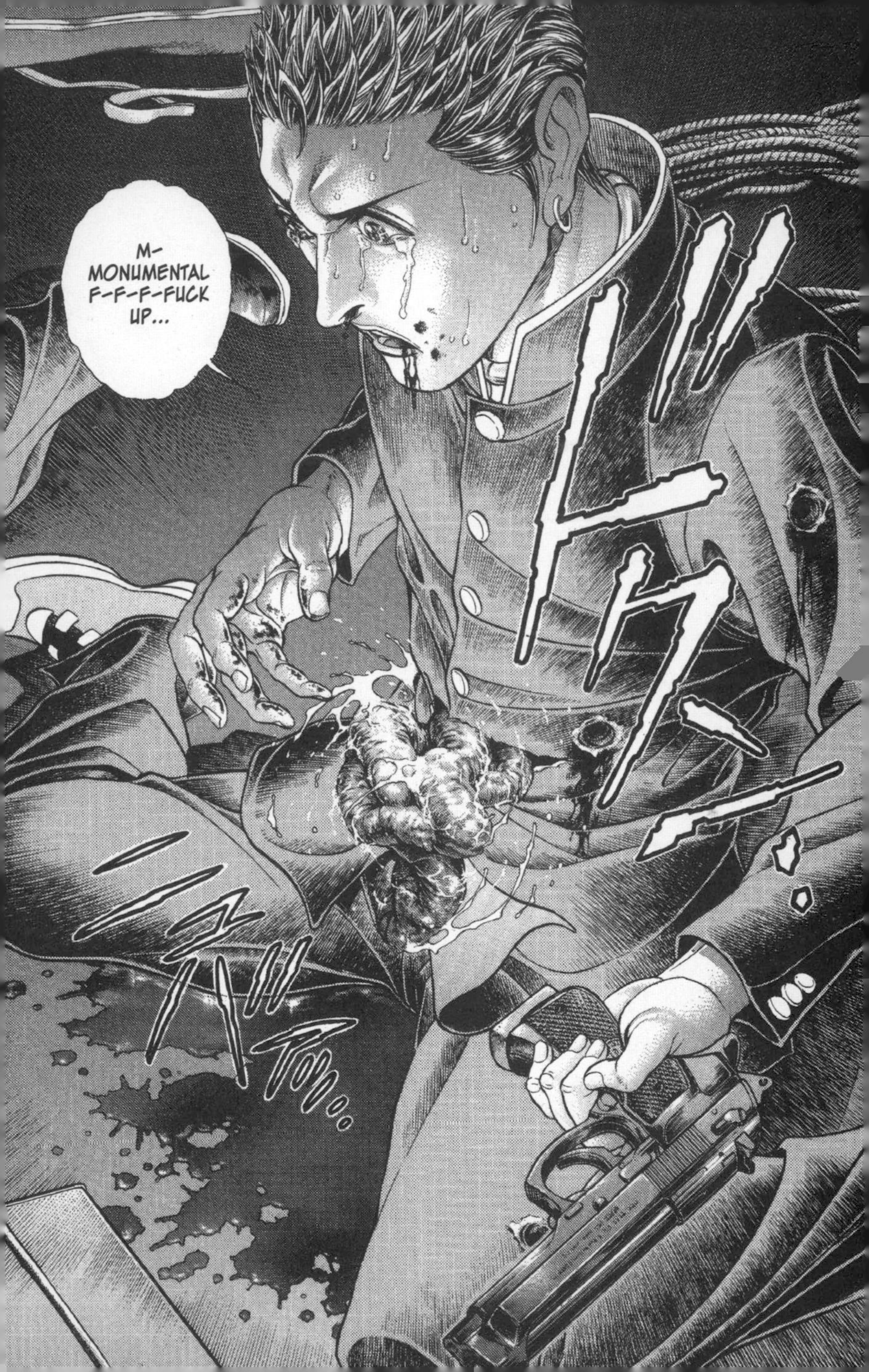
M-MONUMENTAL F-F-F-FUCK UP...

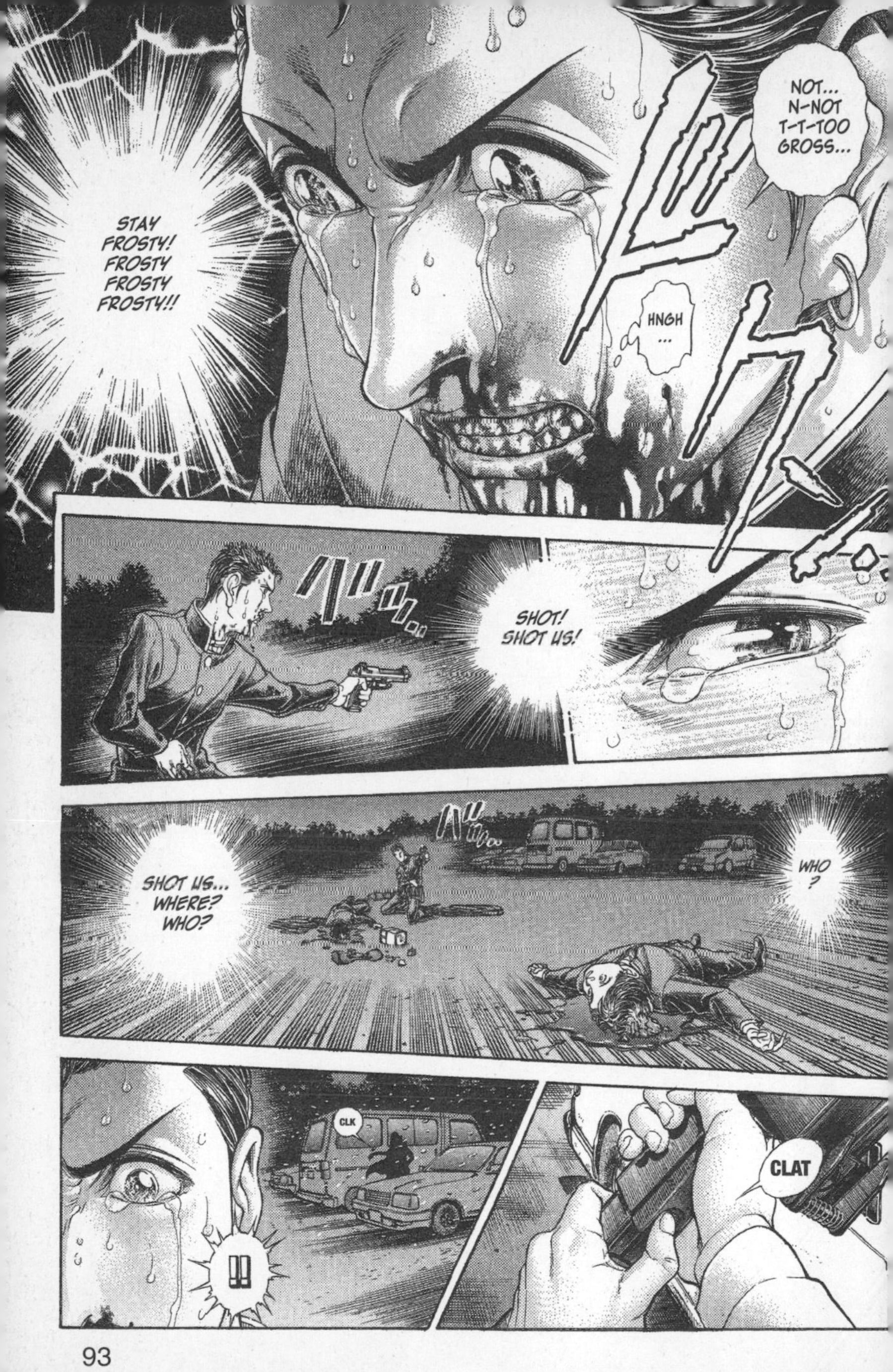
NOT... N-NOT T-T-TOO GROSS...
HNGH ...
STAY FROSTY! FROSTY FROSTY FROSTY!!
SHOT! SHOT US!
WHO ?
SHOT US... WHERE? WHO?
CLAT
CLK
!!

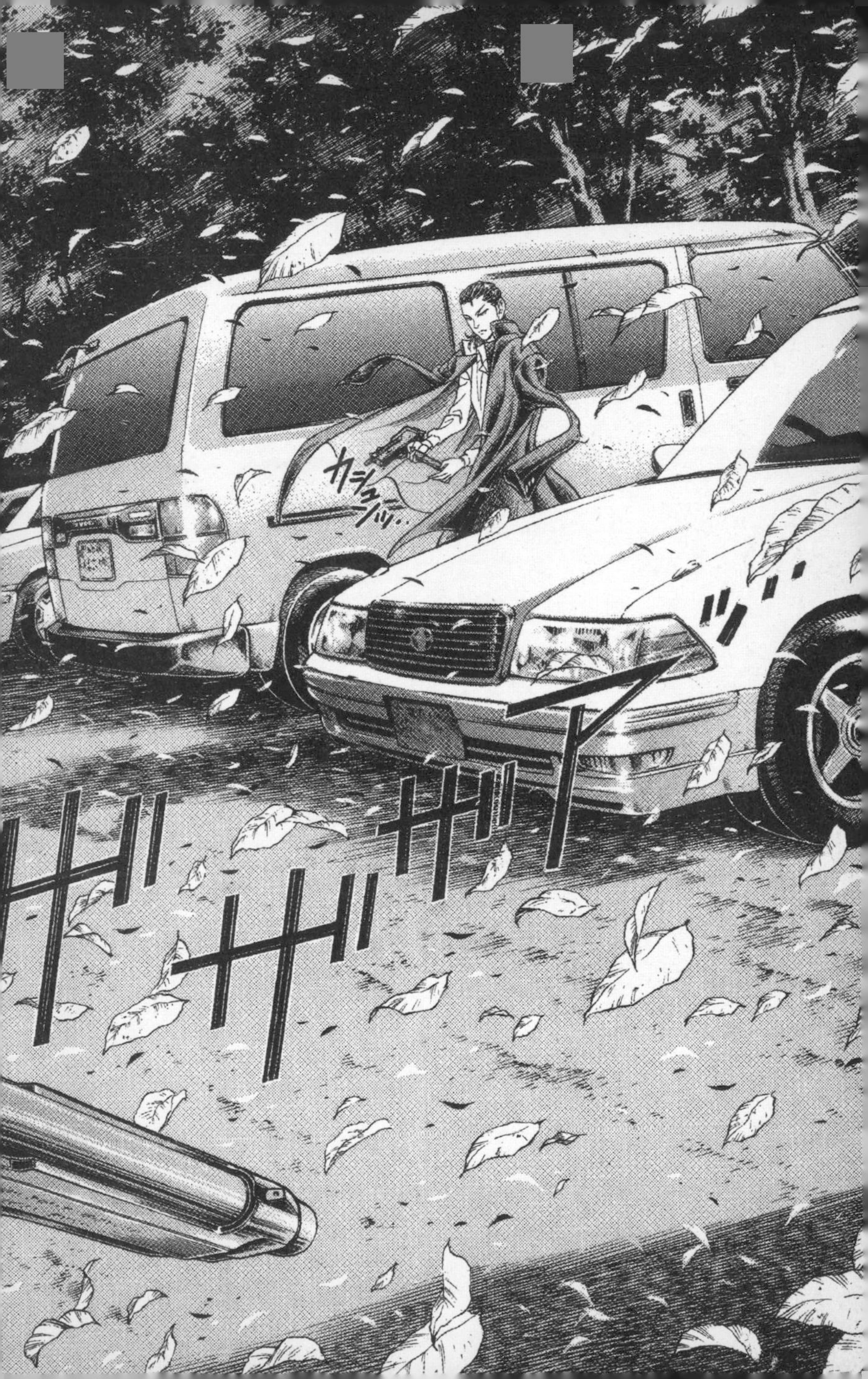
カシュンッ..
ザザザザッ

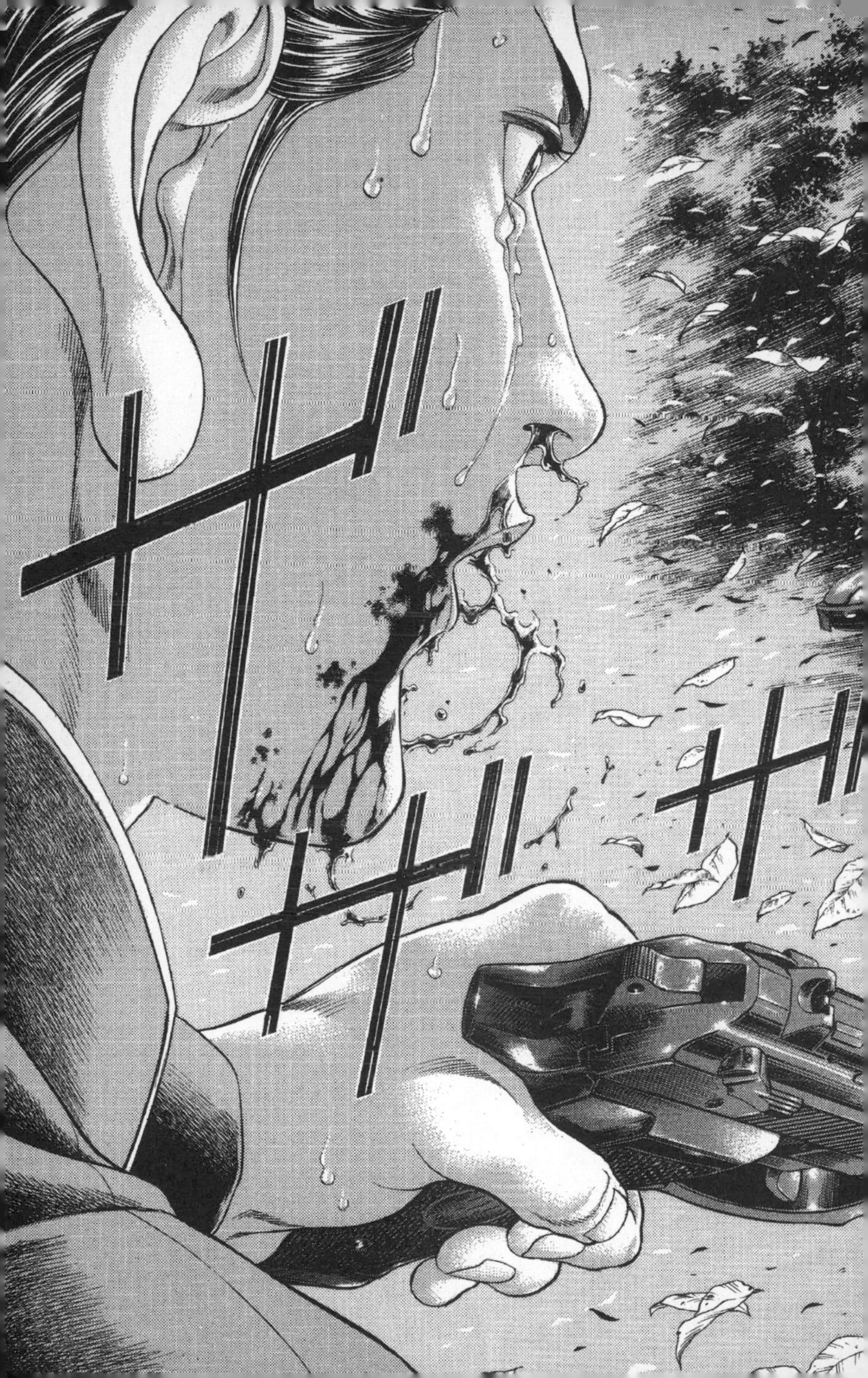

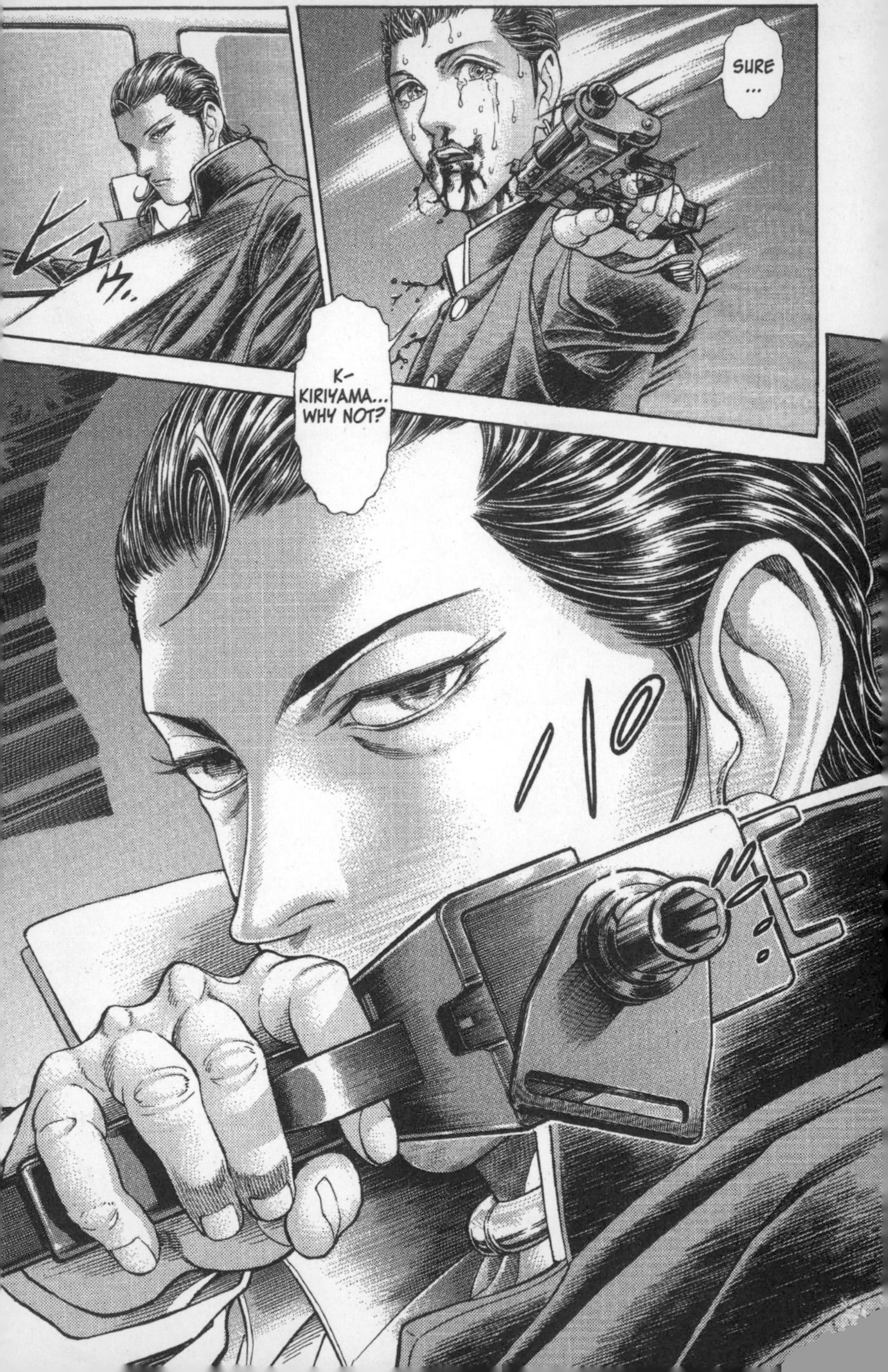
SURE ...
K-KIRIYAMA... WHY NOT?

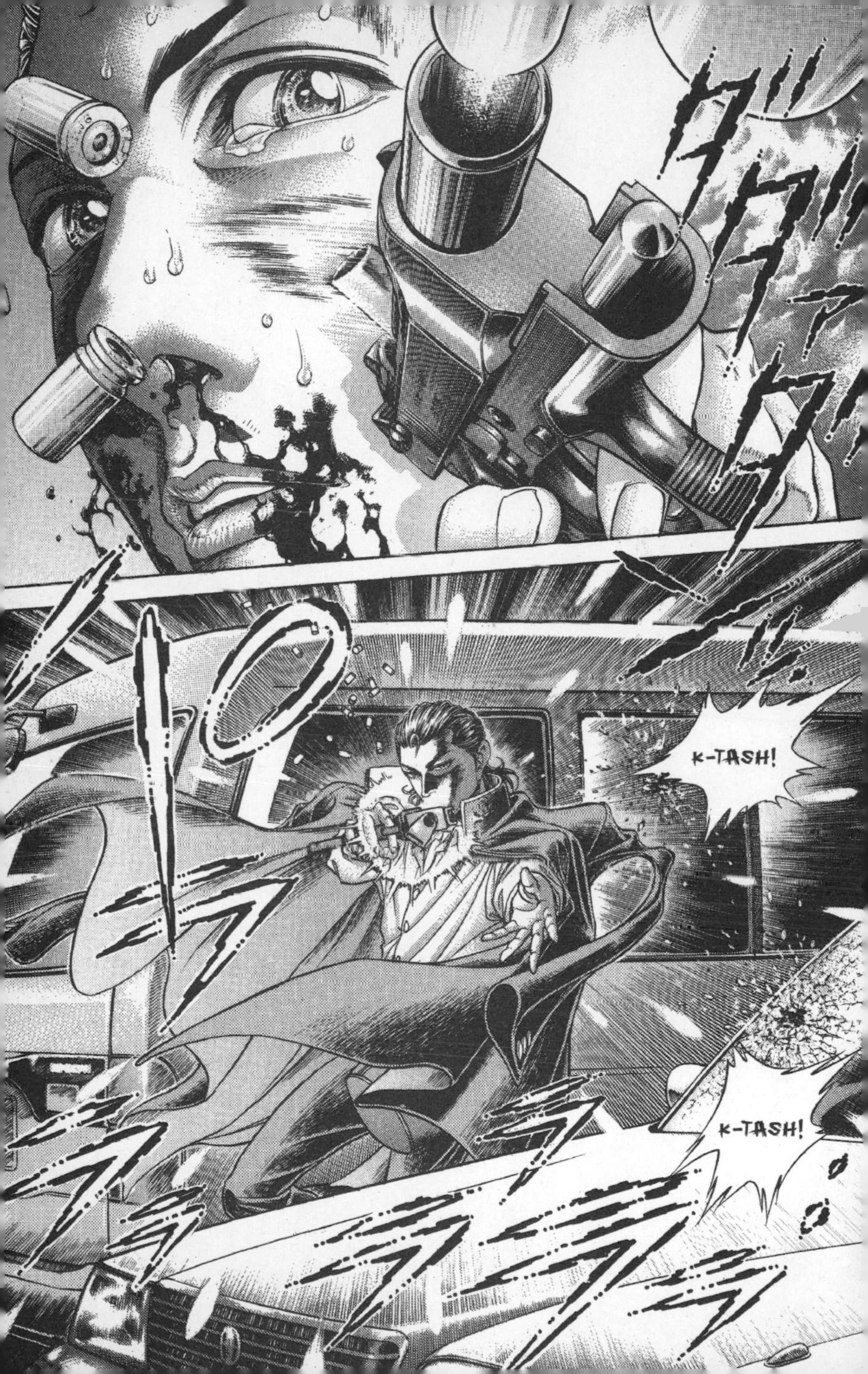
K-TASH!
K-TASH!

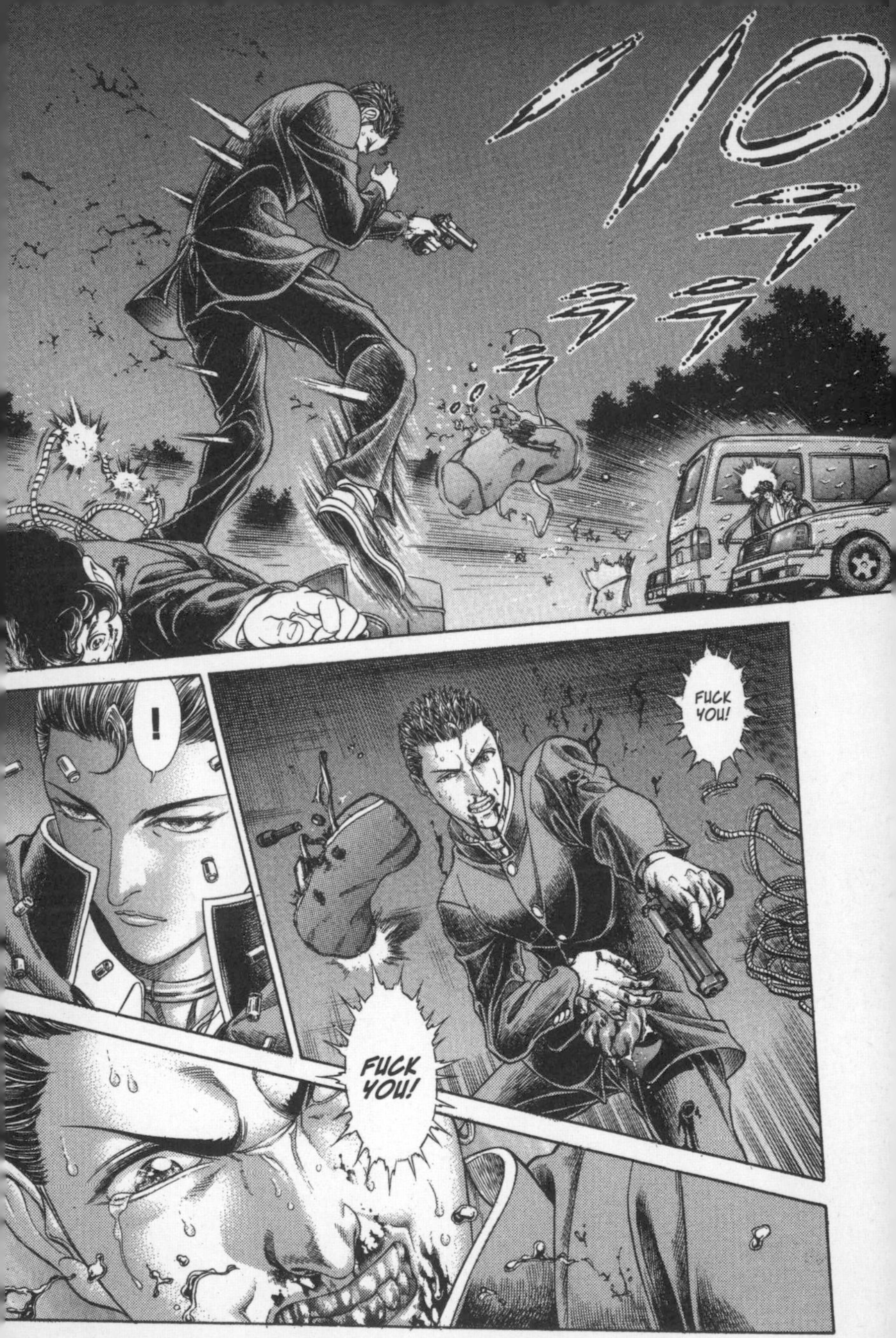
FUCK YOU!
!
FUCK YOU!

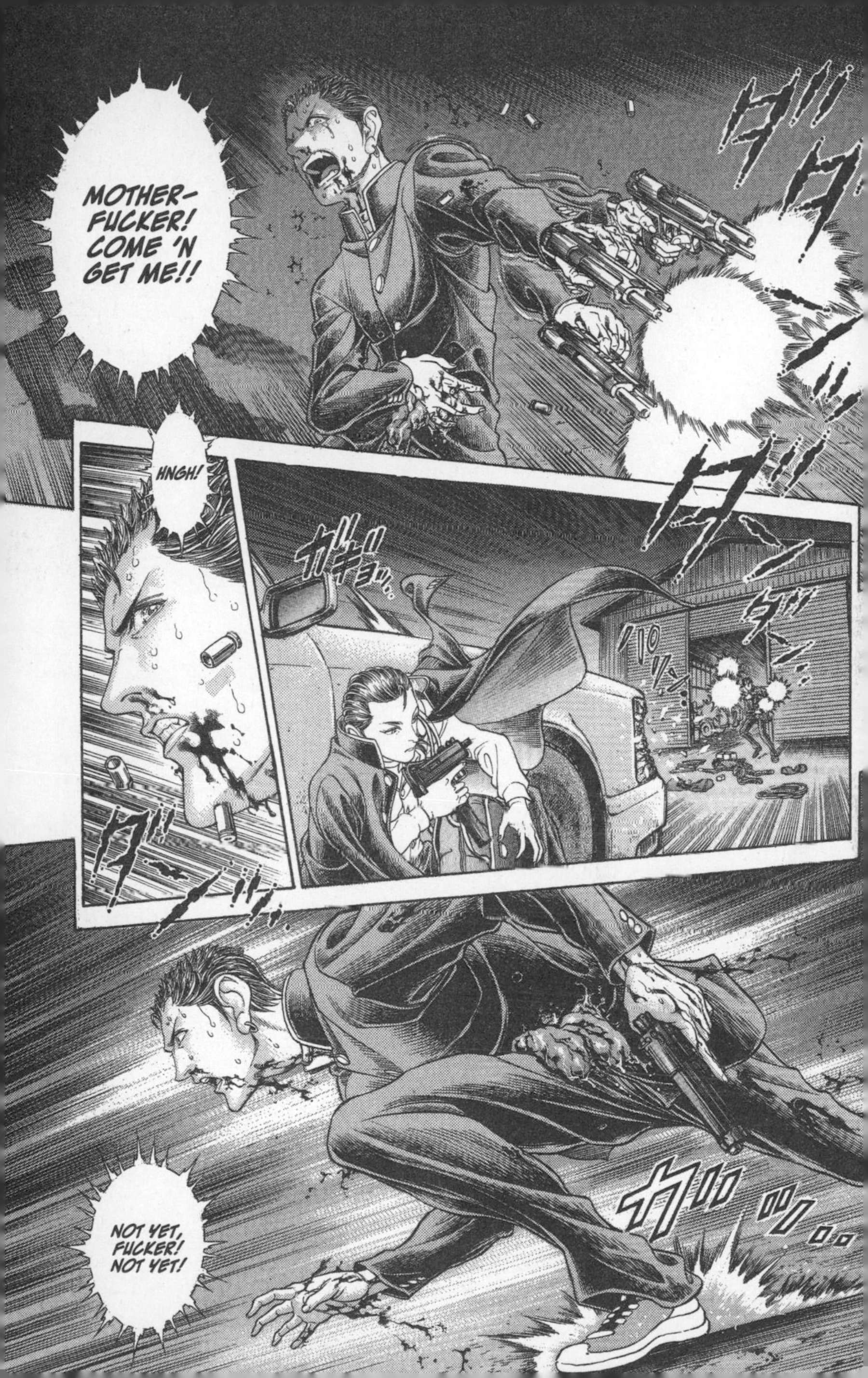
MOTHER-FUCKER! COME 'N GET ME!!
HNGH!
NOT YET, FUCKER! NOT YET!

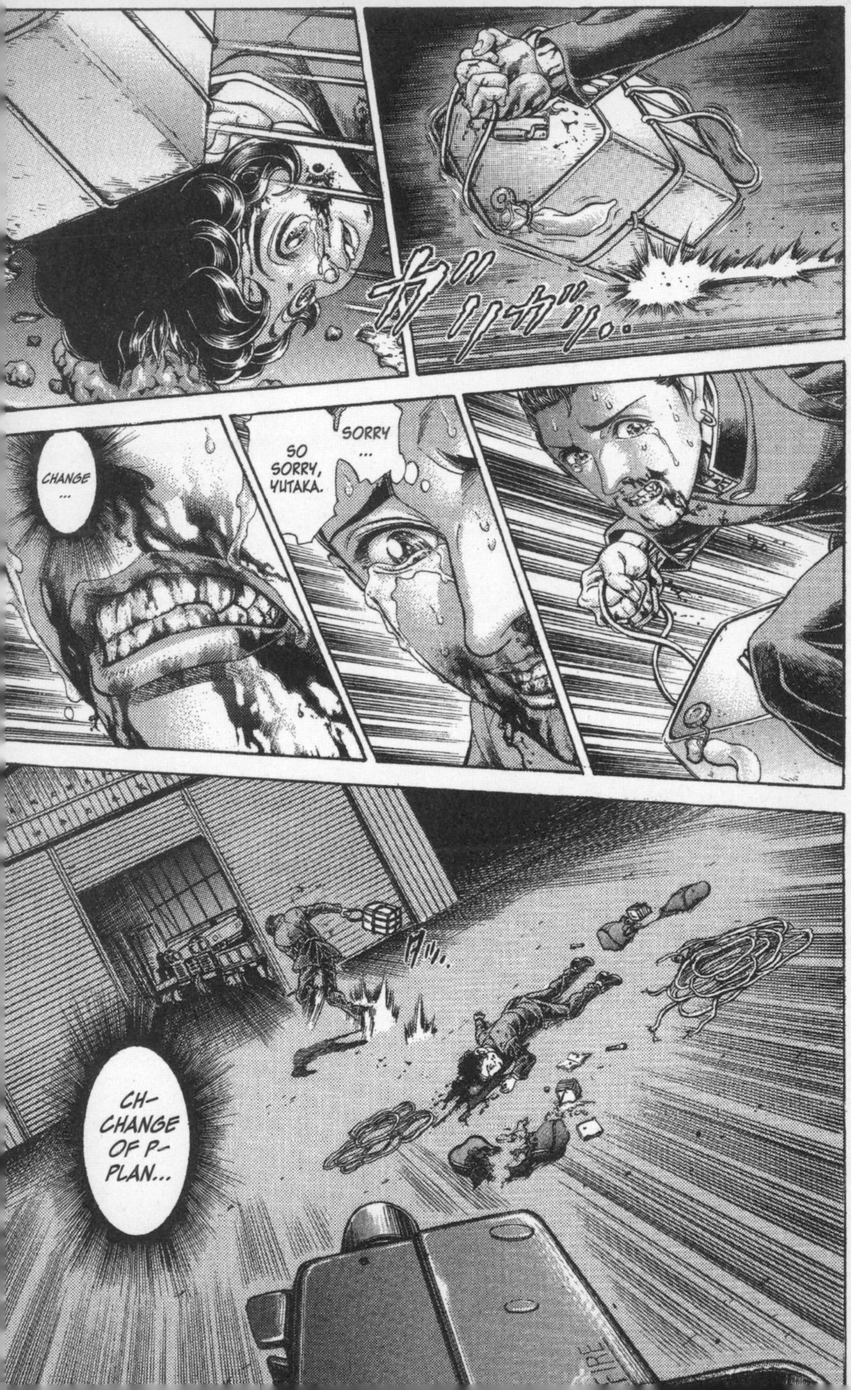
SORRY ...
SO SORRY, YUTAKA.
CHANGE ...
CH-CHANGE OF P-PLAN...

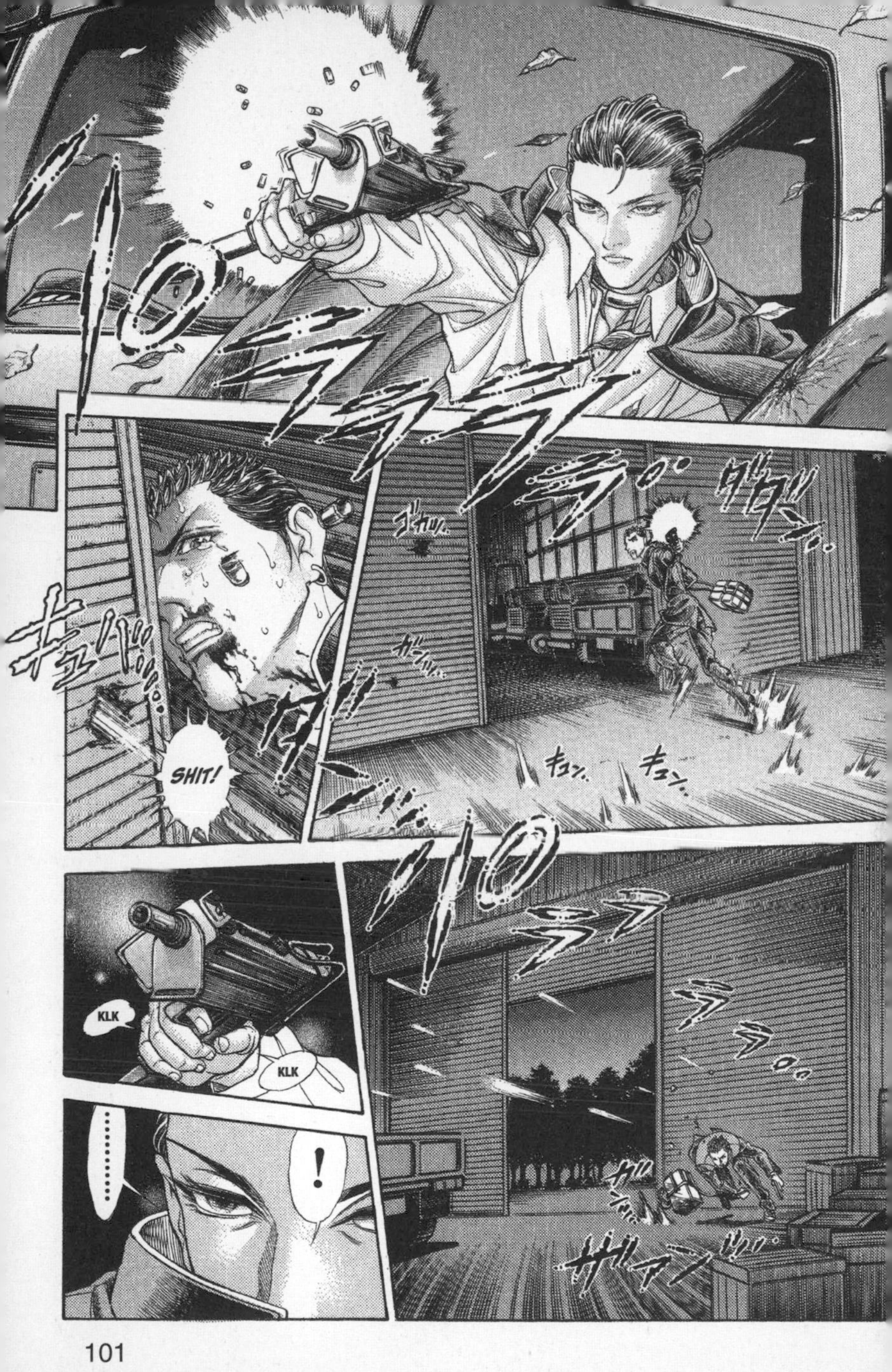
SHIT!
KLK
KLK
!
......

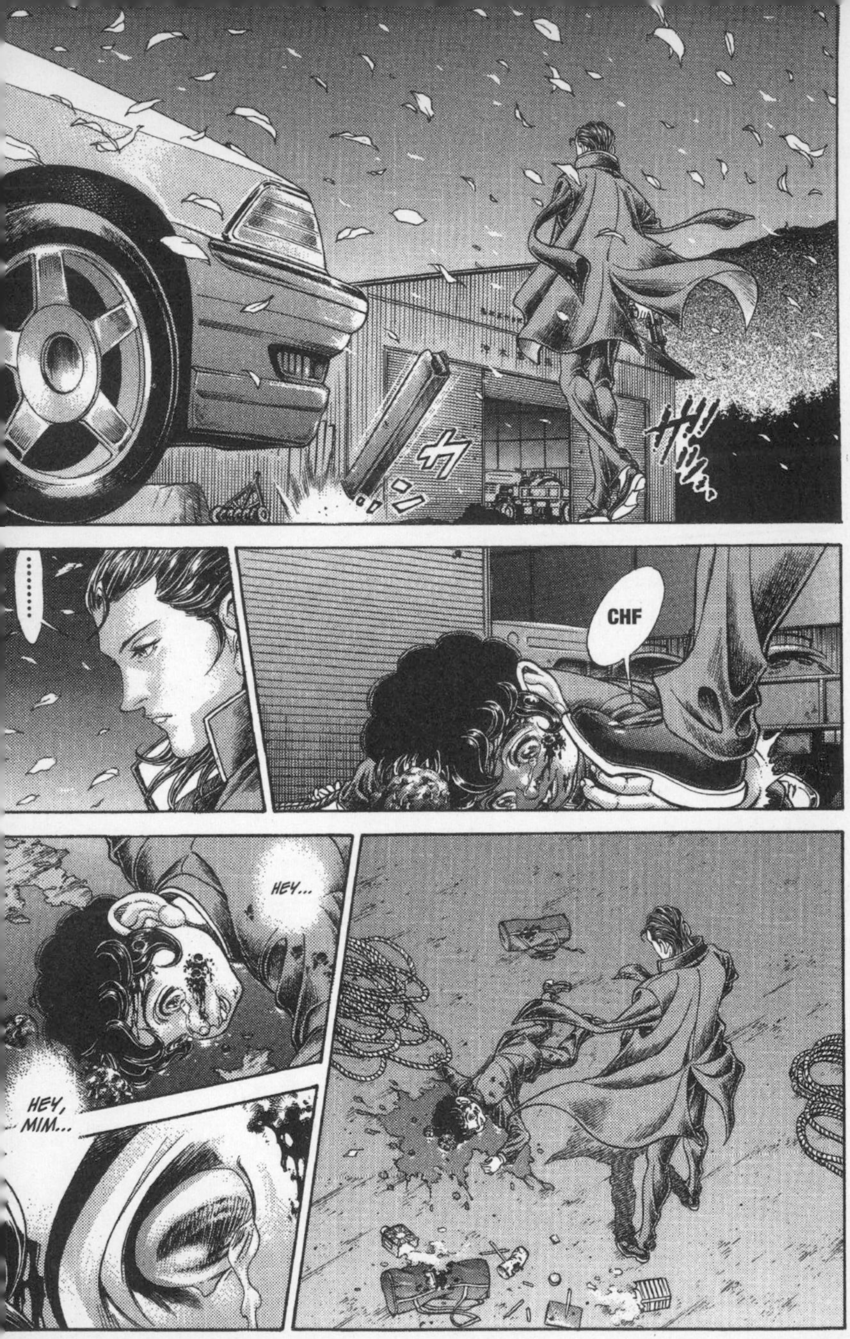
CHF
......
HEY...
HEY, MIM...

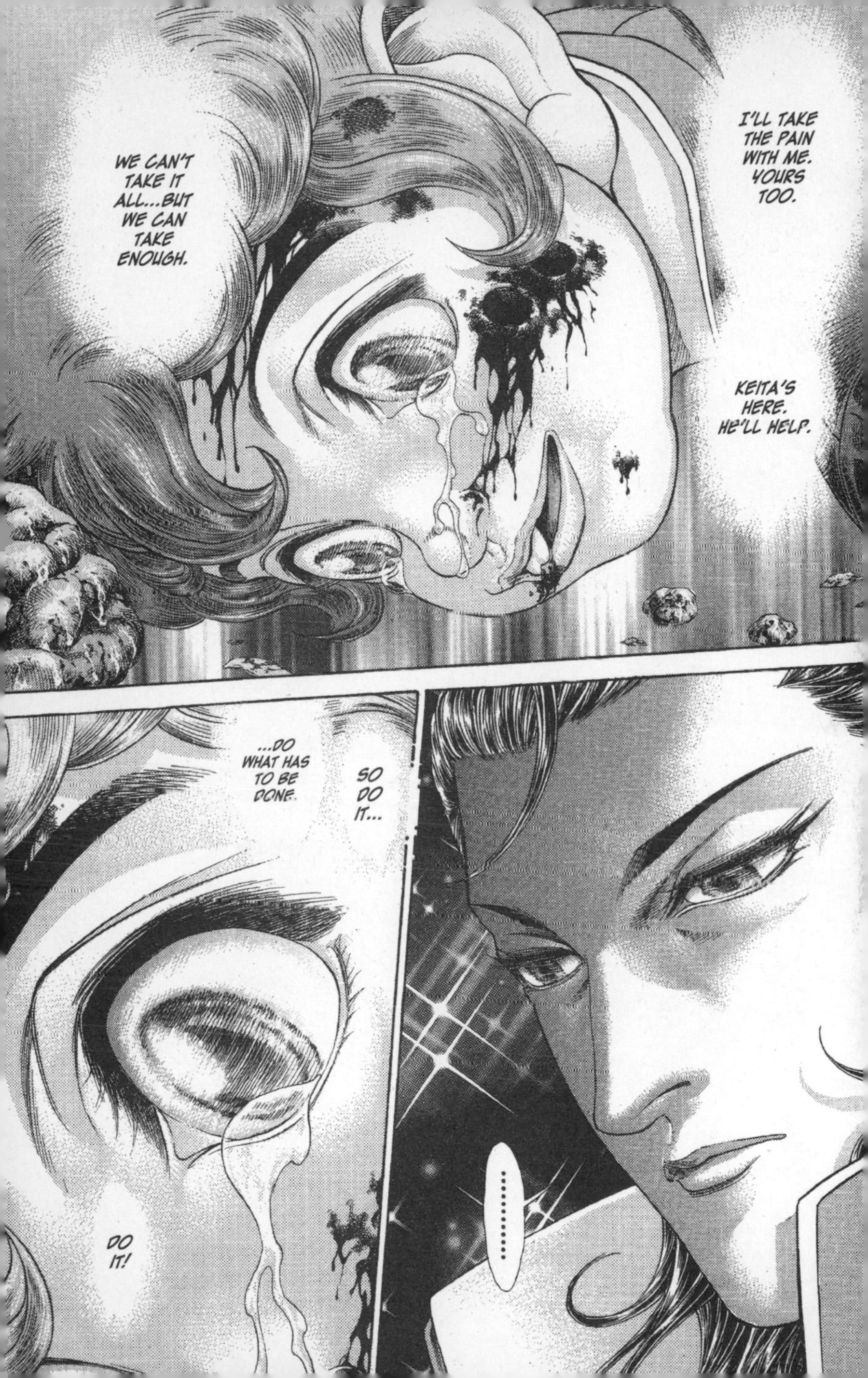
I'LL TAKE THE PAIN WITH ME. YOURS TOO.
WE CAN'T TAKE IT ALL...BUT WE CAN TAKE ENOUGH.
KEITA'S HERE. HE'LL HELP.
....
SO DO IT...
...DO WHAT HAS TO BE DONE.
DO IT!

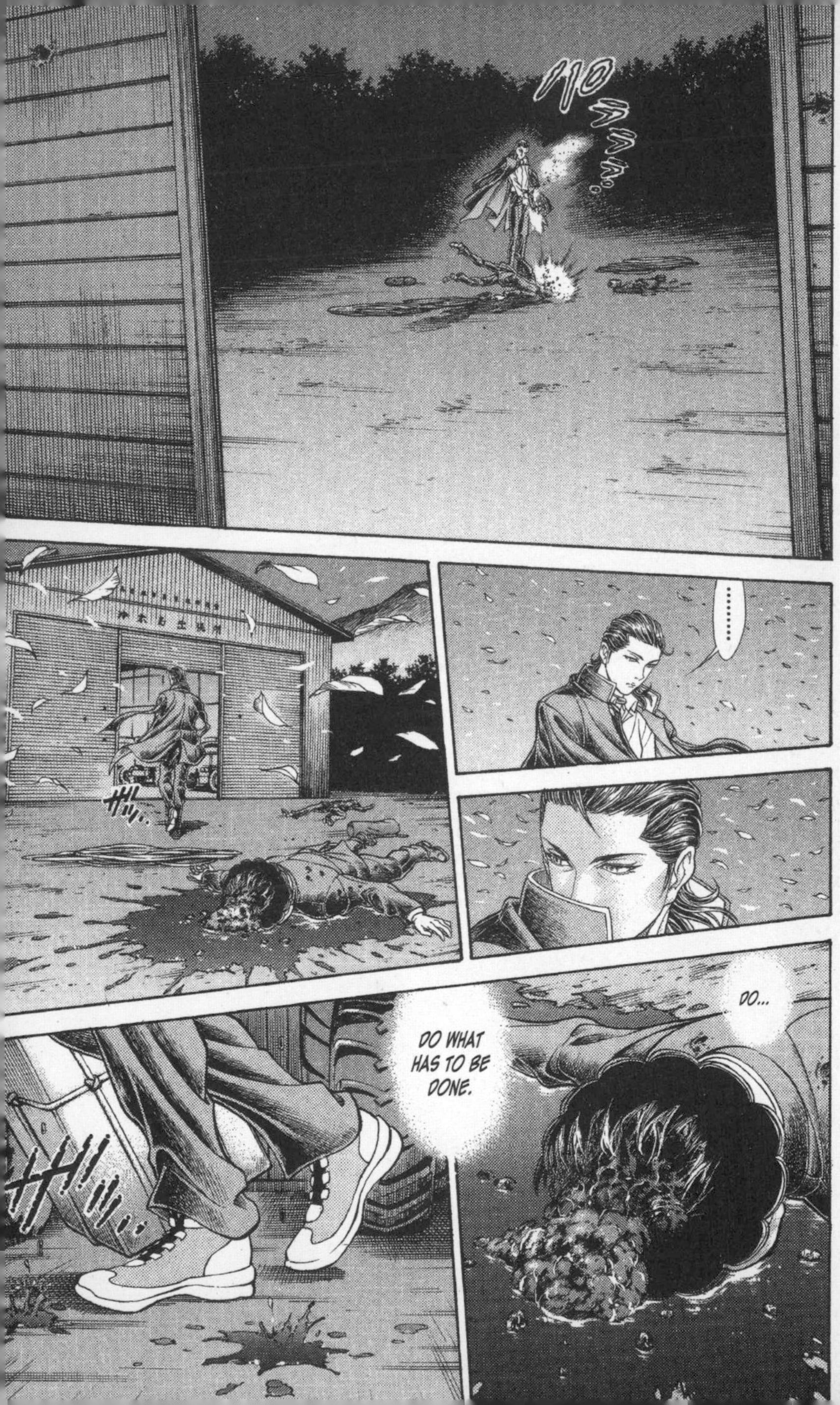
....
DO...
DO WHAT HAS TO BE DONE.

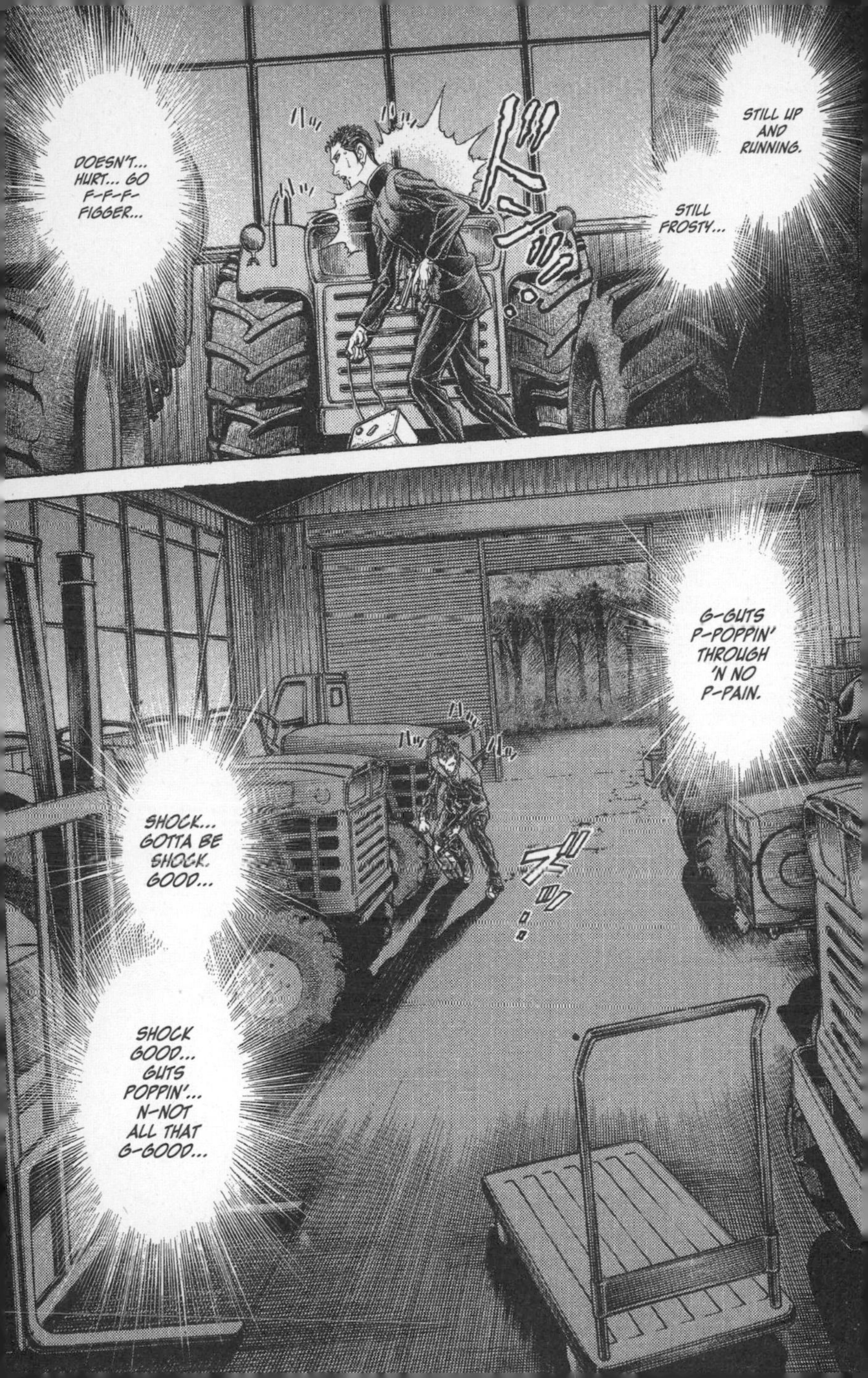
STILL UP AND RUNNING.
STILL FROSTY...
DOESN'T... HURT... GO F-F-F-FIGGER...
G-GUTS P-POPPIN' THROUGH 'N NO P-PAIN.
SHOCK... GOTTA BE SHOCK. GOOD...
SHOCK GOOD... GUTS POPPIN'... N-NOT ALL THAT G-GOOD...

HUH...
SLIPPERY 'S ALL GET OUT.
HARD T' HOLD ON T'... SLIPPERY...
N-NOT TOO FUCKIN' STOMACH-CHURNIN'...
HUH... STOMACH... WONDER IF THAT'S N-NEXT TH-THING OUT...
......
FUCK!
HANDS ALL... SLICKERY.
'ZAT A WORD? S-SLICKERY?
FOCUS!
GOT TO... GOT TO...
'FORE TH' P-PAIN HITS... GOTTA...

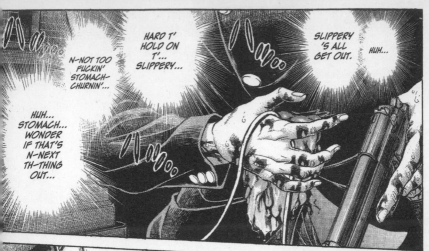

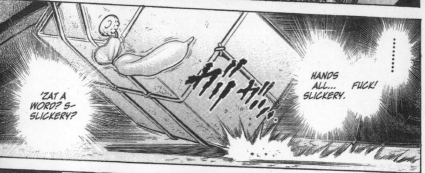

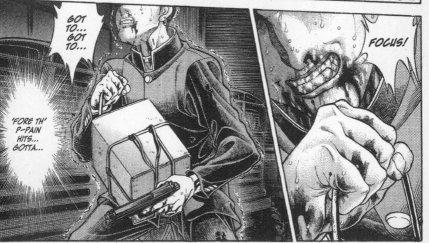

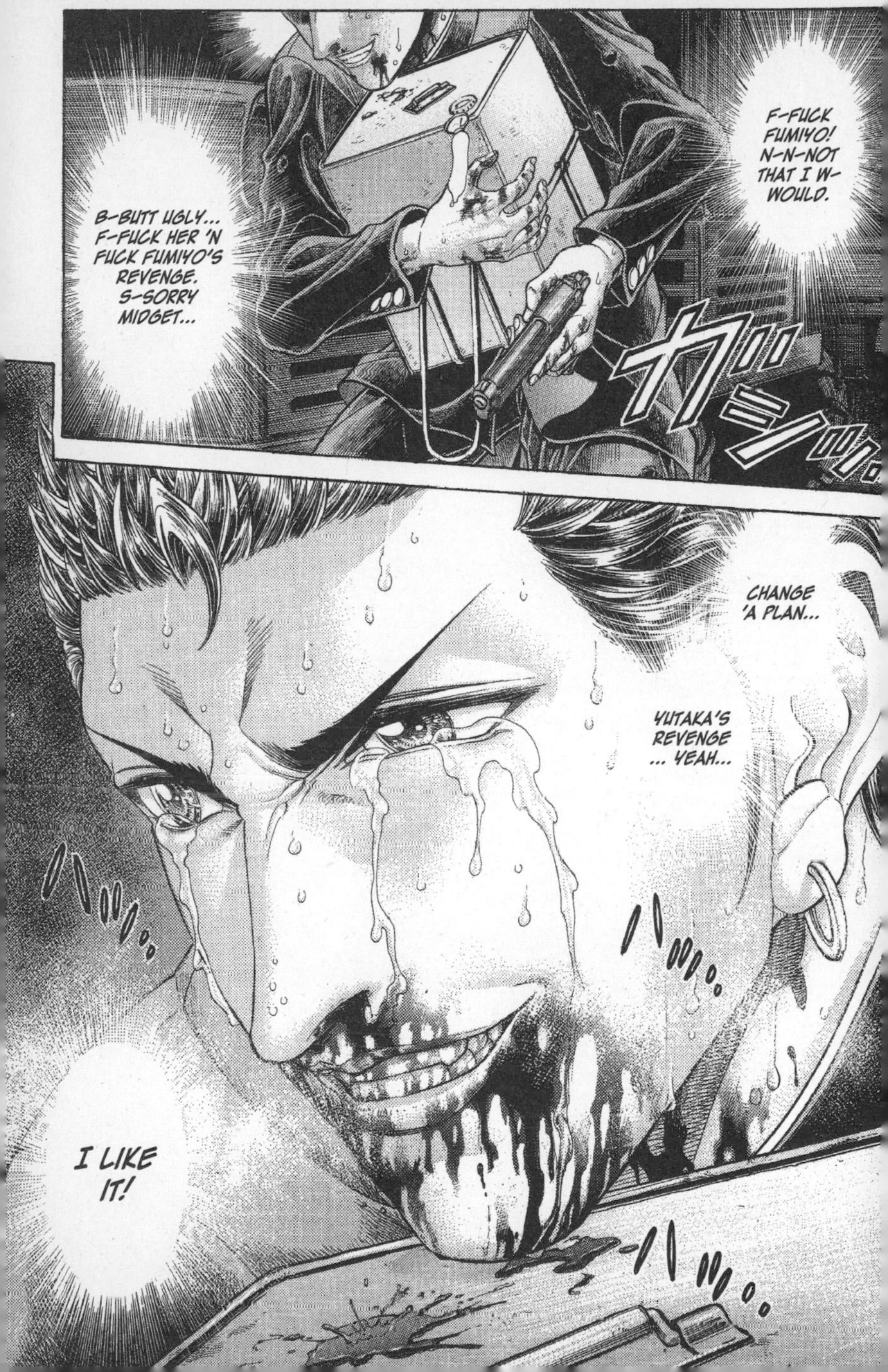
B-BUTT UGLY... F-FUCK HER 'N FUCK FUMIYO'S REVENGE. S-SORRY MIDGET...
F-FUCK FUMIYO! N-N-NOT THAT I W-WOULD.
CHANGE 'A PLAN...
YUTAKA'S REVENGE ... YEAH...
I LIKE IT!

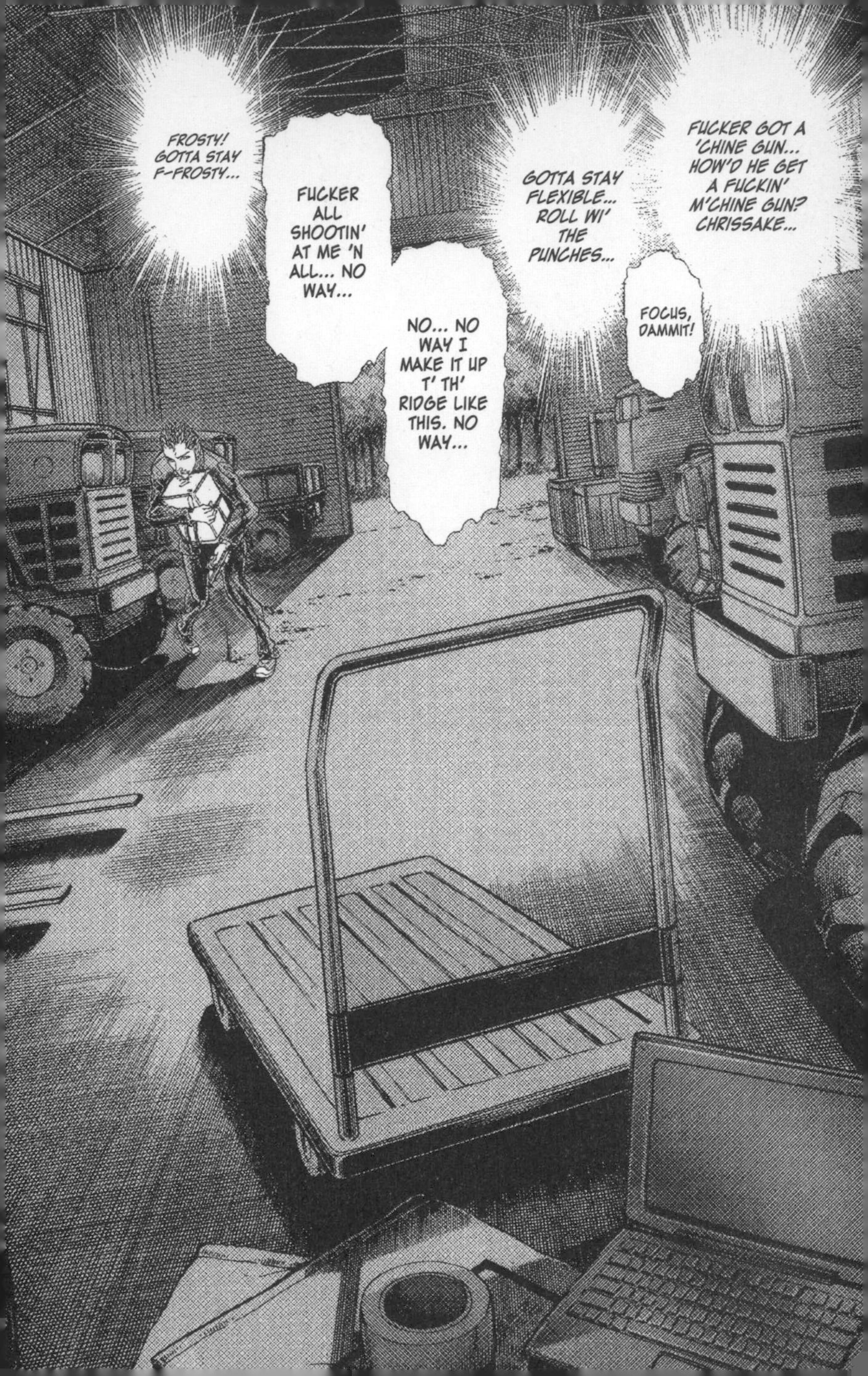
FUCKER GOT A 'CHINE GUN... HOW'D HE GET A FUCKIN' M'CHINE GUN? CHRISSAKE...
GOTTA STAY FLEXIBLE... ROLL WI' THE PUNCHES...
FOCUS, DAMMIT!
NO... NO WAY I MAKE IT UP T' TH' RIDGE LIKE THIS. NO WAY...
FUCKER ALL SHOOTIN' AT ME 'N ALL... NO WAY...
FROSTY! GOTTA STAY F-FROSTY...

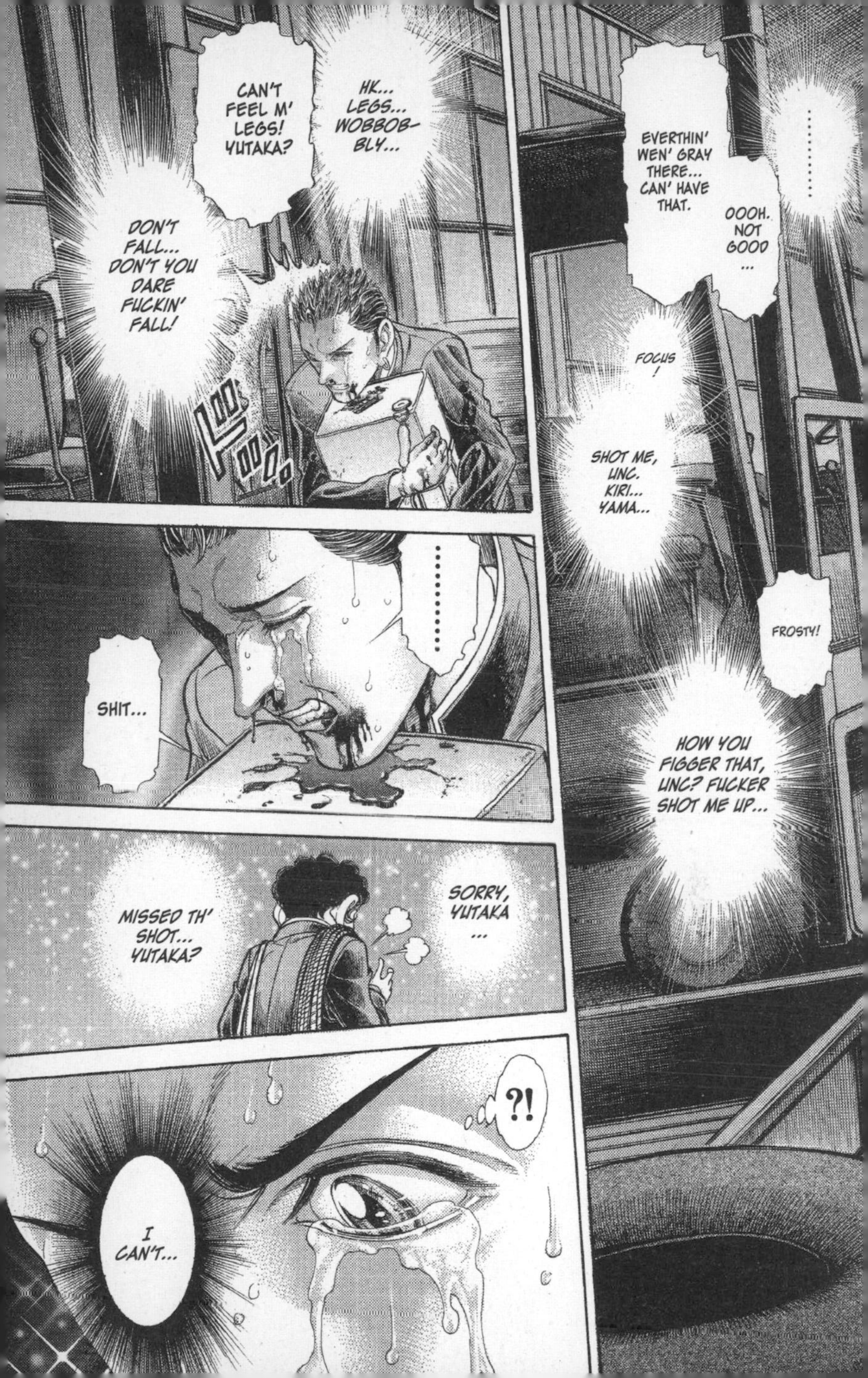
......
EVERTHIN' WEN' GRAY THERE... CAN' HAVE THAT.
OOOH. NOT GOOD ...
FOCUS !
SHOT ME, UNC. KIRI... YAMA...
FROSTY!
HOW YOU FIGGER THAT, UNC? FUCKER SHOT ME UP...
HK... LEGS... WOBBOB-BLY...
CAN'T FEEL M' LEGS! YUTAKA?
DON'T FALL... DON'T YOU DARE FUCKIN' FALL!
......
SHIT...
SORRY, YUTAKA ...
MISSED TH' SHOT... YUTAKA?
?!
I CAN'T...

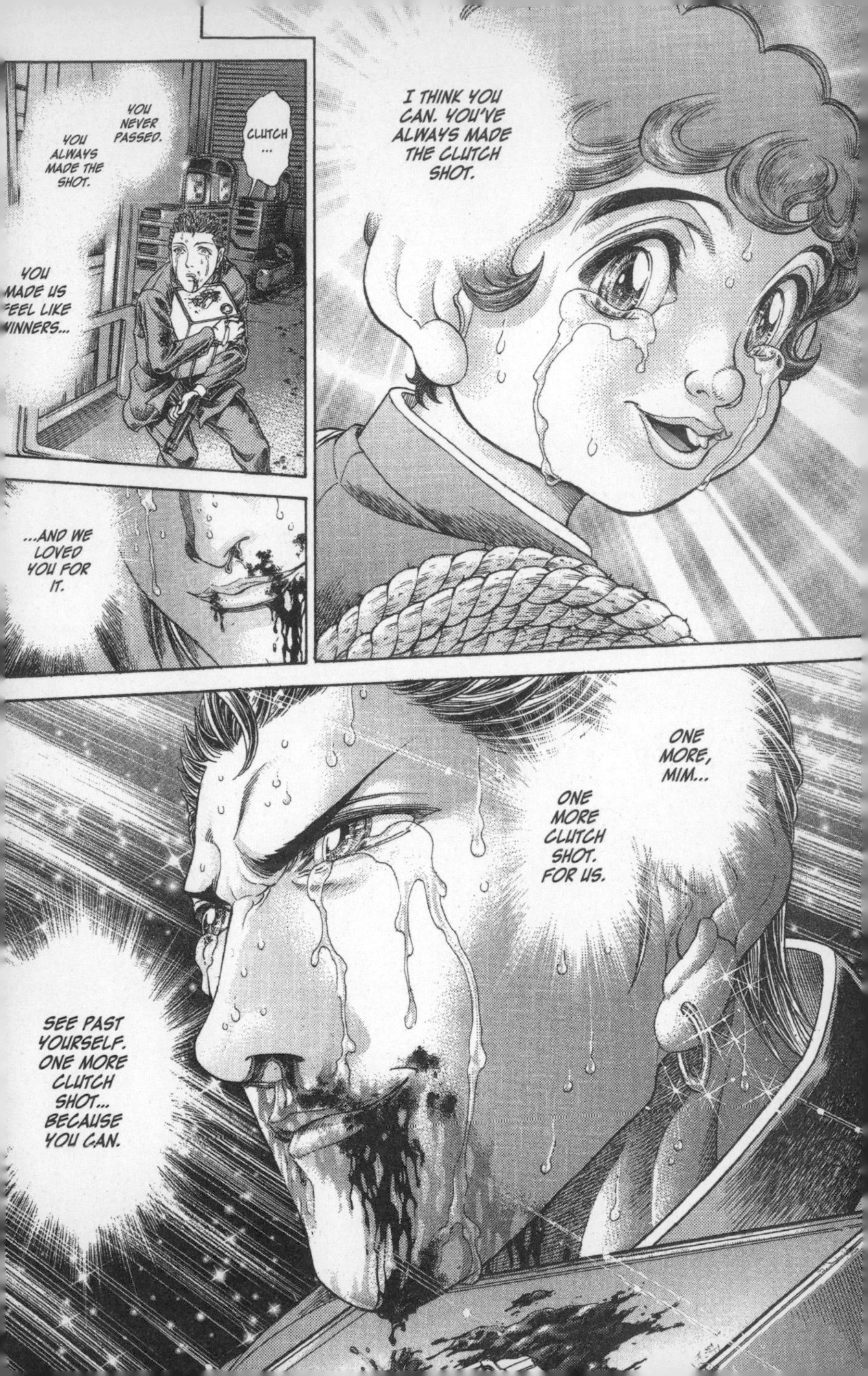
I THINK YOU CAN. YOU'VE ALWAYS MADE THE CLUTCH SHOT.
CLUTCH ...
YOU NEVER PASSED.
YOU ALWAYS MADE THE SHOT.
YOU MADE US FEEL LIKE WINNERS...
...AND WE LOVED YOU FOR IT.
ONE MORE, MIM...
ONE MORE CLUTCH SHOT. FOR US.
SEE PAST YOURSELF. ONE MORE CLUTCH SHOT... BECAUSE YOU CAN.

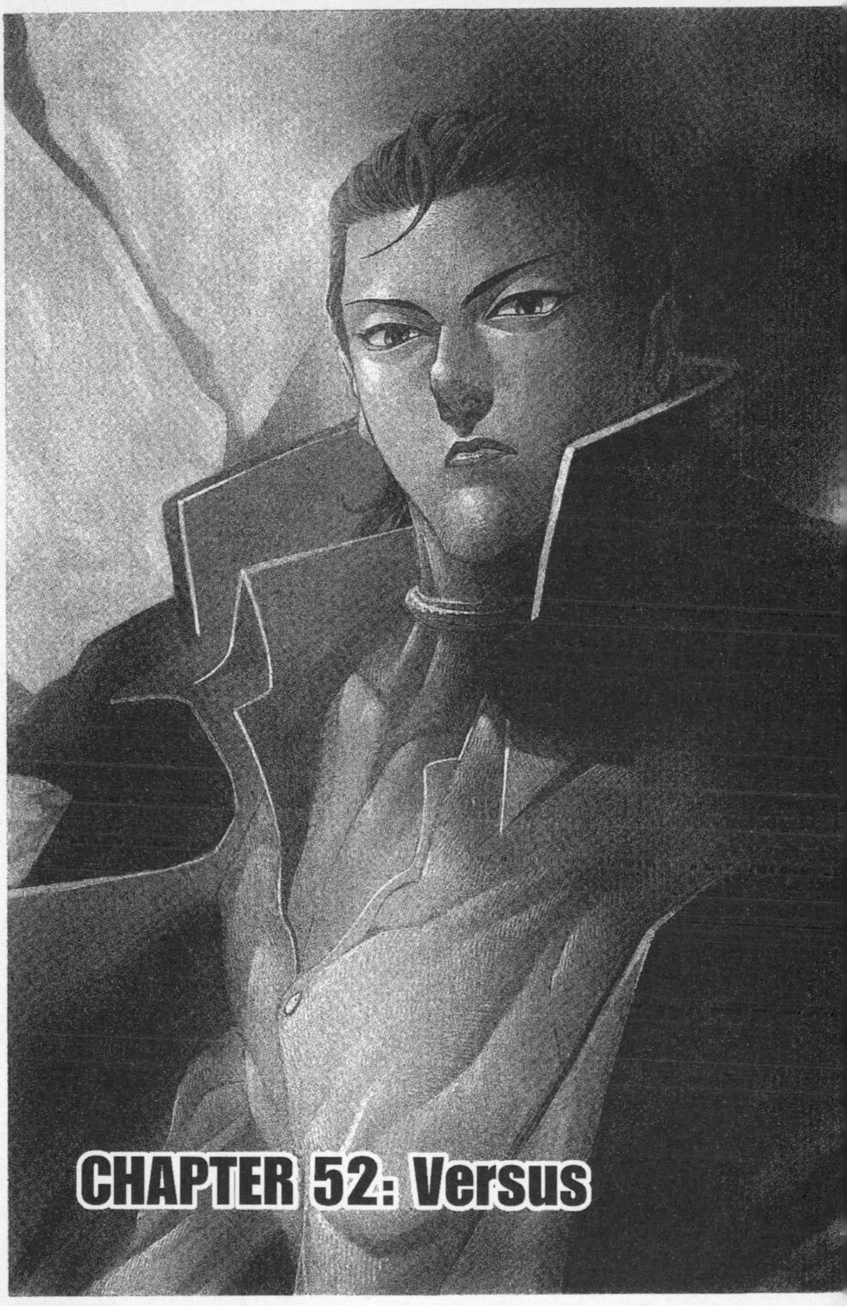
CHAPTER 52: Versus

BATTLE ROYALE

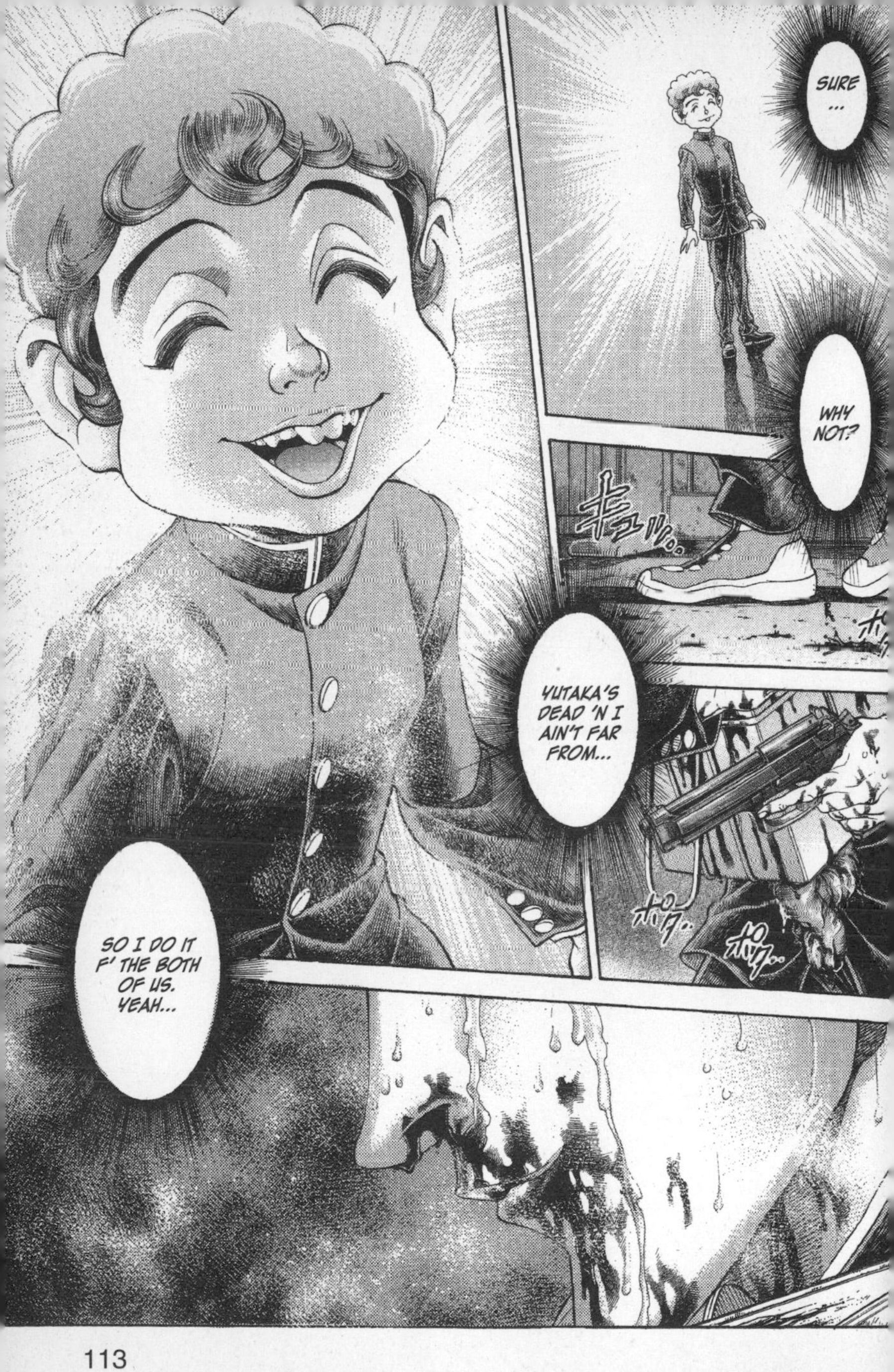
SURE ...
WHY NOT?
YUTAKA'S DEAD 'N I AIN'T FAR FROM...
SO I DO IT F' THE BOTH OF US. YEAH...

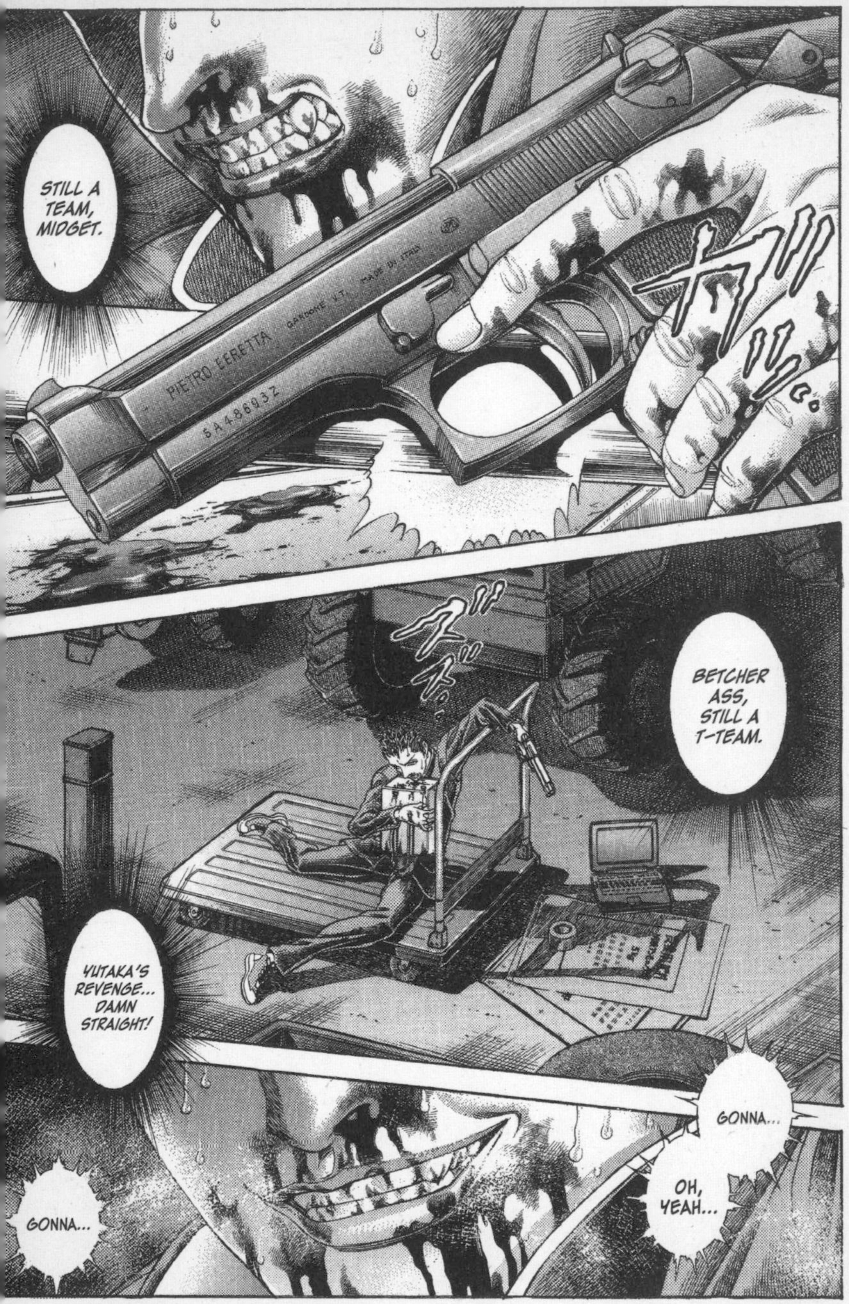
STILL A TEAM, MIDGET.
BETCHER ASS, STILL A T-TEAM.
YUTAKA'S REVENGE... DAMN STRAIGHT!
GONNA...
OH, YEAH...
GONNA...

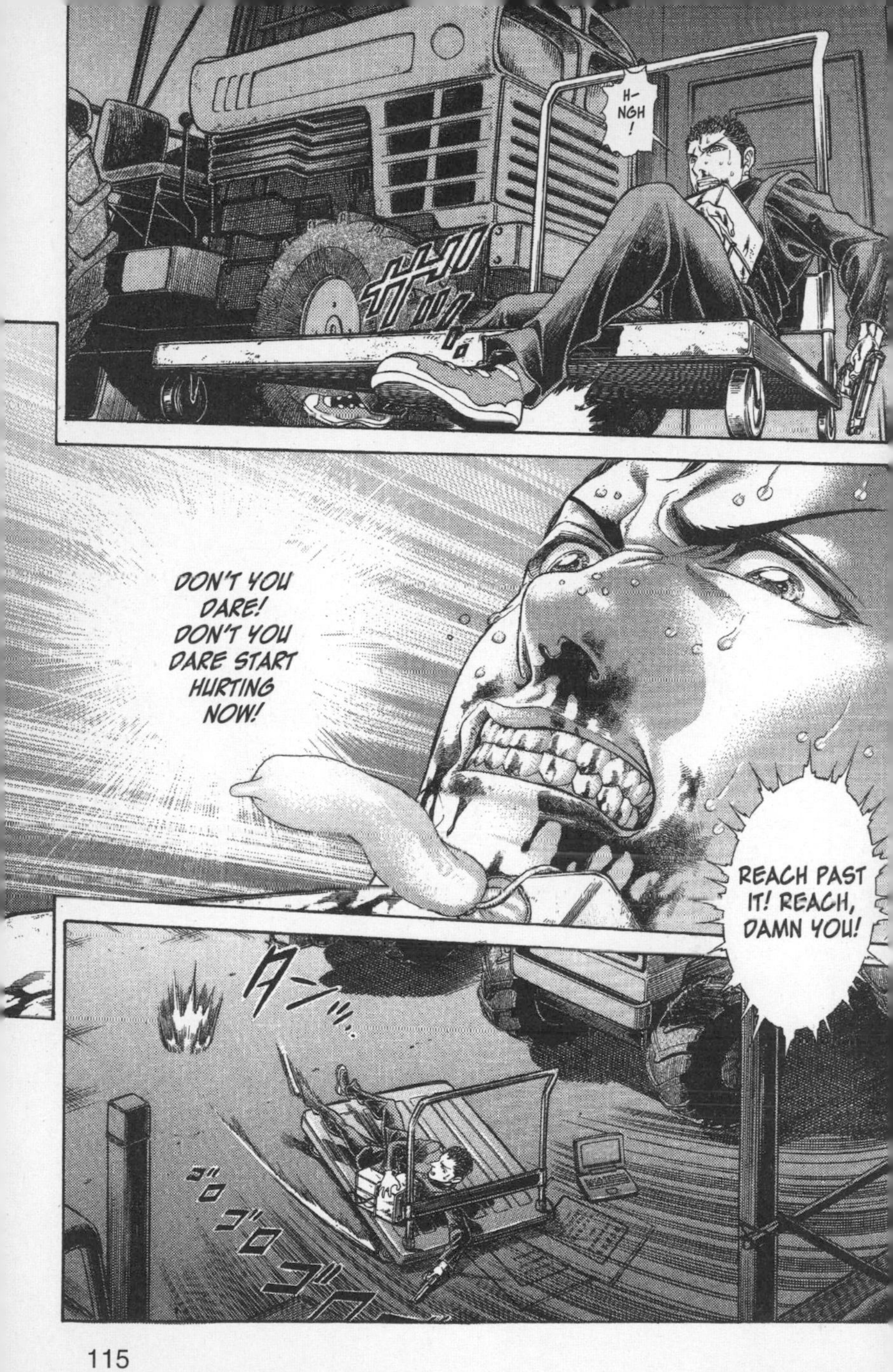
H-NGH!
DON'T YOU DARE! DON'T YOU DARE START HURTING NOW!
REACH PAST IT! REACH, DAMN YOU!

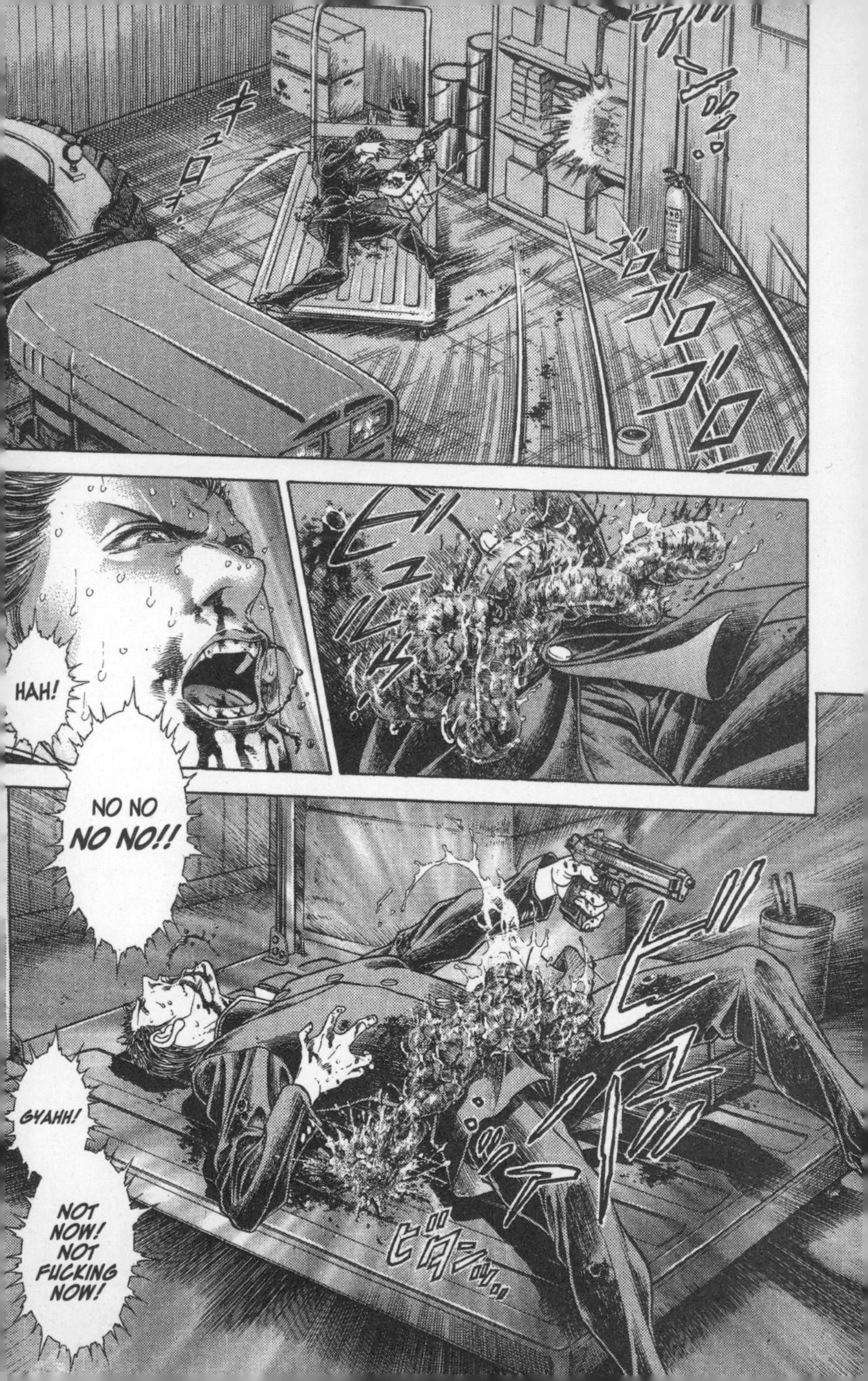
HAH!
NO NO NO NO!!
GYAHH!
NOT NOW! NOT FUCKING NOW!

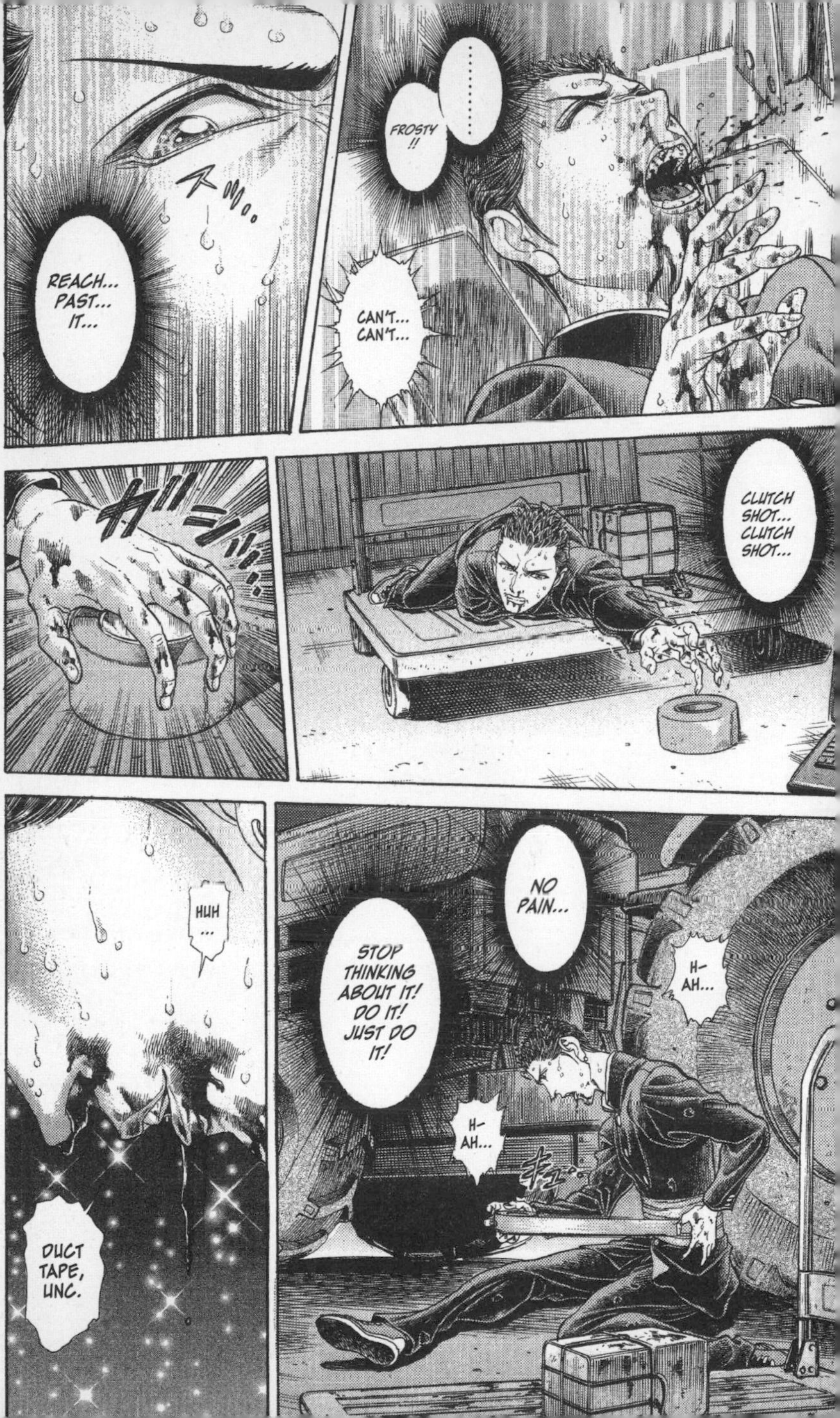
......
FROSTY!!
CAN'T... CAN'T...
REACH... PAST... IT...
CLUTCH SHOT... CLUTCH SHOT...
NO PAIN...
STOP THINKING ABOUT IT! DO IT! JUST DO IT!
H-AH...
H-AH...
HUH...
DUCT TAPE, UNC.

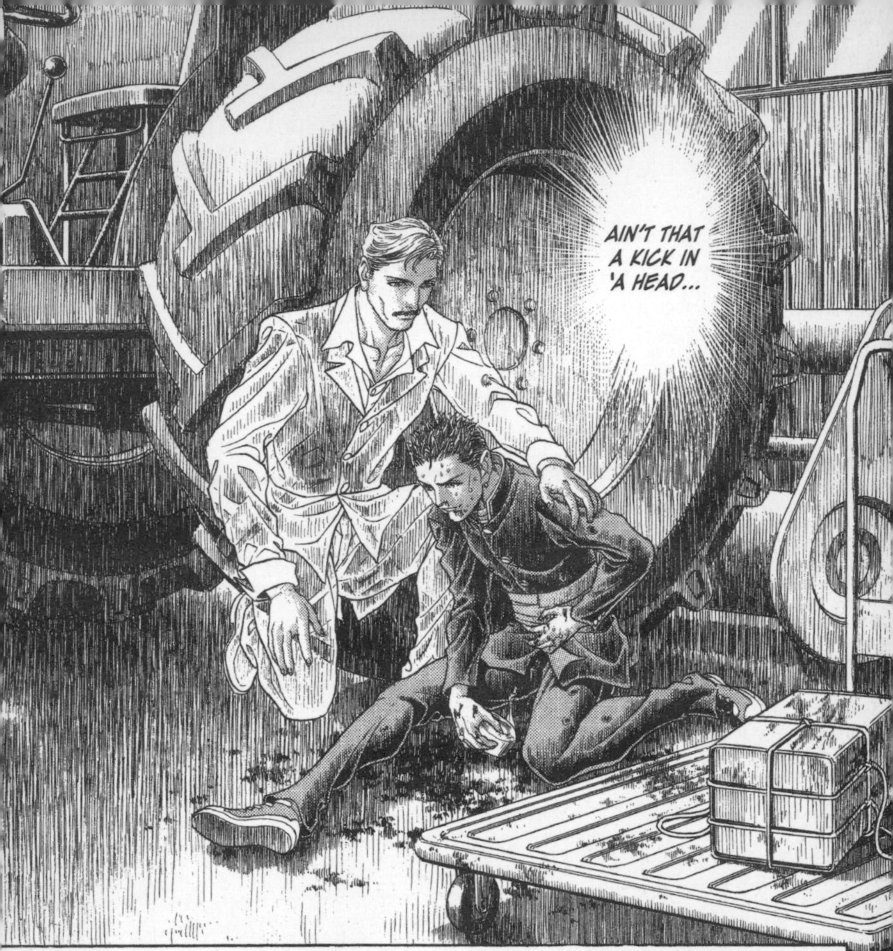
AIN'T THAT A KICK IN 'A HEAD...

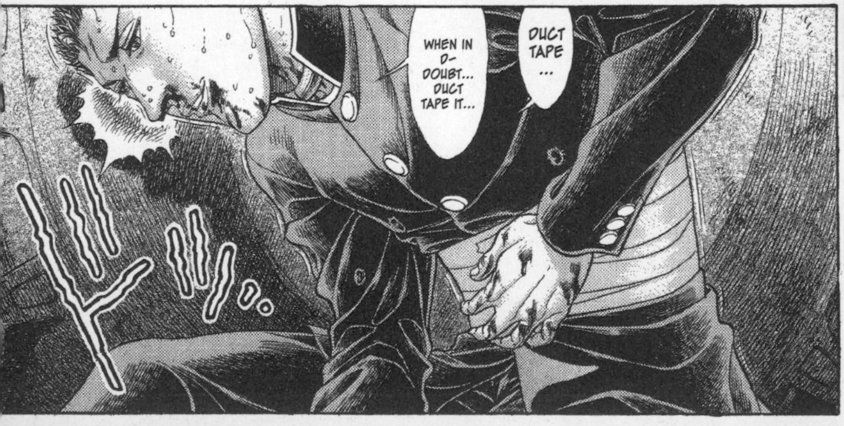
DUCT TAPE ...
WHEN IN D-DOUBT... DUCT TAPE IT...

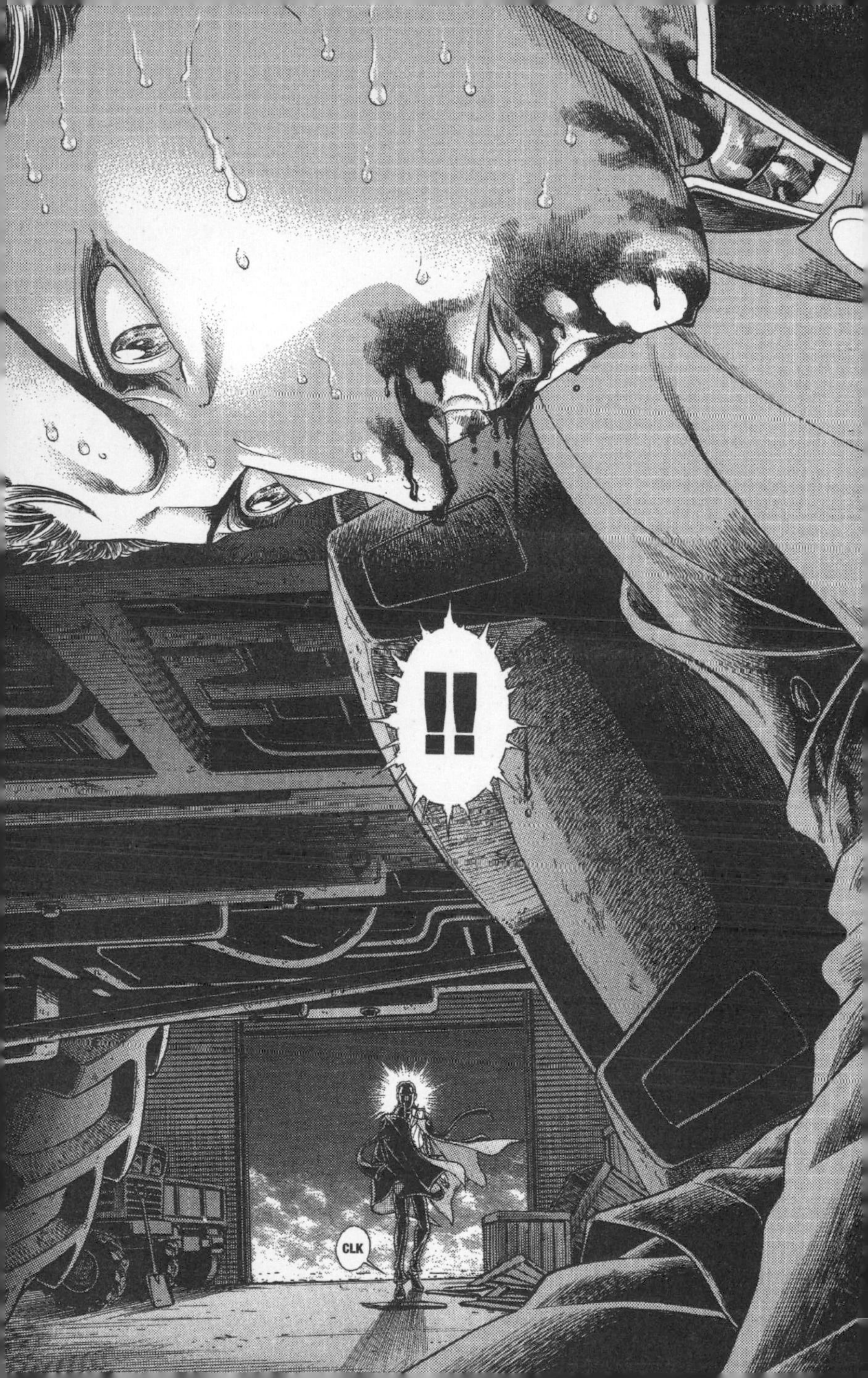
!!
CLK

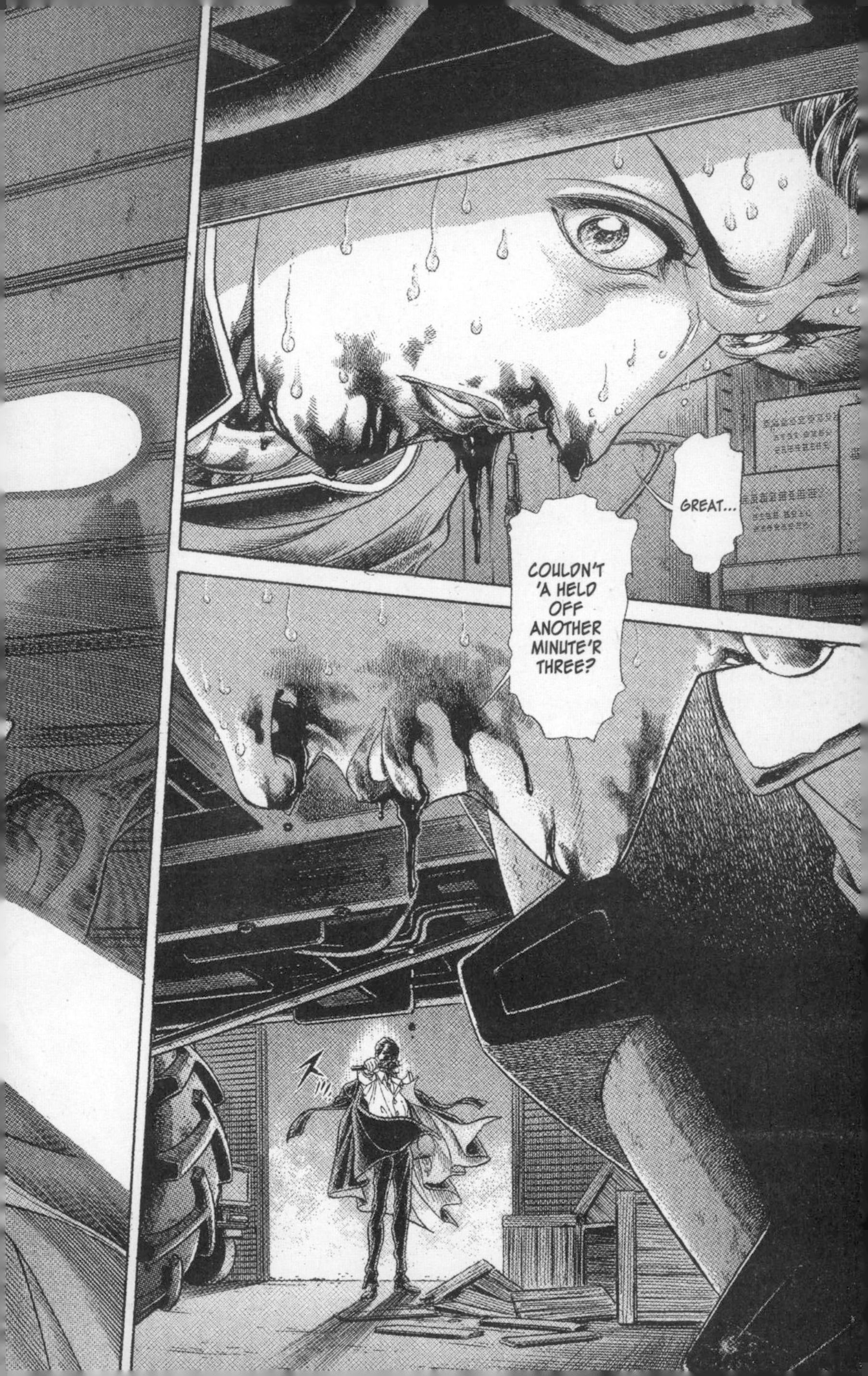
GREAT...
COULDN'T 'A HELD OFF ANOTHER MINUTE'R THREE?

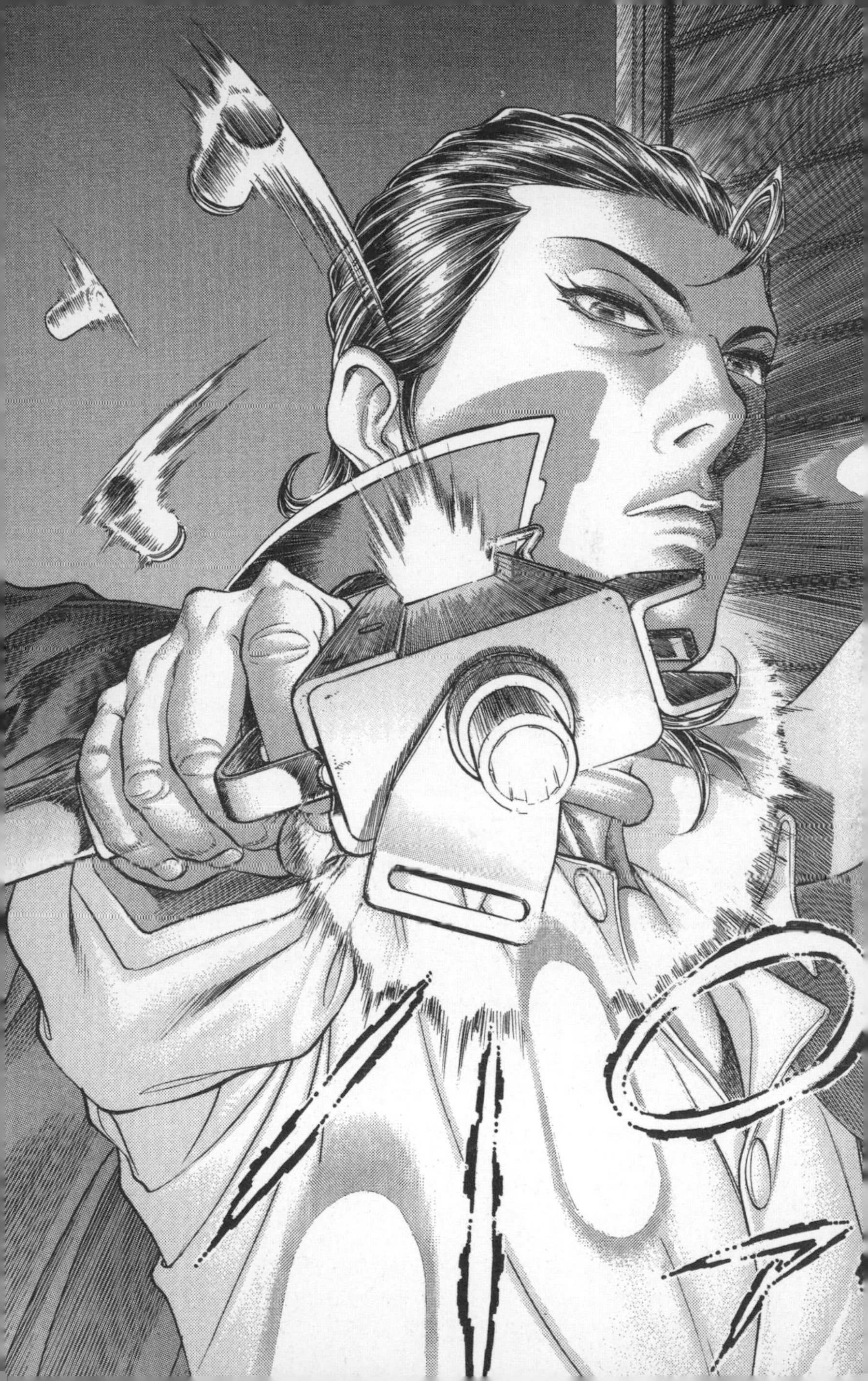

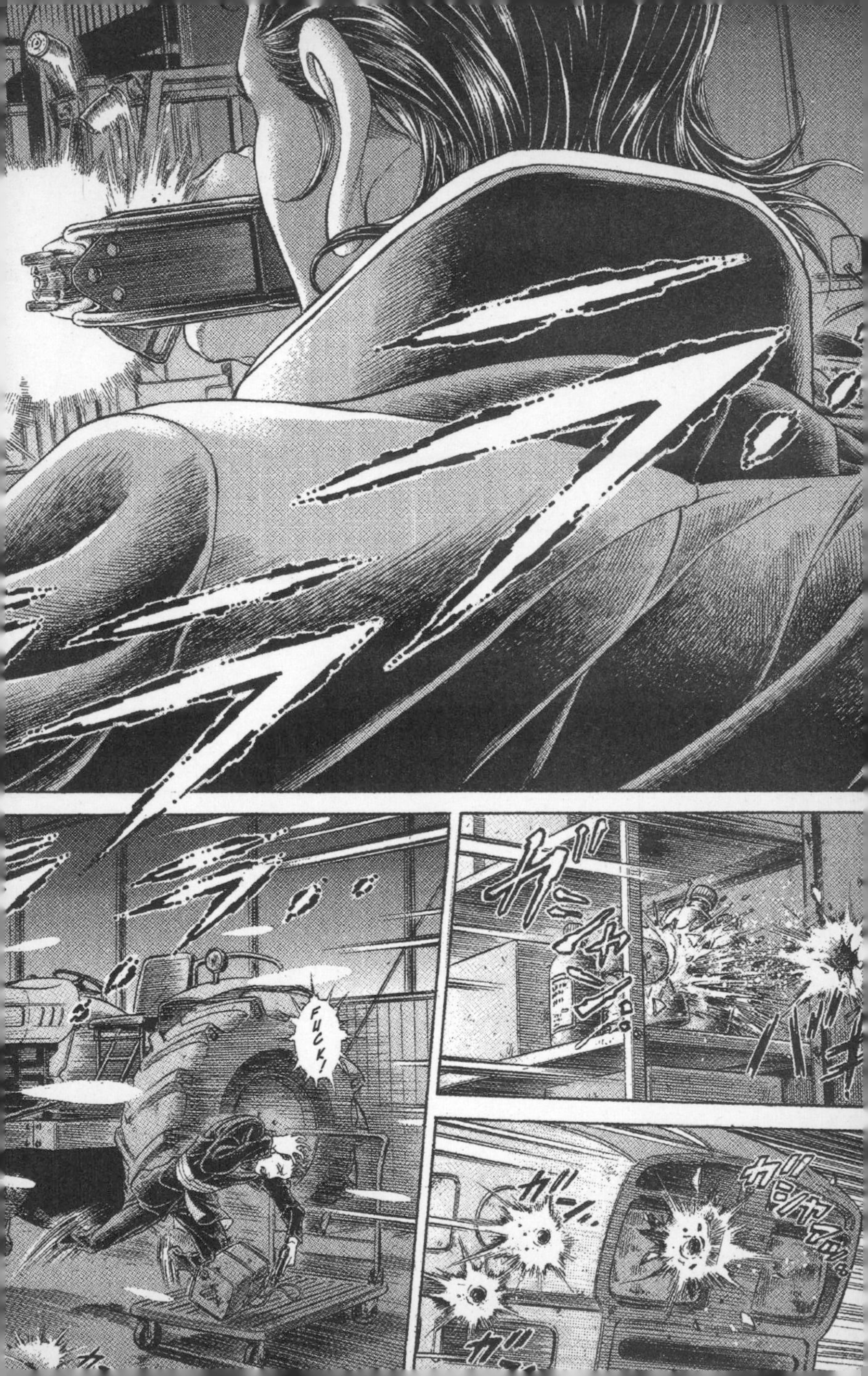
FUCK!

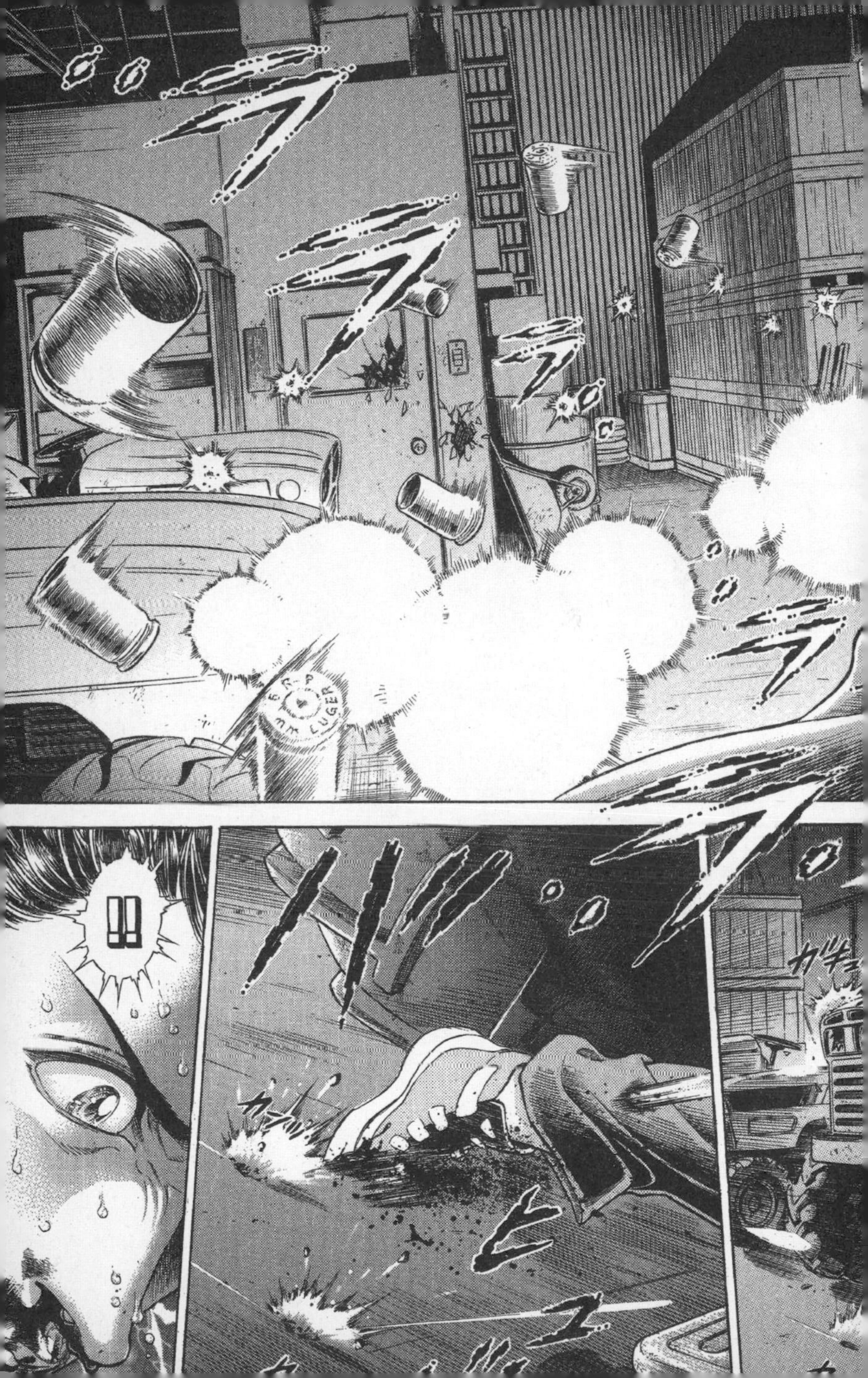
9mm LUGER
!!

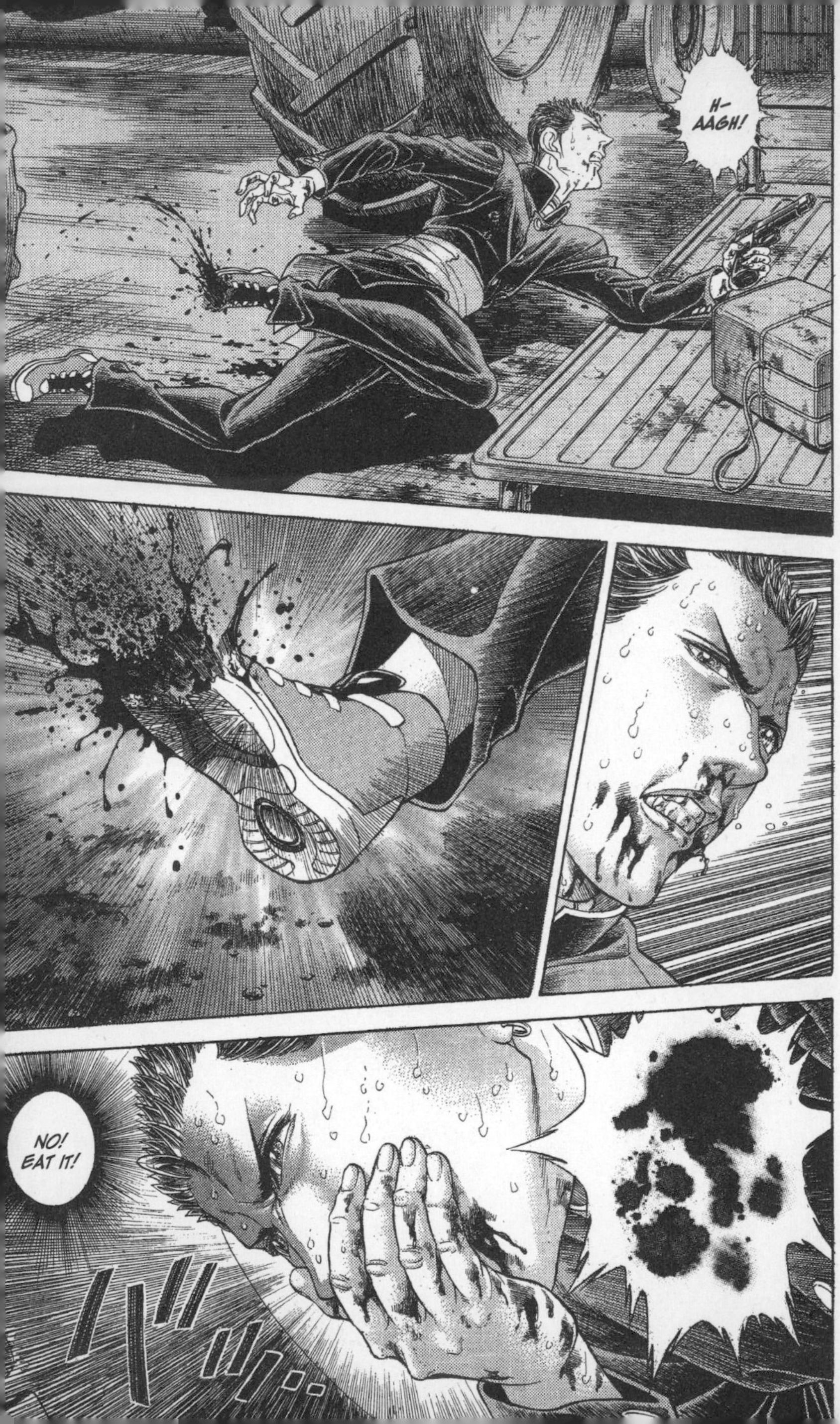
H-
AAGH!
NO!
EAT IT!

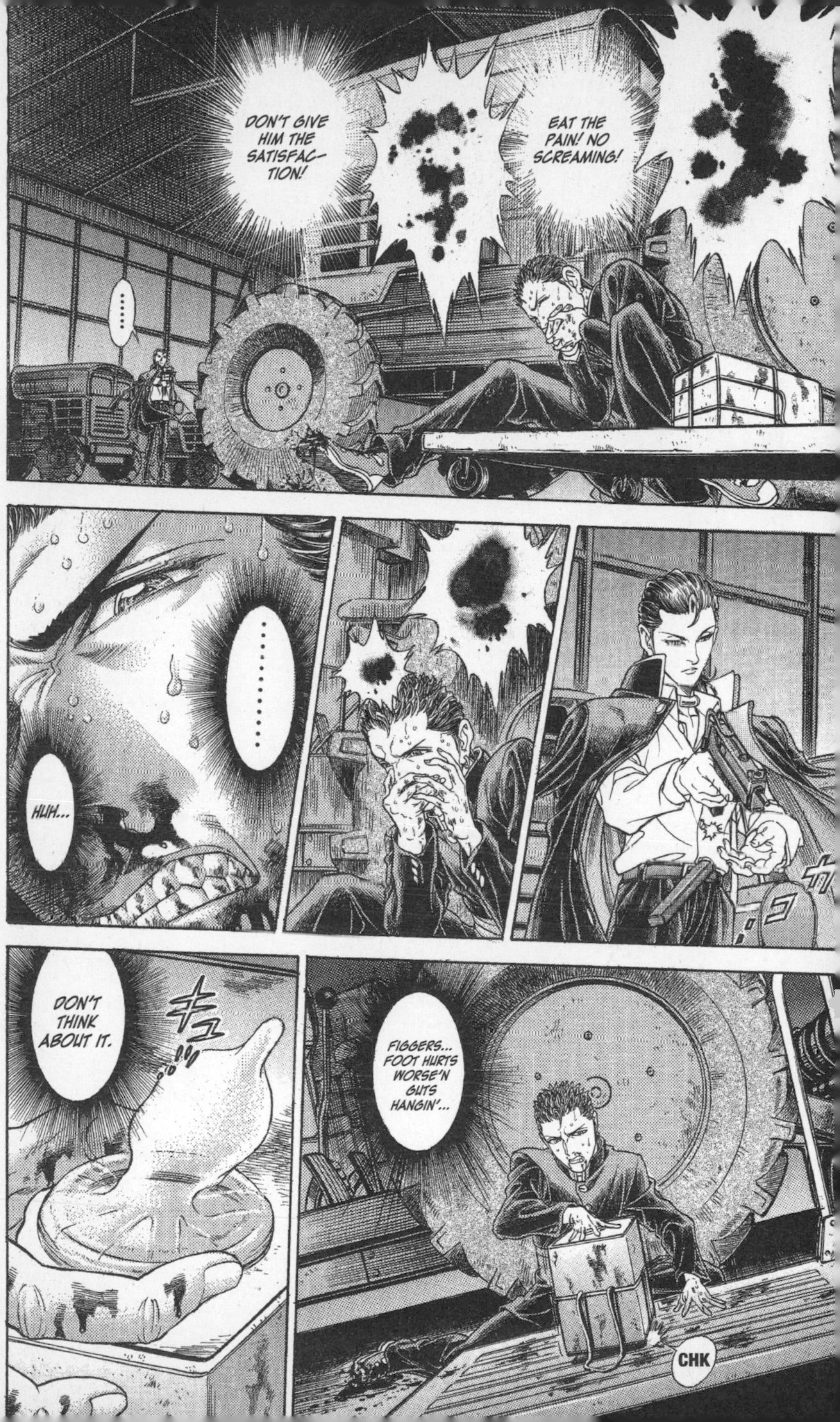
EAT THE PAIN! NO SCREAMING!
DON'T GIVE HIM THE SATISFACTION!
......
....
HUH...
FIGGERS... FOOT HURTS WORSE'N GUTS HANGIN'...
CHK
DON'T THINK ABOUT IT.

CRK-K
KLAK
YOU KNOW YOU GOT ME...
YEH...
SLOW 'N EASY, FUCKER.
gck
...JUST DON'T KNOW HOW BAD.
MIMURA KNOWS BAD. BEST B'LIEVE IT!
thft
FUCKER... YOU DON'T KNOW FROM BAD. STICK...STICK AROUND...

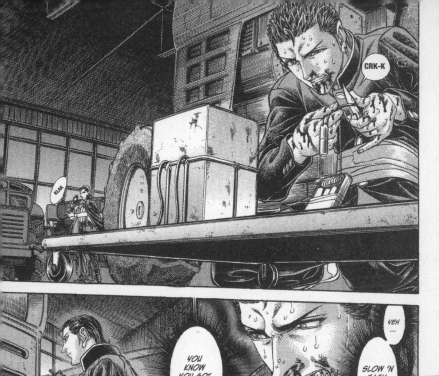

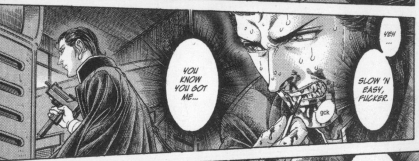

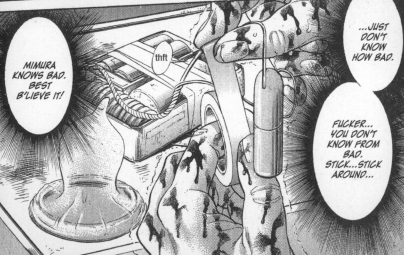

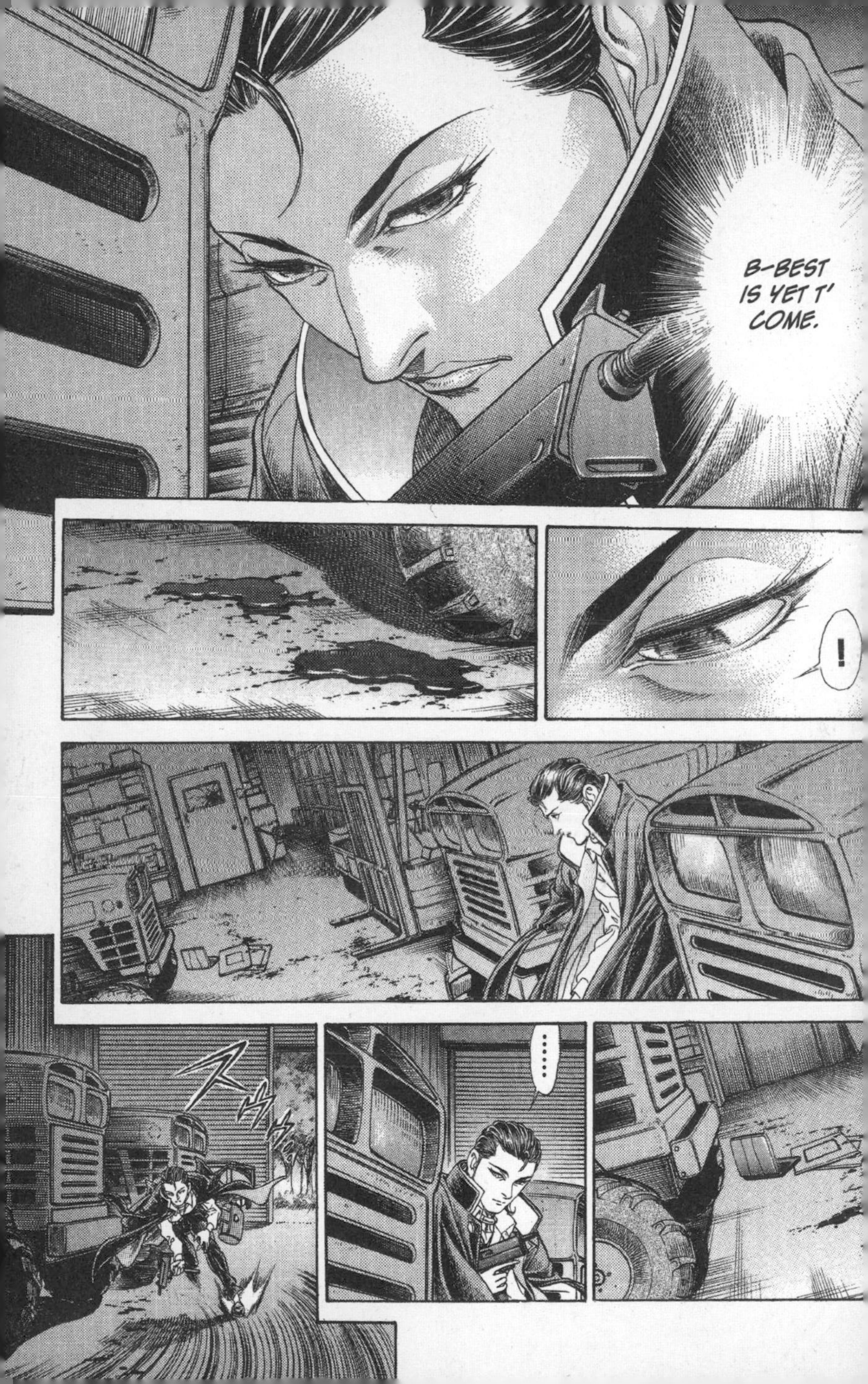
B-BEST IS YET T' COME.
!
......

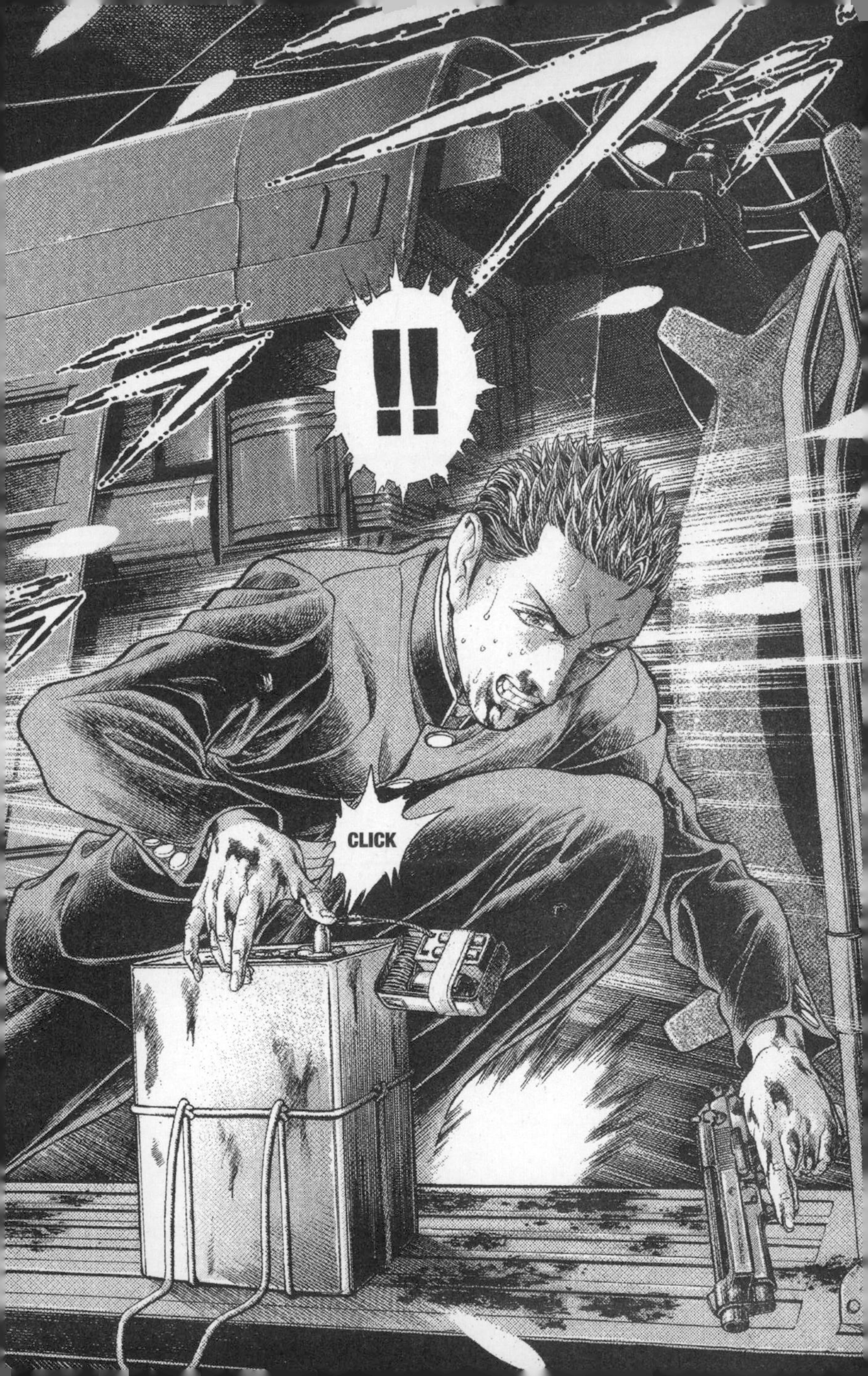
!!
CLICK

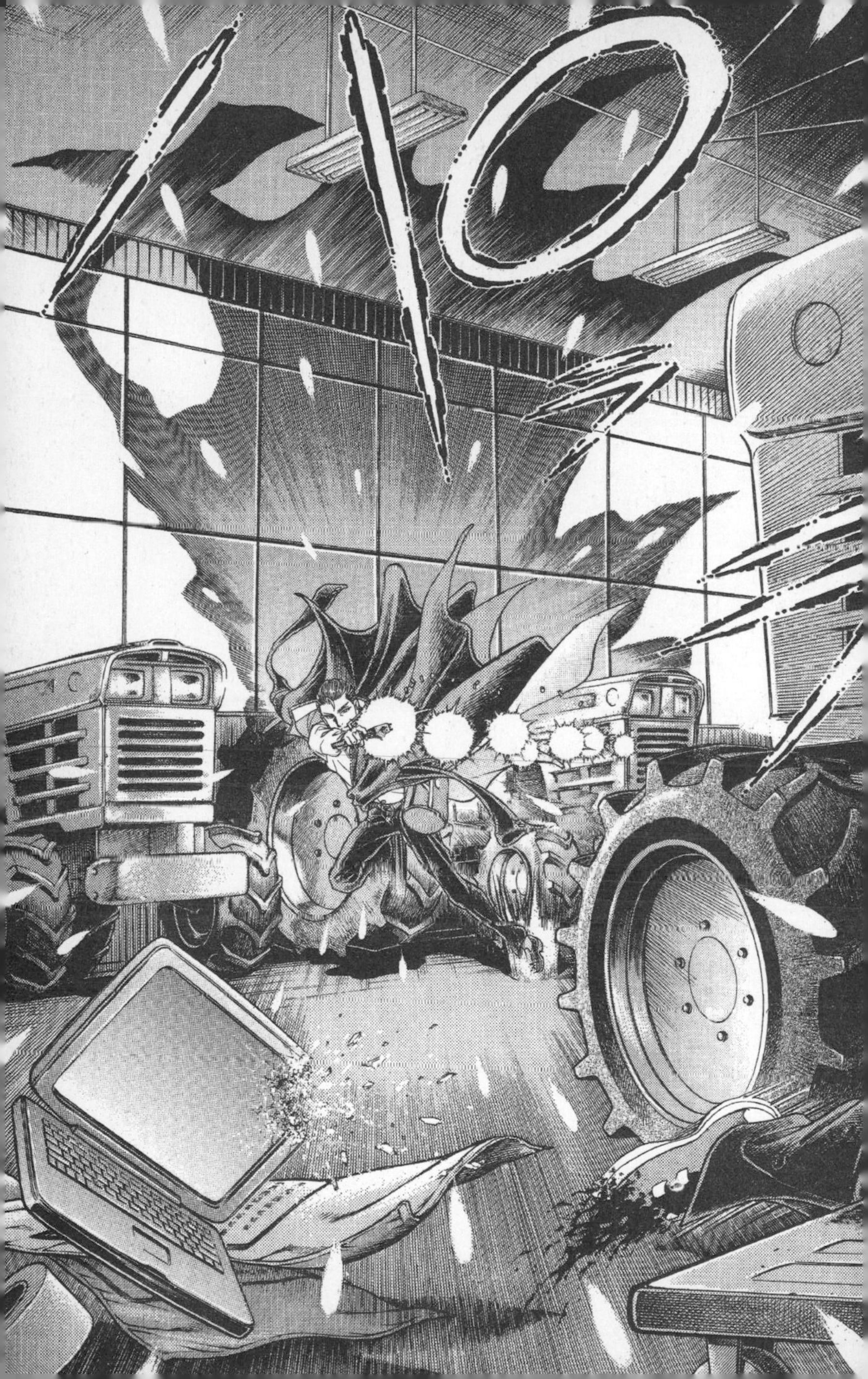

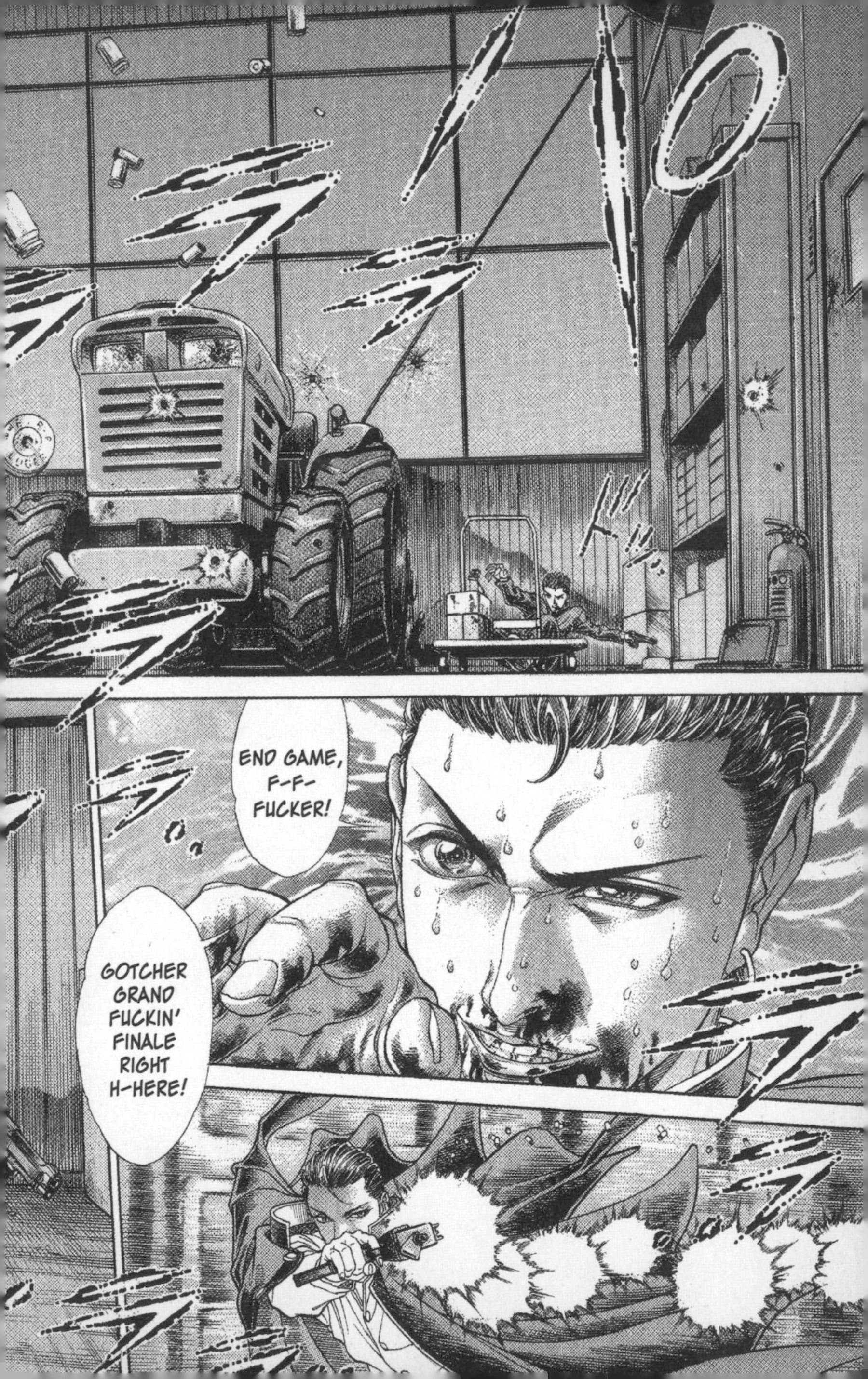
END GAME, F-F-FUCKER!
GOTCHER GRAND FUCKIN' FINALE RIGHT H-HERE!

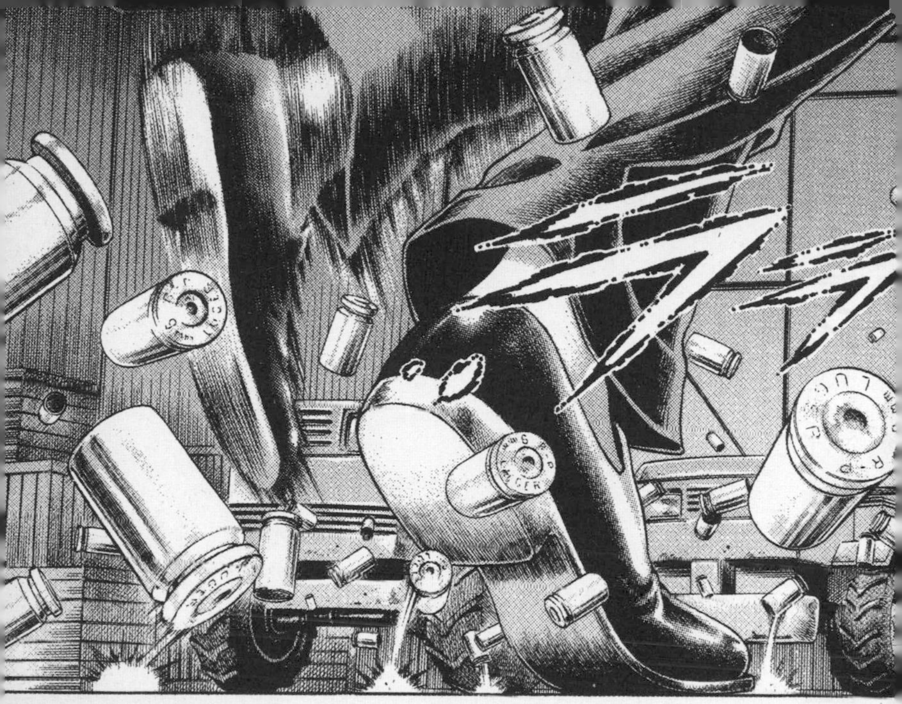

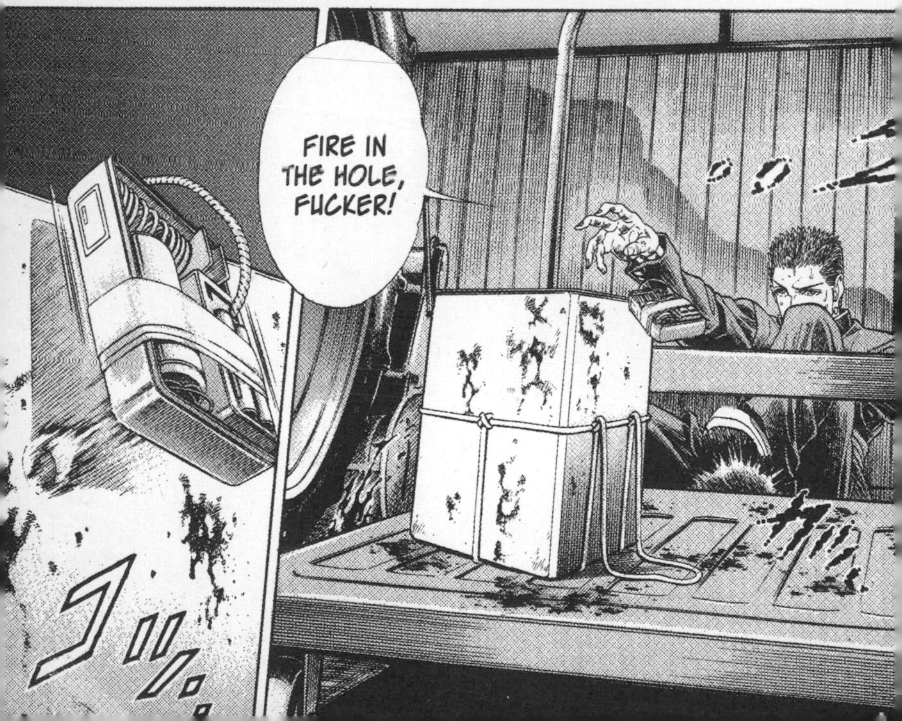
FIRE IN THE HOLE, FUCKER!

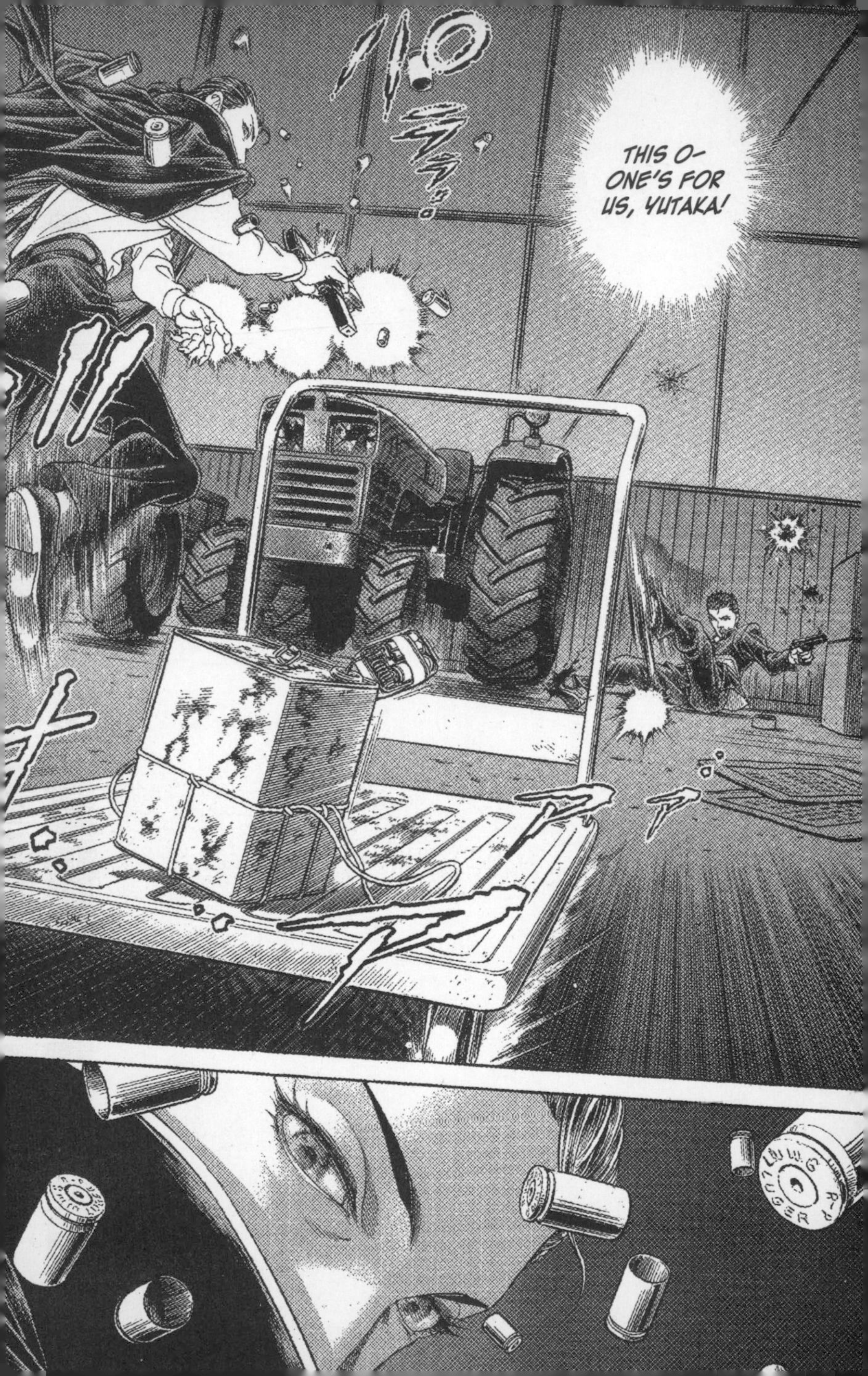
THIS O-ONE'S FOR US, YUTAKA!

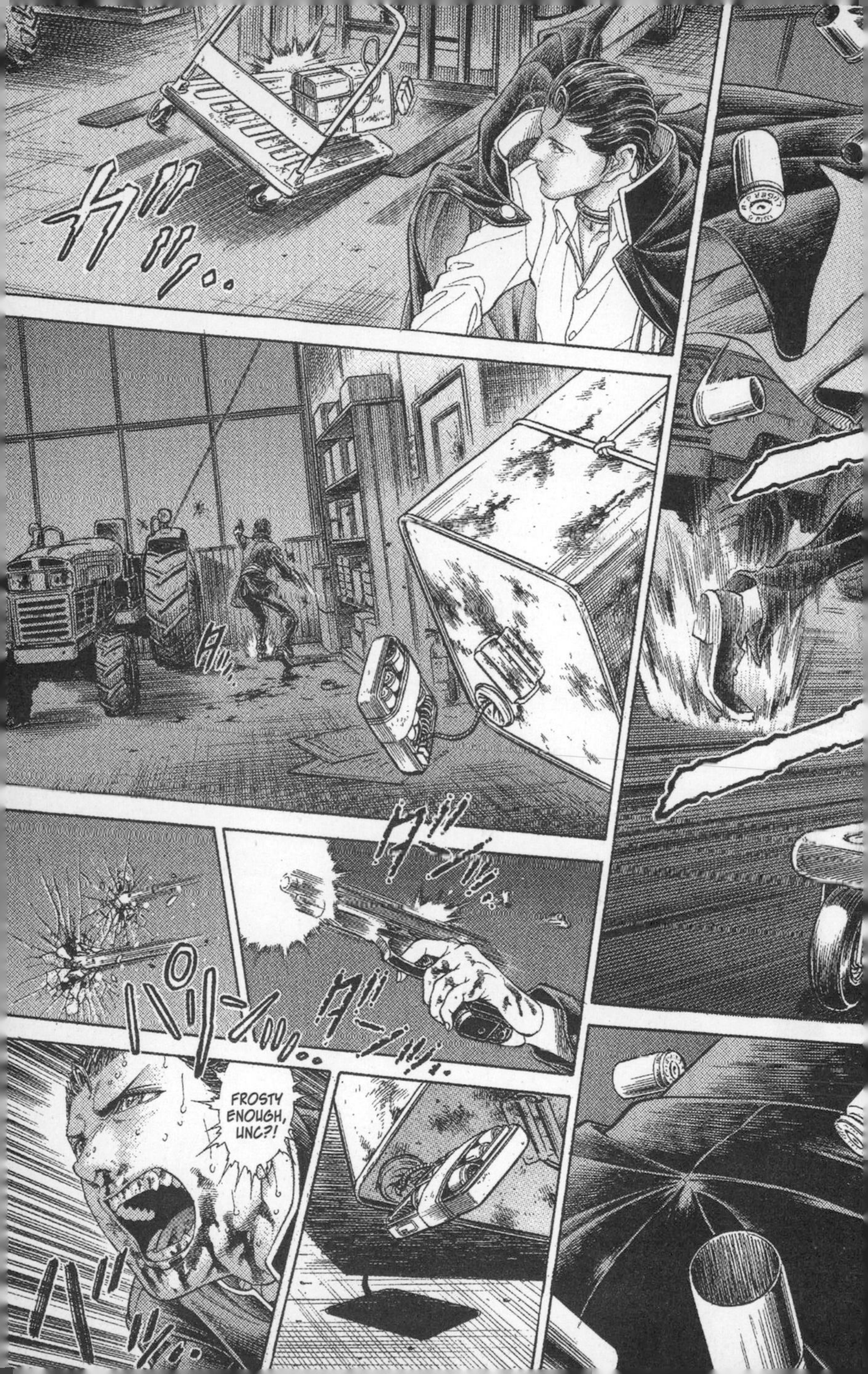
FROSTY ENOUGH, UNC?!

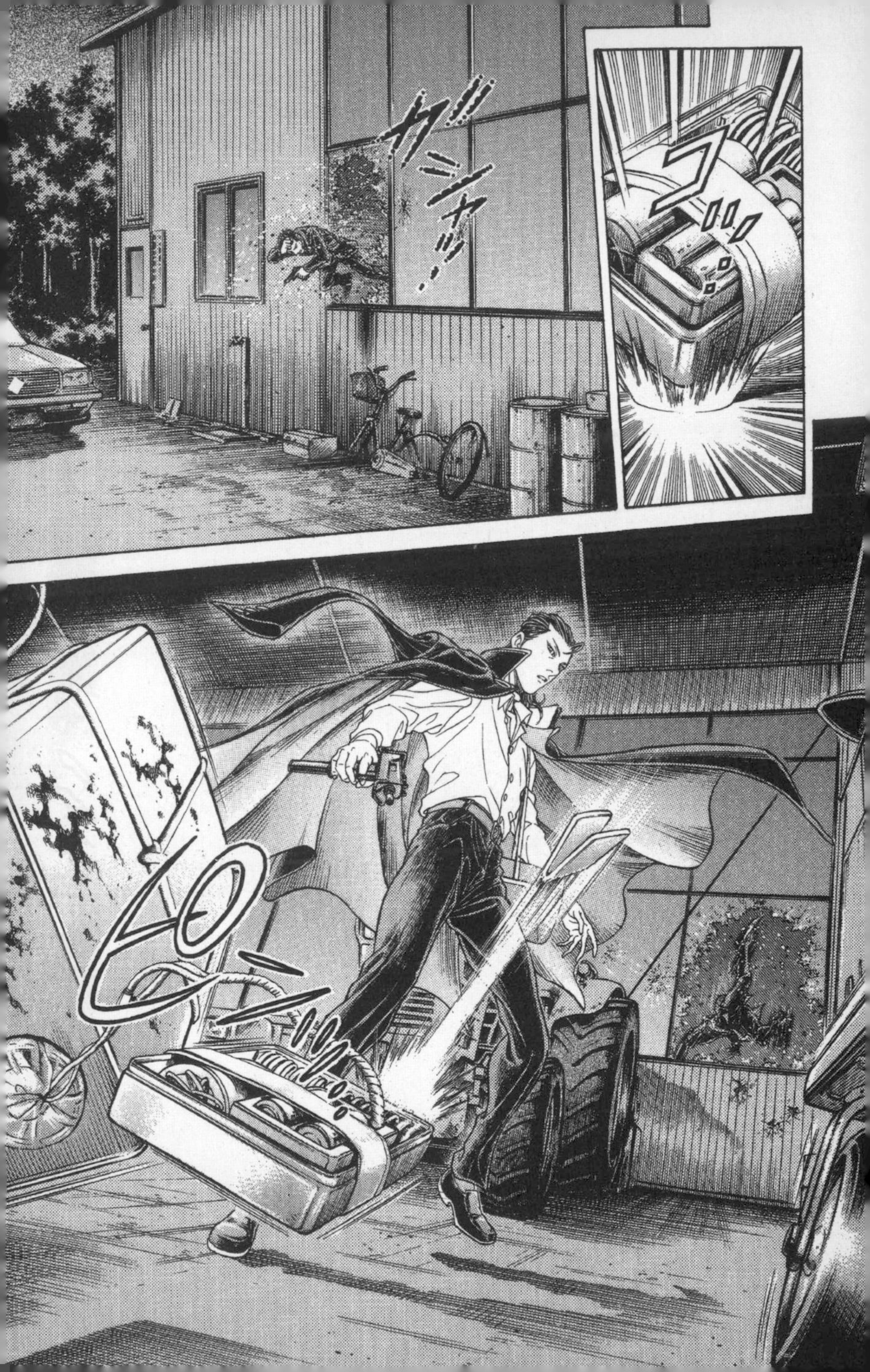

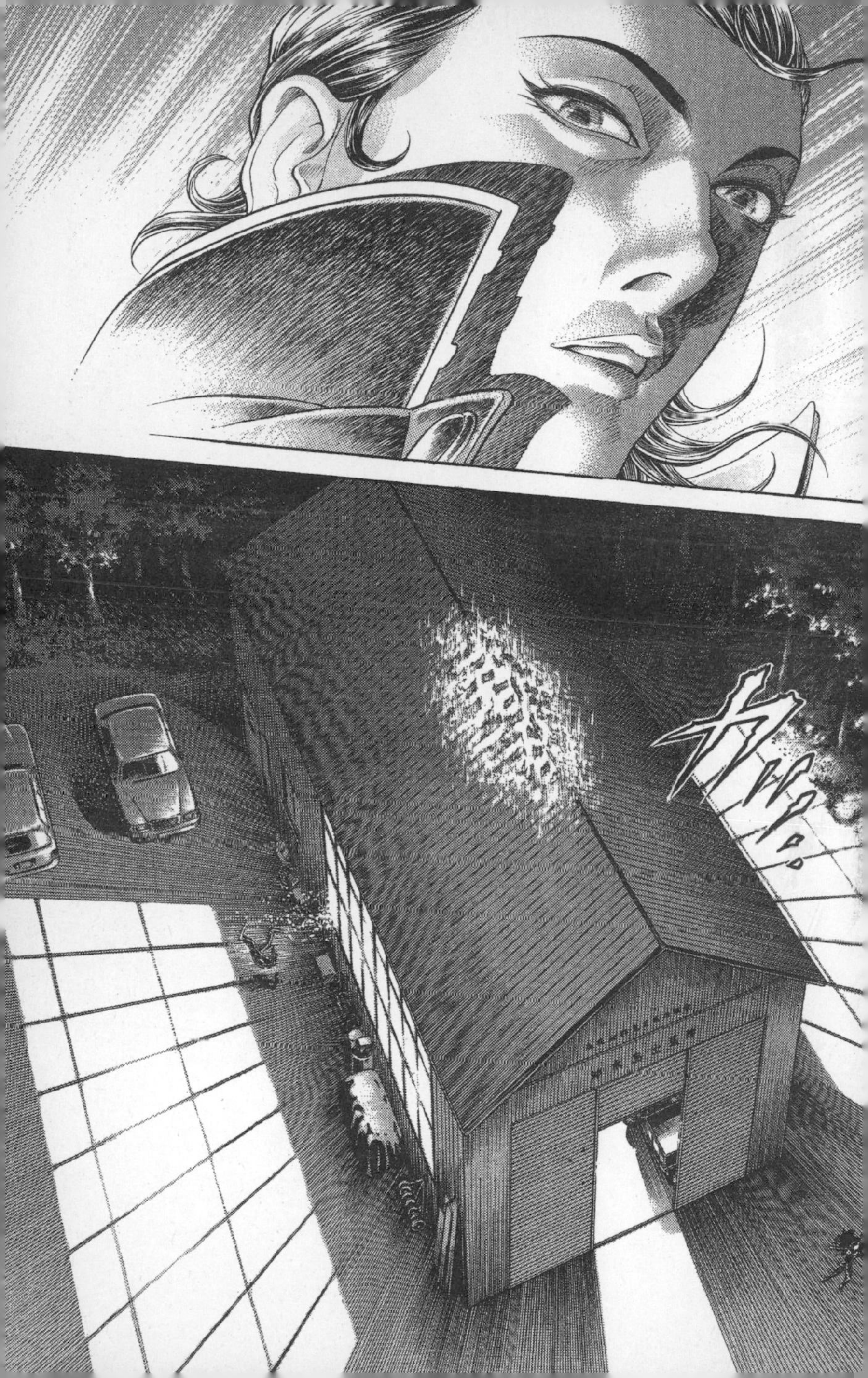

BATTLE ROYALE CONTESTANTS

number fourteen in a series
COLLECT THEM ALL!

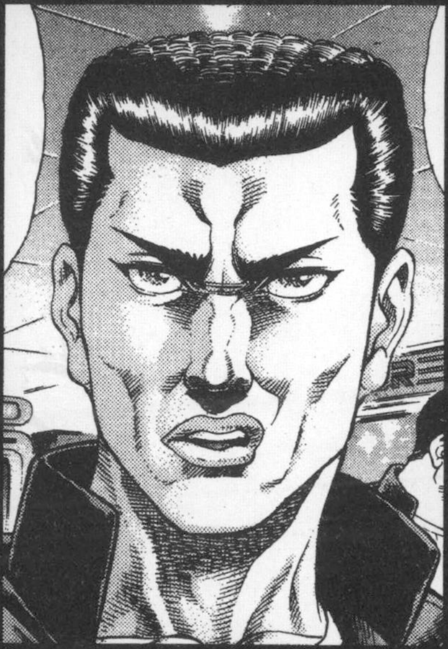

Mitsuru Numai

HEIGHT: 173 cm (5 ft. 8 in.)

WEIGHT: 63 kg (139 lb.)

DESIGNATED WEAPON: Walther P38

SUMMARY: The most physical of the so-called Kiriyama group. Infatuated by Kiriyama's fighting prowess (whether this carries over to emotional infatuation is unknown). Loyal to a fault, the subject will undoubtedly seek out Kiriyama early in The Program.

CONCLUSION(S): A possible dark horse should Kiriyama be eliminated early on.

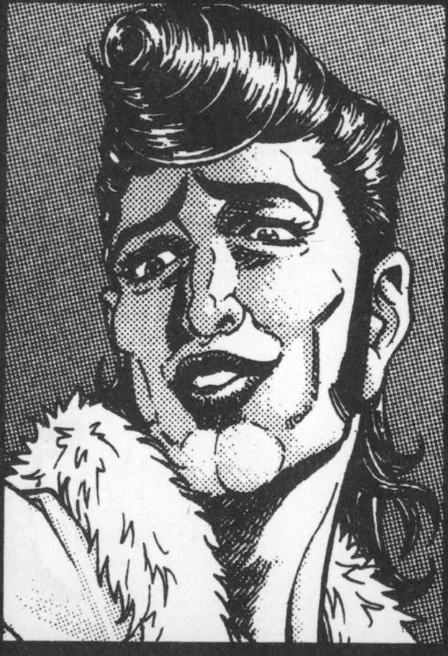

Sho Tsukioka

HEIGHT: 177 cm (5 ft. 10 in.)

WEIGHT: 71 kg (156 lb.)

DESIGNATED WEAPON: Double-shot Derringer

SUMMARY: Borderline alcoholic drag queen (ref: Tsukioka / elder / sub ref: aberrational upbringing). Prone to irrational crushes on heterosexual men / boys (ref: Kazuo Kiriyama: boy #6).

CONCLUSION(S): NOT to leave the island alive under any circumstances (ref: Sexual Deviation Act / sub ref: genetic cleansing).

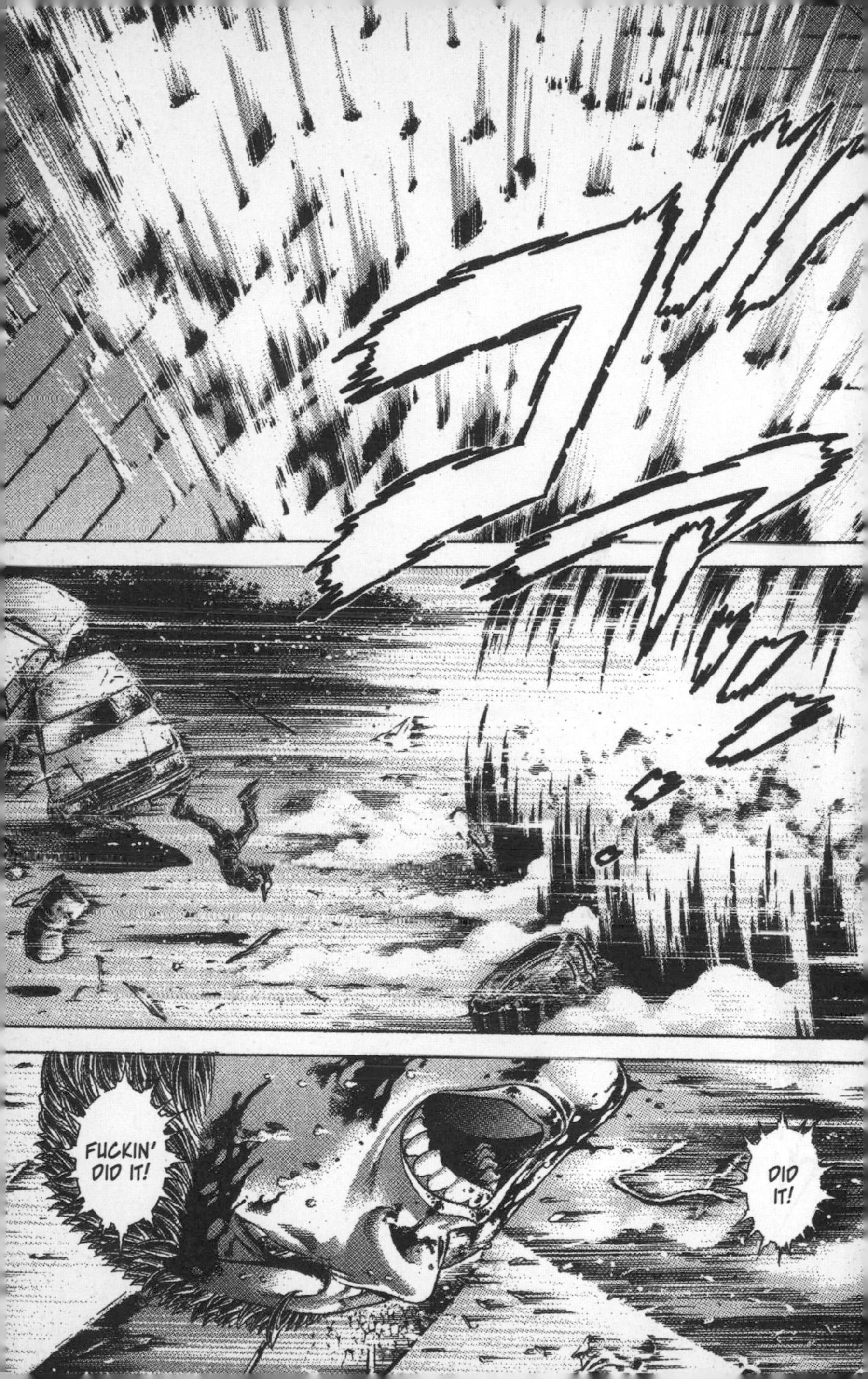
DID IT!
FUCKIN' DID IT!

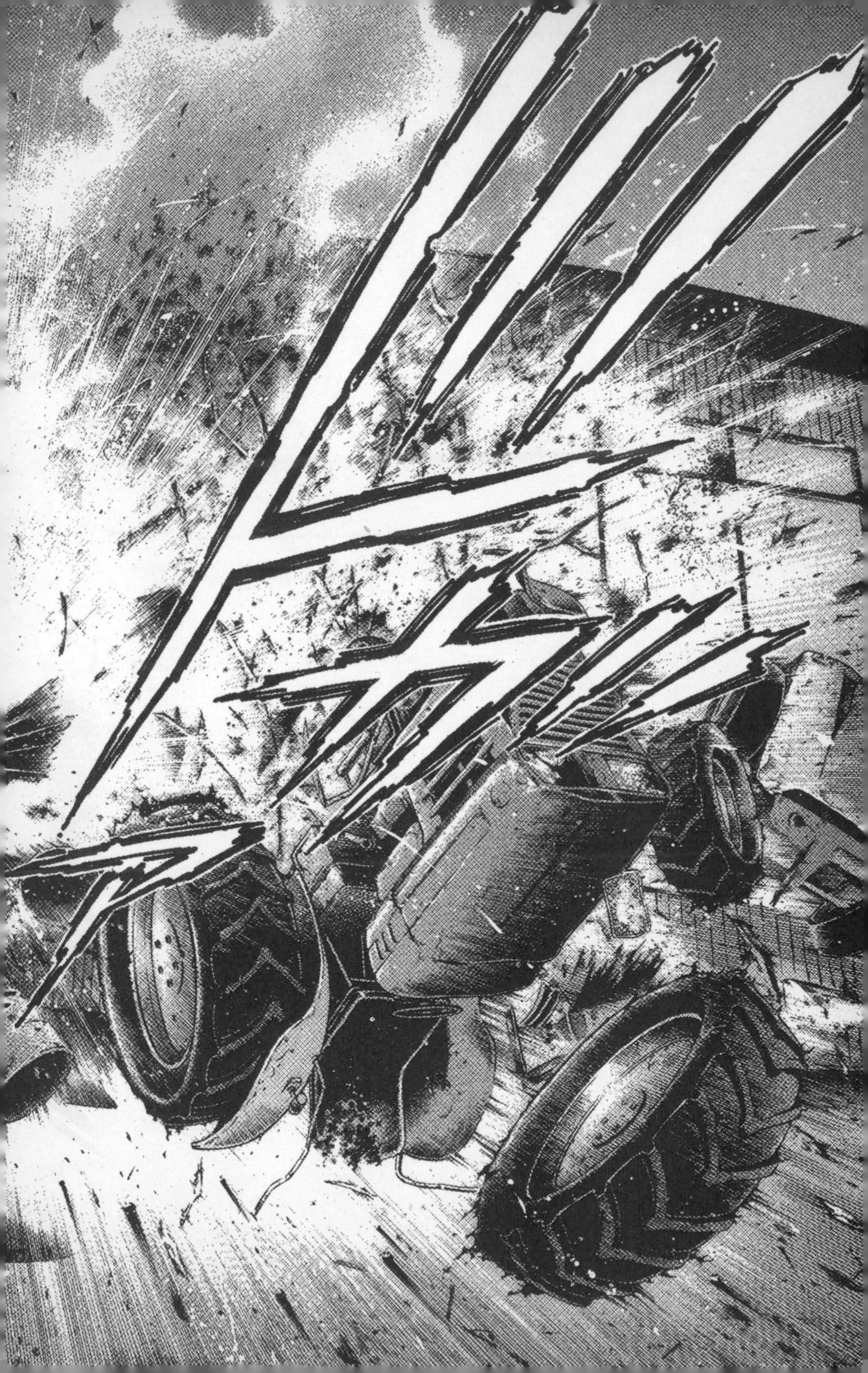

CHAPTER 53: Explosion

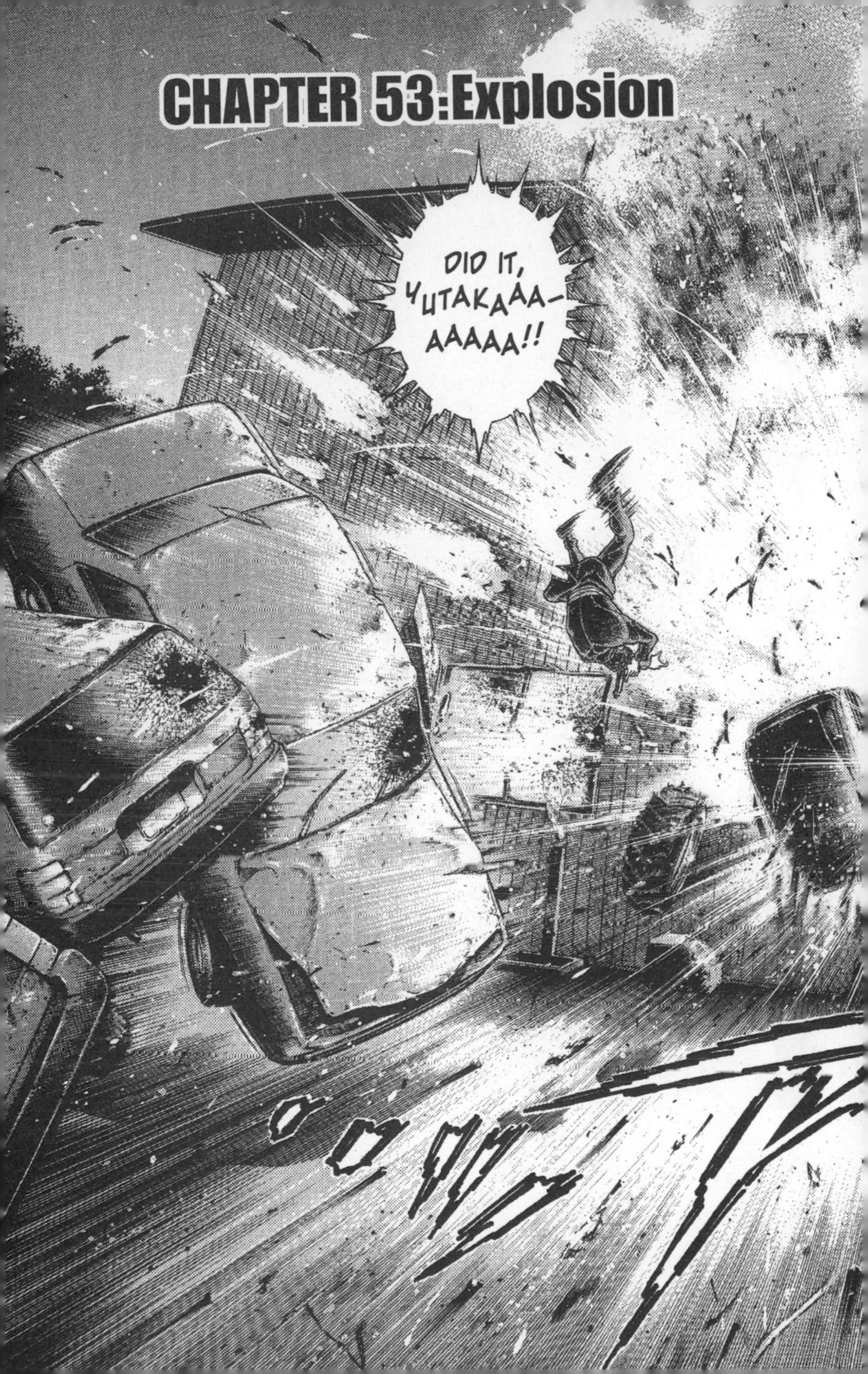
DID IT, YUTAKAAA-AAAAA!!

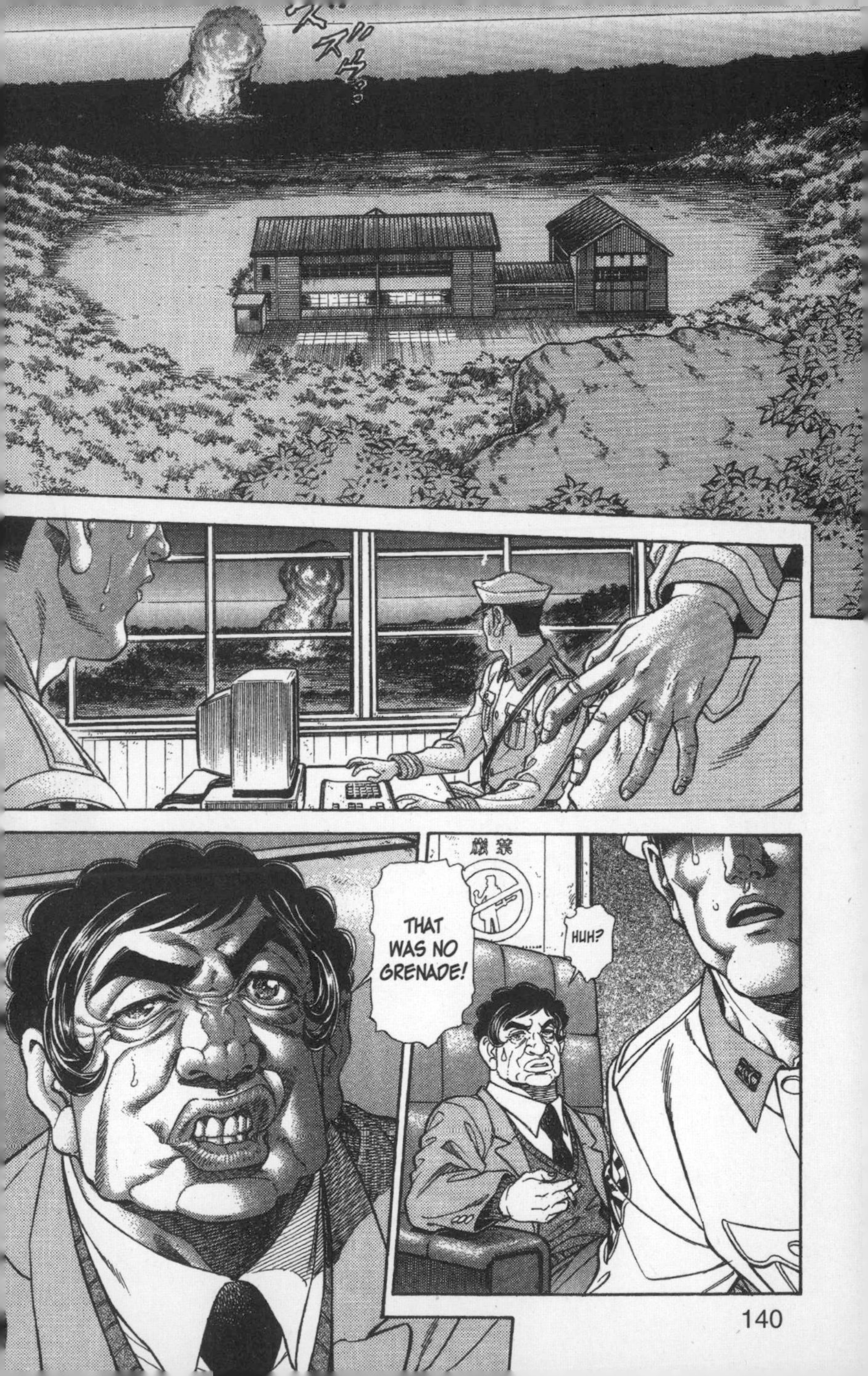
HUH?
THAT WAS NO GRENADE!

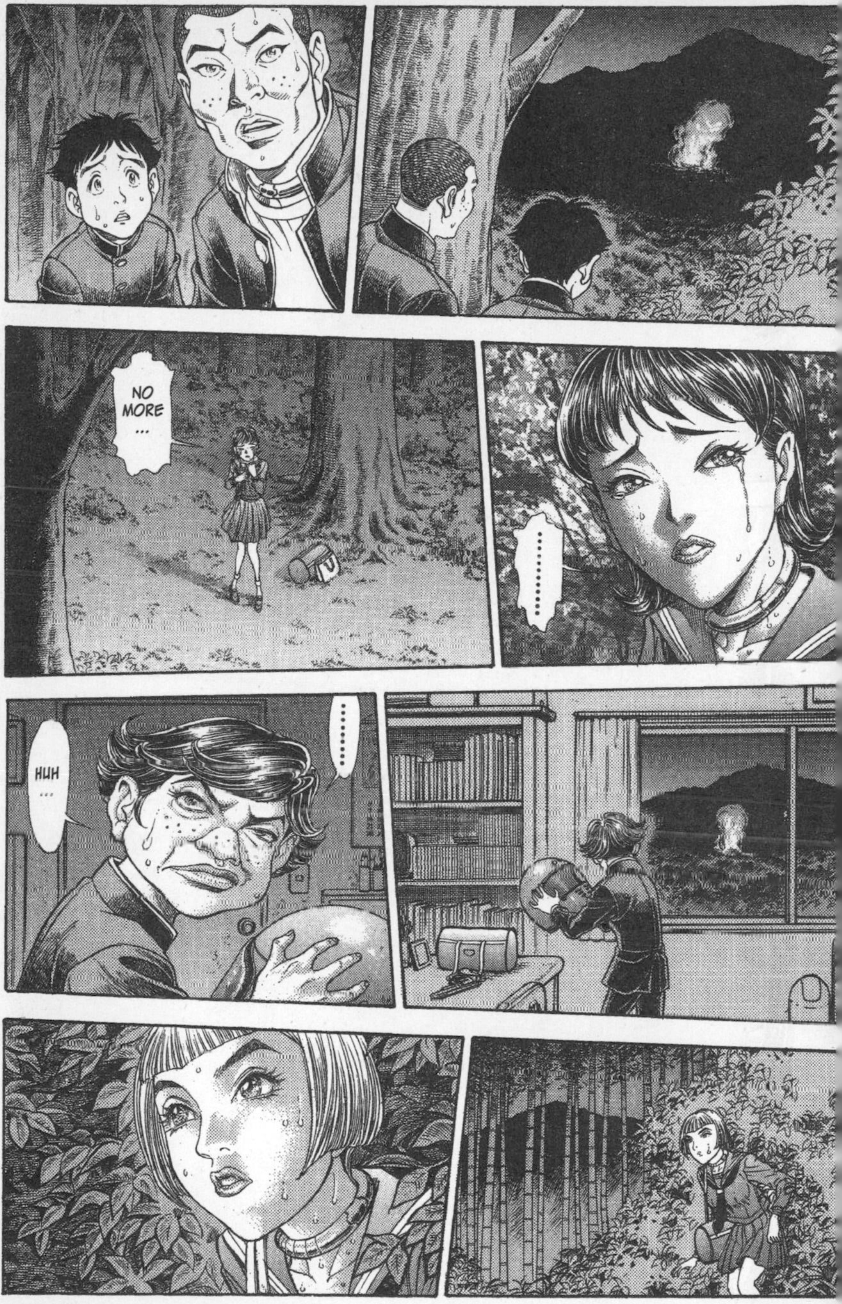
....
NO MORE ...
....
HUH ...

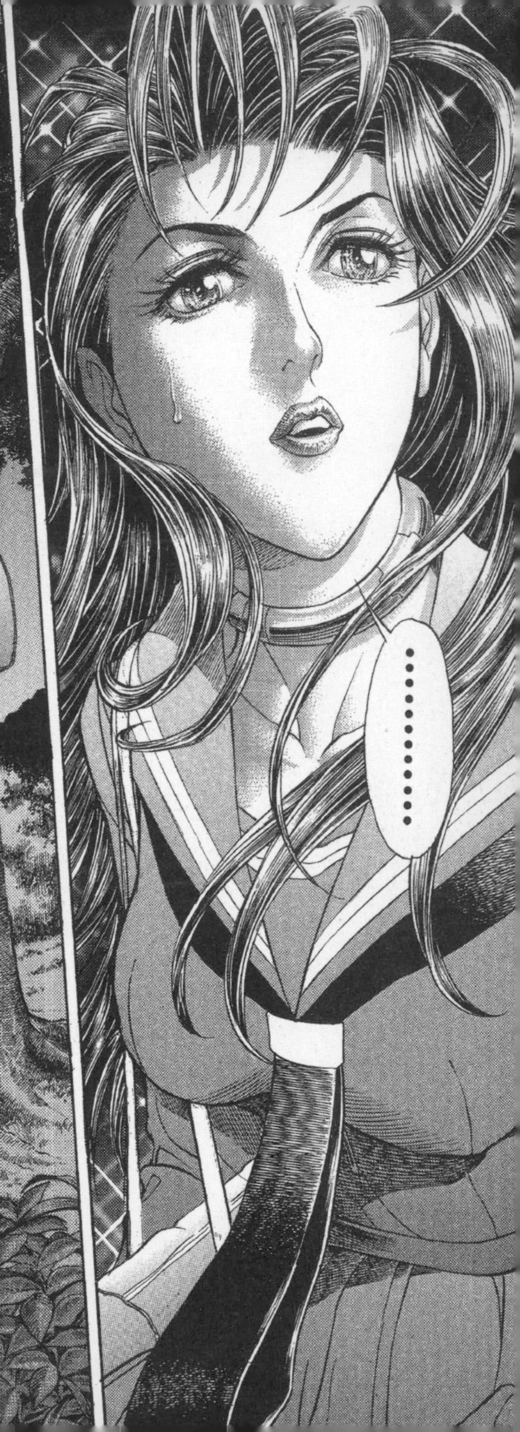
......
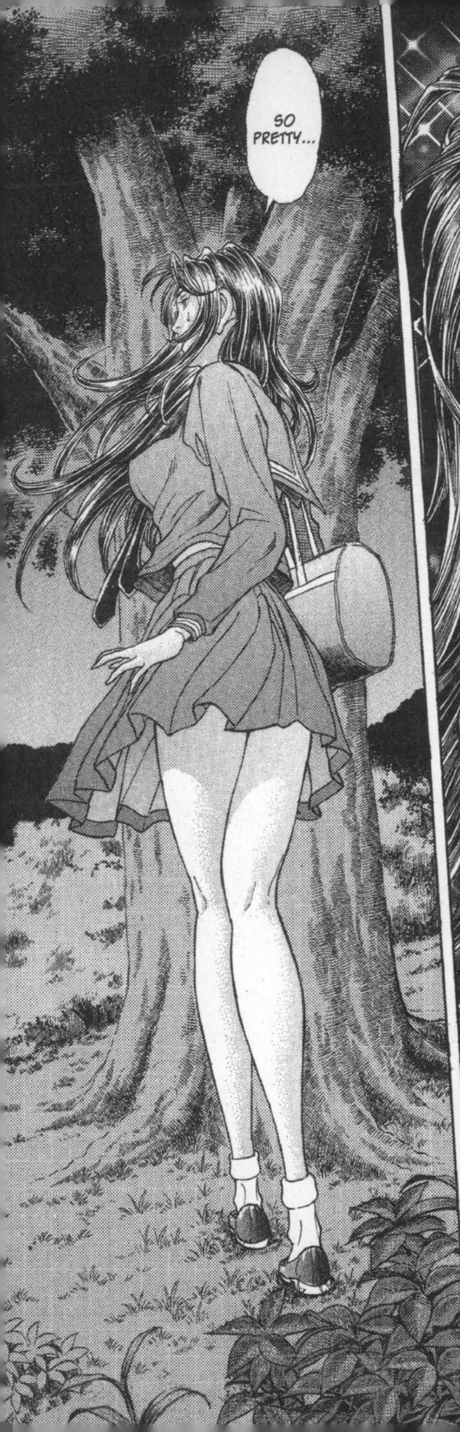
SO PRETTY...

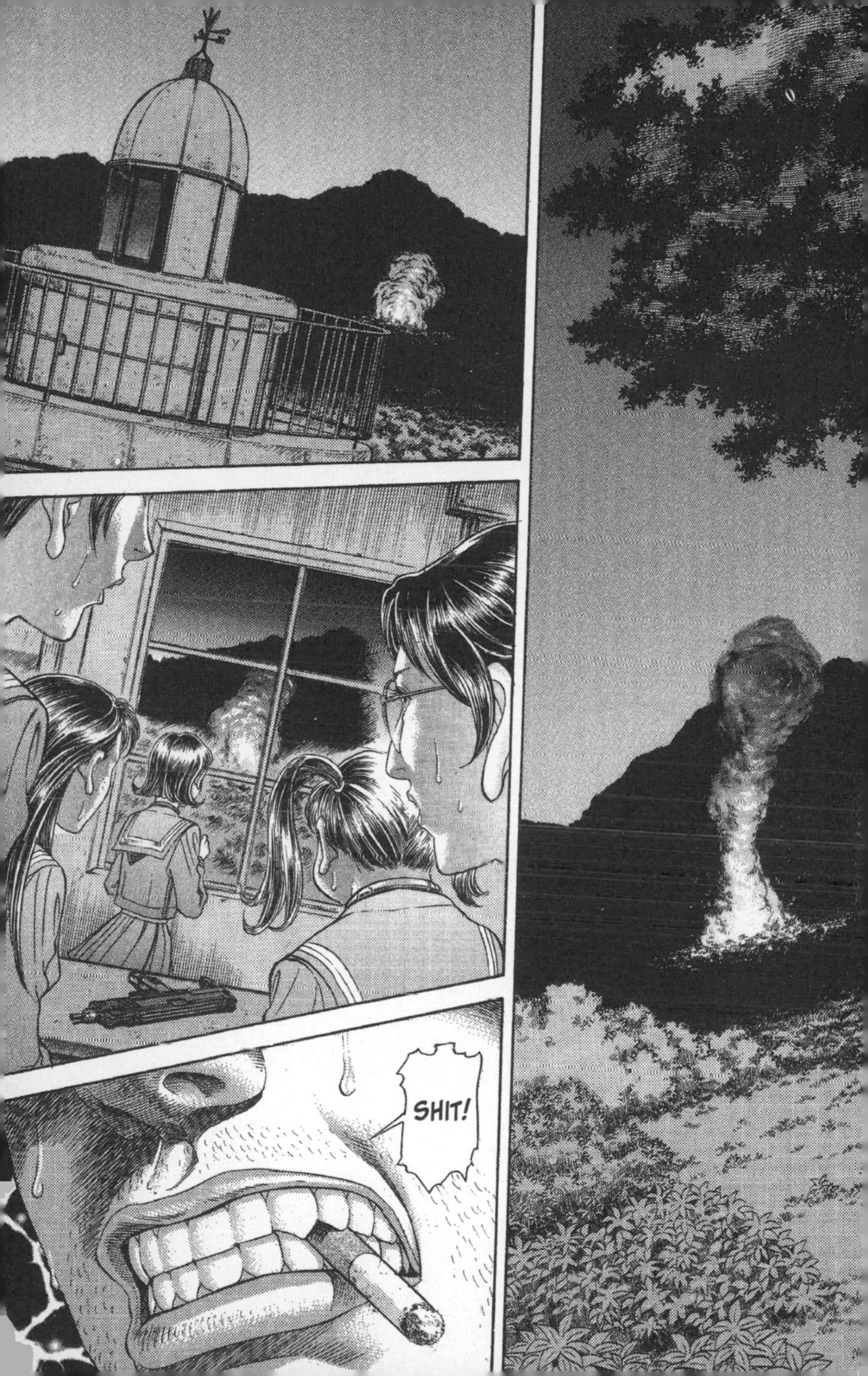
SHIT!

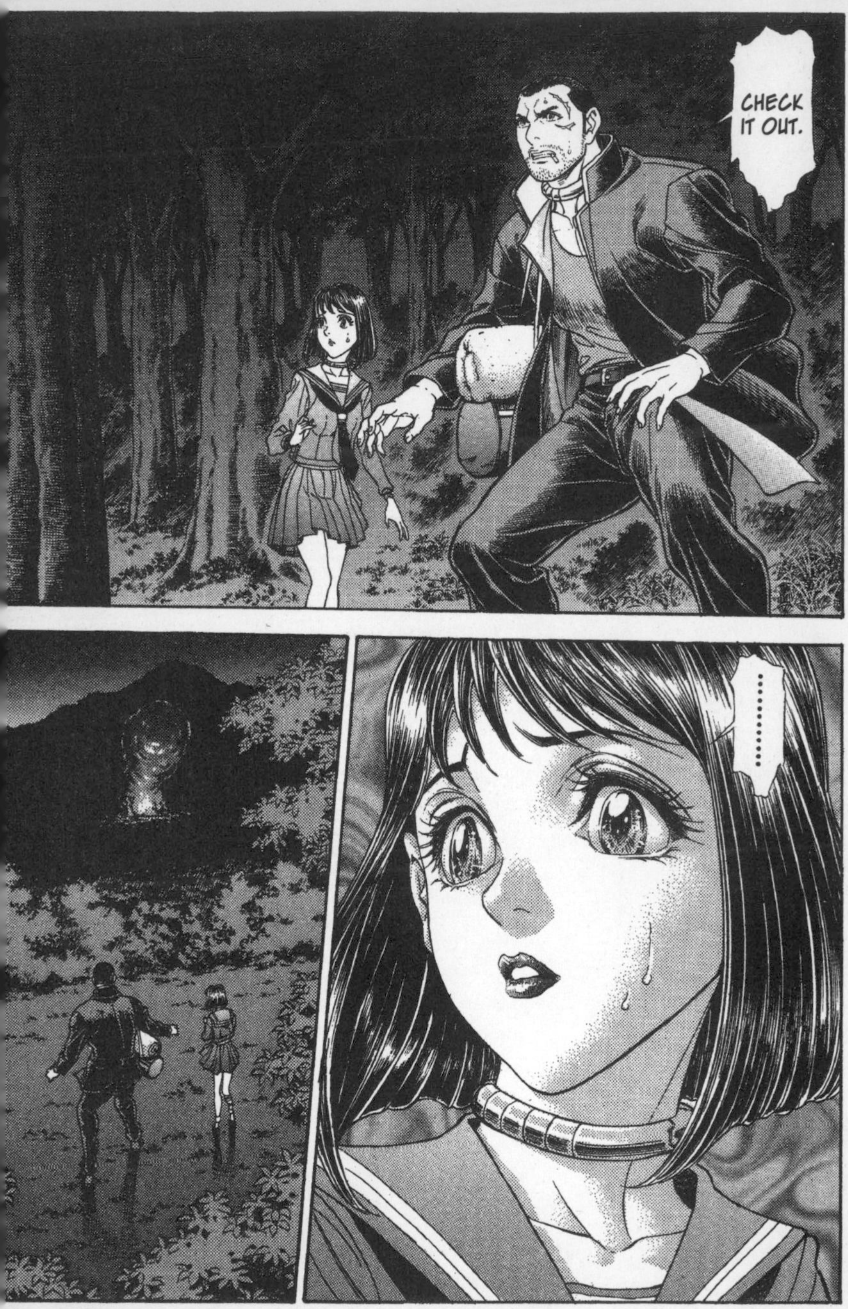
CHECK IT OUT.
....

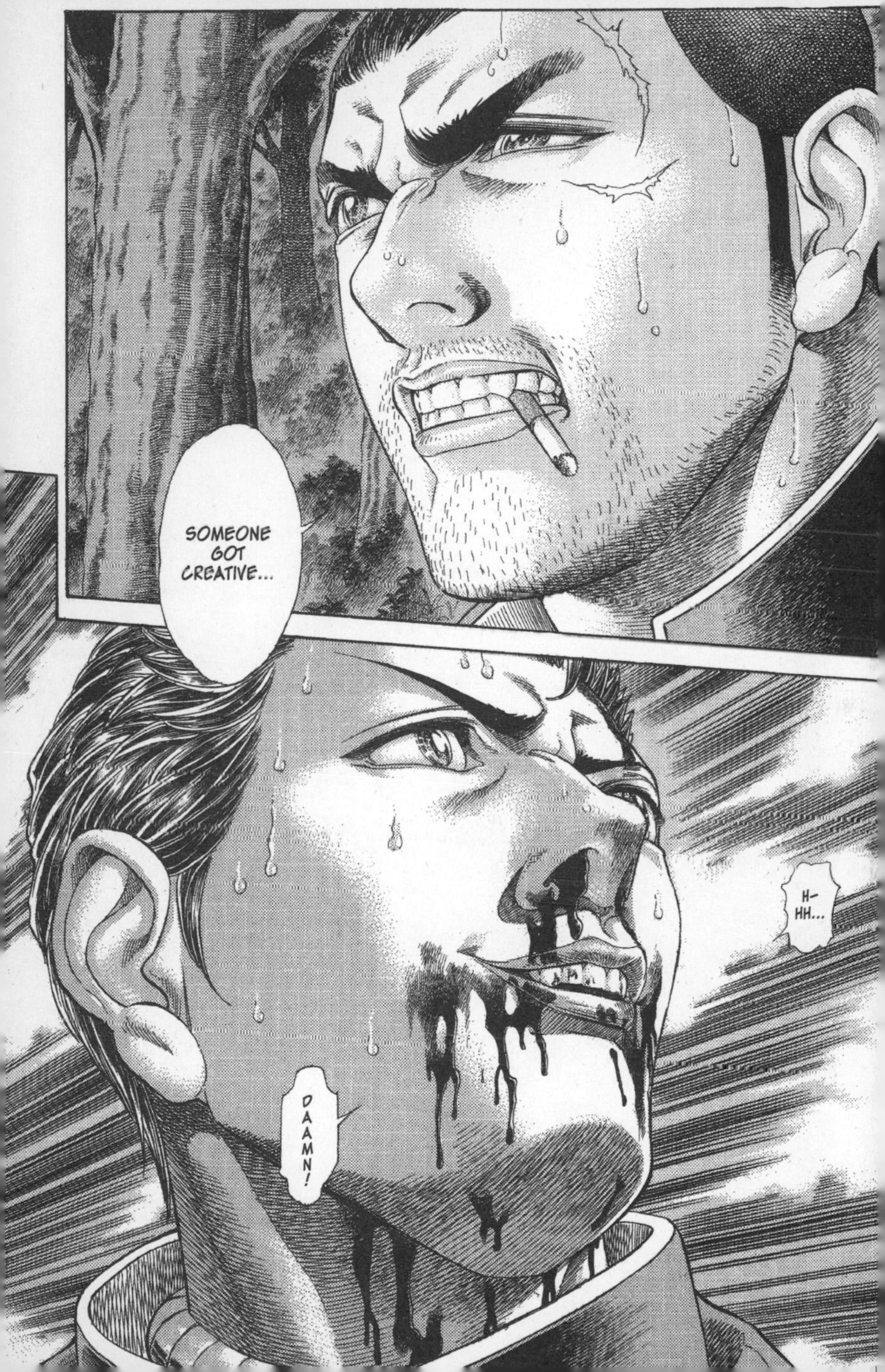
SOMEONE GOT CREATIVE...
H-HH...
DAAMN!

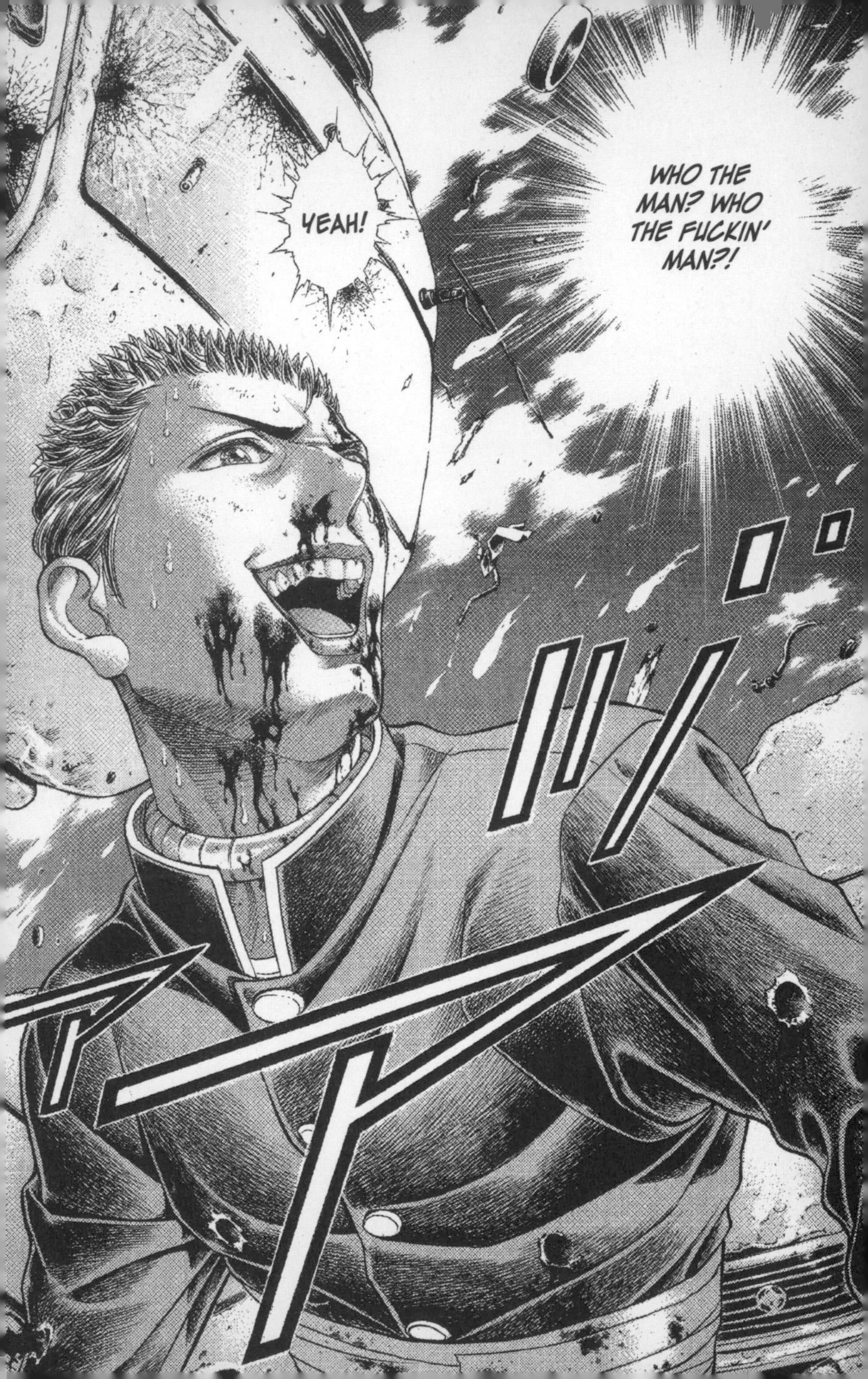
WHO THE MAN? WHO THE FUCKIN' MAN?!
YEAH!

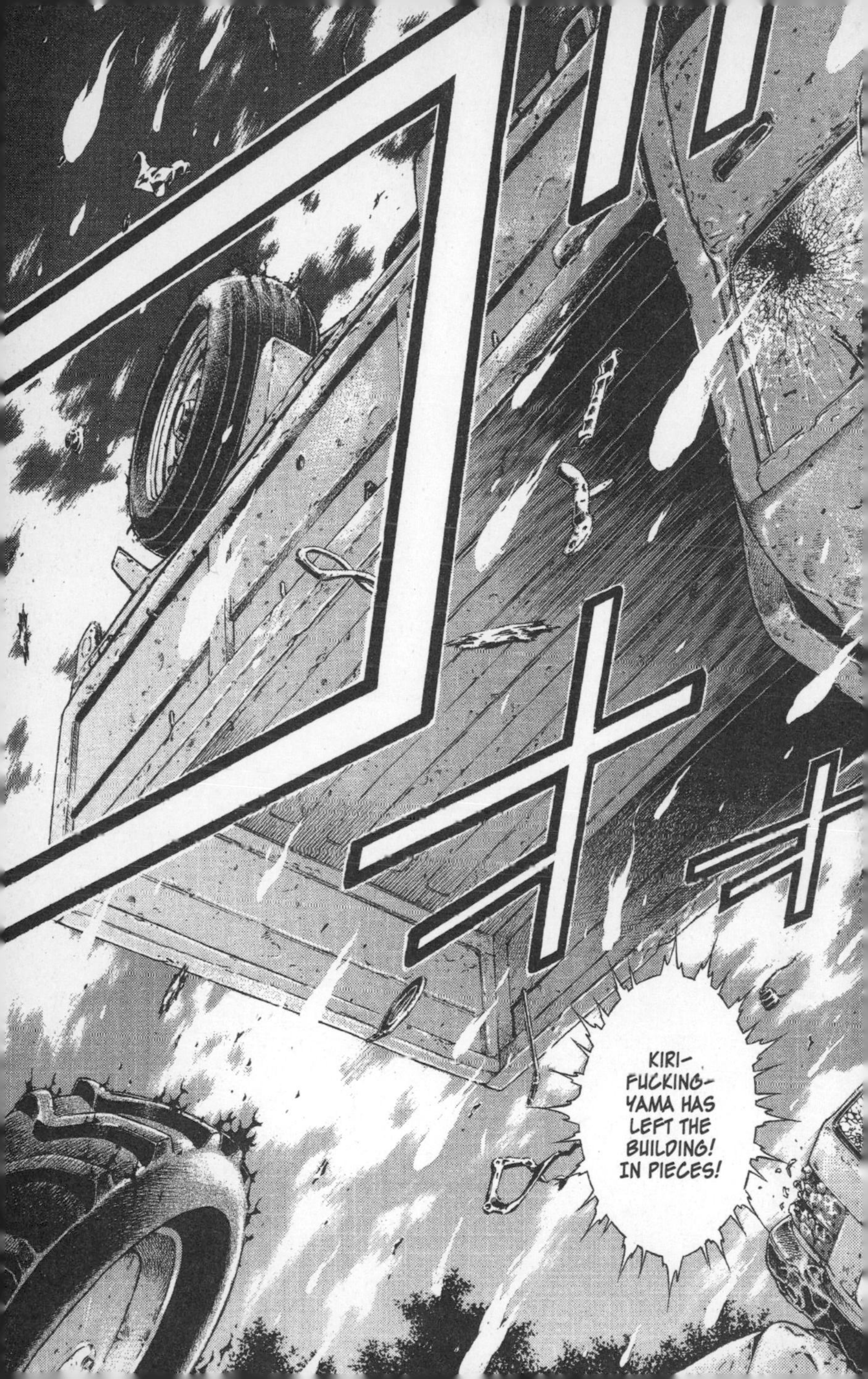
KIRI-FUCKING-YAMA HAS LEFT THE BUILDING! IN PIECES!

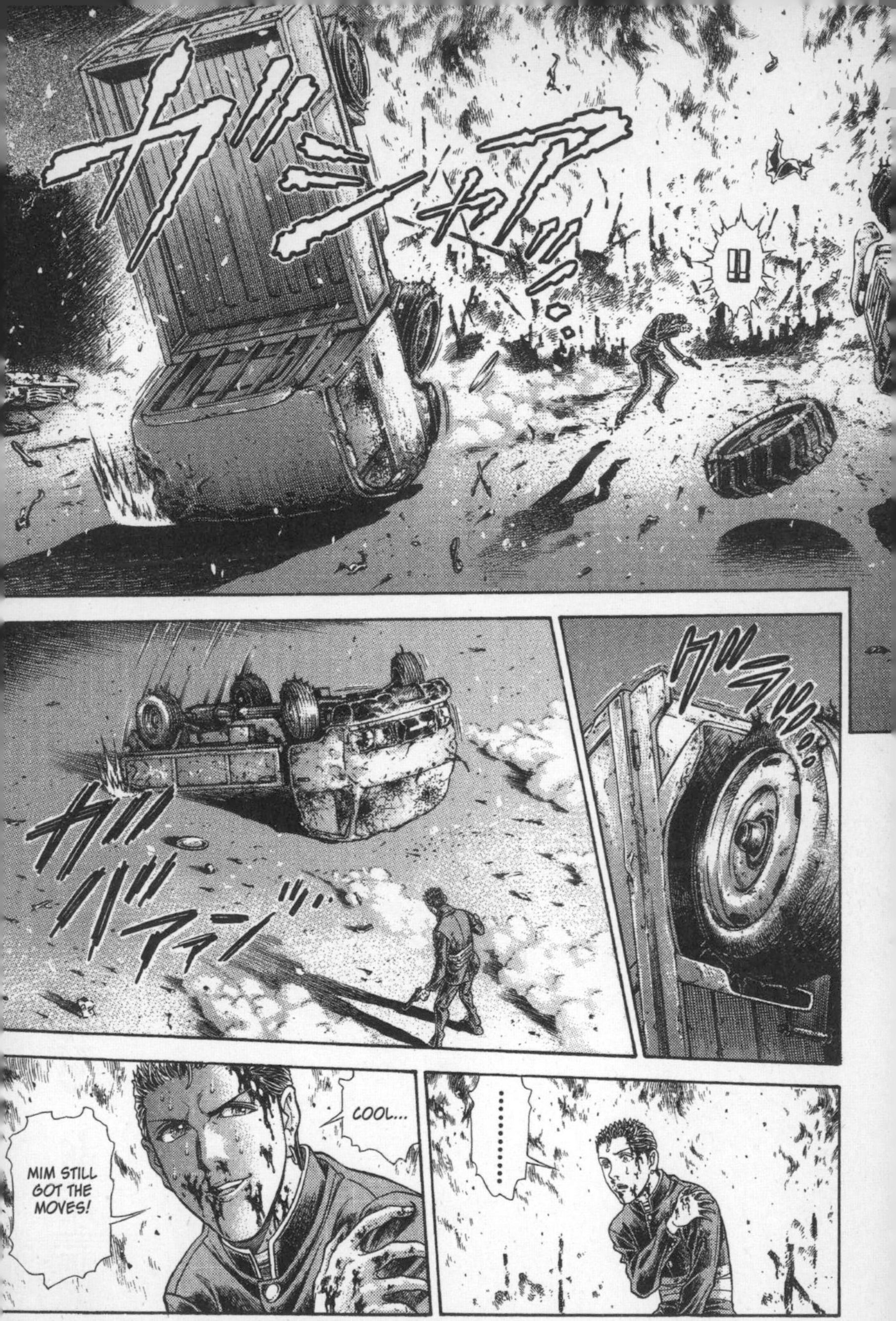
!!
......
COOL...
MIM STILL GOT THE MOVES!

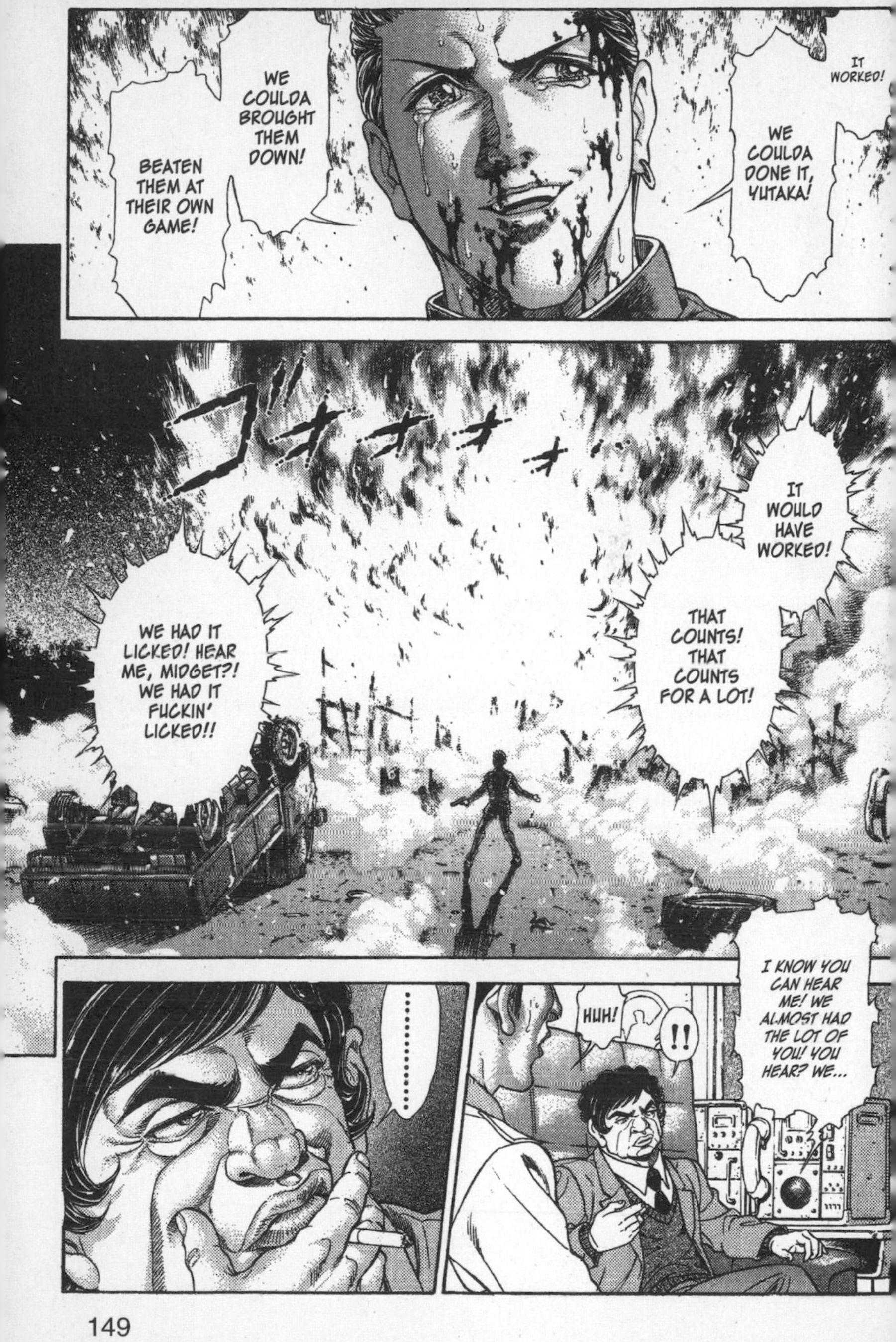
IT WORKED!
WE COULDA DONE IT, YUTAKA!
WE COULDA BROUGHT THEM DOWN!
BEATEN THEM AT THEIR OWN GAME!
IT WOULD HAVE WORKED!
THAT COUNTS! THAT COUNTS FOR A LOT!
WE HAD IT LICKED! HEAR ME, MIDGET?! WE HAD IT FUCKIN' LICKED!!
I KNOW YOU CAN HEAR ME! WE ALMOST HAD THE LOT OF YOU! YOU HEAR? WE...
HUH!
!!
....

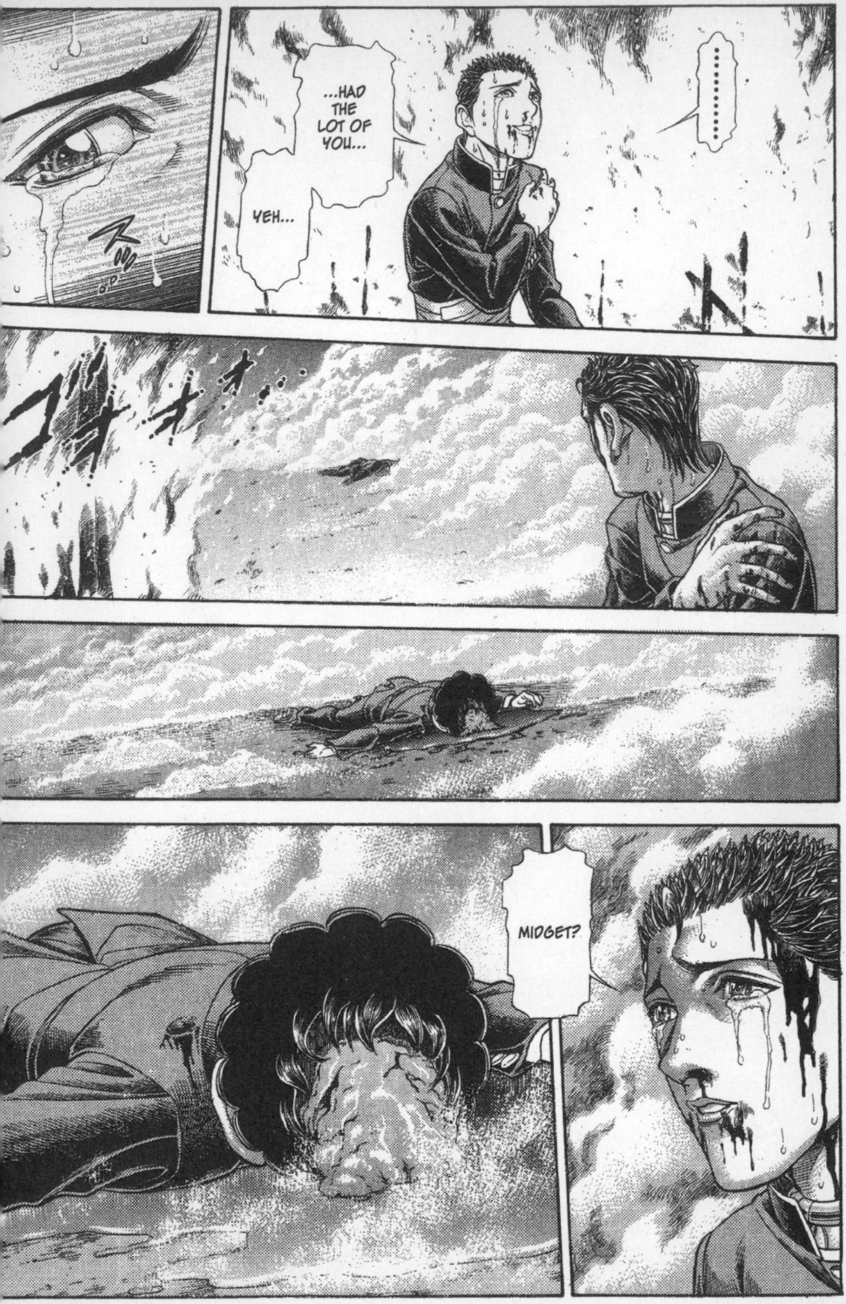
......
...HAD THE LOT OF YOU...
YEH...
MIDGET?

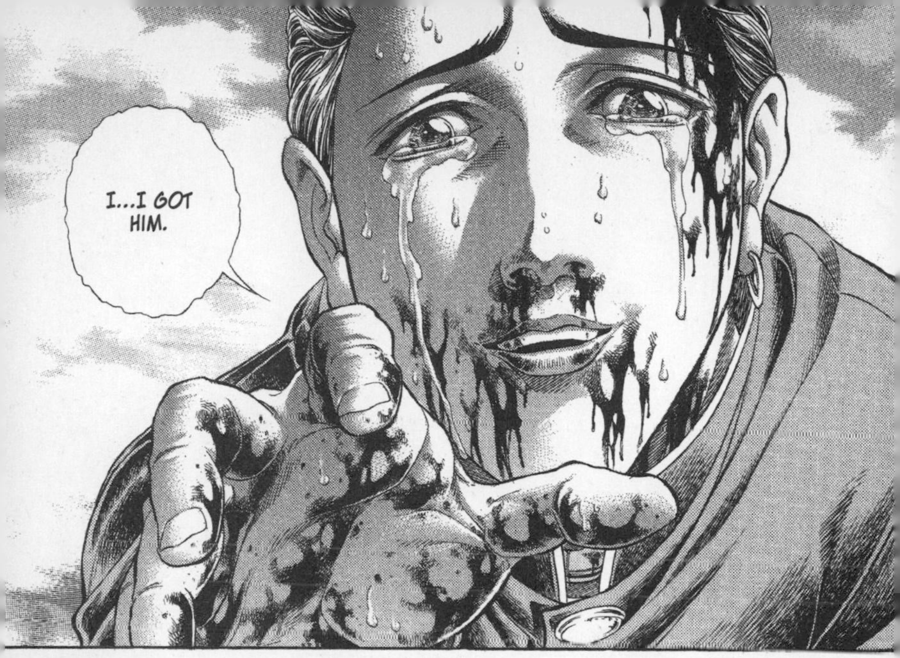
I...I GOT HIM.
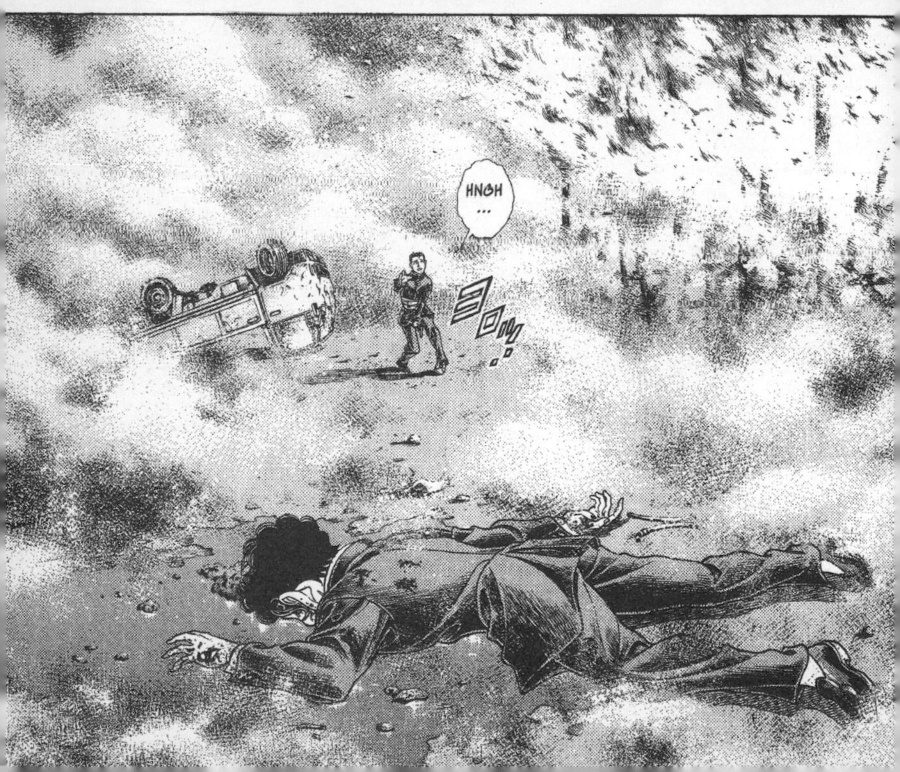
HNGH ...

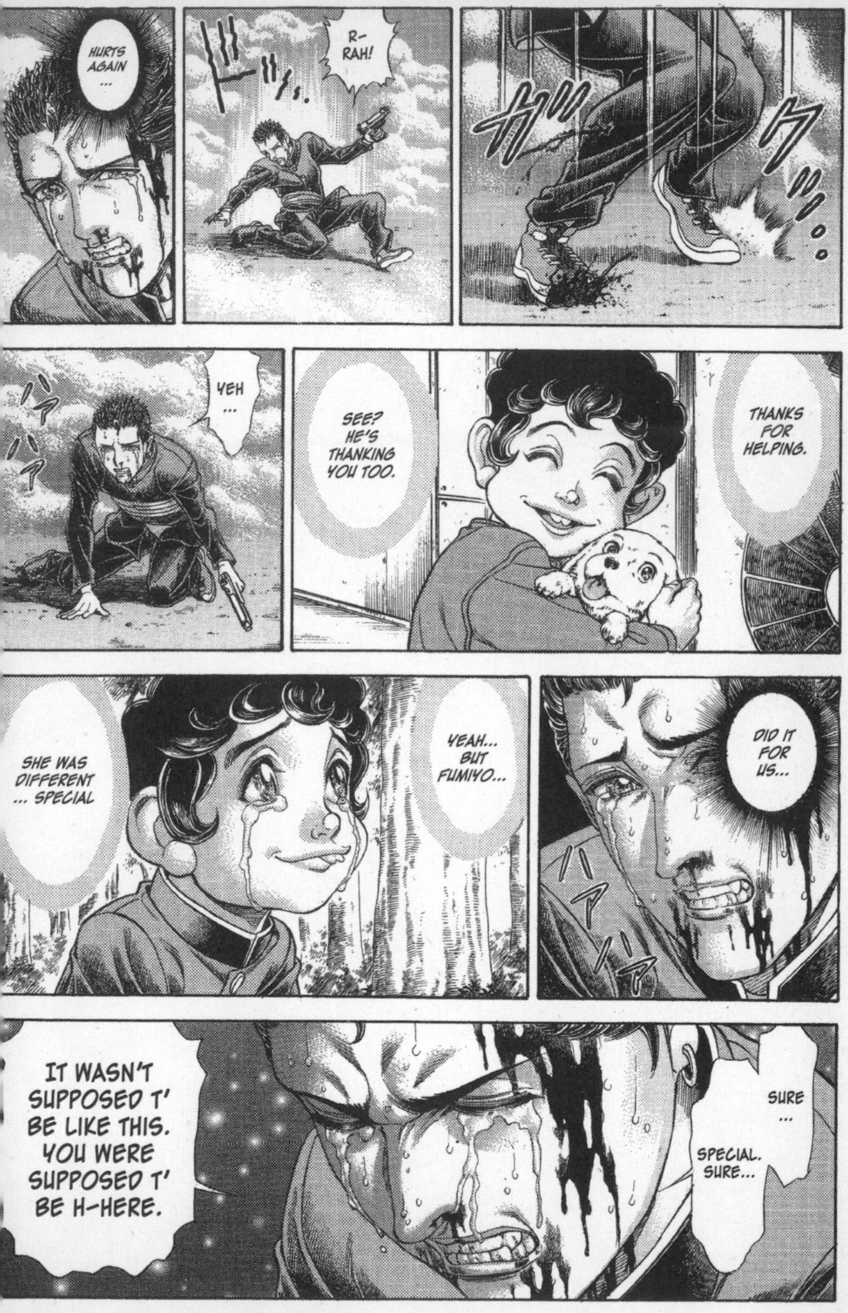
R-RAH!
HURTS AGAIN ...
THANKS FOR HELPING.
SEE? HE'S THANKING YOU TOO.
YEH ...
DID IT FOR US...
YEAH... BUT FUMIYO...
SHE WAS DIFFERENT ... SPECIAL
SURE ...
SPECIAL. SURE...
IT WASN'T SUPPOSED T' BE LIKE THIS. YOU WERE SUPPOSED T' BE H-HERE.

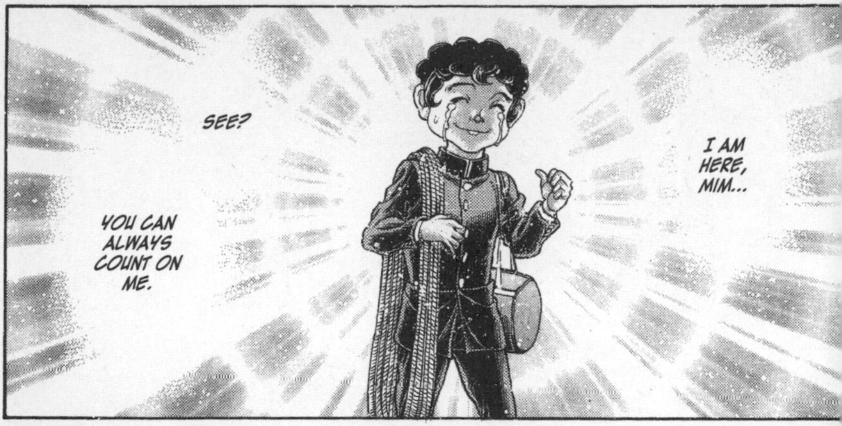
I AM HERE, MIM...
SEE?
YOU CAN ALWAYS COUNT ON ME.

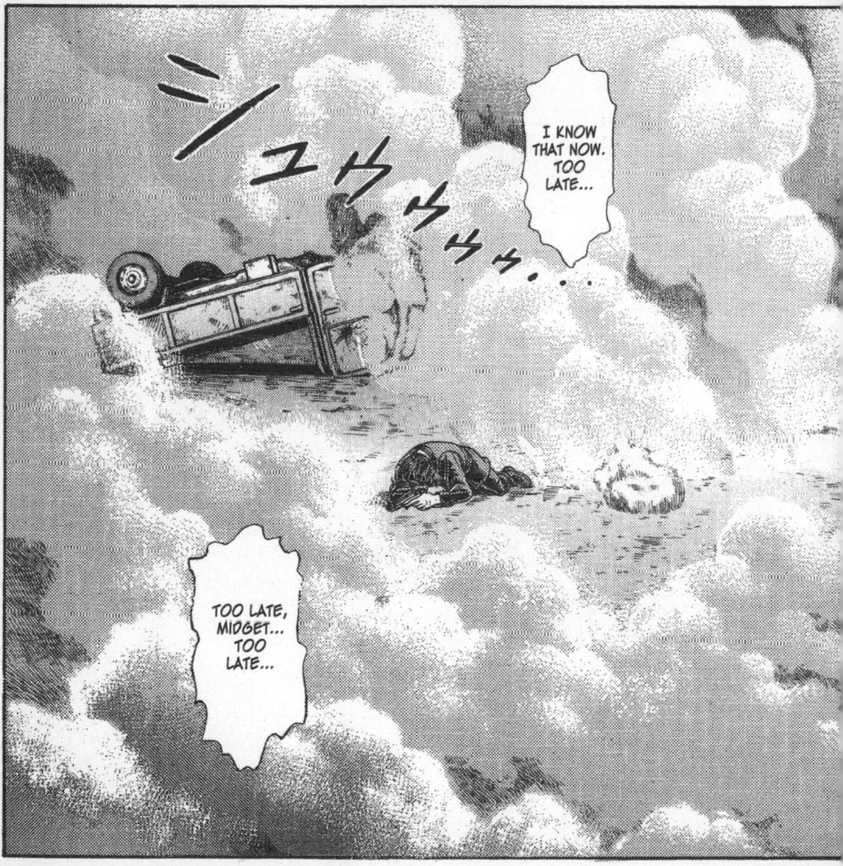
I KNOW THAT NOW. TOO LATE...
シュウゥゥゥ...
TOO LATE, MIDGET... TOO LATE...

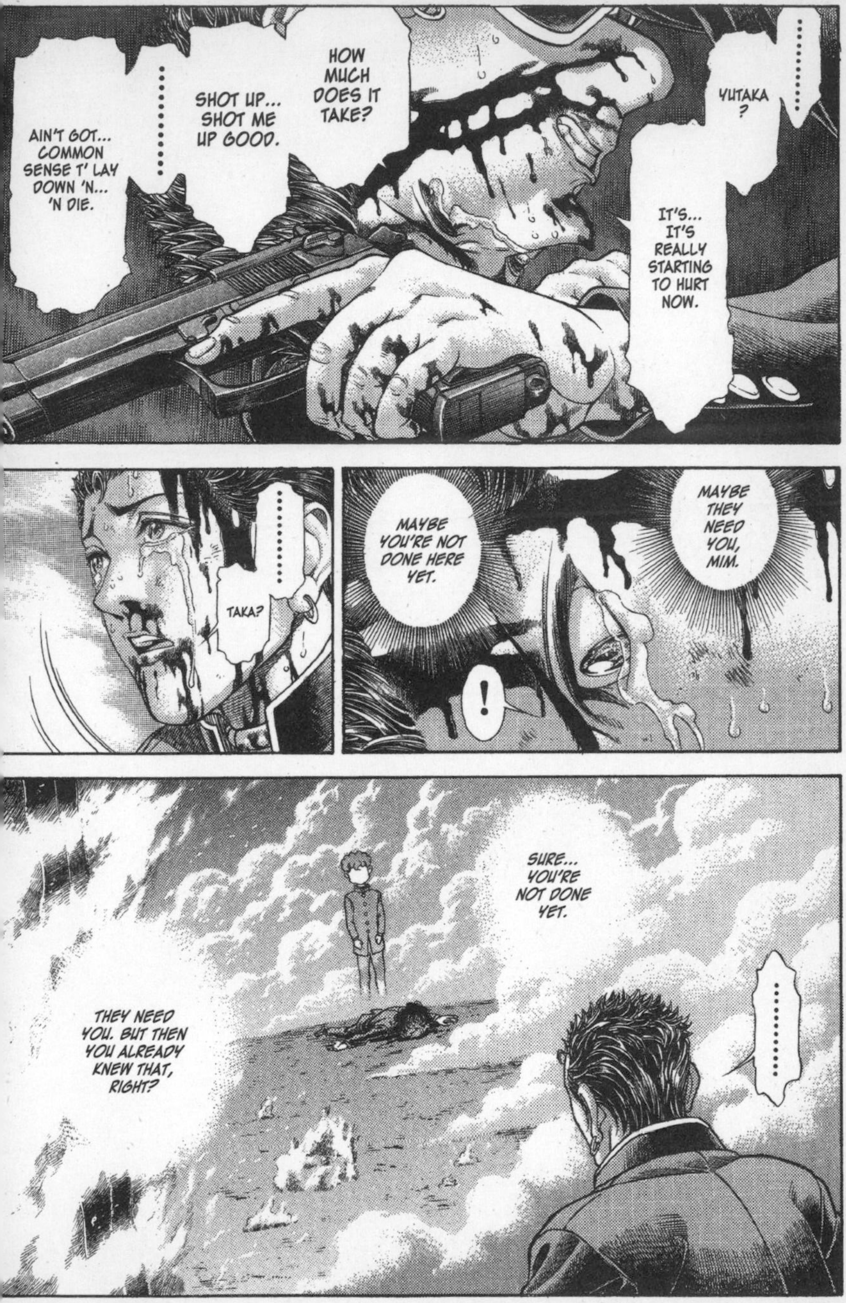
......
YUTAKA?
IT'S... IT'S REALLY STARTING TO HURT NOW.
HOW MUCH DOES IT TAKE?
SHOT UP... SHOT ME UP GOOD.
......
AIN'T GOT... COMMON SENSE T' LAY DOWN 'N... 'N DIE.
MAYBE THEY NEED YOU, MIM.
MAYBE YOU'RE NOT DONE HERE YET.
!
......
TAKA?
SURE... YOU'RE NOT DONE YET.
......
THEY NEED YOU. BUT THEN YOU ALREADY KNEW THAT, RIGHT?

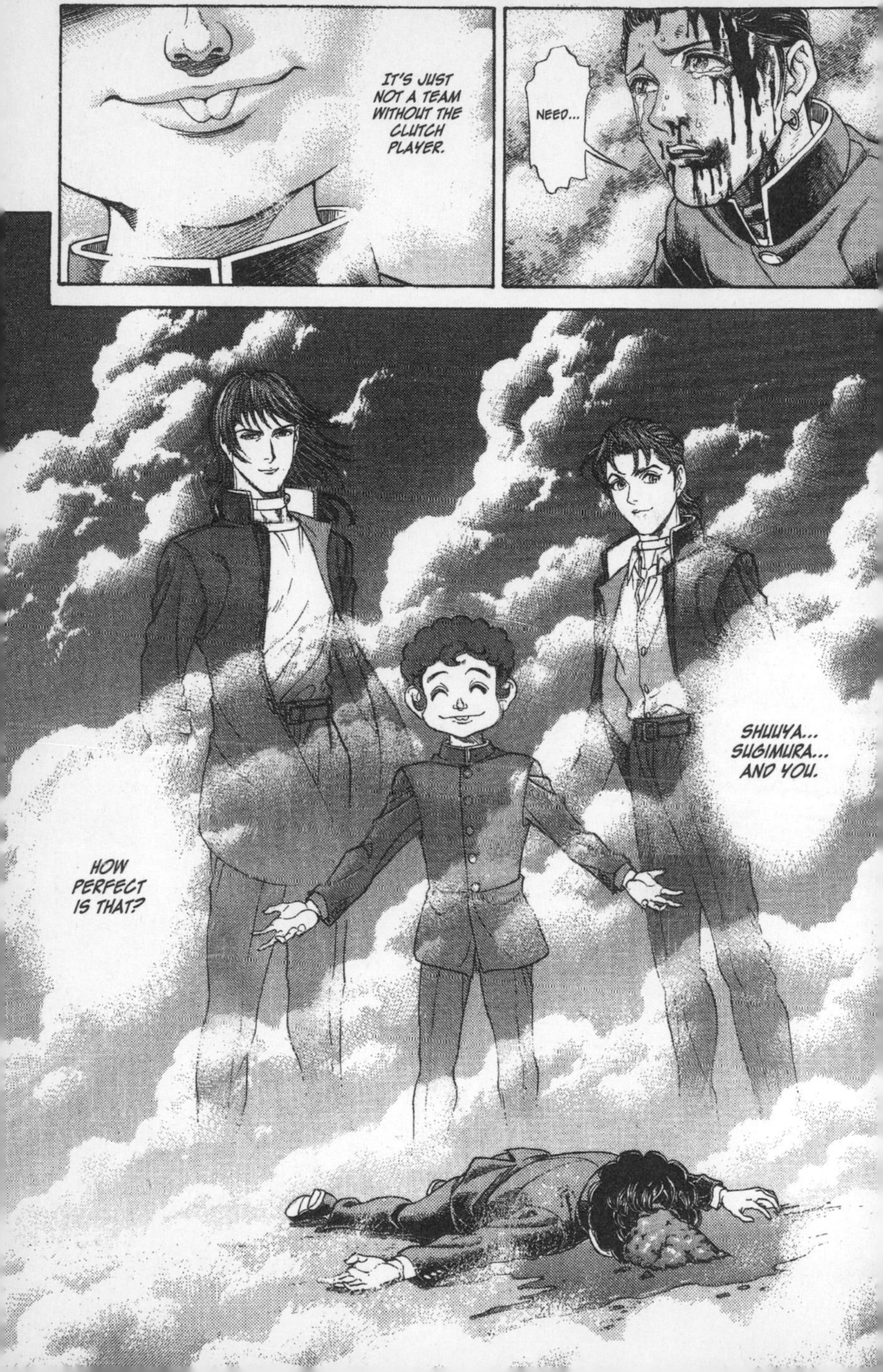
NEED...
IT'S JUST NOT A TEAM WITHOUT THE CLUTCH PLAYER.
SHUUYA... SUGIMURA... AND YOU.
HOW PERFECT IS THAT?

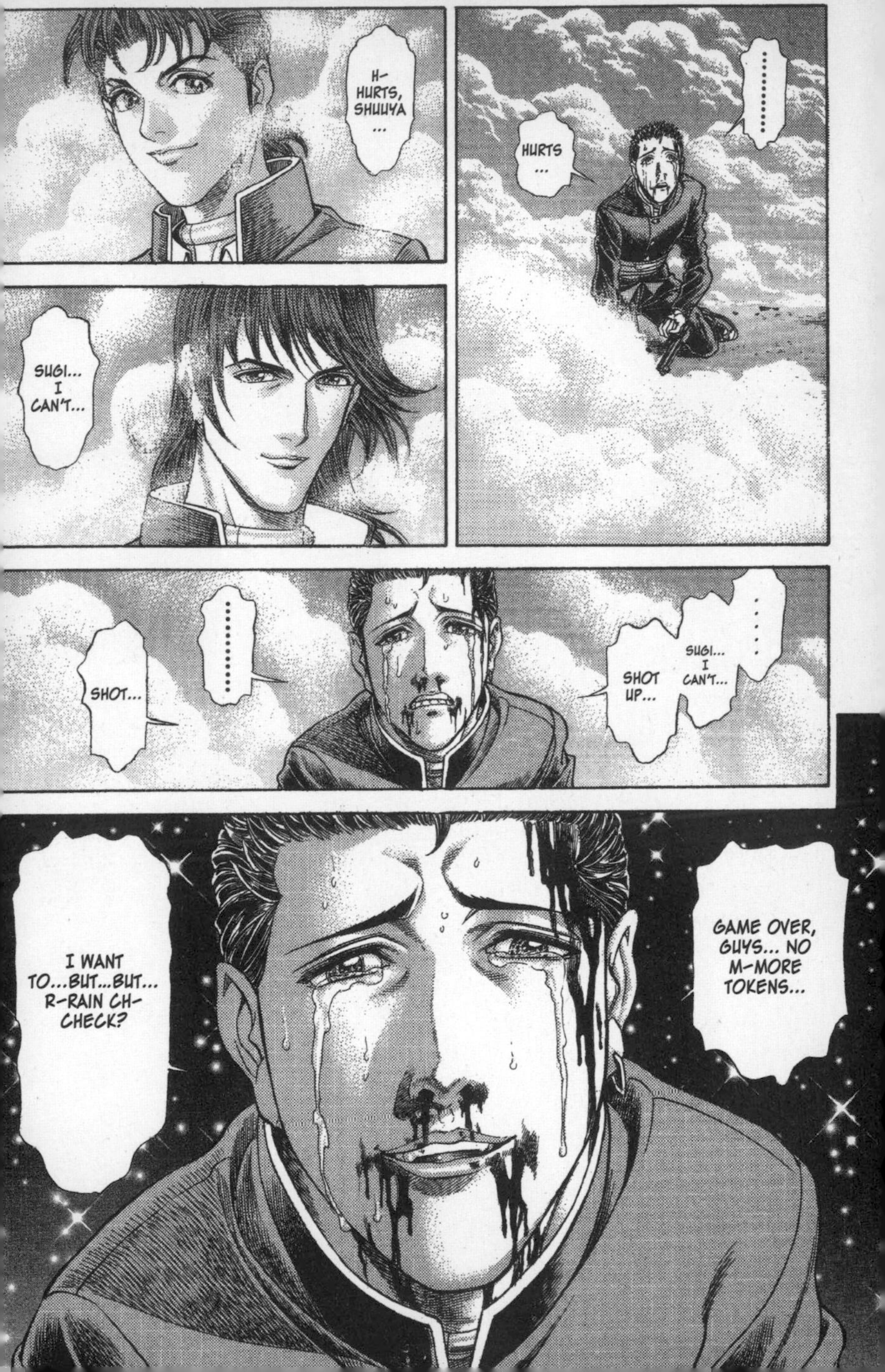
......
HURTS...
H-HURTS, SHUUYA...
SUGI... I CAN'T...
....
SUGI... I CAN'T...
SHOT UP...
......
SHOT...
GAME OVER, GUYS... NO M-MORE TOKENS...
I WANT TO...BUT...BUT... R-RAIN CH-CHECK?

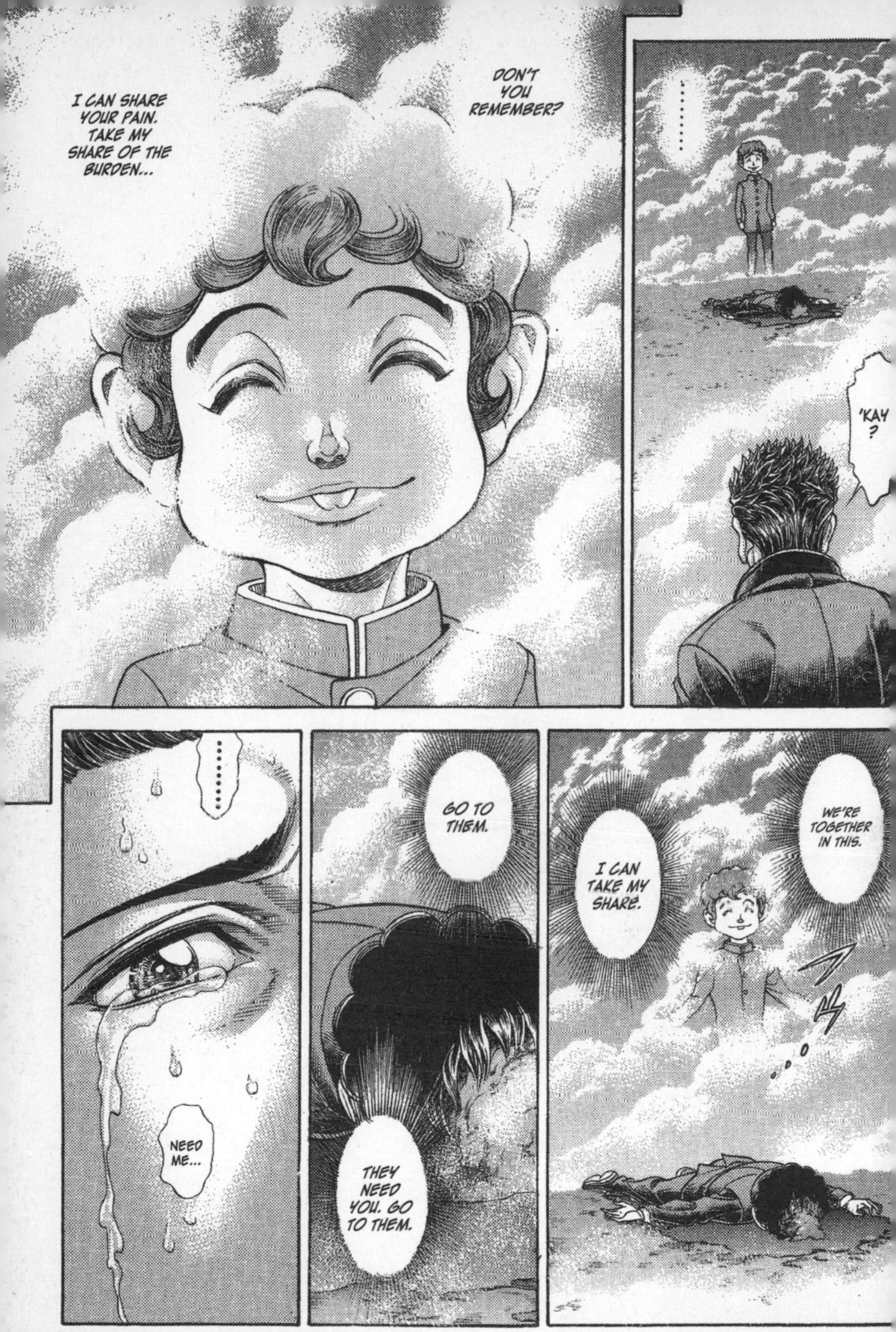
......
'KAY?
DON'T YOU REMEMBER?
I CAN SHARE YOUR PAIN. TAKE MY SHARE OF THE BURDEN...
WE'RE TOGETHER IN THIS.
I CAN TAKE MY SHARE.
GO TO THEM.
THEY NEED YOU. GO TO THEM.
......
NEED ME...

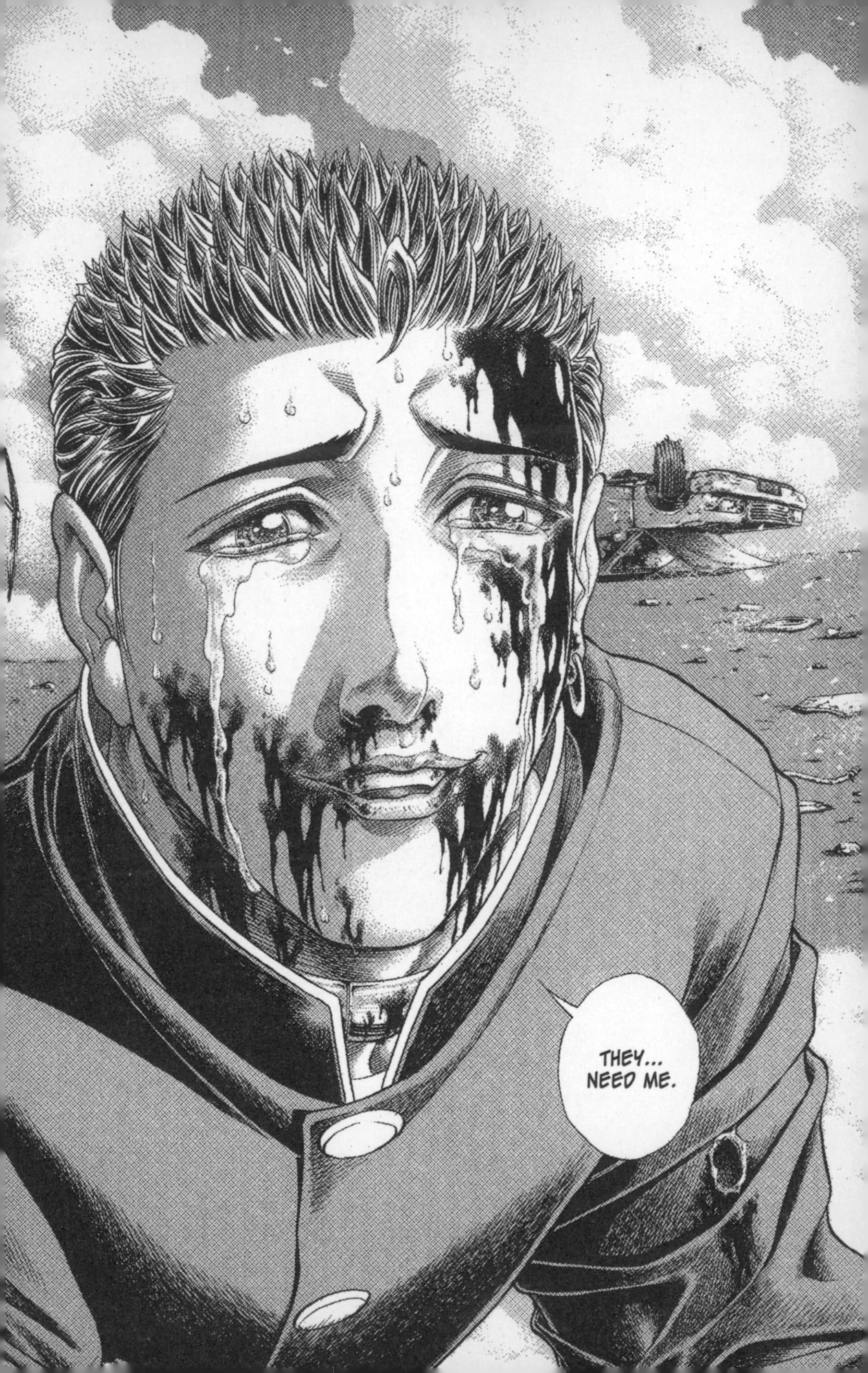
THEY... NEED ME.

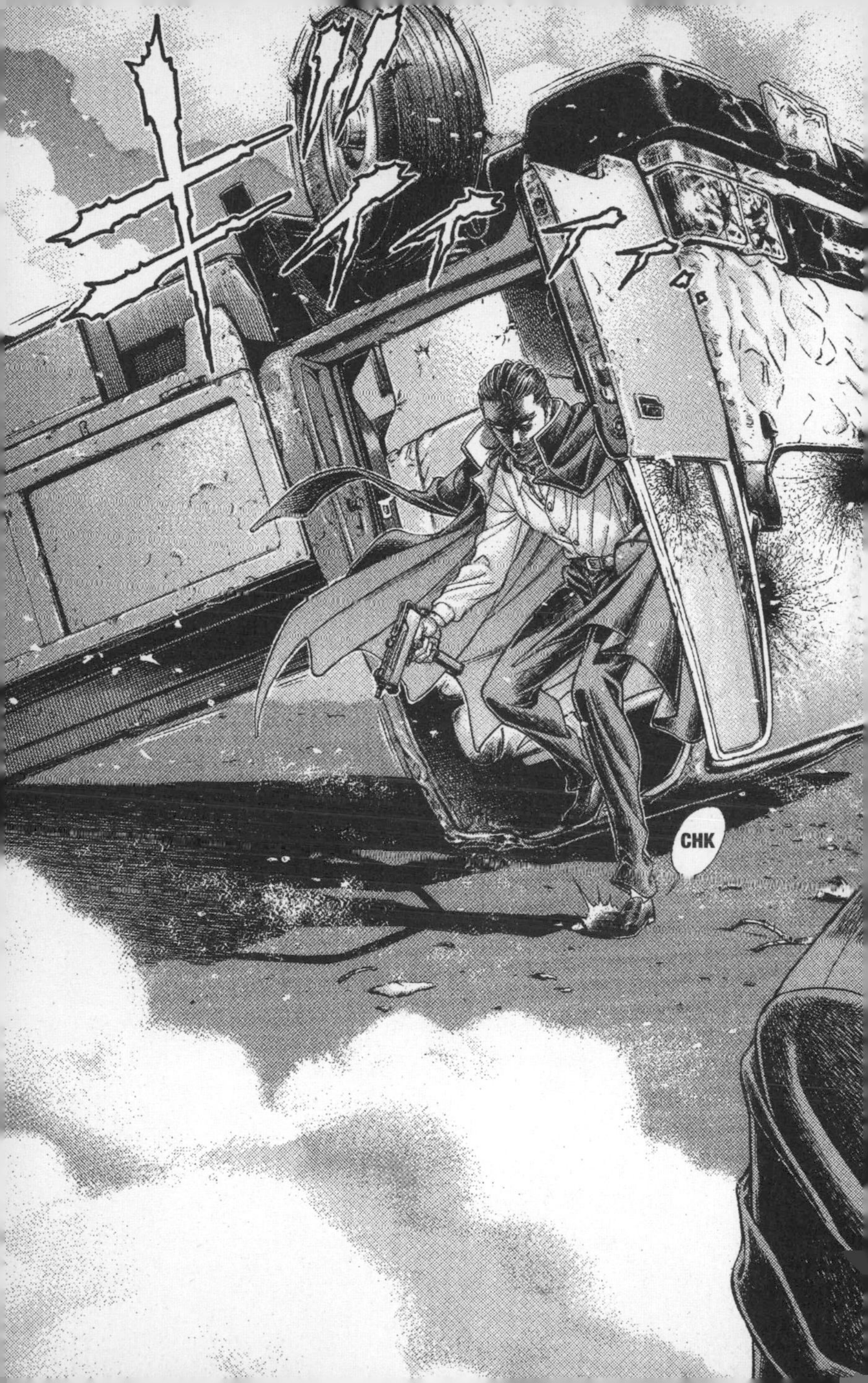
CHK

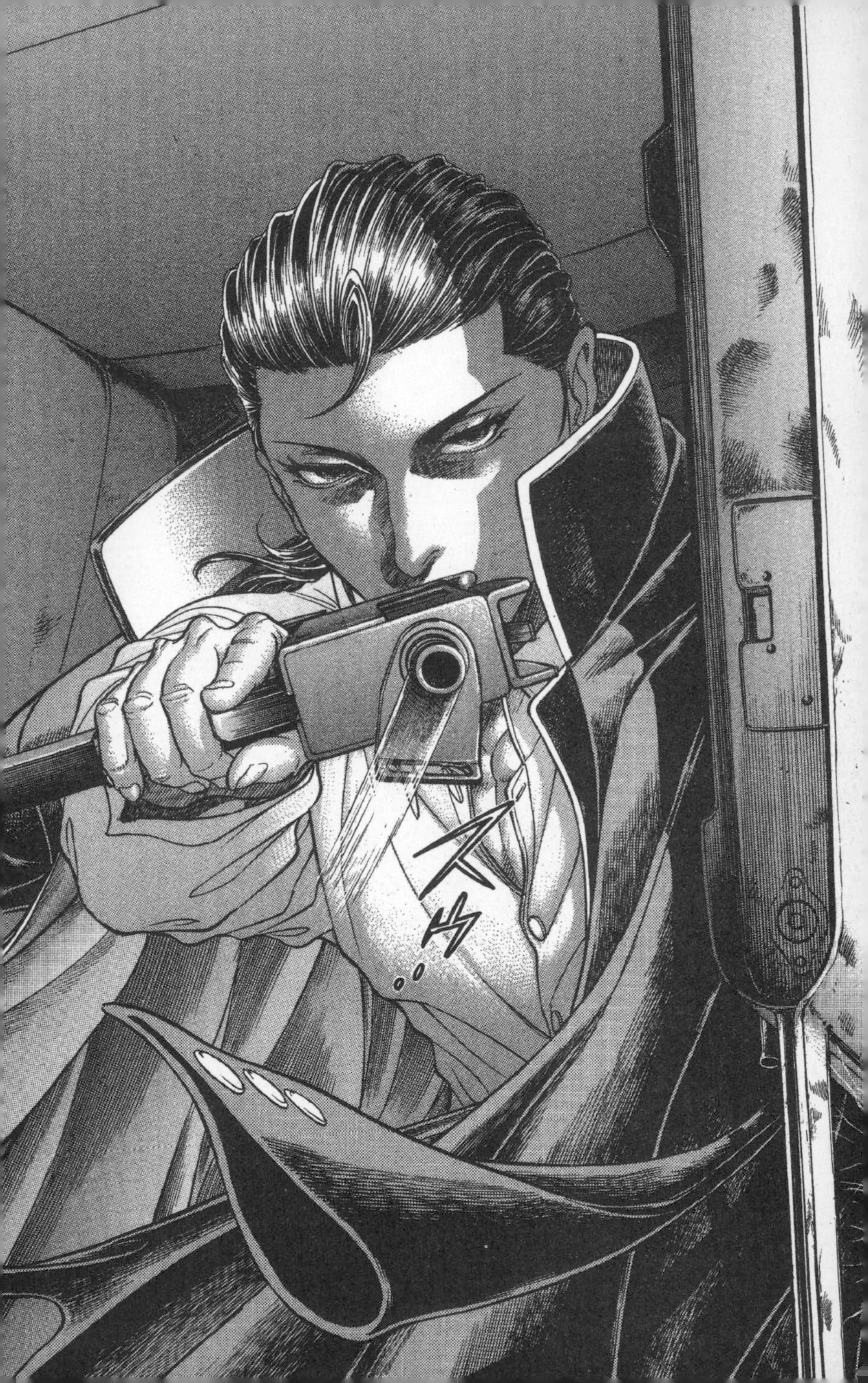
スッ

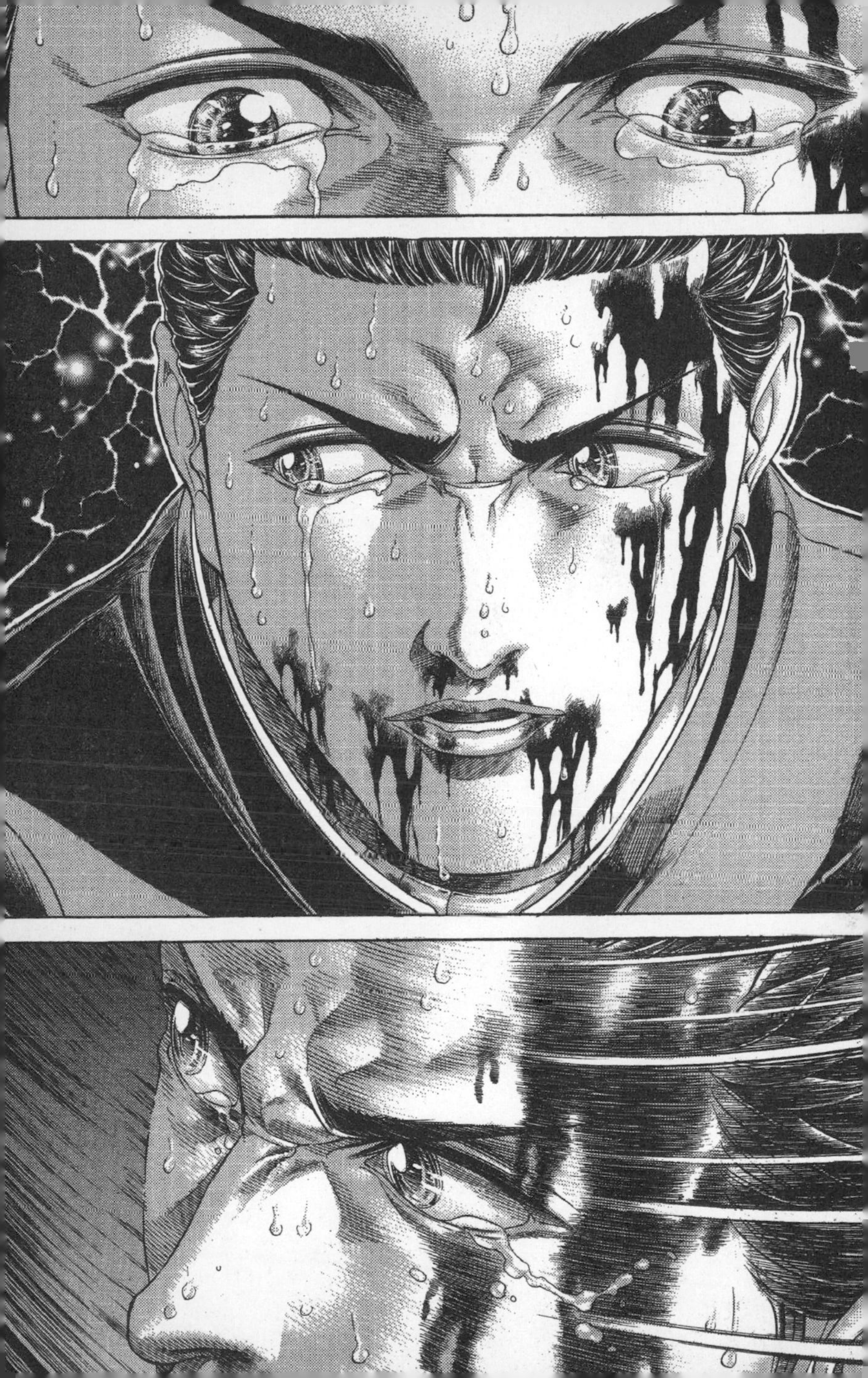

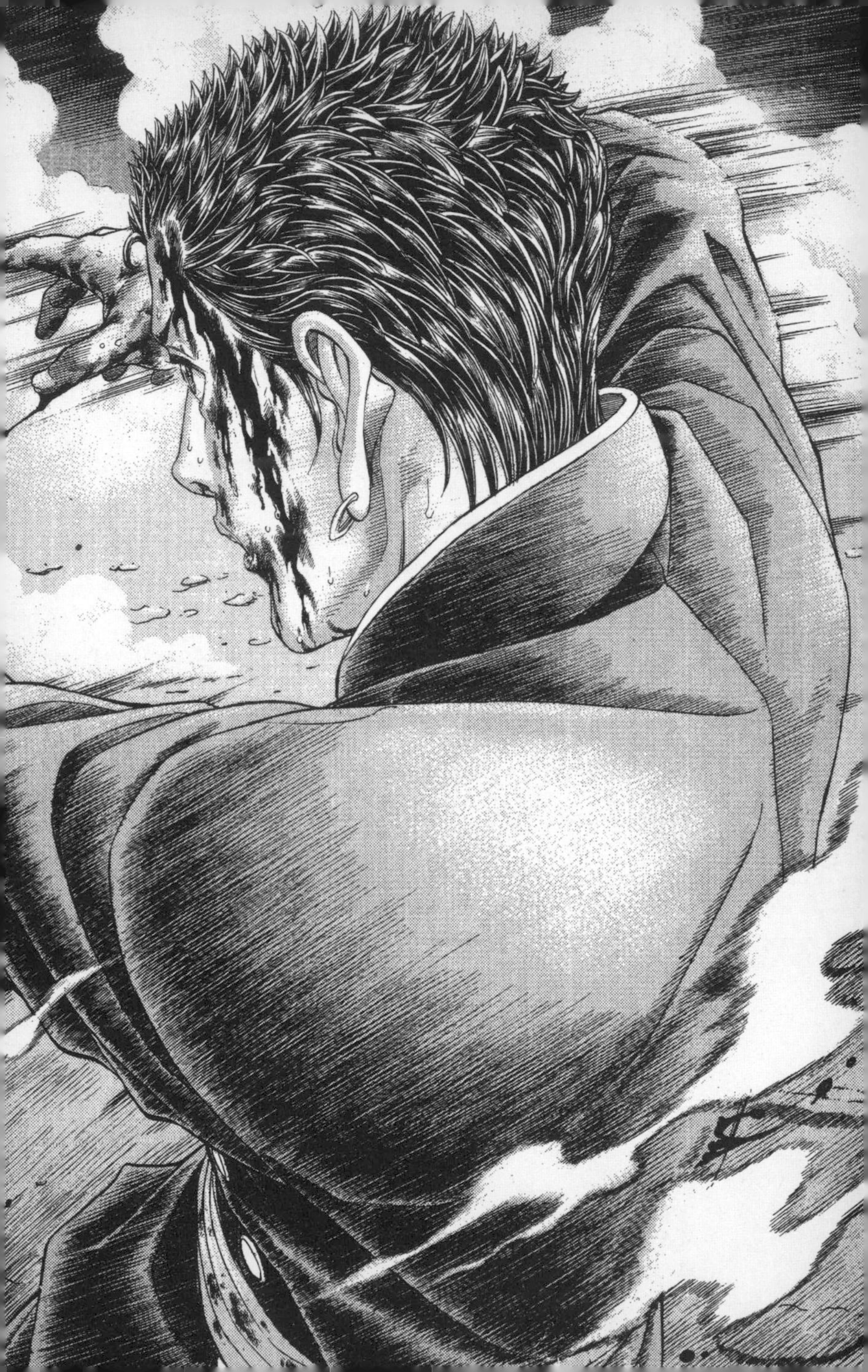

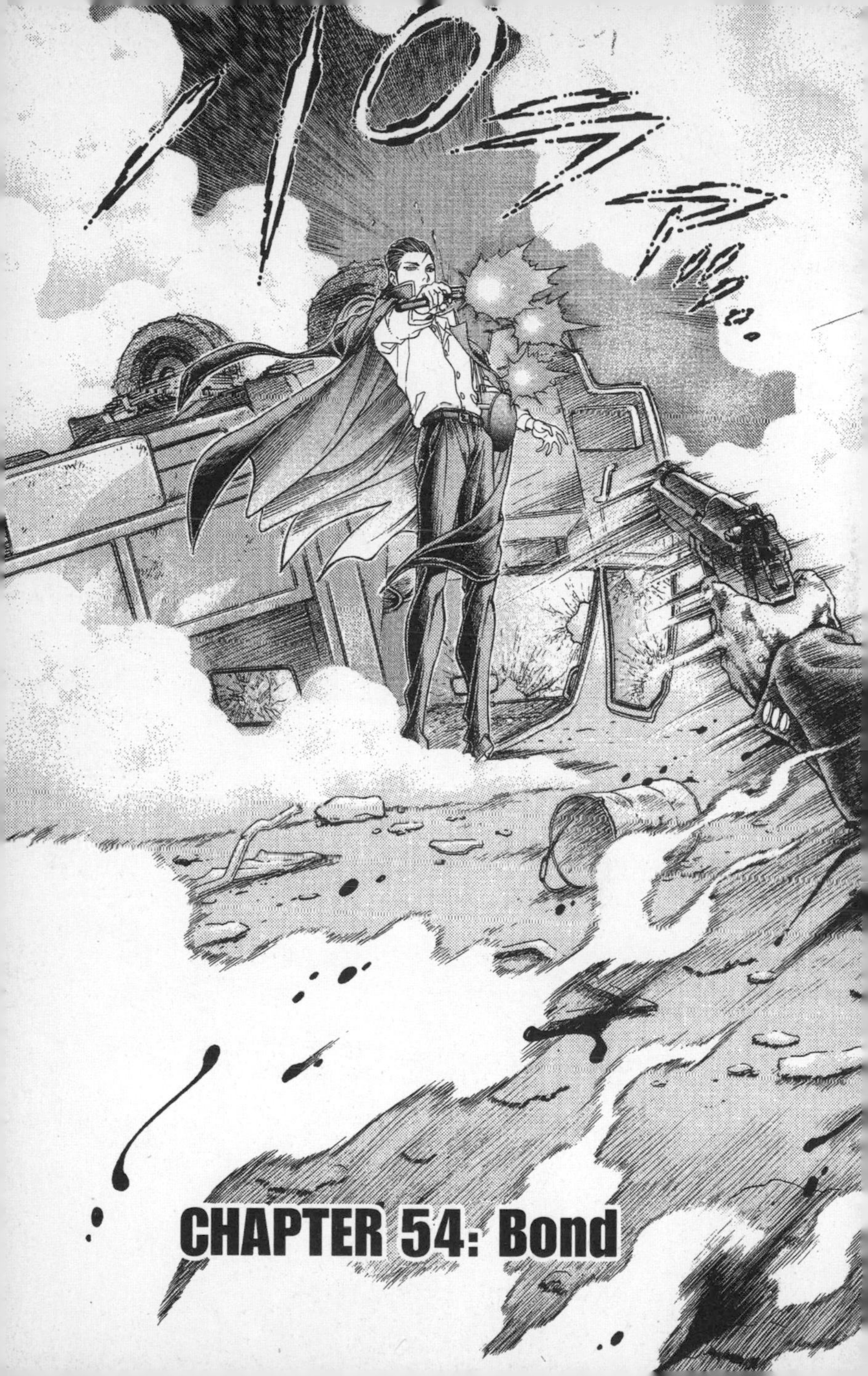

CHAPTER 54: Bond

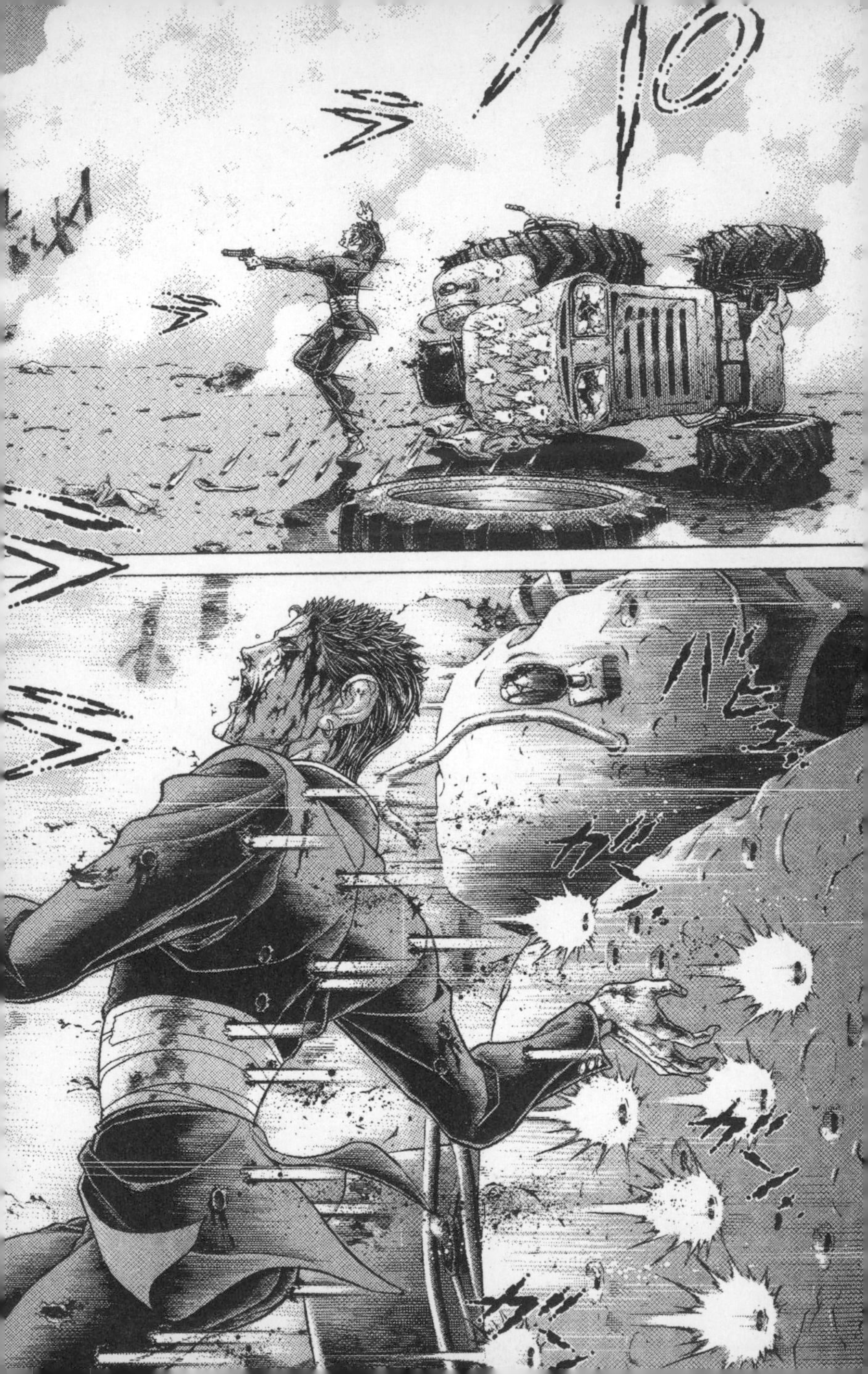

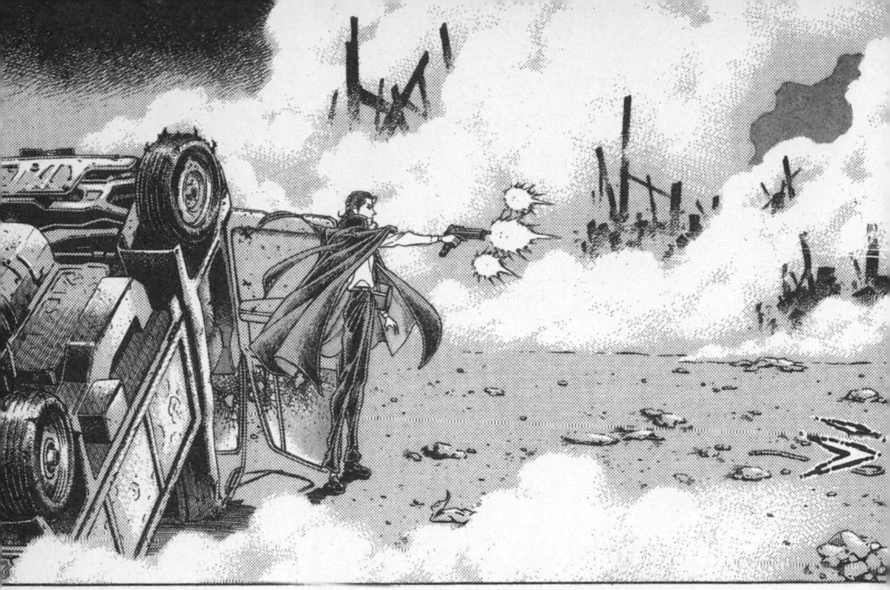

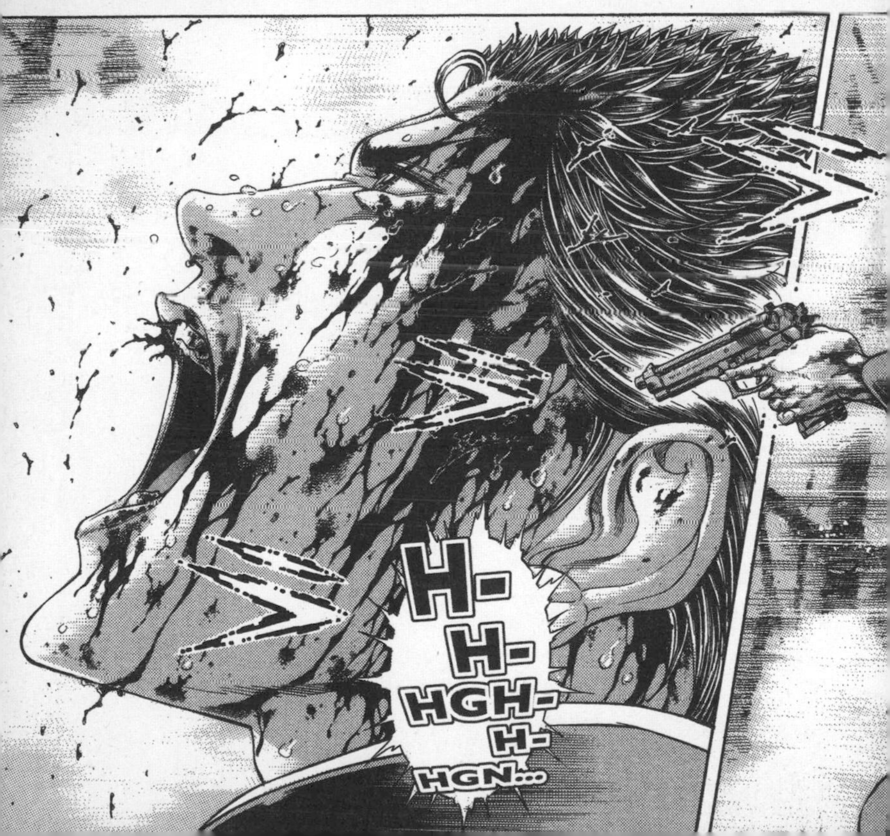
H-
H-
HGH-
H-
HGN...

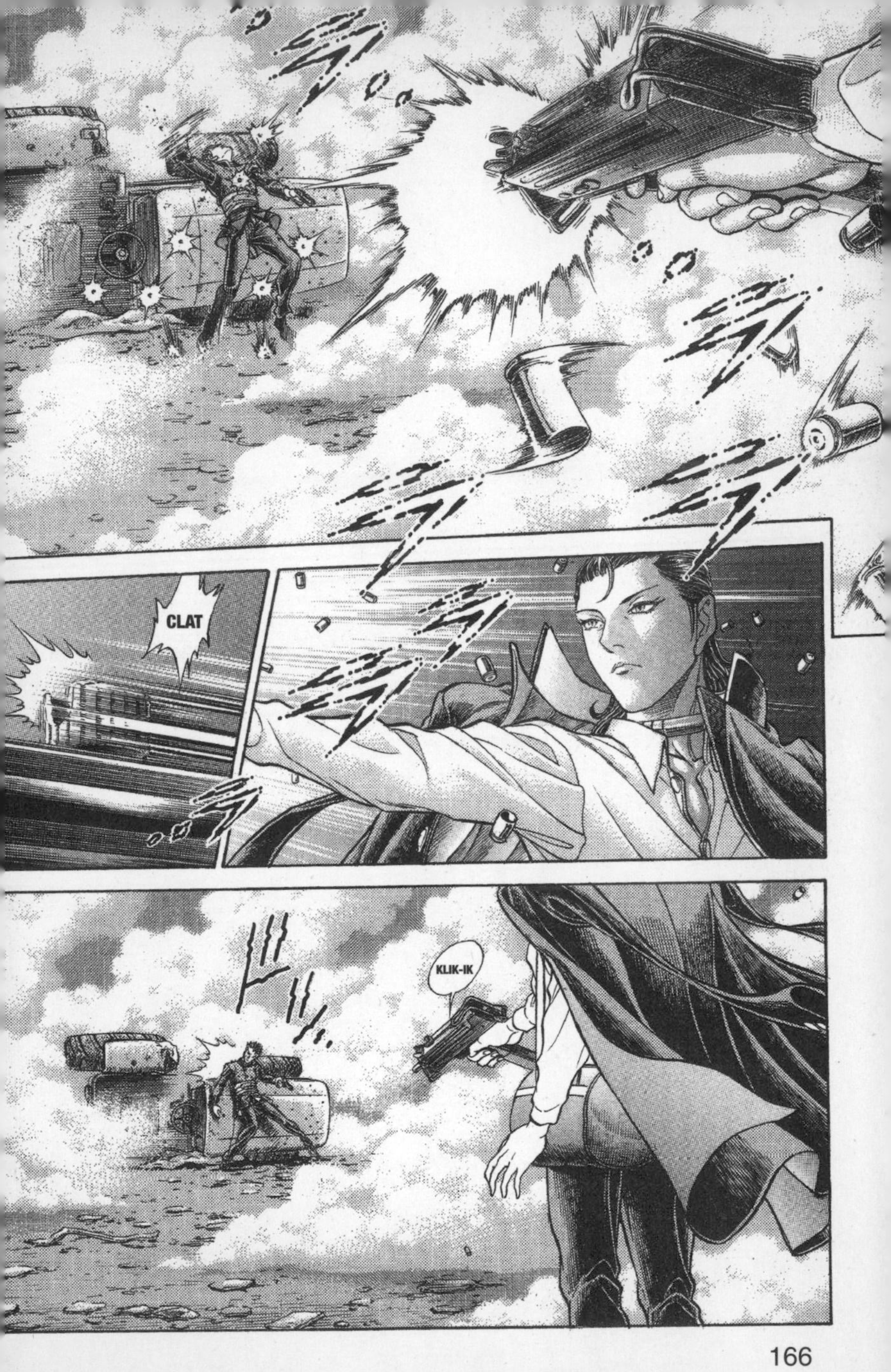
CLAT
KLIK-IK

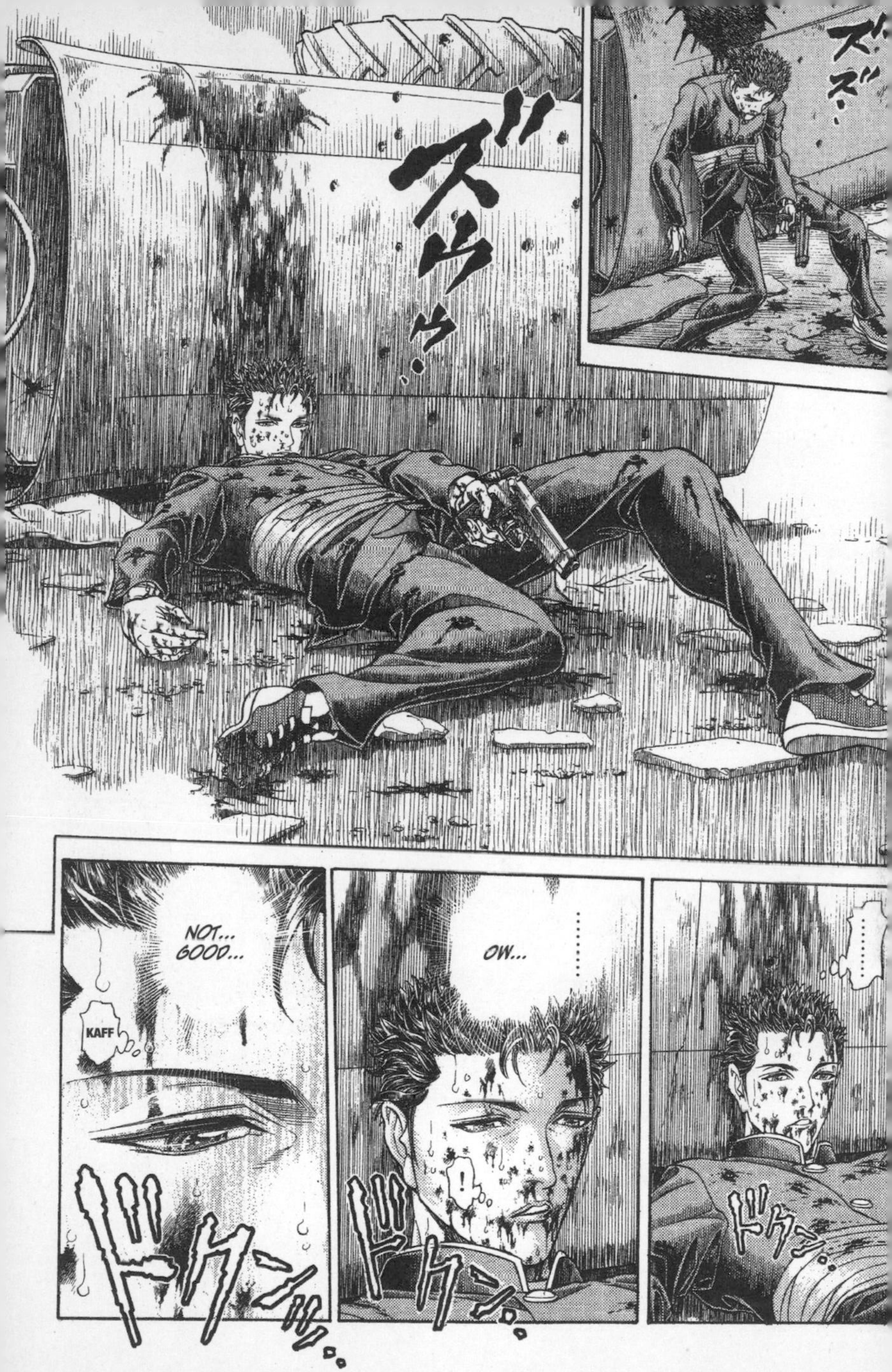

……
ドクン…
OW…
……
!
ドクン…
NOT… GOOD…
KAFF
ドクン…

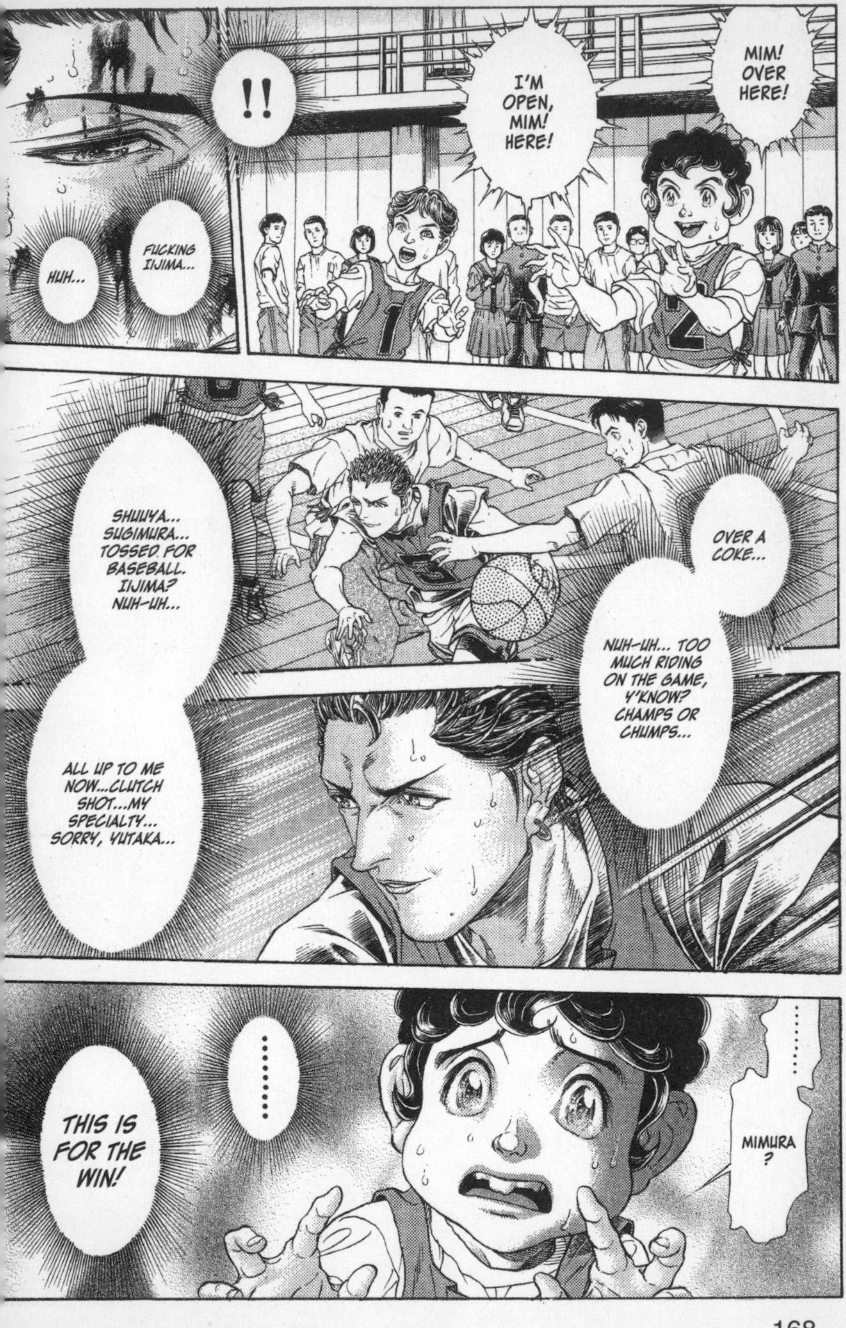
MIM! OVER HERE!
I'M OPEN, MIM! HERE!
!!
FUCKING IIJIMA...
HUH...
SHUUYA... SUGIMURA... TOSSED FOR BASEBALL. IIJIMA? NUH-UH...
OVER A COKE...
NUH-UH... TOO MUCH RIDING ON THE GAME, Y'KNOW? CHAMPS OR CHUMPS...
ALL UP TO ME NOW...CLUTCH SHOT...MY SPECIALTY... SORRY, YUTAKA...
......
MIMURA ?
......
THIS IS FOR THE WIN!

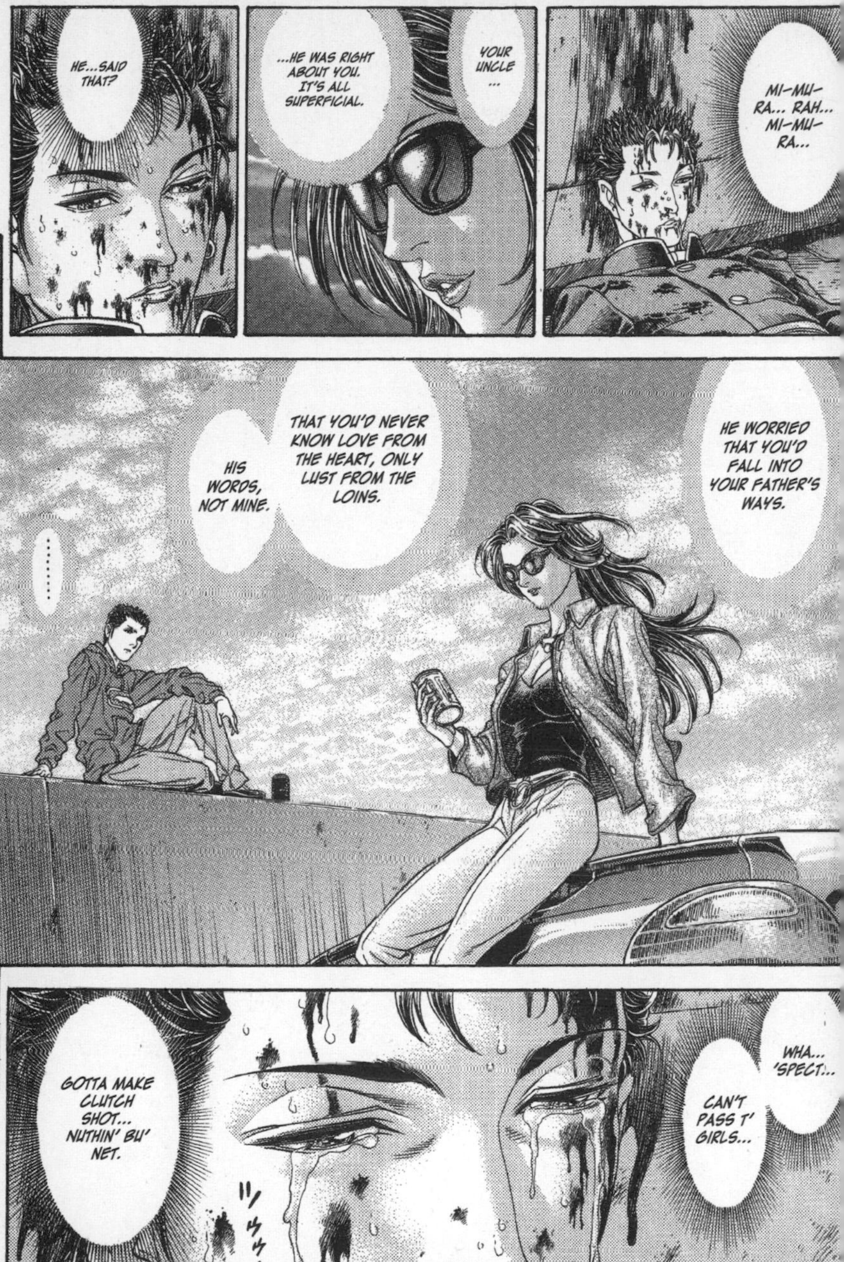
MI-MU-RA... RAH... MI-MU-RA...
YOUR UNCLE ...
...HE WAS RIGHT ABOUT YOU. IT'S ALL SUPERFICIAL.
HE...SAID THAT?
HE WORRIED THAT YOU'D FALL INTO YOUR FATHER'S WAYS.
THAT YOU'D NEVER KNOW LOVE FROM THE HEART, ONLY LUST FROM THE LOINS.
HIS WORDS, NOT MINE.
......
WHA... 'SPECT...
CAN'T PASS T' GIRLS...
GOTTA MAKE CLUTCH SHOT... NUTHIN' BU' NET.

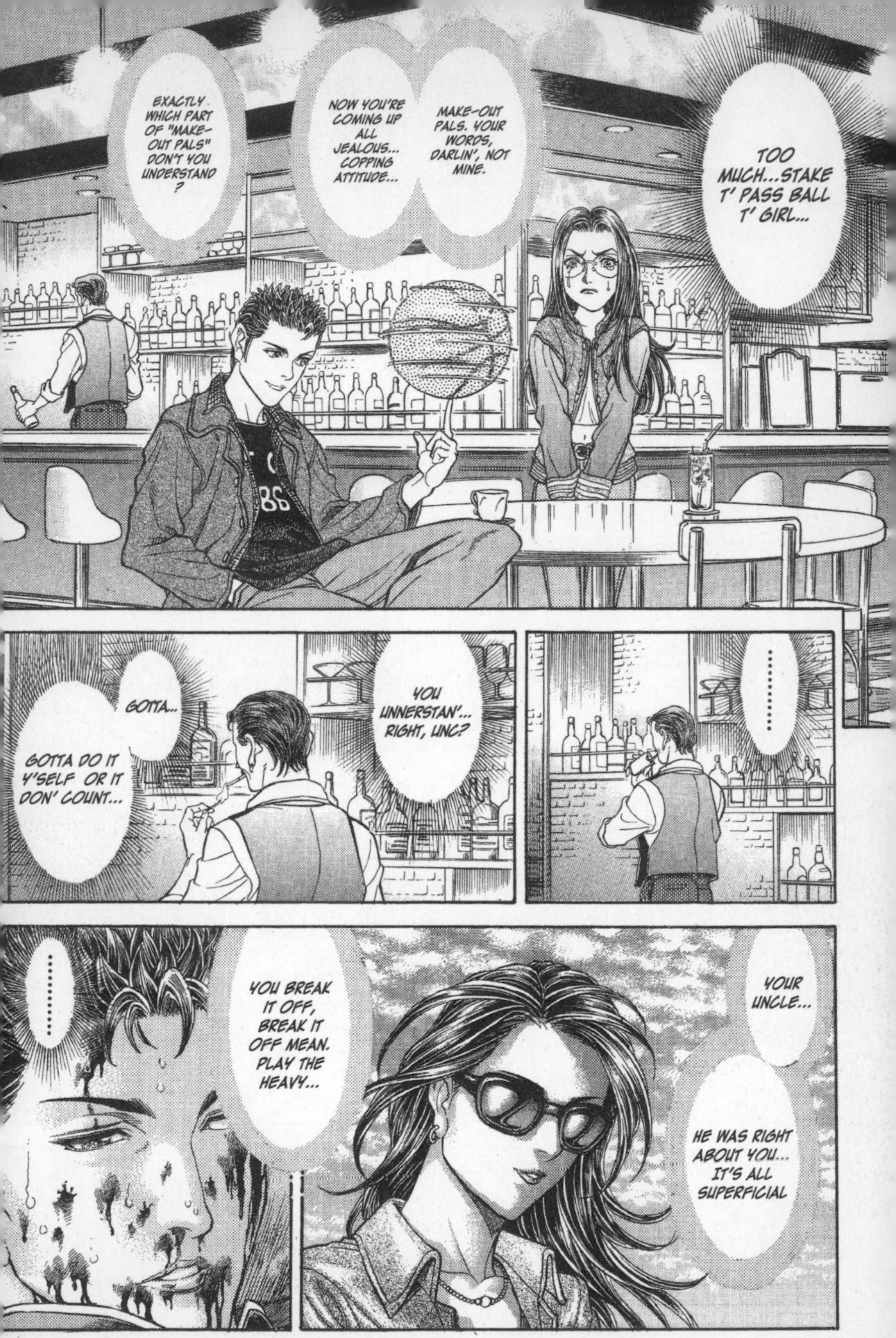
TOO MUCH...STAKE T' PASS BALL T' GIRL...
MAKE-OUT PALS. YOUR WORDS, DARLIN', NOT MINE.
NOW YOU'RE COMING UP ALL JEALOUS... COPPING ATTITUDE...
EXACTLY WHICH PART OF "MAKE-OUT PALS" DON'T YOU UNDERSTAND?
......
YOU UNNERSTAN'... RIGHT, UNC?
GOTTA...
GOTTA DO IT Y'SELF OR IT DON' COUNT...
YOUR UNCLE...
HE WAS RIGHT ABOUT YOU... IT'S ALL SUPERFICIAL
YOU BREAK IT OFF, BREAK IT OFF MEAN. PLAY THE HEAVY...
......

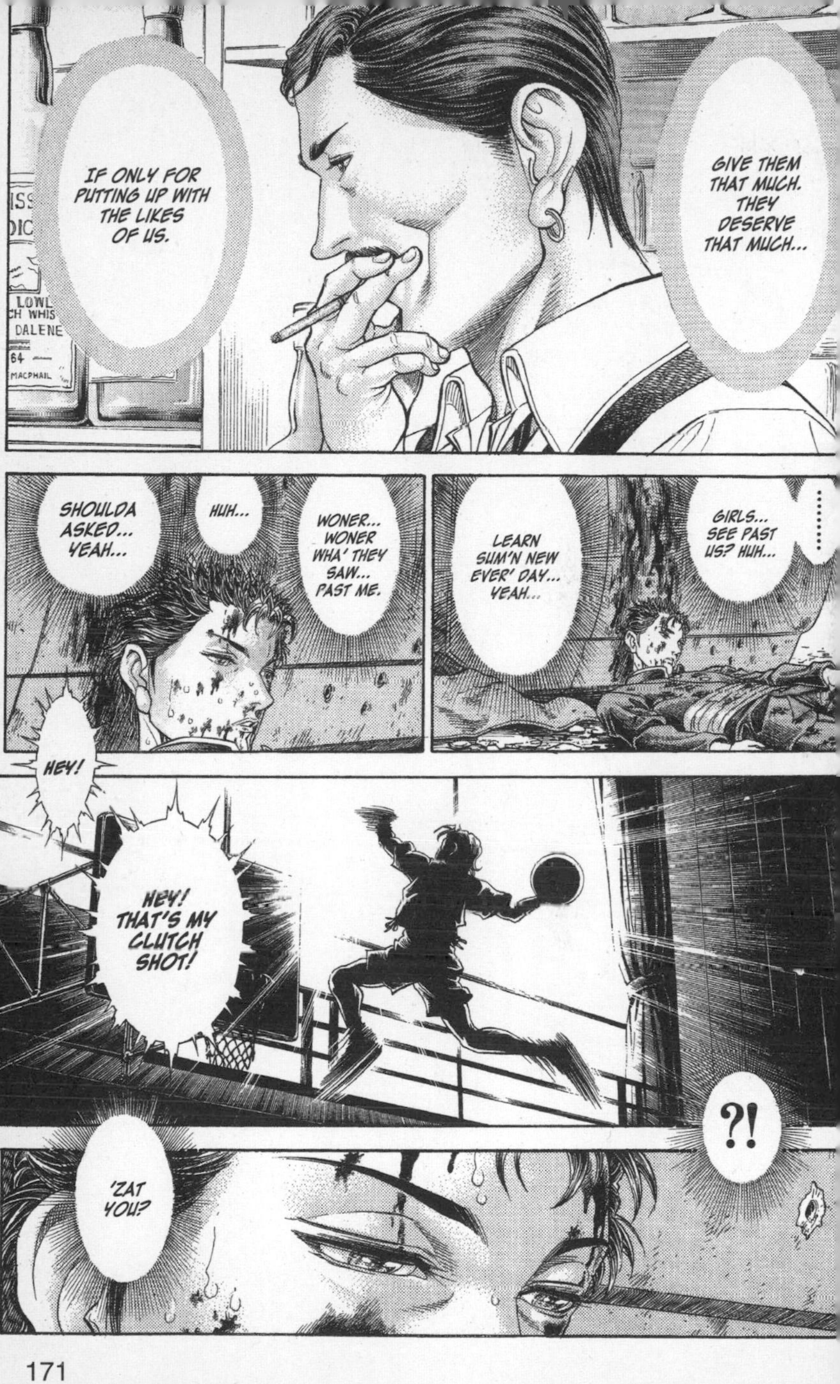

GIVE THEM THAT MUCH. THEY DESERVE THAT MUCH...
IF ONLY FOR PUTTING UP WITH THE LIKES OF US.
......
GIRLS... SEE PAST US? HUH...
LEARN SUM'N NEW EVER' DAY... YEAH...
WONER... WONER WHA' THEY SAW... PAST ME.
HUH...
SHOULDA ASKED... YEAH...
HEY!
HEY! THAT'S MY CLUTCH SHOT!
?!
'ZAT YOU?

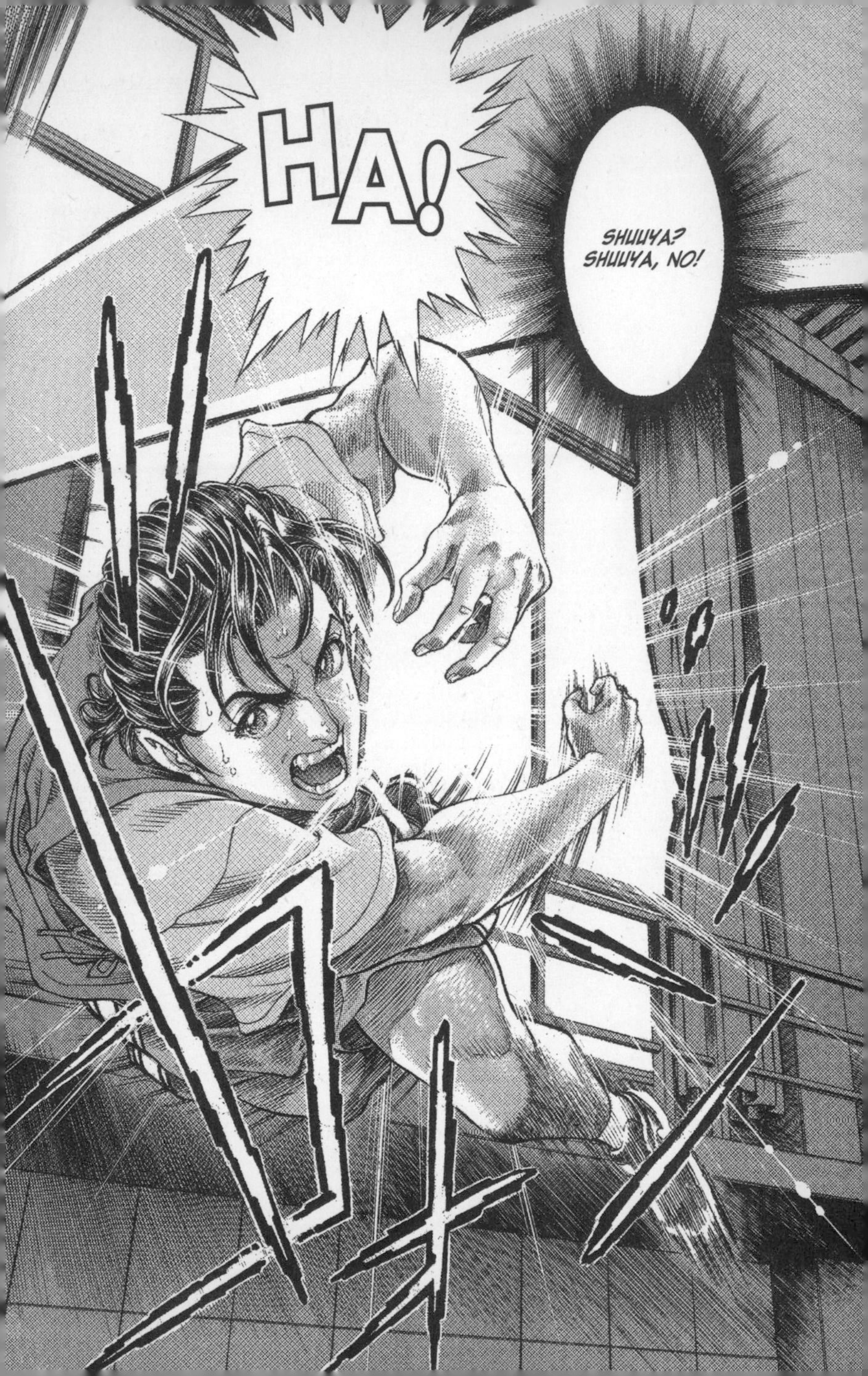
HA!
SHUUYA?
SHUUYA, NO!

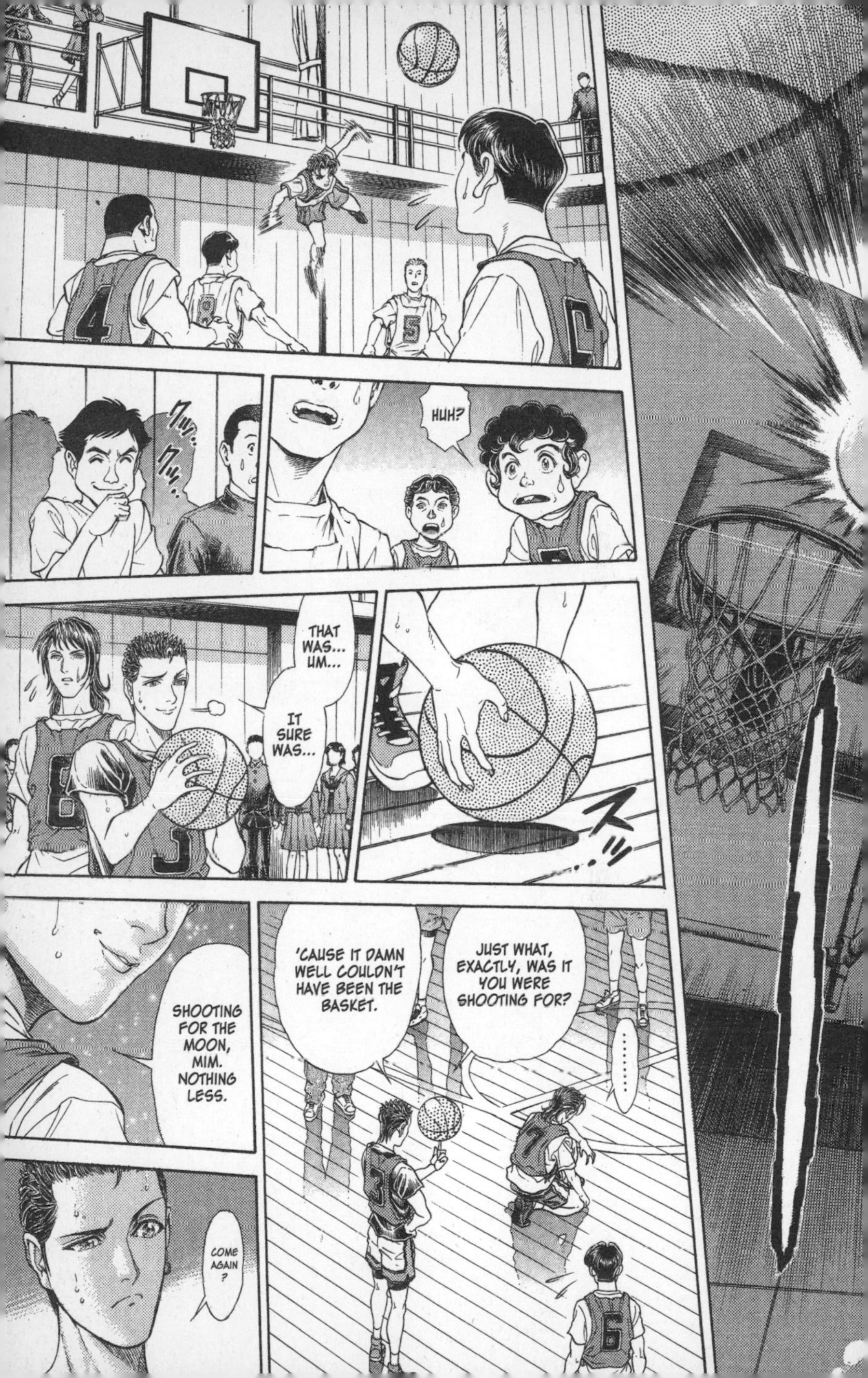
HUH?
THAT WAS... UM...
IT SURE WAS...
JUST WHAT, EXACTLY, WAS IT YOU WERE SHOOTING FOR?
'CAUSE IT DAMN WELL COULDN'T HAVE BEEN THE BASKET.
......
SHOOTING FOR THE MOON, MIM. NOTHING LESS.
COME AGAIN?

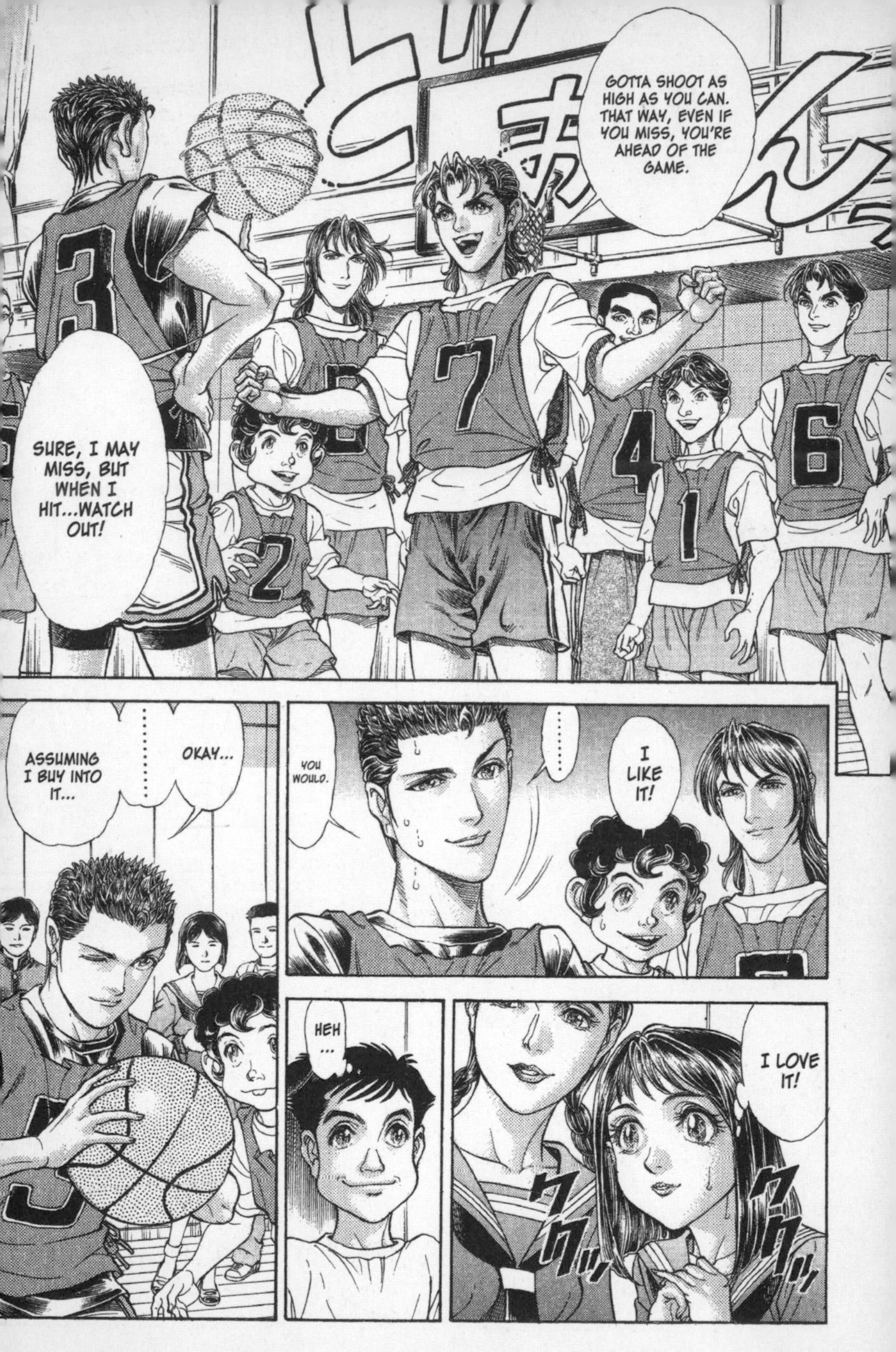
GOTTA SHOOT AS HIGH AS YOU CAN. THAT WAY, EVEN IF YOU MISS, YOU'RE AHEAD OF THE GAME.
SURE, I MAY MISS, BUT WHEN I HIT...WATCH OUT!
......
I LIKE IT!
YOU WOULD.
I LOVE IT!
HEH ...
......
OKAY...
ASSUMING I BUY INTO IT...

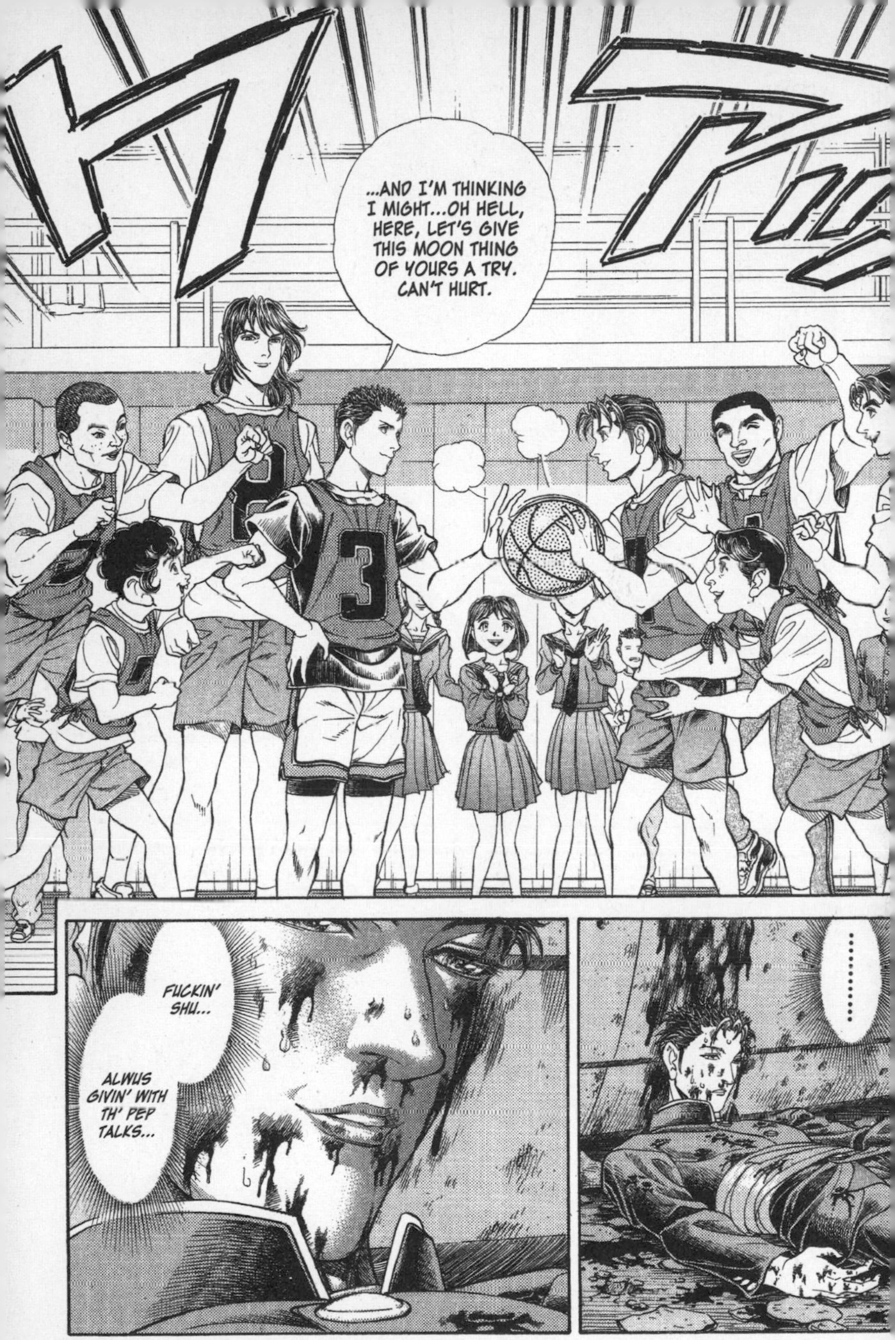
...AND I'M THINKING I MIGHT...OH HELL, HERE, LET'S GIVE THIS MOON THING OF YOURS A TRY. CAN'T HURT.
......
FUCKIN' SHU...
ALWUS GIVIN' WITH TH' PEP TALKS...

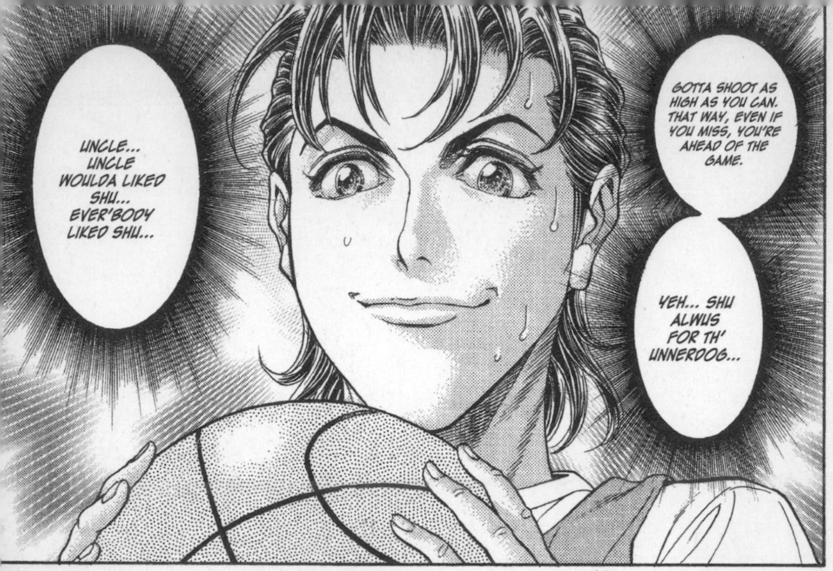
GOTTA SHOOT AS HIGH AS YOU CAN. THAT WAY, EVEN IF YOU MISS, YOU'RE AHEAD OF THE GAME.
YEH... SHU ALWUS FOR TH' UNNERDOG...
UNCLE... UNCLE WOULDA LIKED SHU... EVER'BODY LIKED SHU...

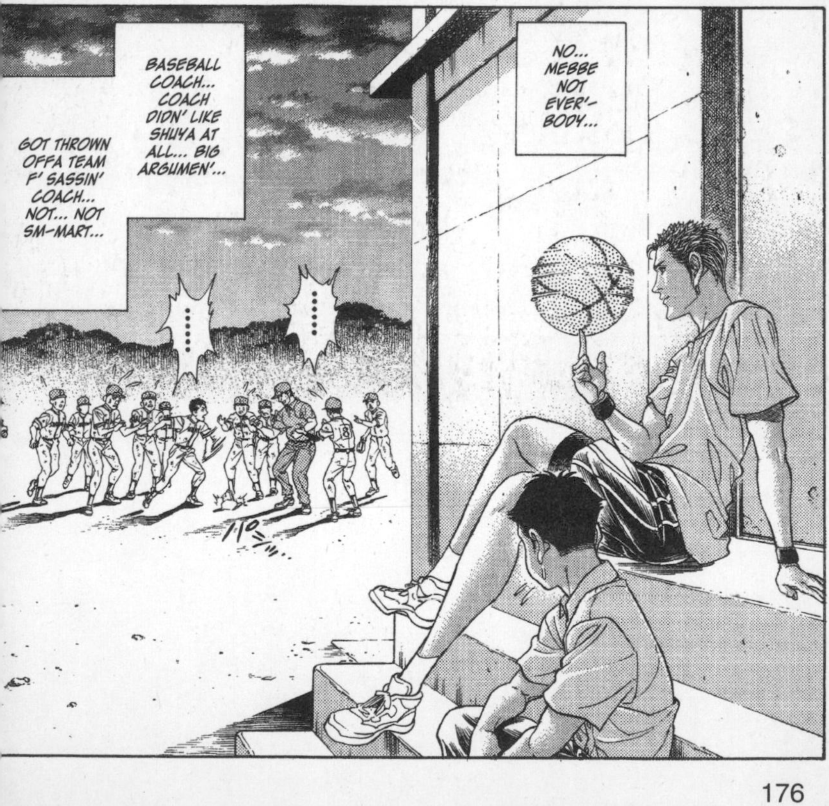
NO... MEBBE NOT EVER'-BODY...
BASEBALL COACH... COACH DIDN' LIKE SHUYA AT ALL... BIG ARGUMEN'...
GOT THROWN OFFA TEAM F' SASSIN' COACH... NOT... NOT SM-MART...

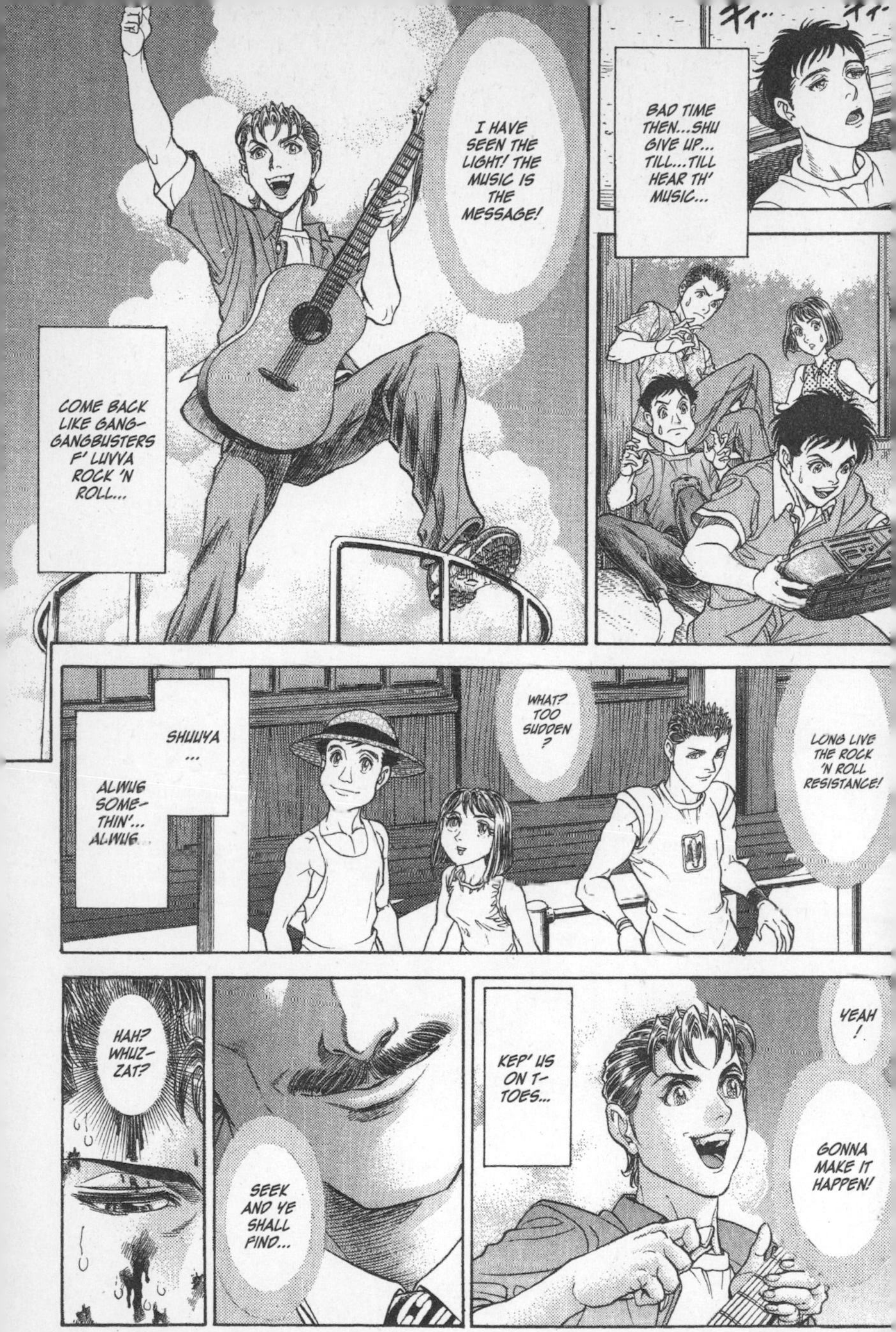
BAD TIME THEN...SHU GIVE UP... TILL...TILL HEAR TH' MUSIC...
I HAVE SEEN THE LIGHT! THE MUSIC IS THE MESSAGE!
COME BACK LIKE GANG-GANGBUSTERS F' LUVVA ROCK 'N ROLL...
LONG LIVE THE ROCK 'N ROLL RESISTANCE!
WHAT? TOO SUDDEN?
SHUUYA ...
ALWUG SOME-THIN'... ALWUG...
YEAH!
GONNA MAKE IT HAPPEN!
KEP' US ON T-TOES...
SEEK AND YE SHALL FIND...
HAH? WHUZ-ZAT?

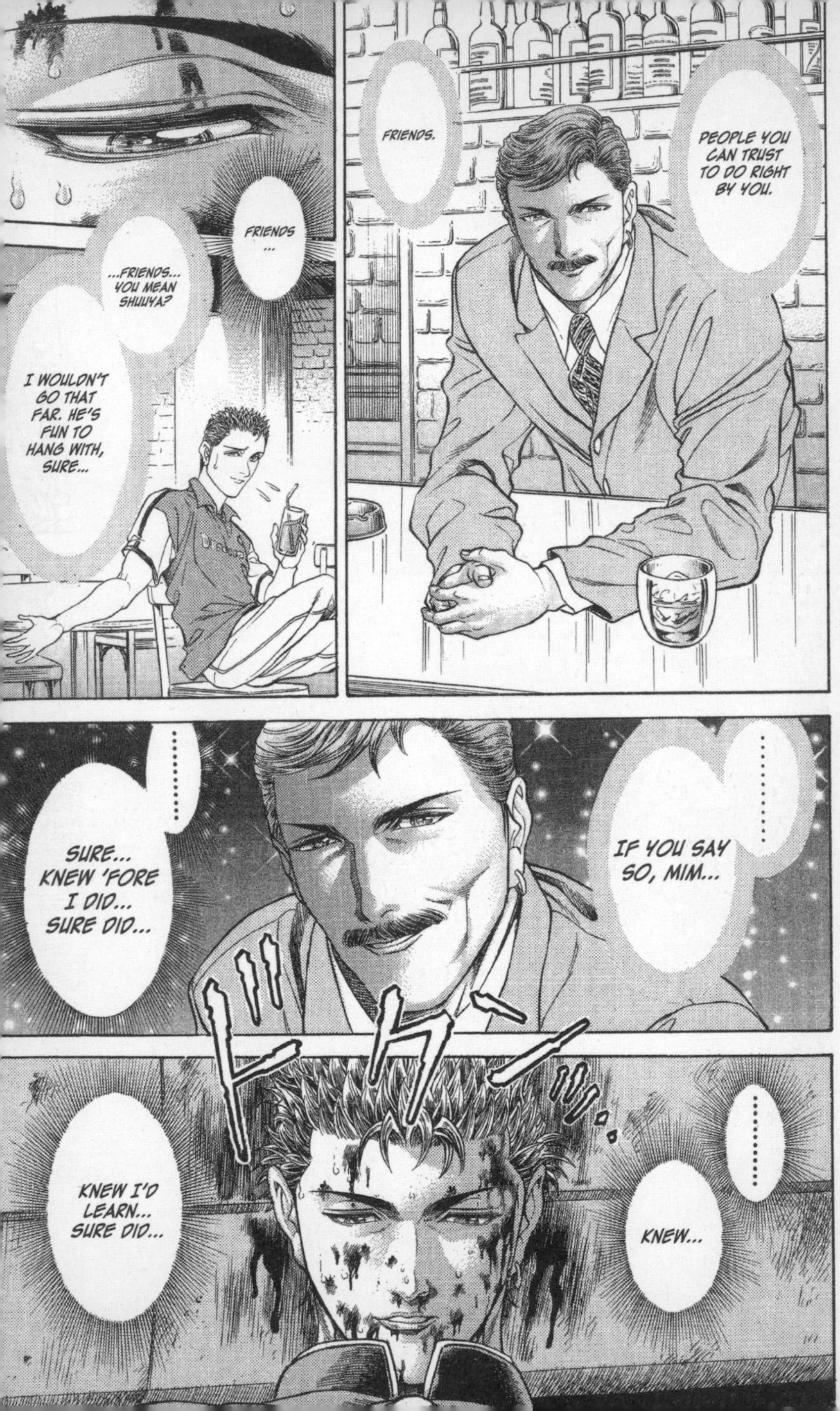
PEOPLE YOU CAN TRUST TO DO RIGHT BY YOU.
FRIENDS.
FRIENDS ...
...FRIENDS... YOU MEAN SHUUYA?
I WOULDN'T GO THAT FAR. HE'S FUN TO HANG WITH, SURE...
......
IF YOU SAY SO, MIM...
......
SURE... KNEW 'FORE I DID... SURE DID...
ドカーッ
......
KNEW...
KNEW I'D LEARN... SURE DID...

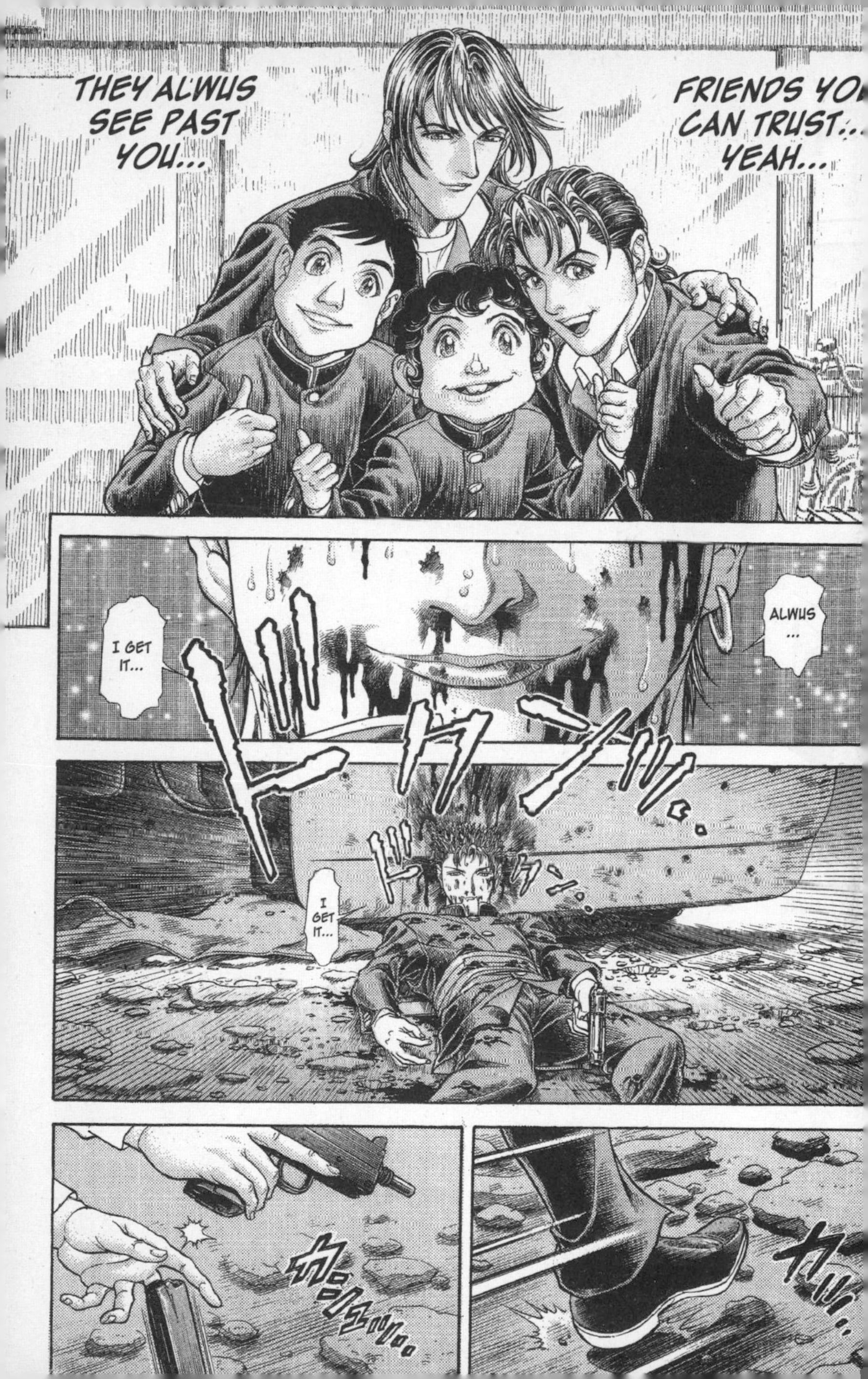
FRIENDS YO CAN TRUST... YEAH...
THEY ALWUS SEE PAST YOU...
ALWUS ...
I GET IT...
I GET IT...

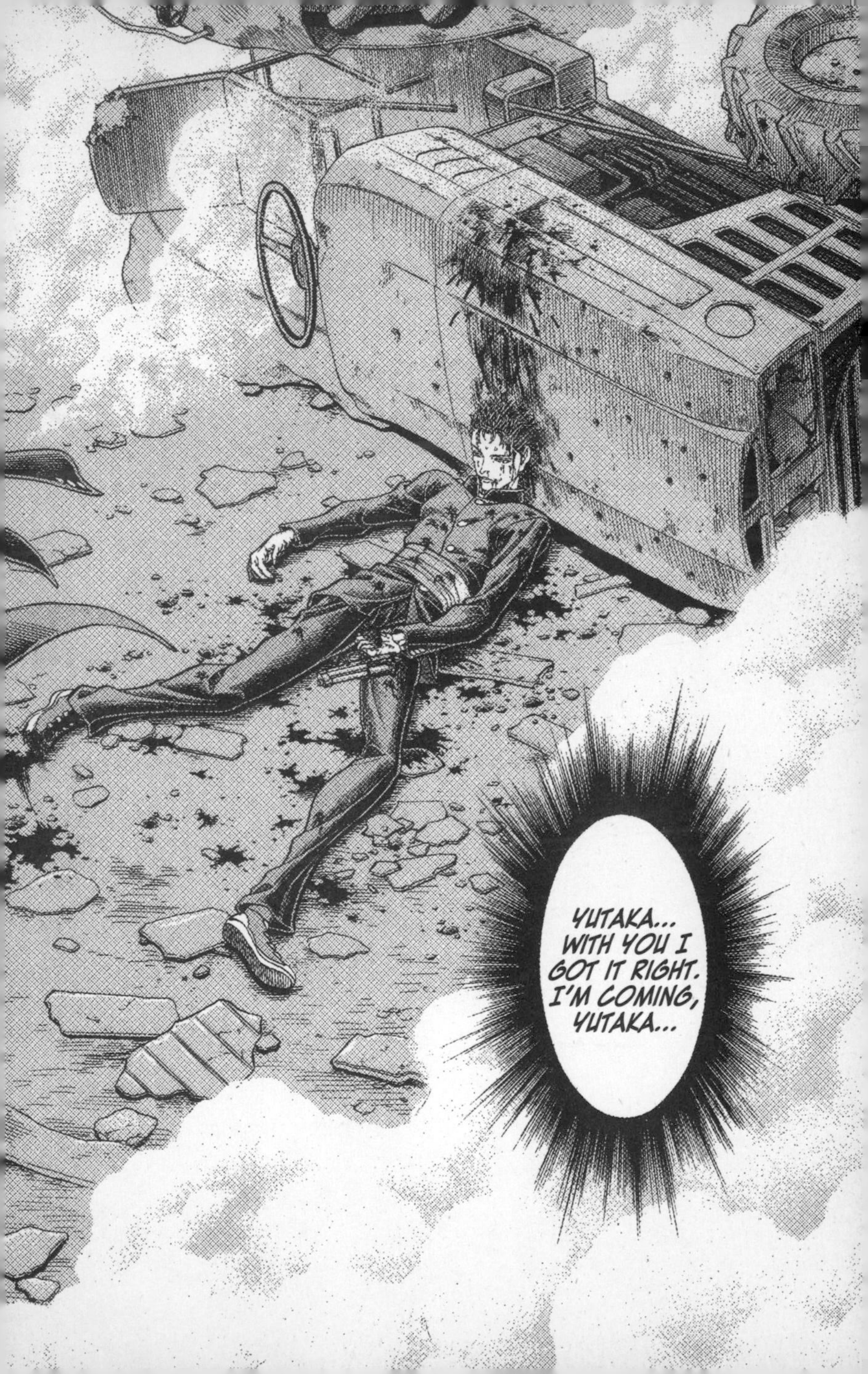
YUTAKA... WITH YOU I GOT IT RIGHT. I'M COMING, YUTAKA...

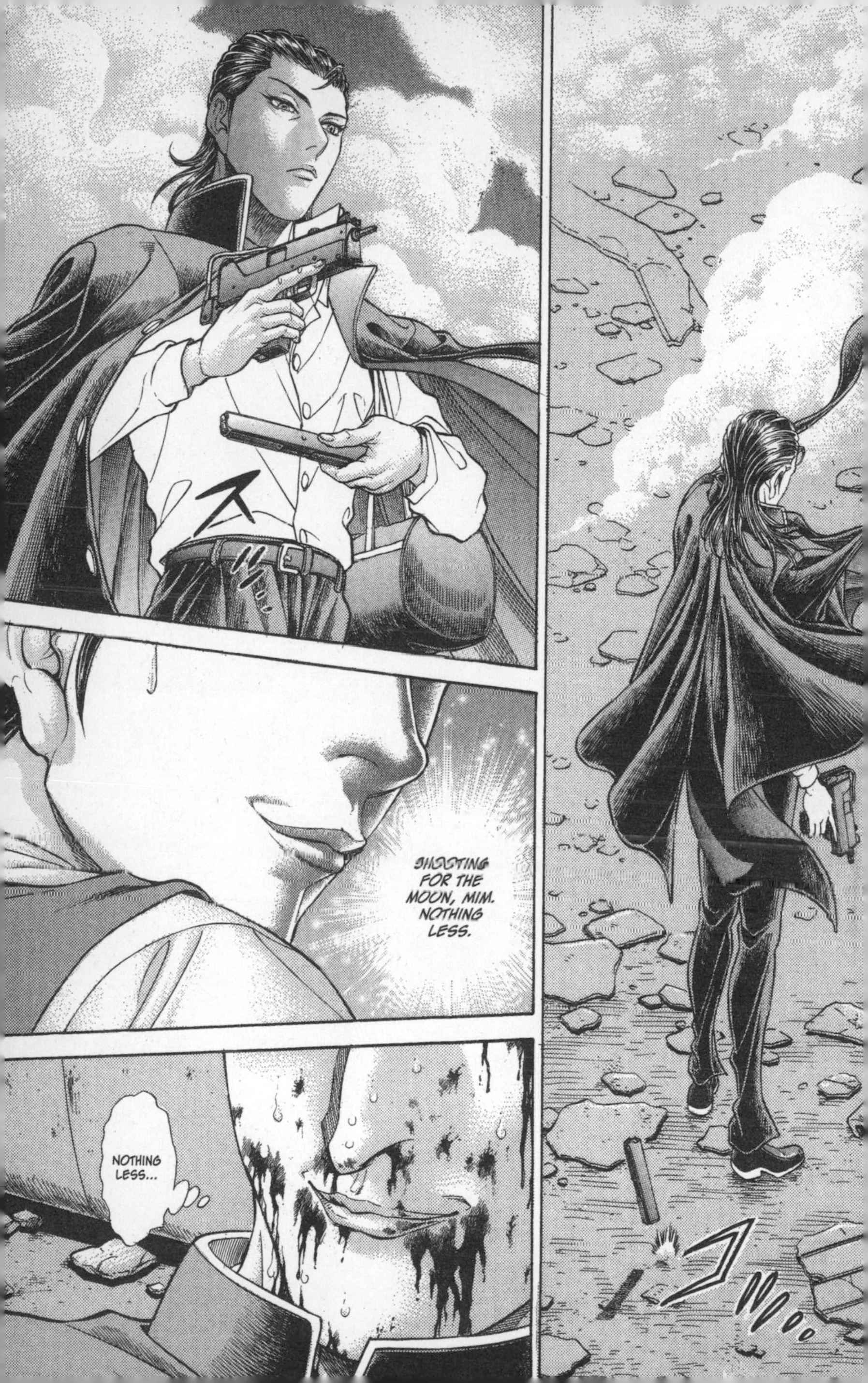
SHOOTING FOR THE MOON, MIM. NOTHING LESS.
NOTHING LESS...

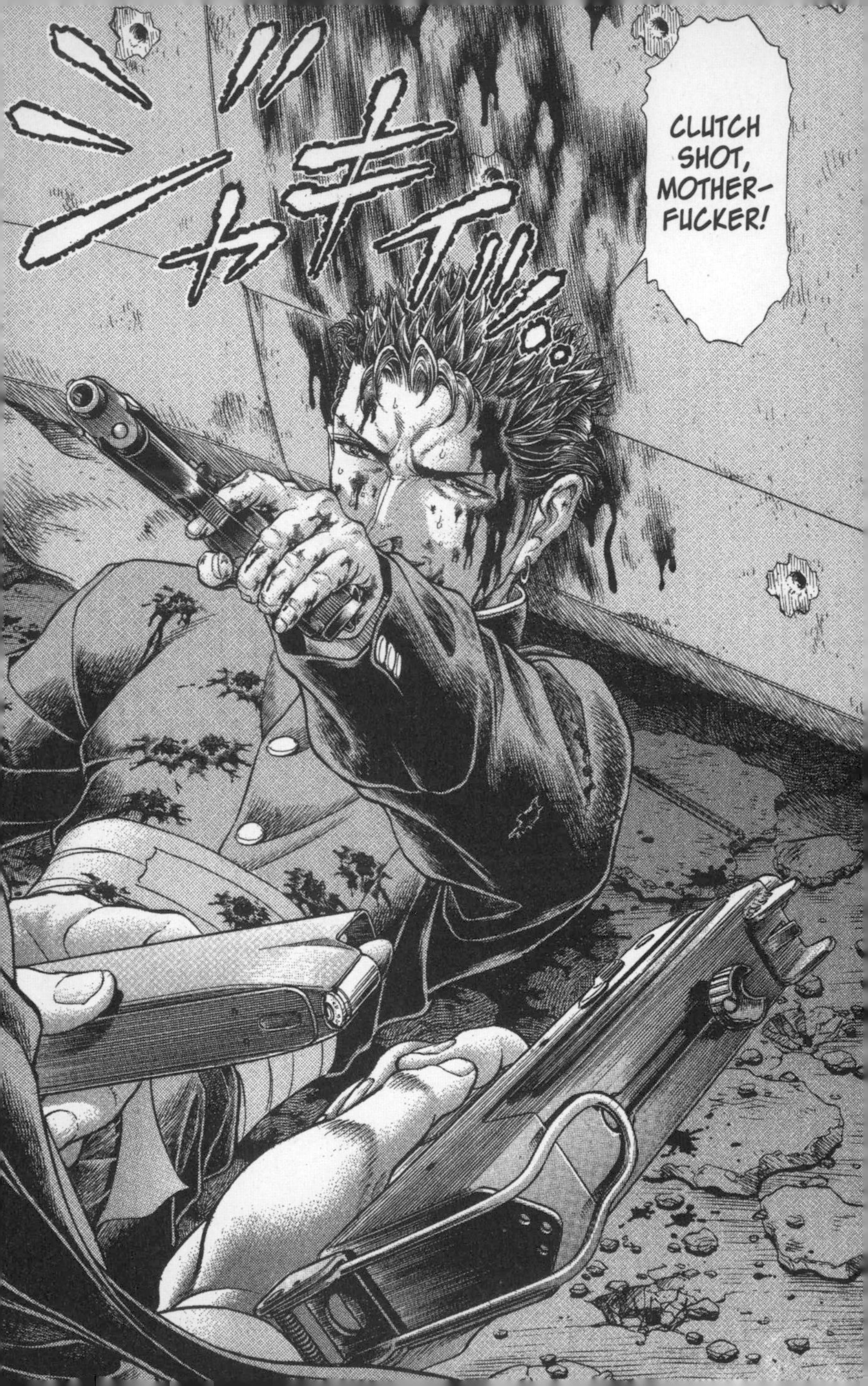
CLUTCH SHOT, MOTHER-FUCKER!

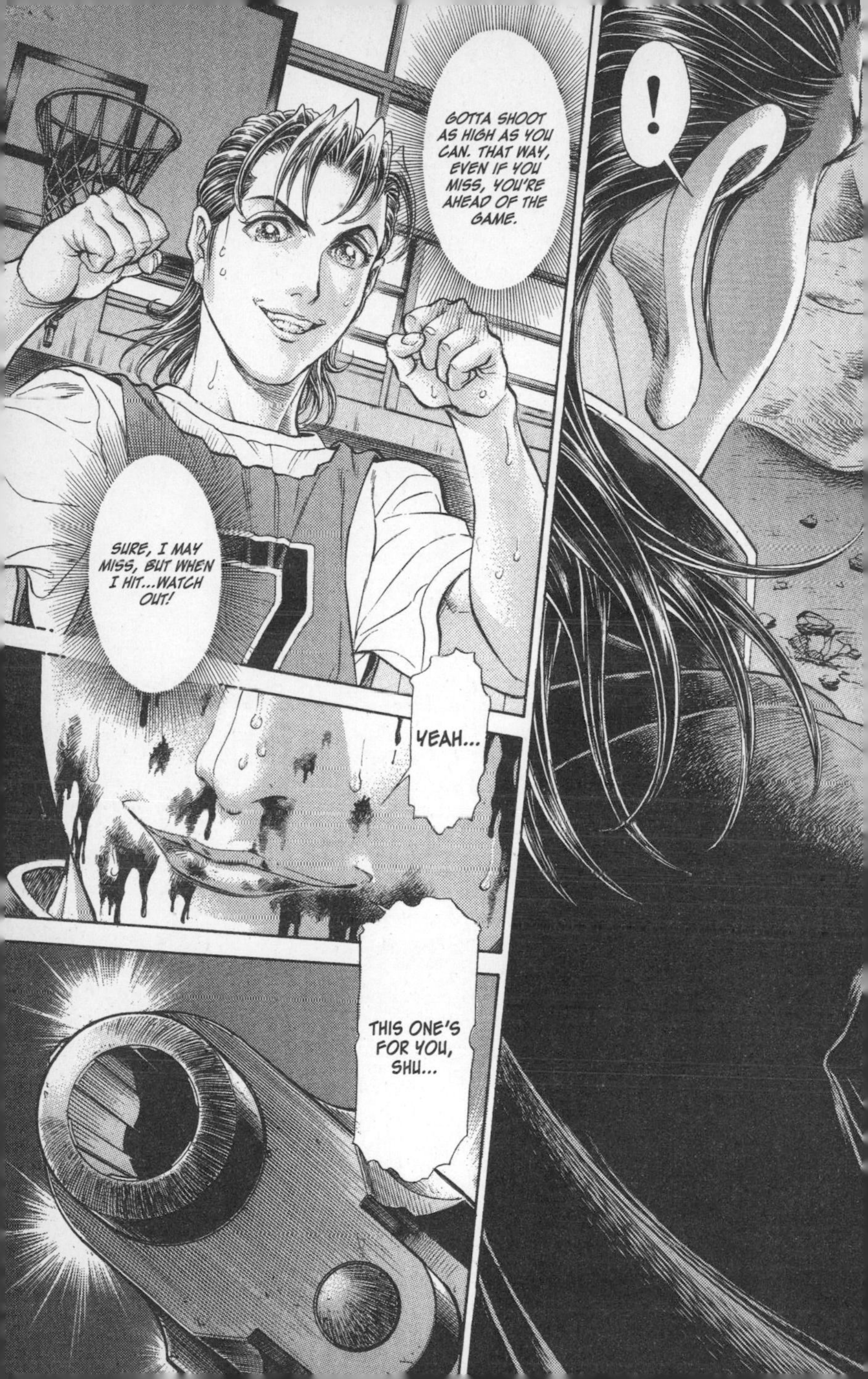
!
GOTTA SHOOT AS HIGH AS YOU CAN. THAT WAY, EVEN IF YOU MISS, YOU'RE AHEAD OF THE GAME.
SURE, I MAY MISS, BUT WHEN I HIT...WATCH OUT!
YEAH...
THIS ONE'S FOR YOU, SHU...

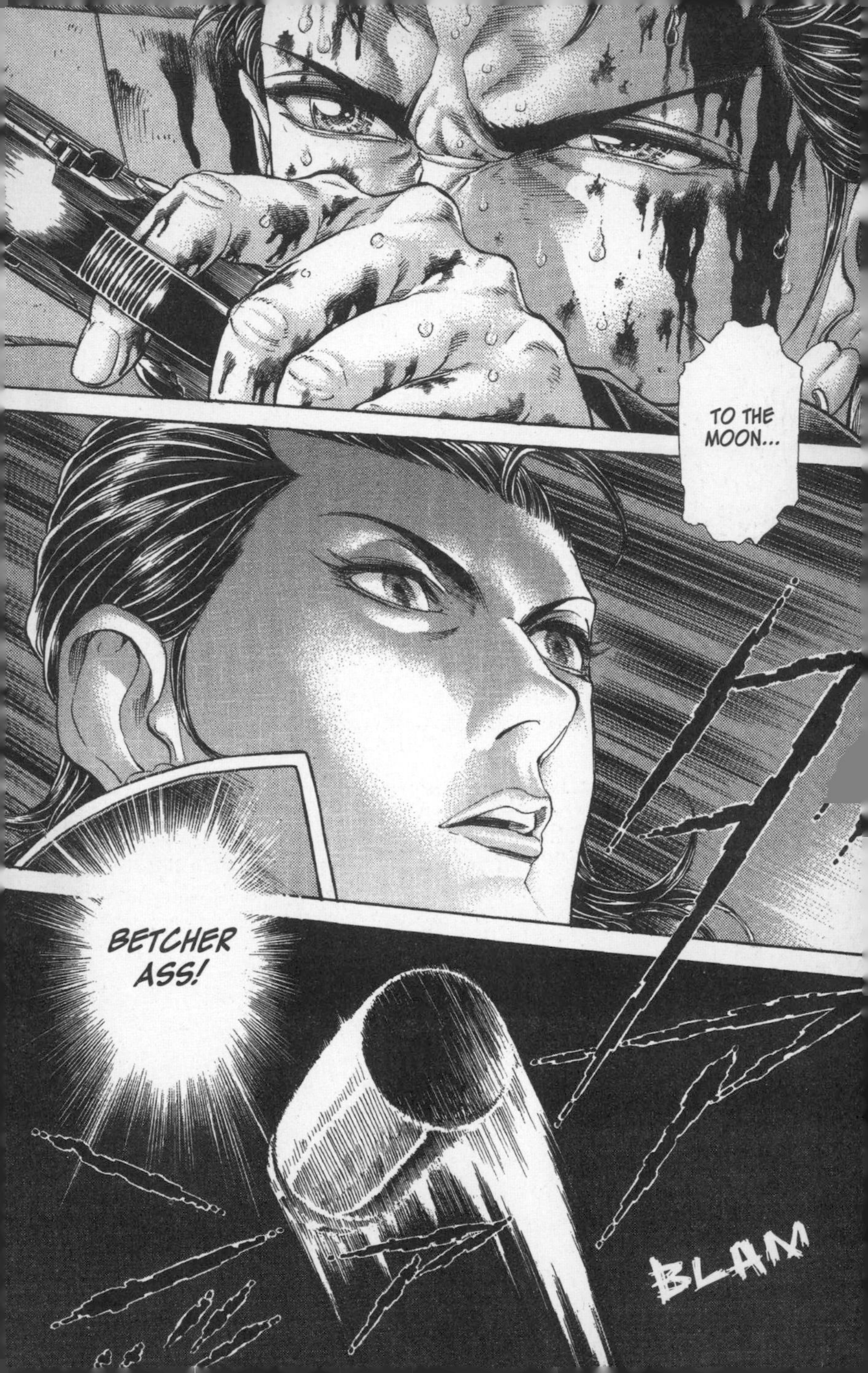
TO THE MOON...
BETCHER ASS!
BLAM

BATTLE ROYALE

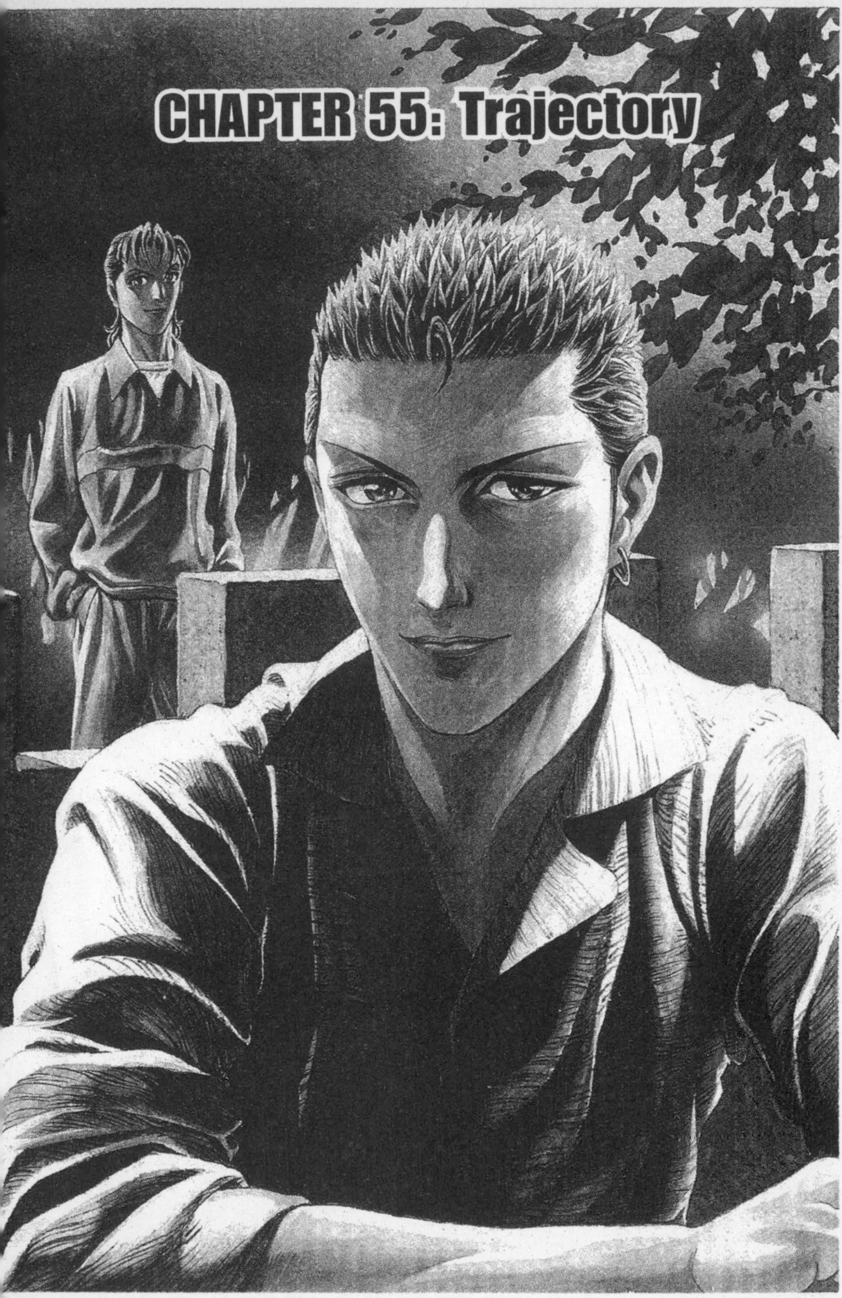
CHAPTER 55: Trajectory

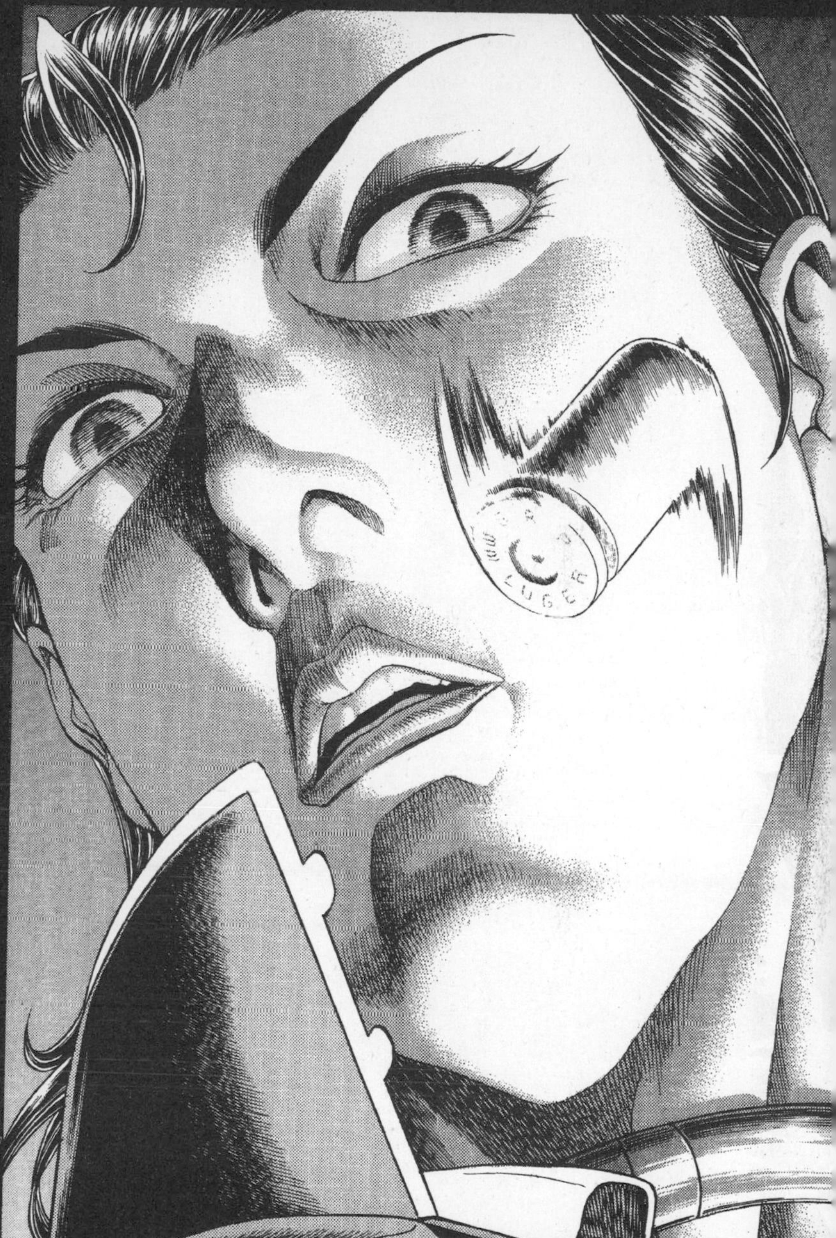
LUGER

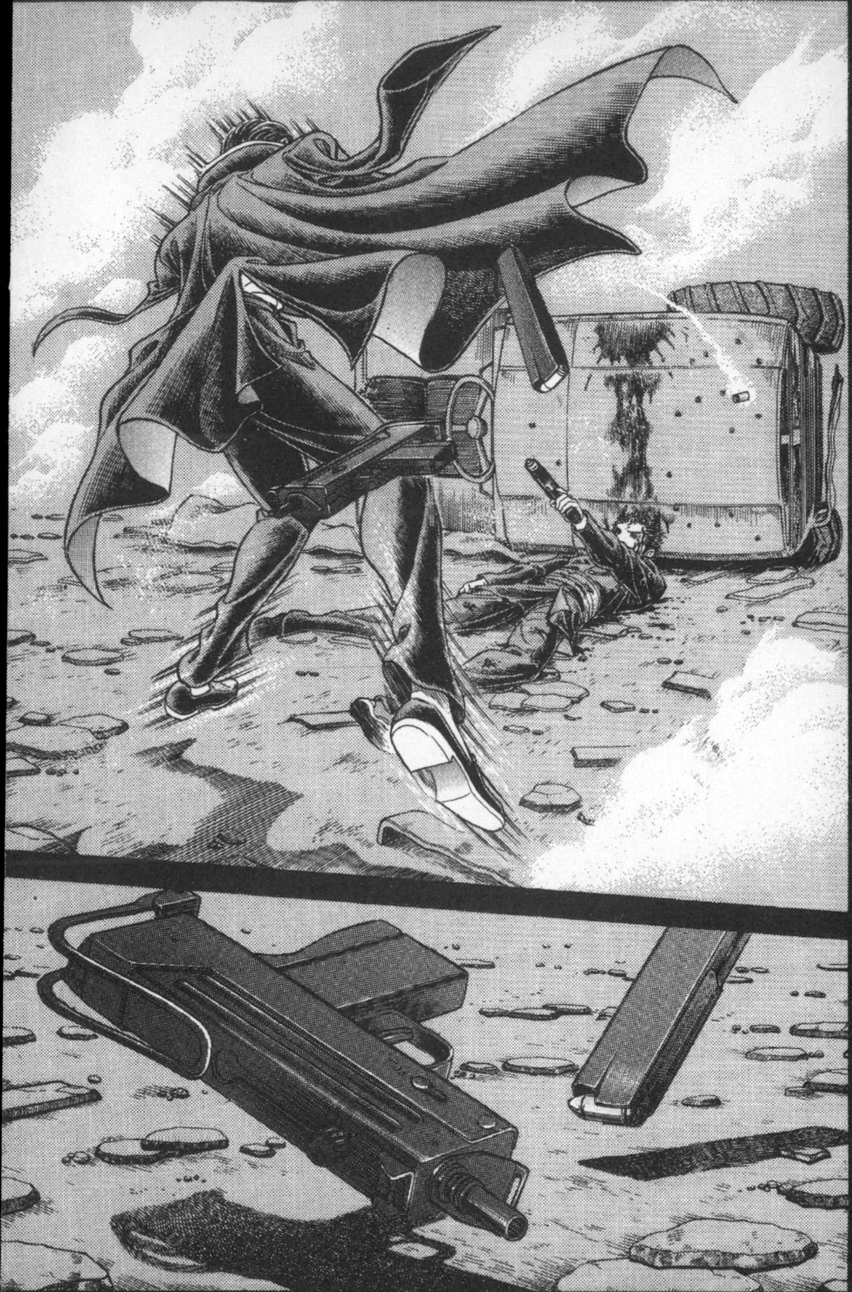

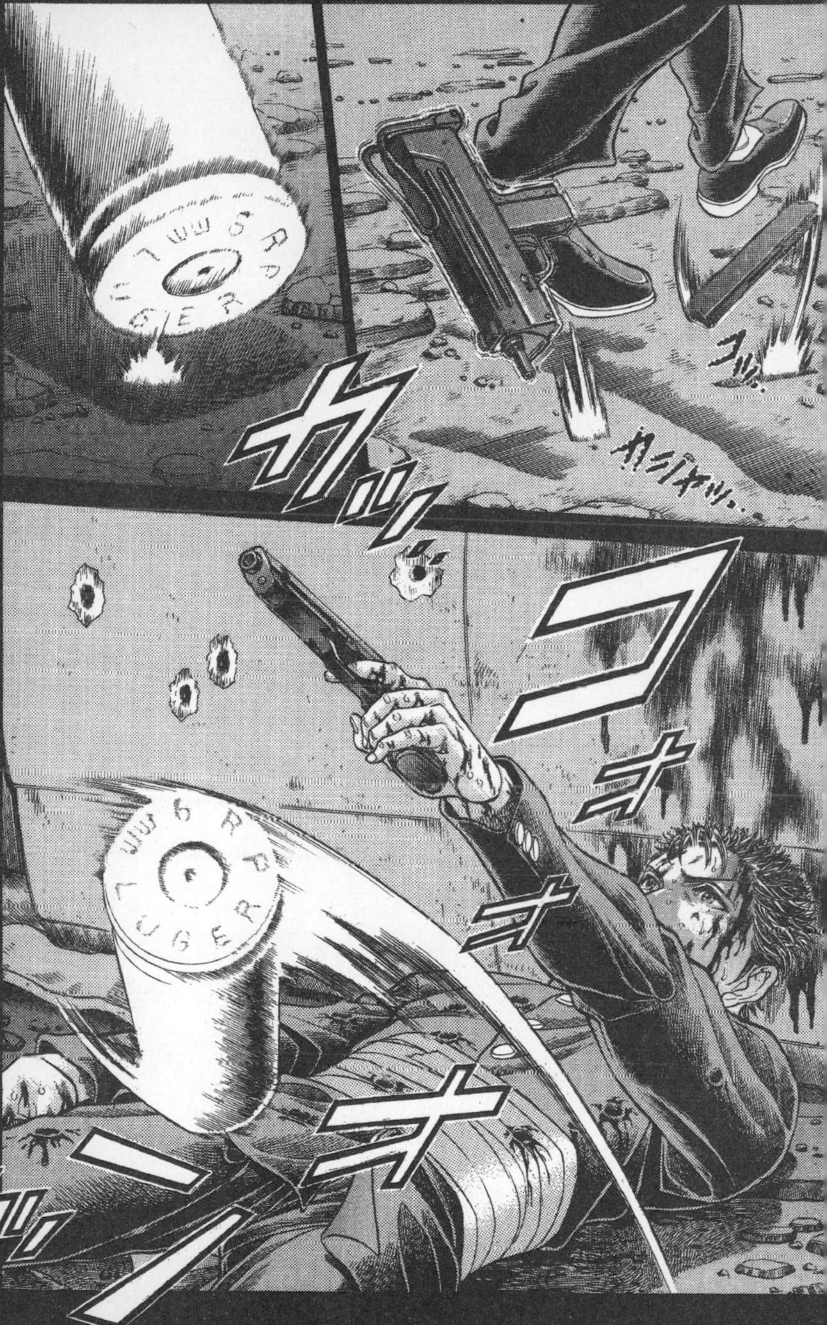
カッ
コッ…
カシャッ…
コォオオーーッ

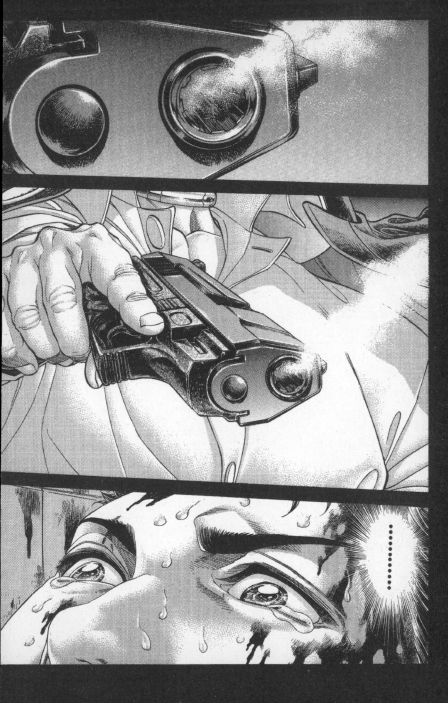

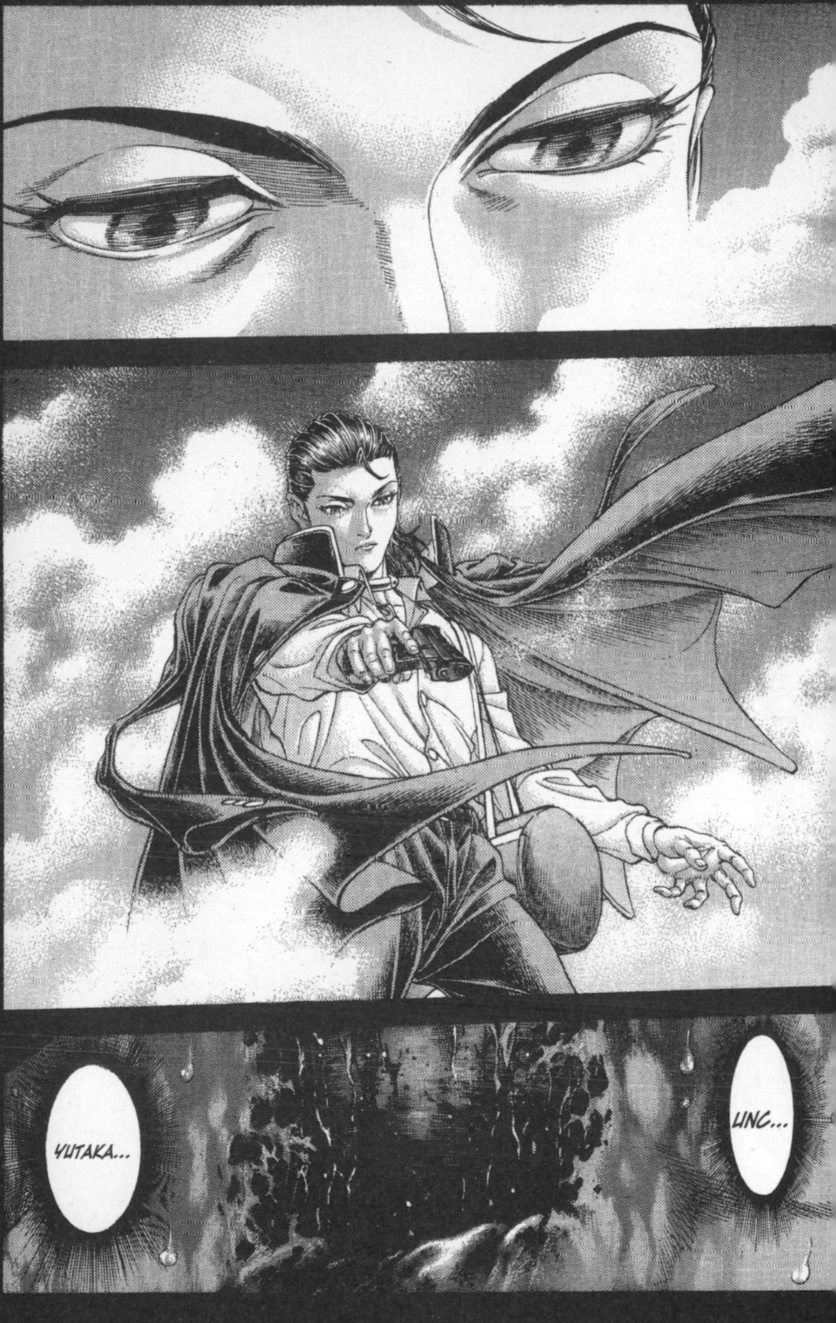
UNC...
YUTAKA...

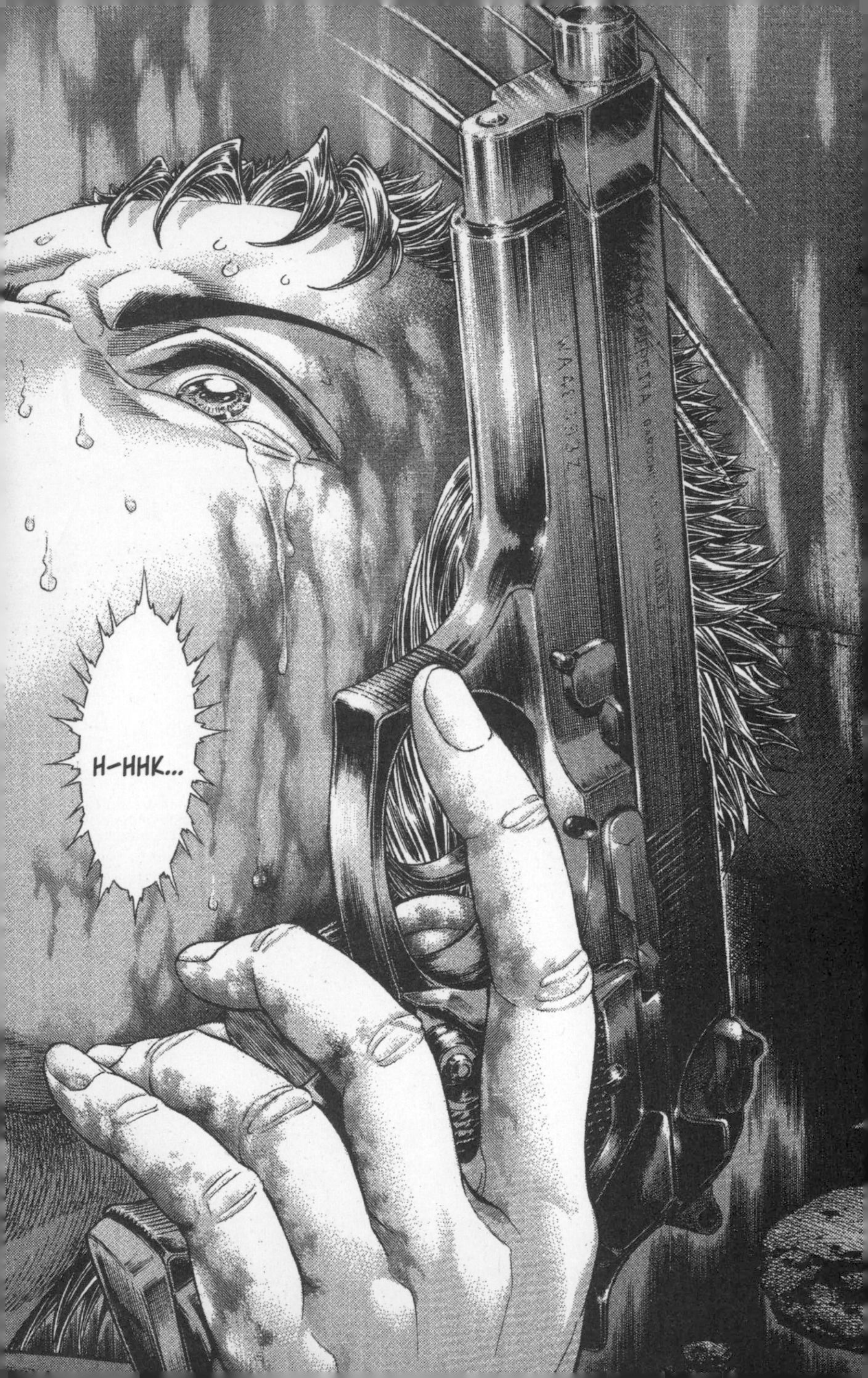
H-HHK...

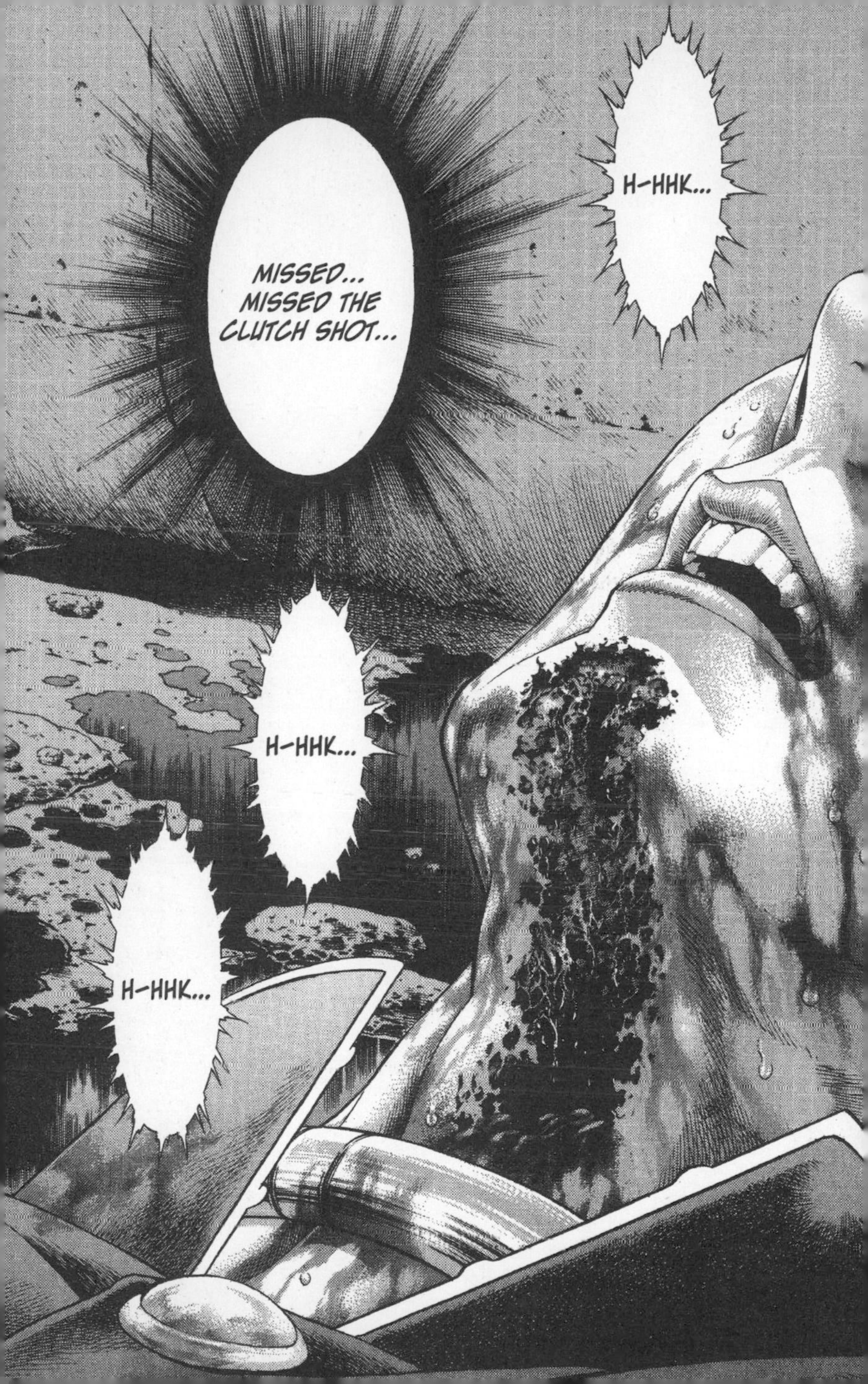
H-HHK...
MISSED... MISSED THE CLUTCH SHOT...
H-HHK...
H-HHK...

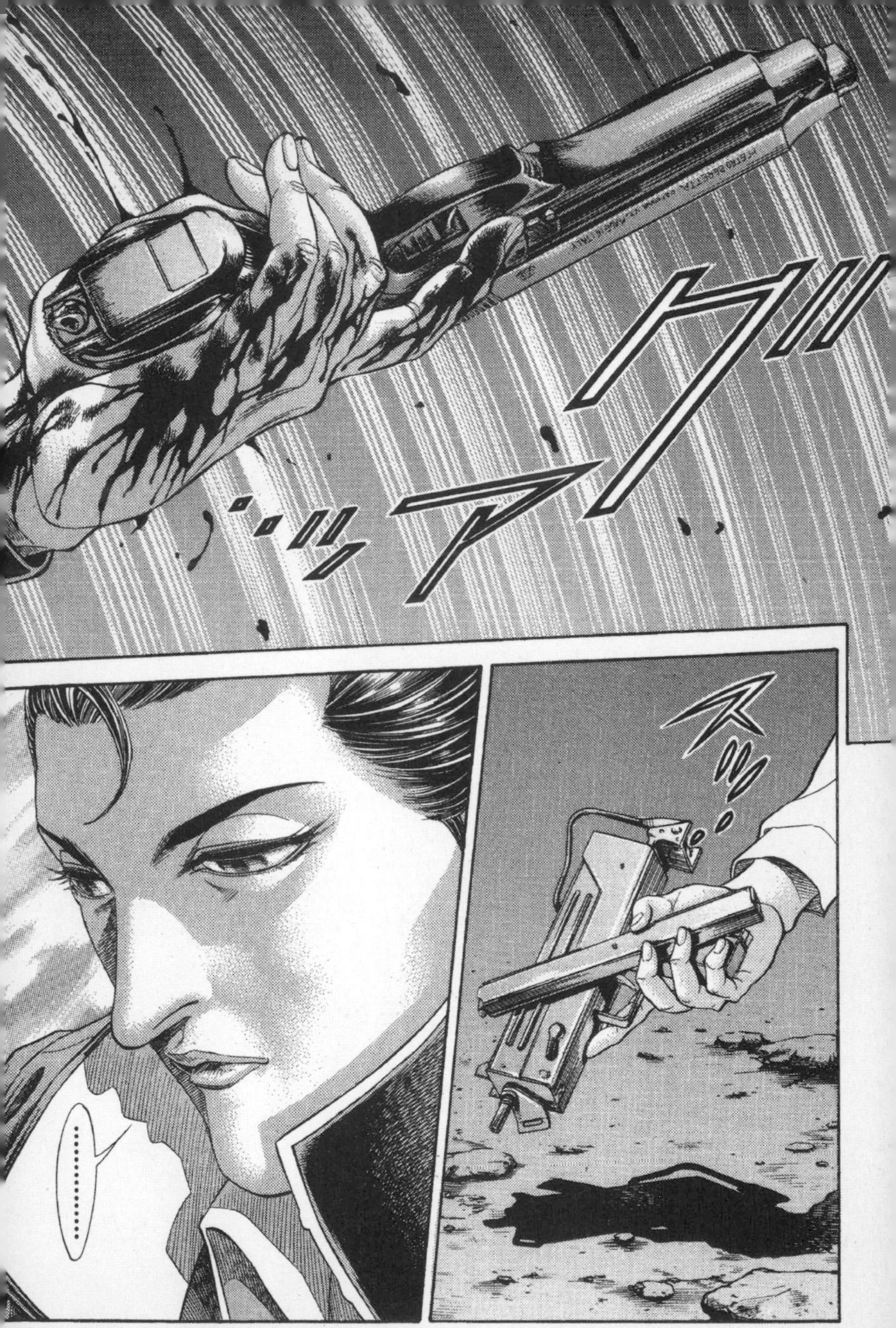
グアッ
スッ…
…………

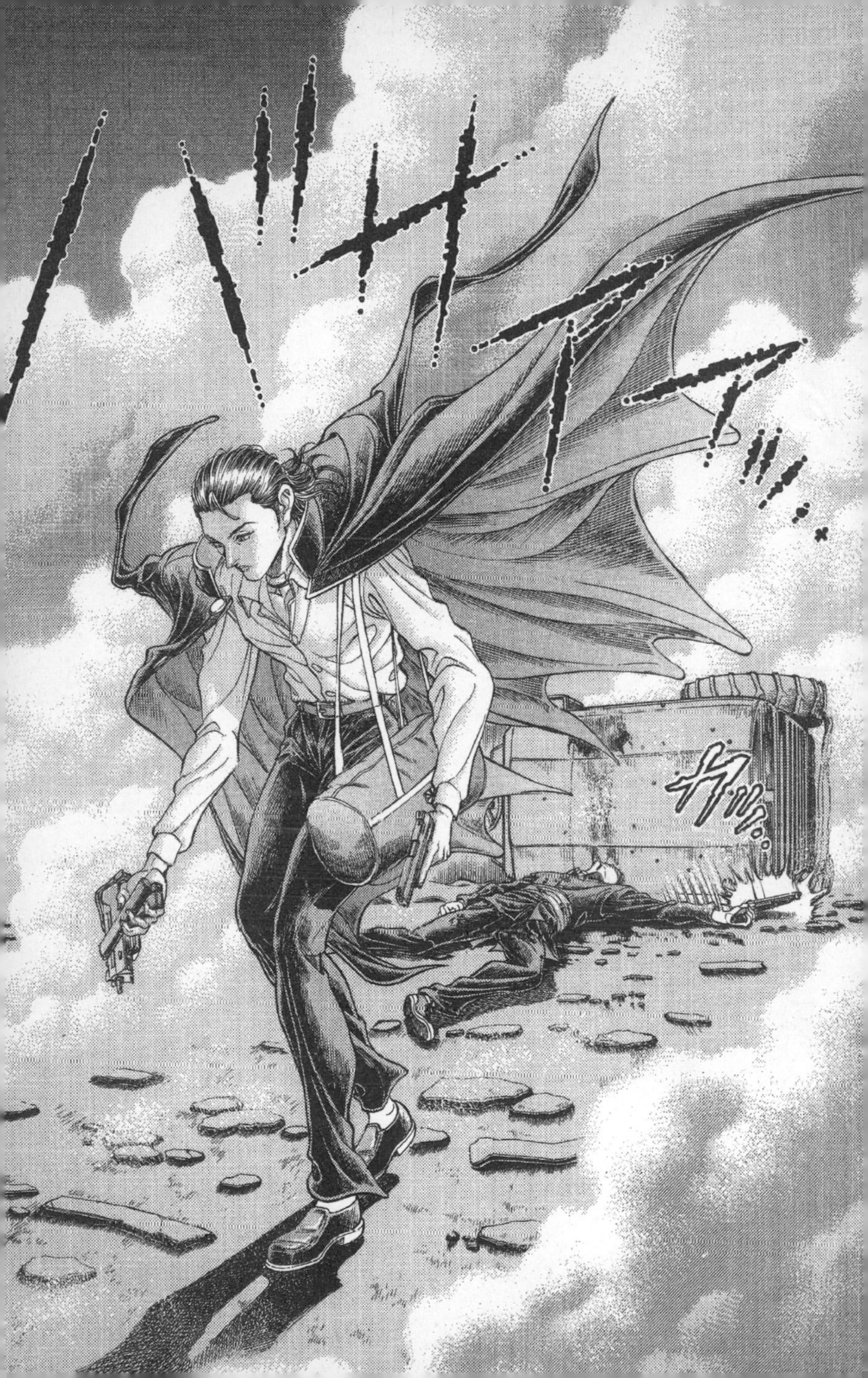

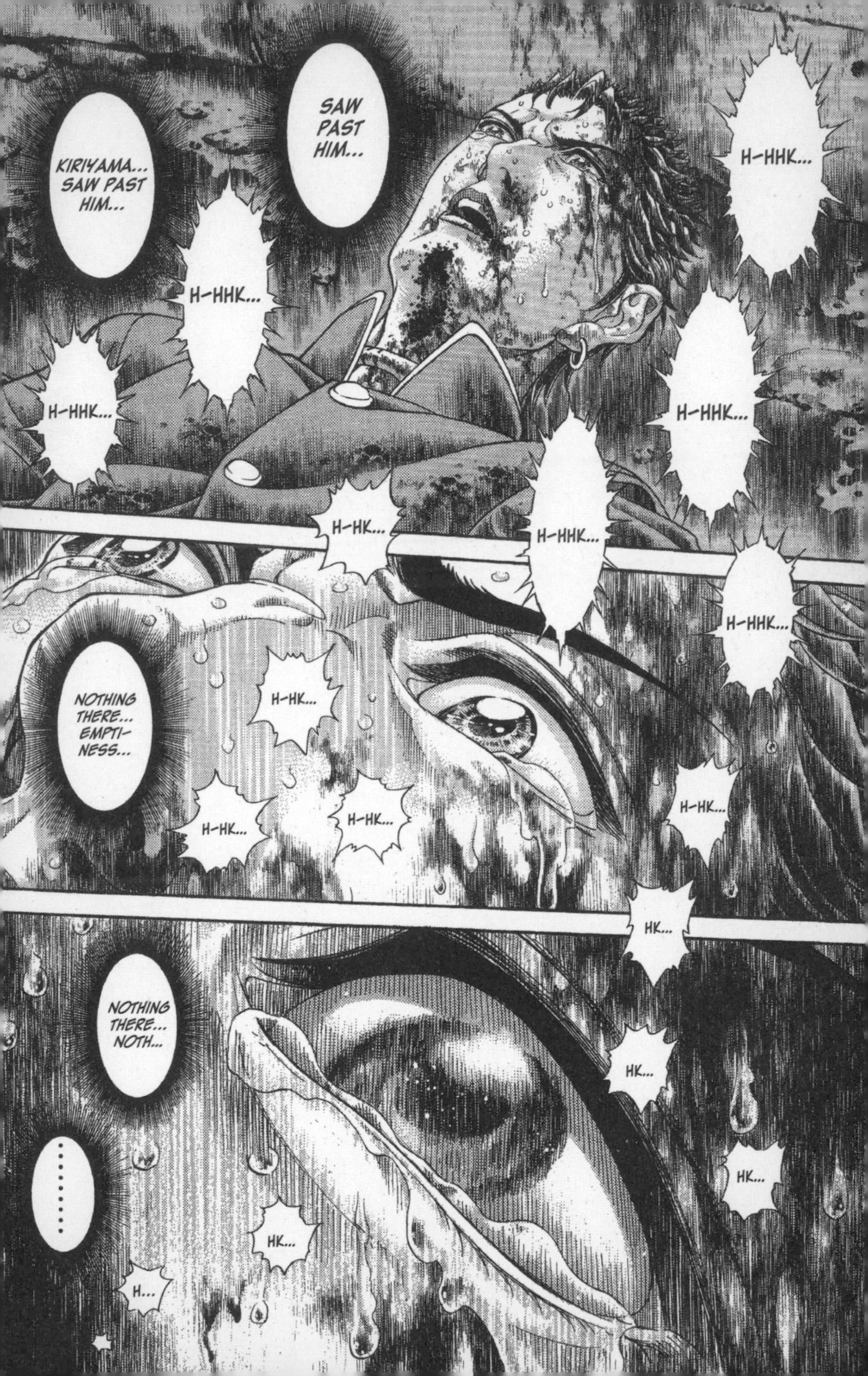
H-HHK...
SAW PAST HIM...
KIRIYAMA... SAW PAST HIM...
H-HHK...
H-HHK...
H-HHK...
H-HK...
H-HHK...
H-HHK...
H-HK...
H-HK...
NOTHING THERE... EMPTINESS...
H-HK...
H-HK...
HK...
HK...
NOTHING THERE... NOTH...
HK...
......
HK...
H...

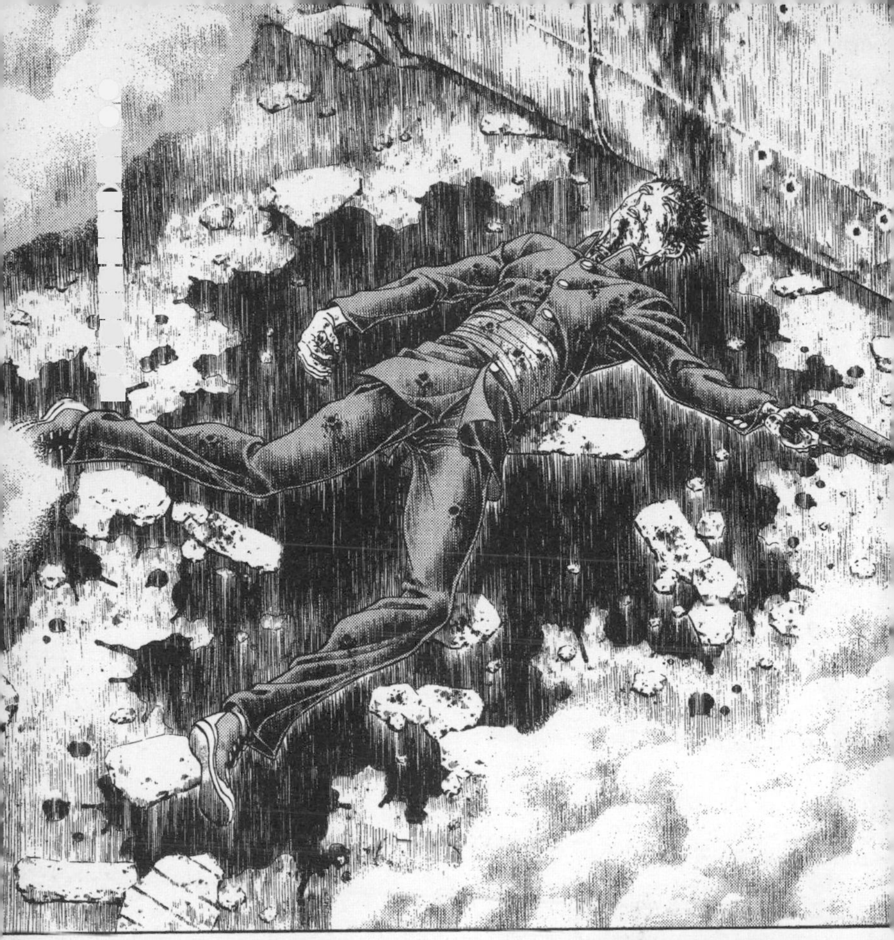
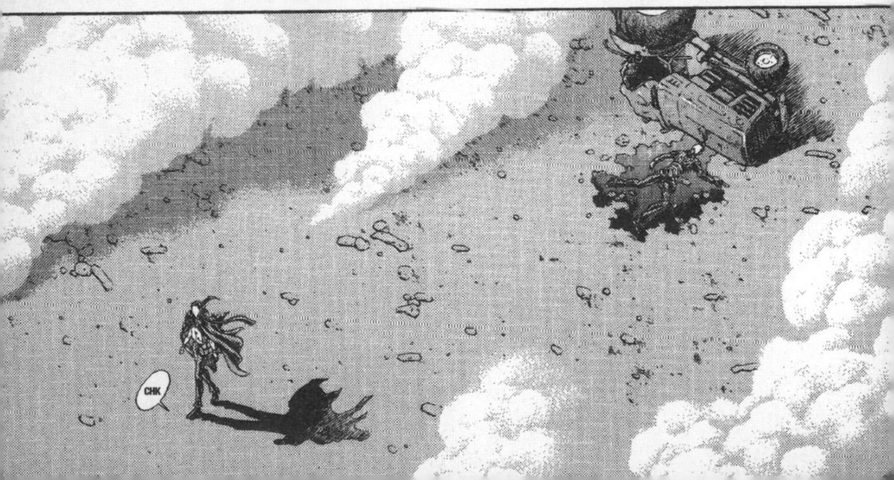
CHK

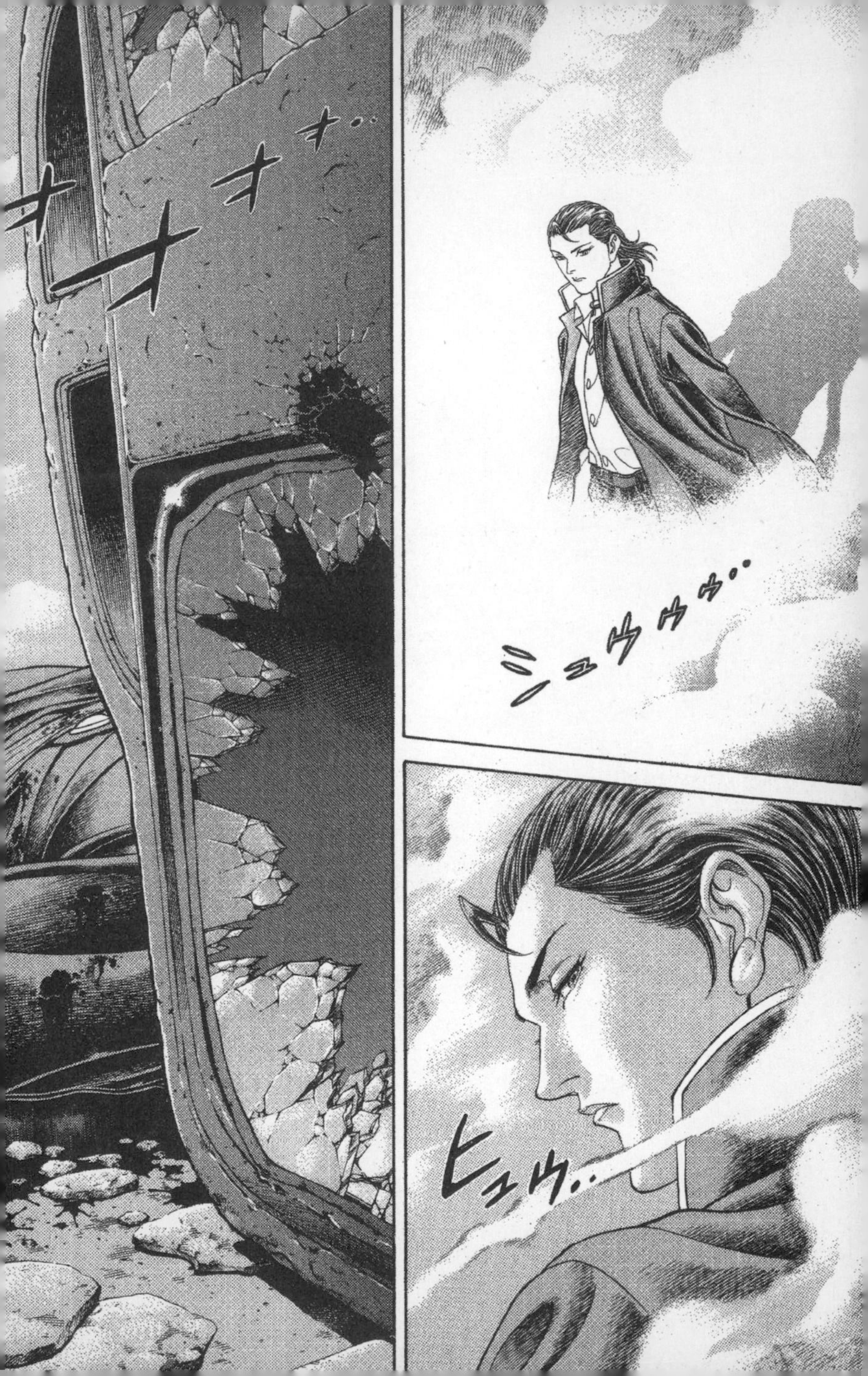

シュウウヴ..
ヒュウ..
オオオオ..

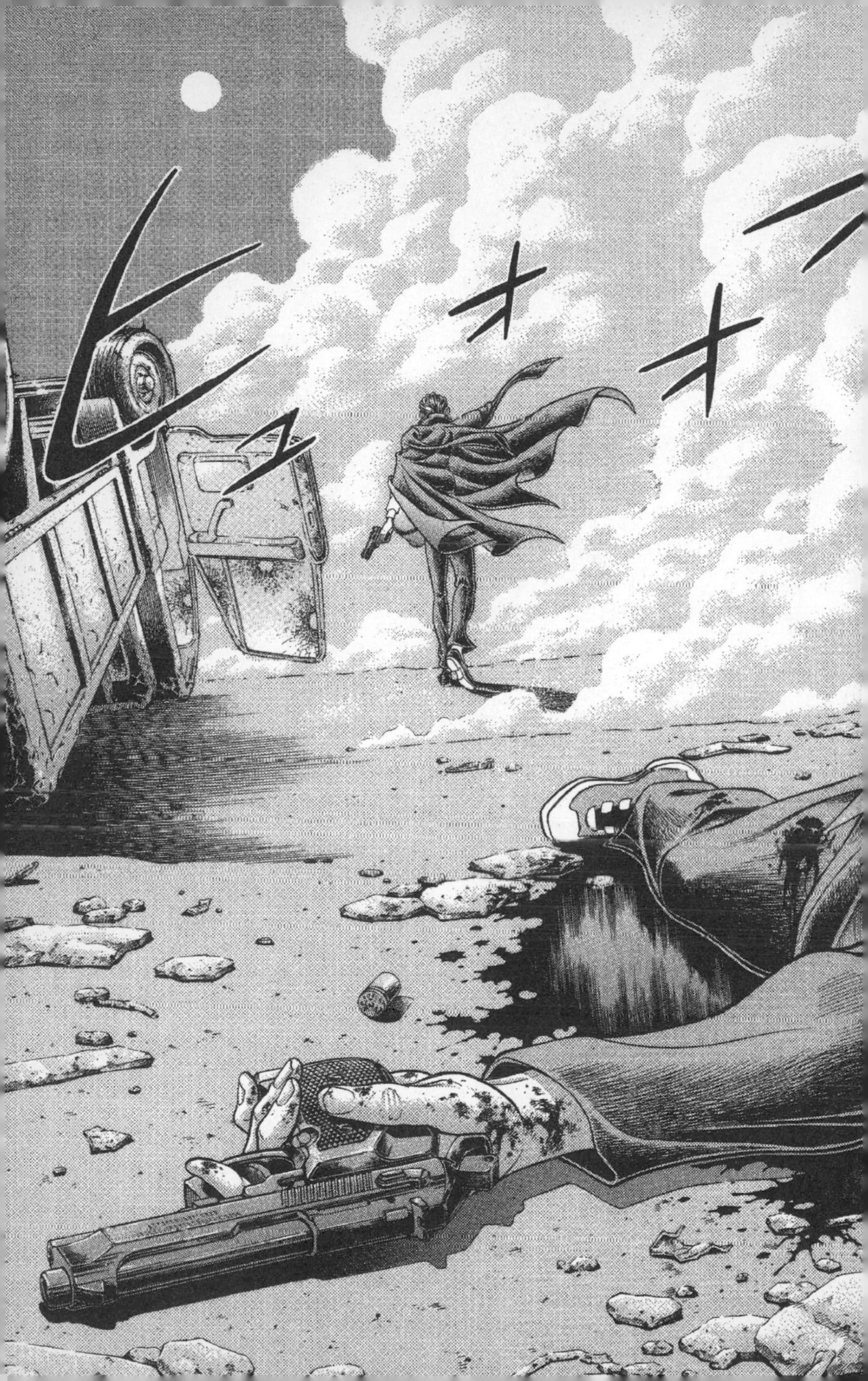
ヒュォォォ

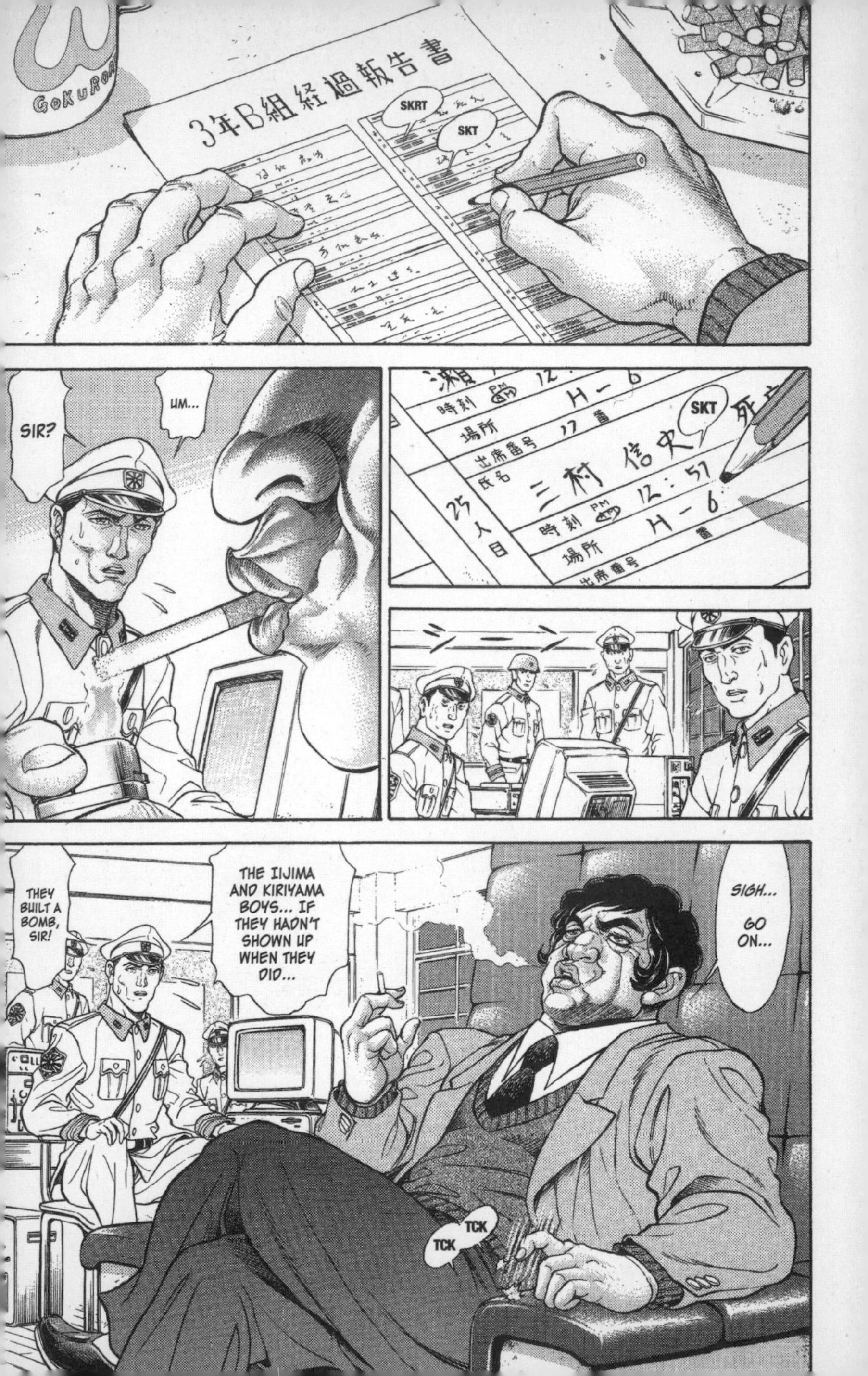
3年B組経過報告書
SKRT
SKT
SKT
時刻 PM 12:
H-6
場所
出席番号 17番
氏名 三村信史
25人目
時刻 PM 12:57
H-6
場所
出席番号
UM...
SIR?
SIGH...
GO ON...
THE IIJIMA AND KIRIYAMA BOYS... IF THEY HADN'T SHOWN UP WHEN THEY DID...
THEY BUILT A BOMB, SIR!
TCK
TCK

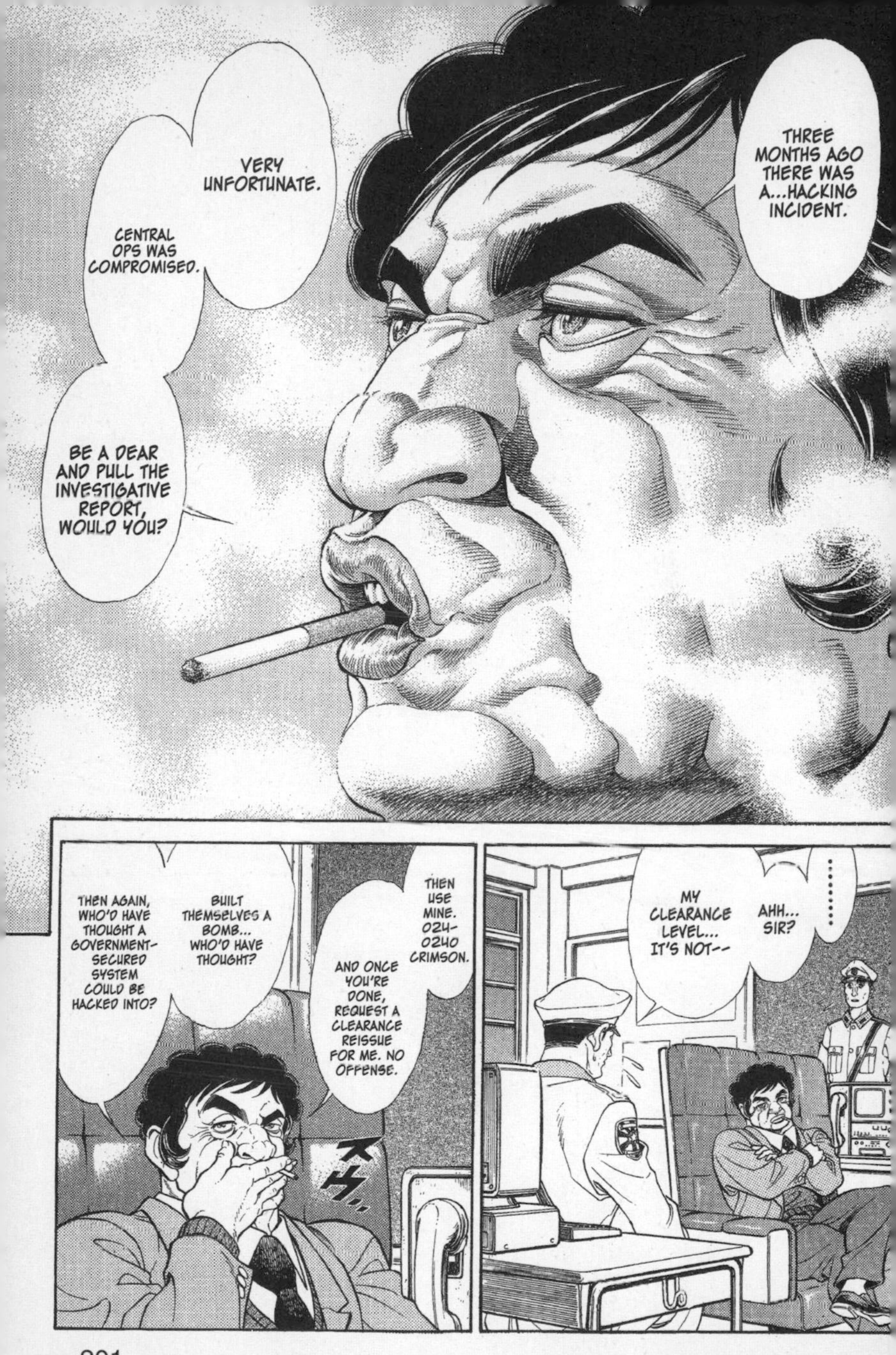
THREE MONTHS AGO THERE WAS A...HACKING INCIDENT.
VERY UNFORTUNATE.
CENTRAL OPS WAS COMPROMISED.
BE A DEAR AND PULL THE INVESTIGATIVE REPORT, WOULD YOU?
....
AHH... SIR?
MY CLEARANCE LEVEL... IT'S NOT--
THEN USE MINE. 024-0240 CRIMSON.
AND ONCE YOU'RE DONE, REQUEST A CLEARANCE REISSUE FOR ME. NO OFFENSE.
BUILT THEMSELVES A BOMB... WHO'D HAVE THOUGHT?
THEN AGAIN, WHO'D HAVE THOUGHT A GOVERNMENT-SECURED SYSTEM COULD BE HACKED INTO?
スッ..

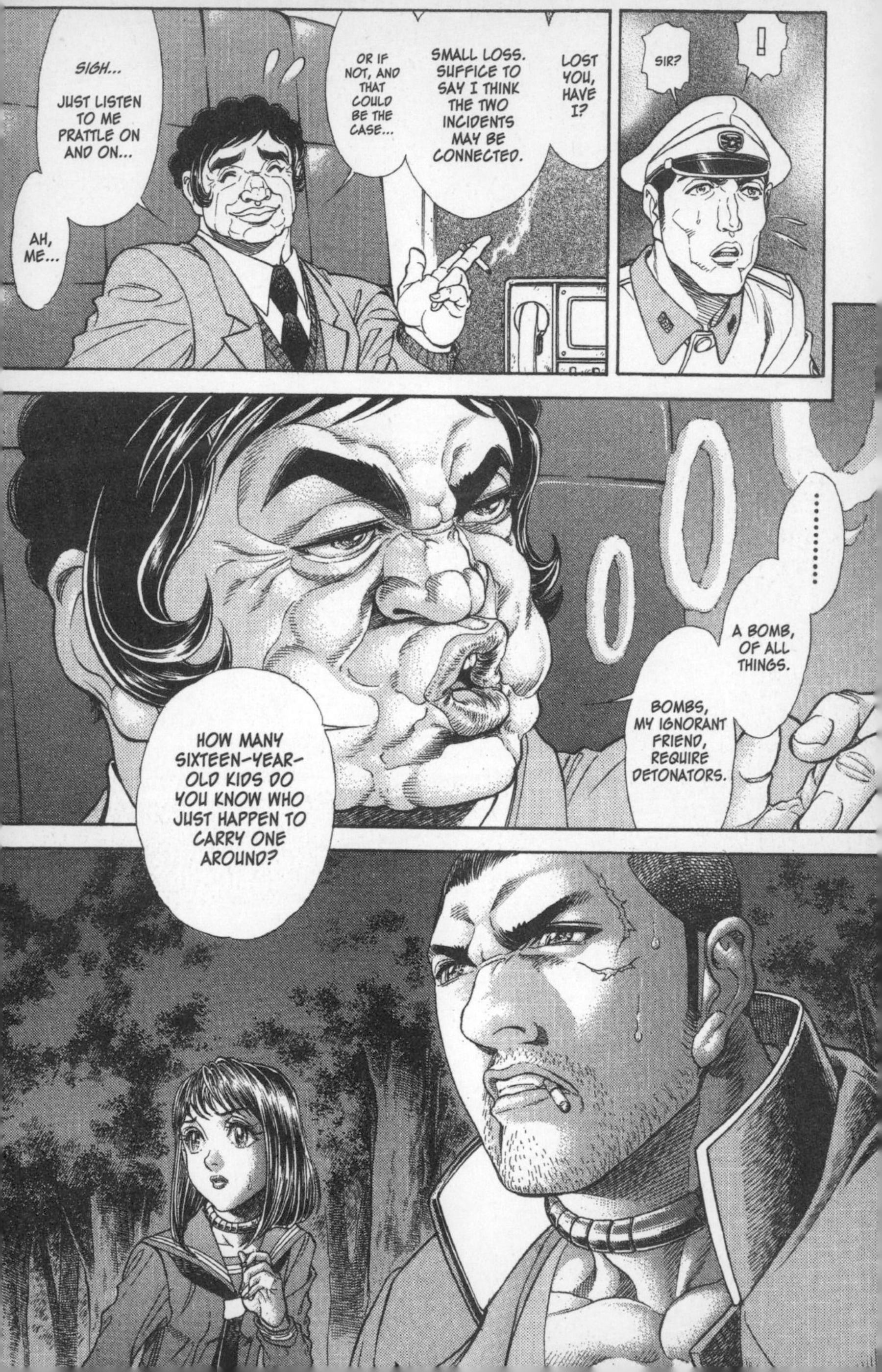
!
SIR?
LOST YOU, HAVE I?
SMALL LOSS. SUFFICE TO SAY I THINK THE TWO INCIDENTS MAY BE CONNECTED.
OR IF NOT, AND THAT COULD BE THE CASE...
SIGH... JUST LISTEN TO ME PRATTLE ON AND ON...
AH, ME...
....
A BOMB, OF ALL THINGS.
BOMBS, MY IGNORANT FRIEND, REQUIRE DETONATORS.
HOW MANY SIXTEEN-YEAR-OLD KIDS DO YOU KNOW WHO JUST HAPPEN TO CARRY ONE AROUND?

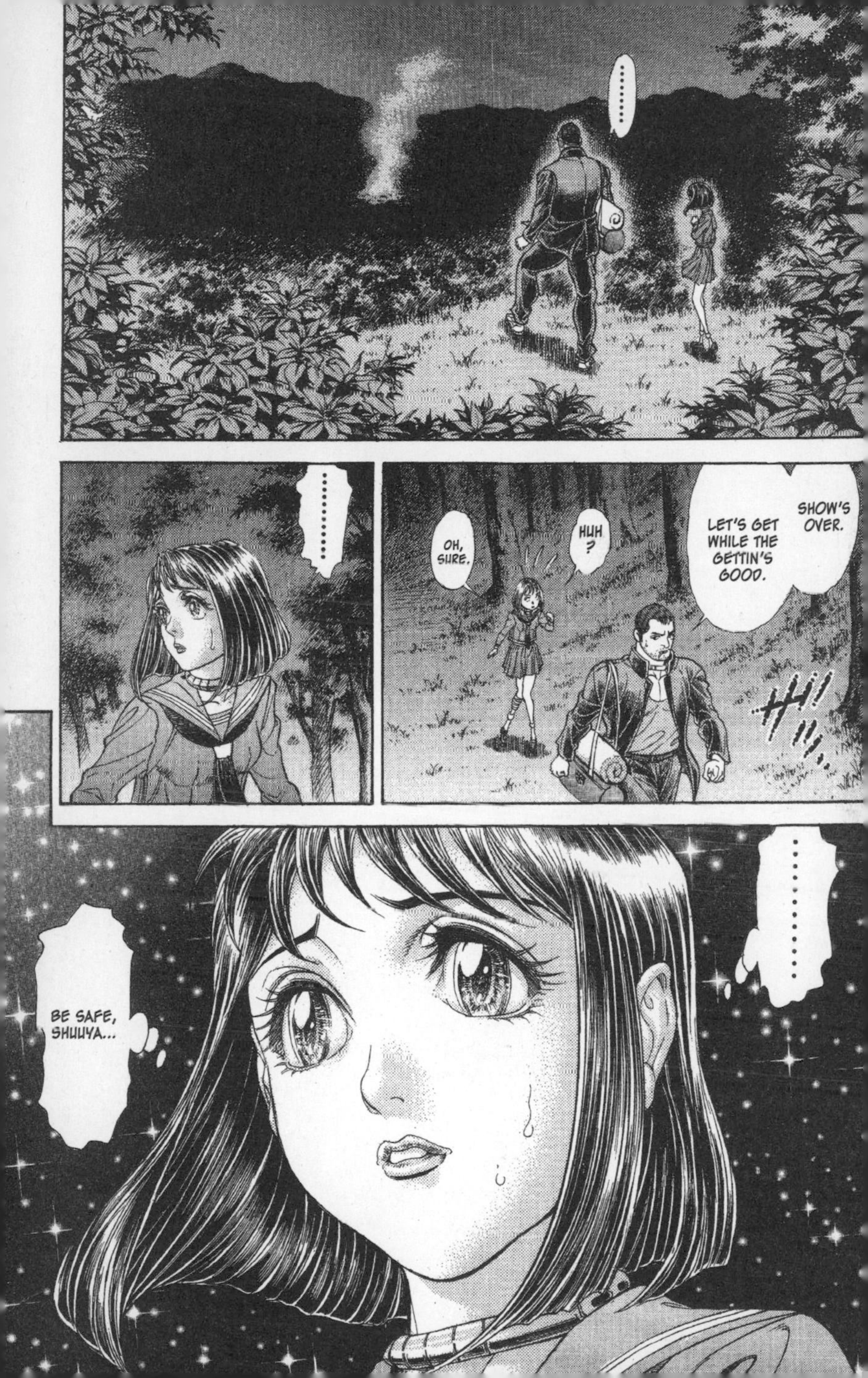
......
SHOW'S OVER.
LET'S GET WHILE THE GETTIN'S GOOD.
HUH?
OH, SURE.
......
......
BE SAFE, SHUUYA...

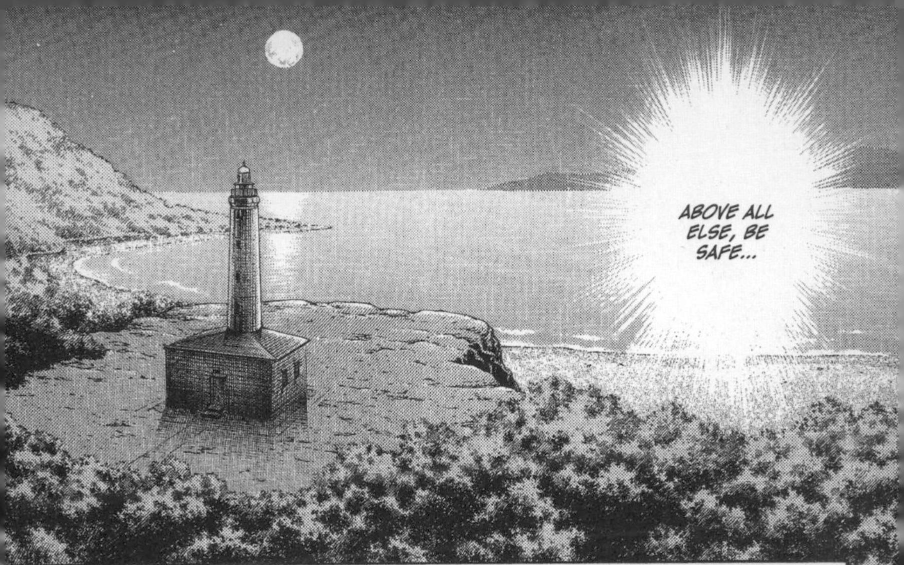
ABOVE ALL ELSE, BE SAFE...
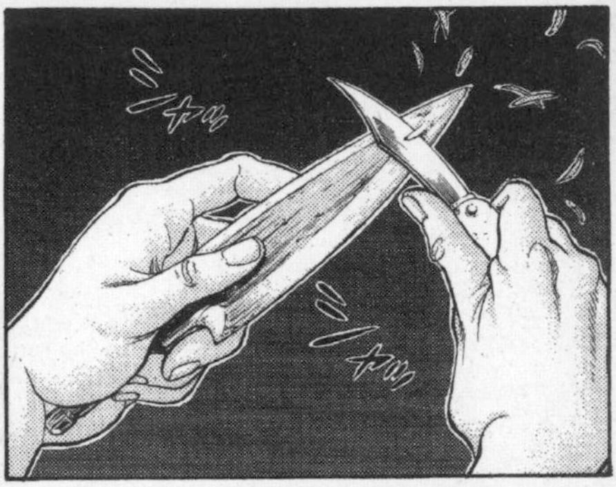
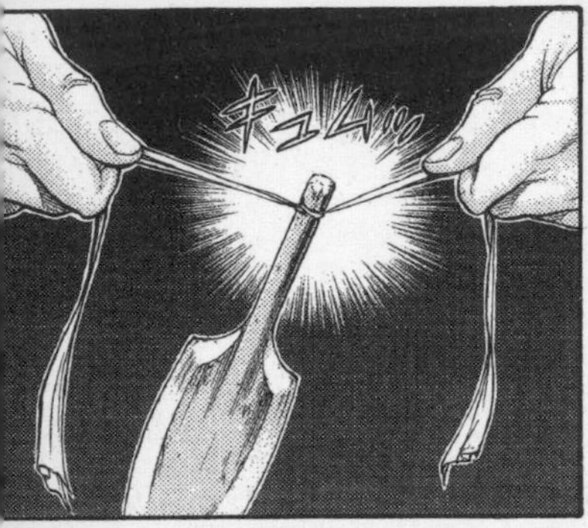
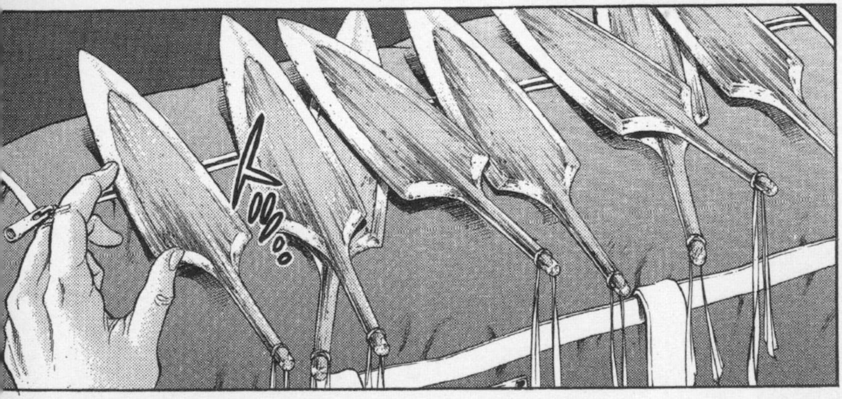

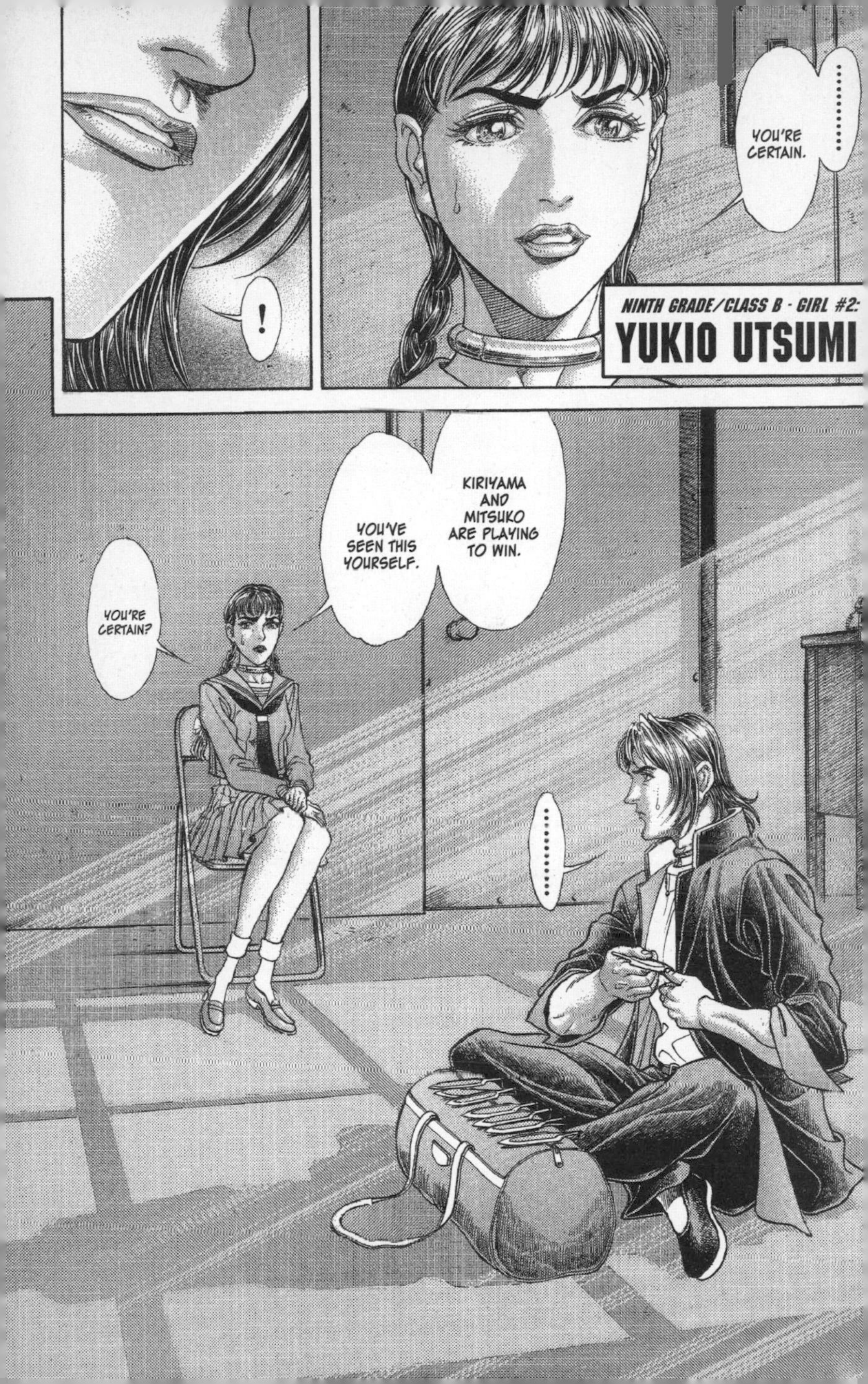
......
YOU'RE CERTAIN.
NINTH GRADE/CLASS B - GIRL #2:
YUKIO UTSUMI
!
KIRIYAMA AND MITSUKO ARE PLAYING TO WIN.
YOU'VE SEEN THIS YOURSELF.
YOU'RE CERTAIN?
......

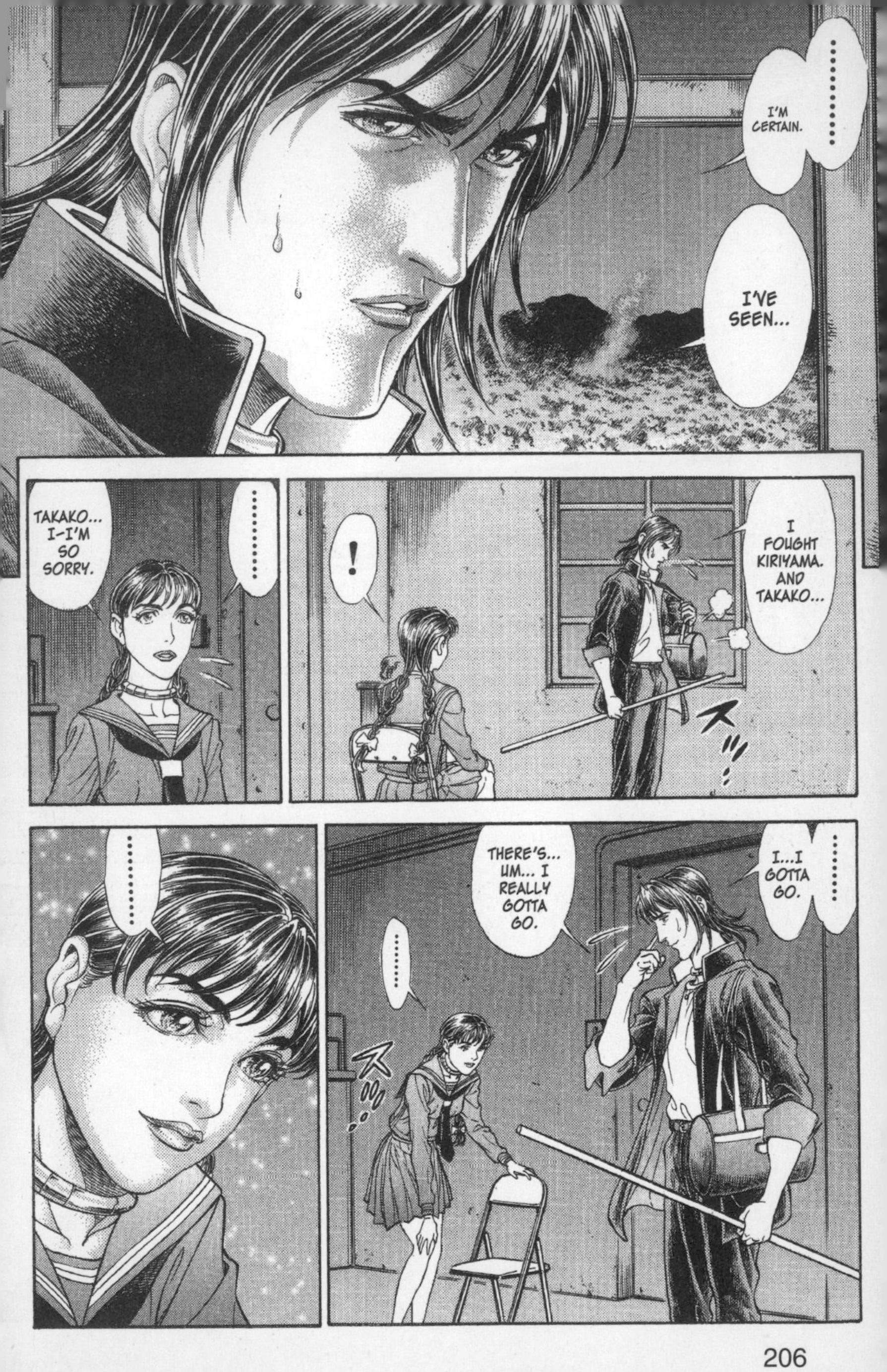
......
I'M CERTAIN.
I'VE SEEN...
I FOUGHT KIRIYAMA. AND TAKAKO...
!
......
TAKAKO... I-I'M SO SORRY.
......
I...I GOTTA GO.
THERE'S... UM... I REALLY GOTTA GO.
......
......

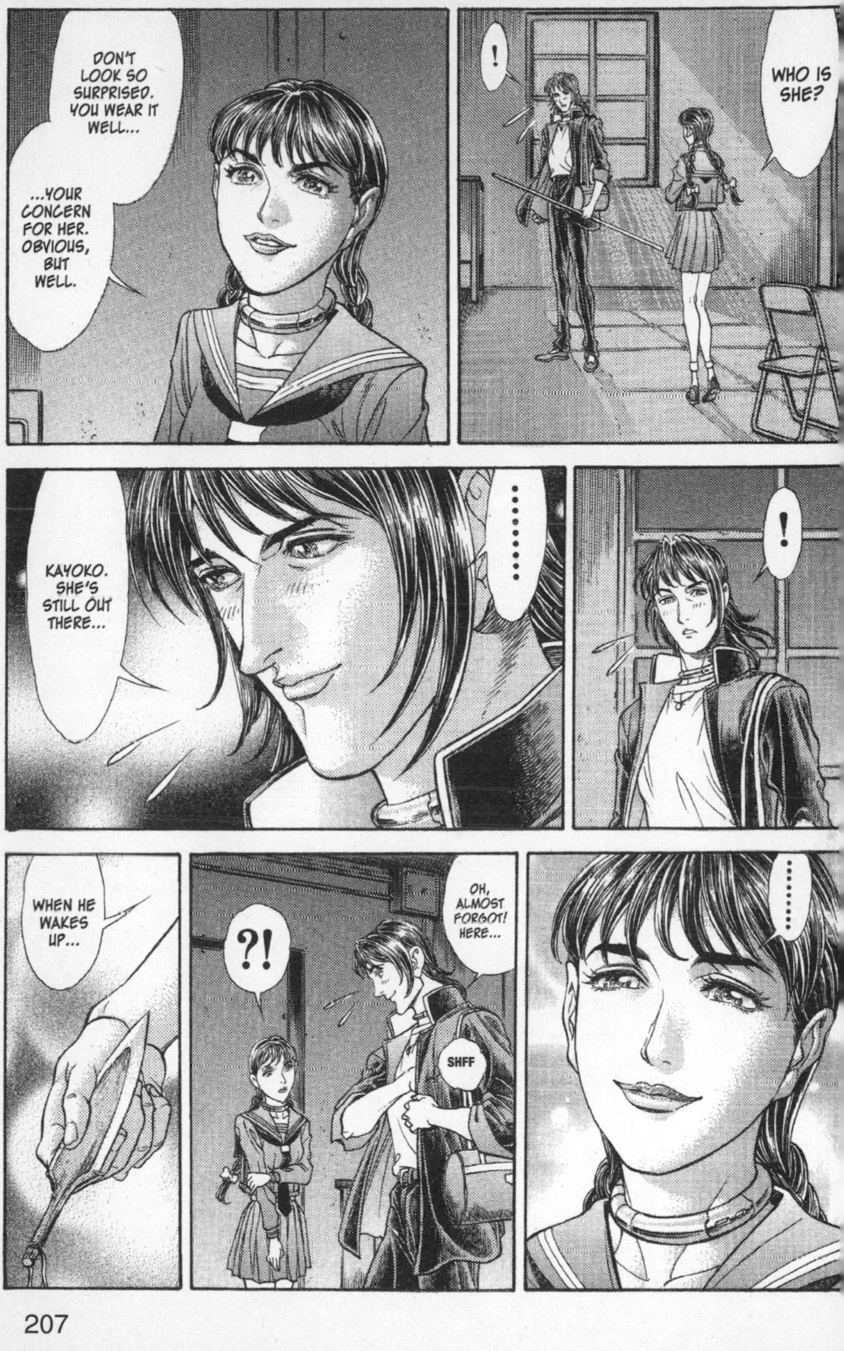
WHO IS SHE?
!
DON'T LOOK SO SURPRISED. YOU WEAR IT WELL...
...YOUR CONCERN FOR HER. OBVIOUS, BUT WELL.
!
......
KAYOKO. SHE'S STILL OUT THERE...
......
OH, ALMOST FORGOT! HERE...
?!
SHFF
WHEN HE WAKES UP...

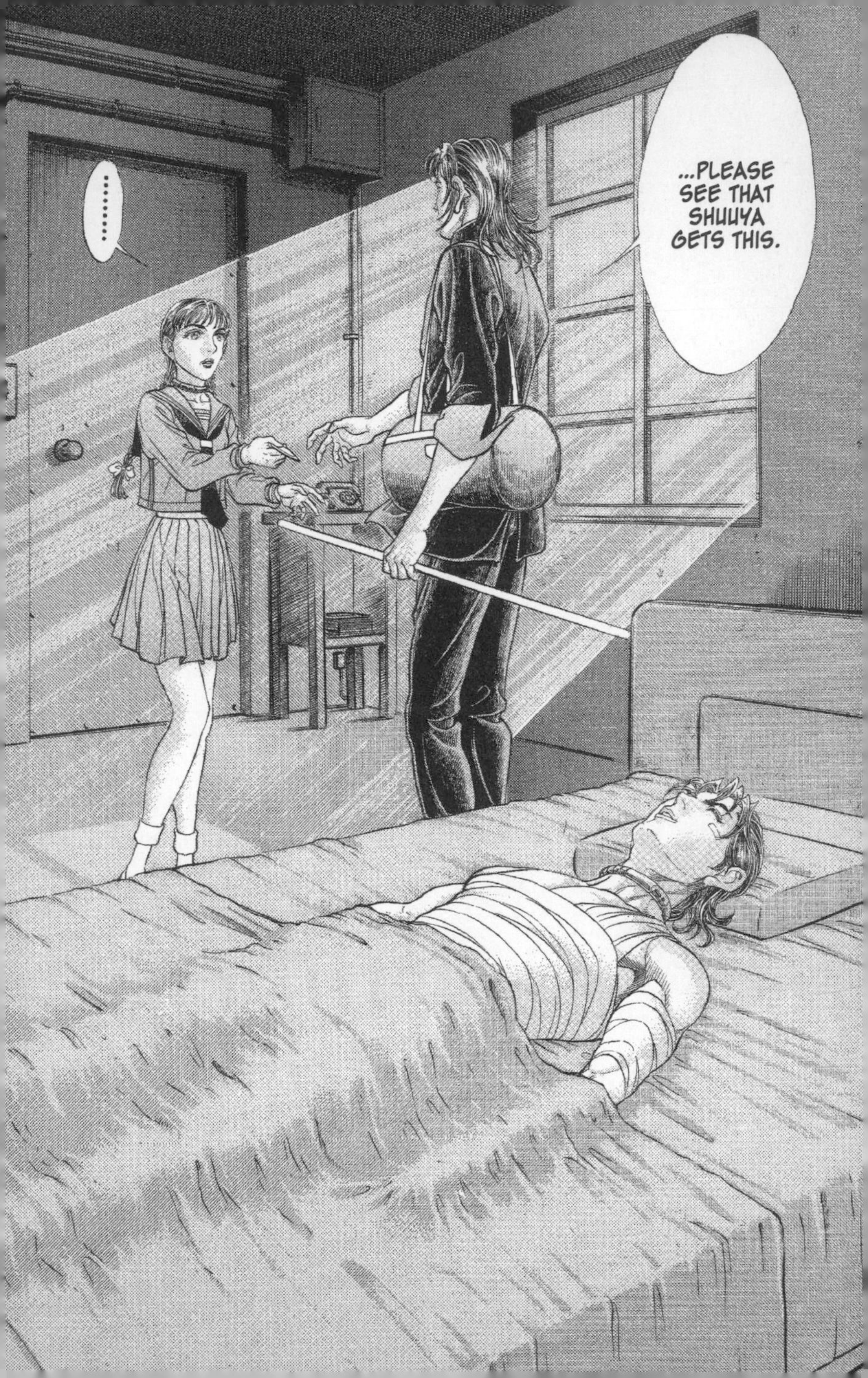
...PLEASE SEE THAT SHUUYA GETS THIS.
......

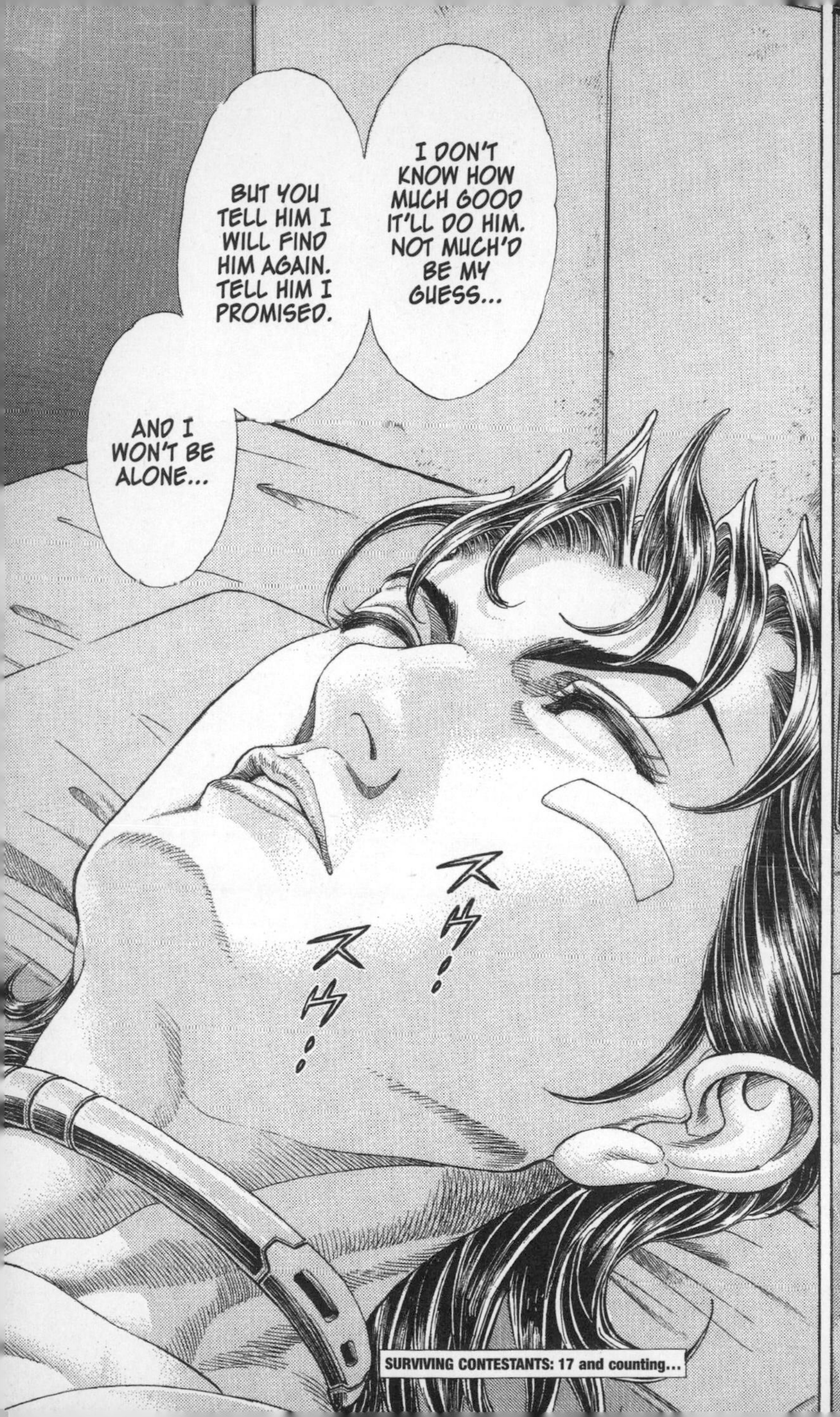
I DON'T KNOW HOW MUCH GOOD IT'LL DO HIM. NOT MUCH'D BE MY GUESS...
BUT YOU TELL HIM I WILL FIND HIM AGAIN. TELL HIM I PROMISED.
AND I WON'T BE ALONE...
スゥ...
スゥ...
SURVIVING CONTESTANTS: 17 and counting...

SHIRO IWA Junior High School - Grade 9/Class B - Student Roster

Boys: 21 - Girls: 21 - Total: 42

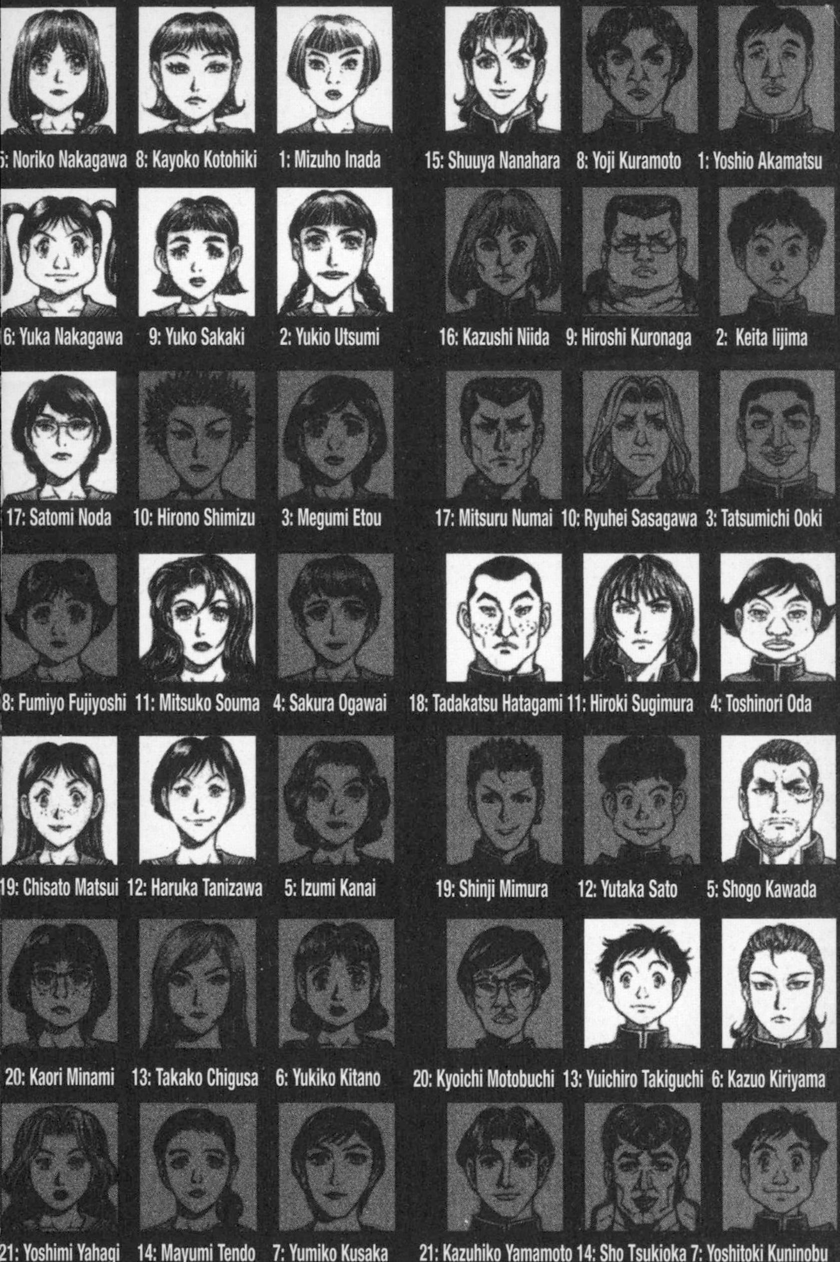
: Noriko Nakagawa
8: Kayoko Kotohiki
1: Mizuho Inada
15: Shuuya Nanahara
8: Yoji Kuramoto
1: Yoshio Akamatsu
6: Yuka Nakagawa
9: Yuko Sakaki
2: Yukio Utsumi
16: Kazushi Niida
9: Hiroshi Kuronaga
2: Keita Iijima
17: Satomi Noda
10: Hirono Shimizu
3: Megumi Etou
17: Mitsuru Numai
10: Ryuhei Sasagawa
3: Tatsumichi Ooki
8: Fumiyo Fujiyoshi
11: Mitsuko Souma
4: Sakura Ogawai
18: Tadakatsu Hatagami
11: Hiroki Sugimura
4: Toshinori Oda
19: Chisato Matsui
12: Haruka Tanizawa
5: Izumi Kanai
19: Shinji Mimura
12: Yutaka Sato
5: Shogo Kawada
20: Kaori Minami
13: Takako Chigusa
6: Yukiko Kitano
20: Kyoichi Motobuchi
13: Yuichiro Takiguchi
6: Kazuo Kiriyama
21: Yoshimi Yahagi
14: Mayumi Tendo
7: Yumiko Kusaka
21: Kazuhiko Yamamoto
14: Sho Tsukioka
7: Yoshitoki Kuninobu

BATTLE ROYALE

THE PROGRAM: UPDATE
CHAPTERS 48-55

PROGRAM CONDITIONS:
All members of the class must kill each other until one survivor remains. All students are supplied with a ration of food, a map of the island and a weapon. All students will wear an explosive bomb collar which also monitors life signs. Students are free to move about the island but must stay out of designated danger zones that will frequently change locations. If there is more than one survivor at the end of the game, the remaining bomb collars will be detonated.

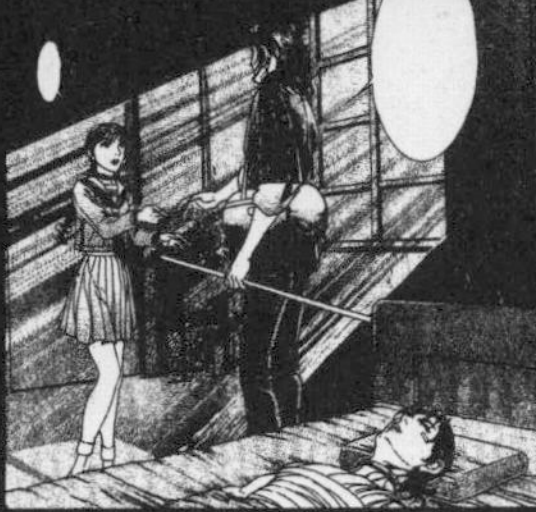

CHAPTER 55
Sugimura leaves Shuuya and the girls.

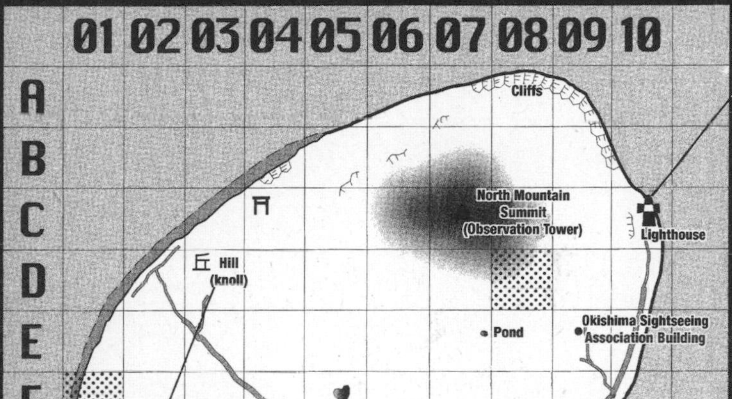

01 02 03 04 05 06 07 08 09 10
A
B
C
D
E
F
G
H
I
J
Cliffs
North Mountain Summit (Observation Tower)
Lighthouse
Hill (knoll)
Pond
Okishima Sightseeing Association Building
Pond
Clinic
School Grounds: Permanent Danger Zone
Pond
Farming Association Building
Fishing Association Building
South Mountain Summit
Hill (knoll)
Reservoir
Port
Sandy Beach
N
0
0.5
1km

CHAPTER 53
Kawada and Noriko hear Mim's bomb.

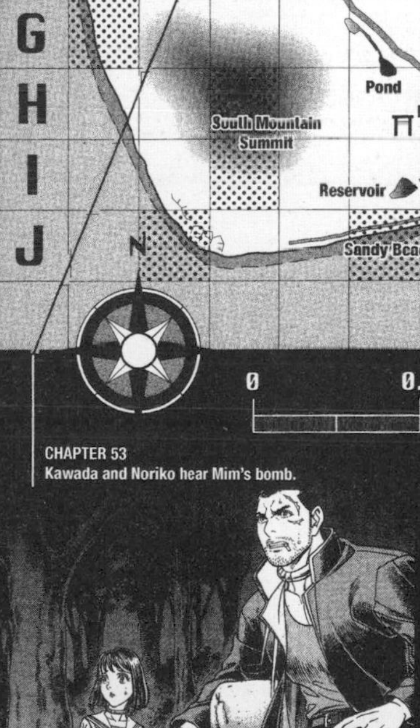

CHAPTERS 48-55
Shinji Mimura battles Kirigama.

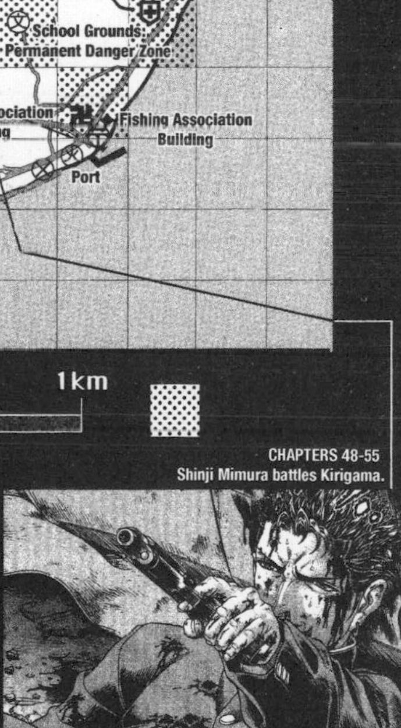

BATTLE ROYALE

KOUSHUN TAKAMI & MASAYUKI TAGUCHI

On the next exciting episode of *The Program!*

Mitsuko Souma is a sexy little siren with a mind for murder and a soul for sin. She boasts a lethal combination of cunning and curves and always makes sure her victims go out smiling. But when a twist of fate leaves her tied up and at the mercy of two of her classmates, our girl will stop at nothing to get back on top. And we mean nothing! Mitsuko's accumulated an impressive set of weapons, but the heat she packs comes from a different "set" entirely. Can our hardcore hottie handle two men at once? Or will it be Mitsuko who goes down in the big finish? One thing's for certain, it'll all end with one hell of a climax...

Close the curtains and put the kids to bed—you're in for one wild ride!

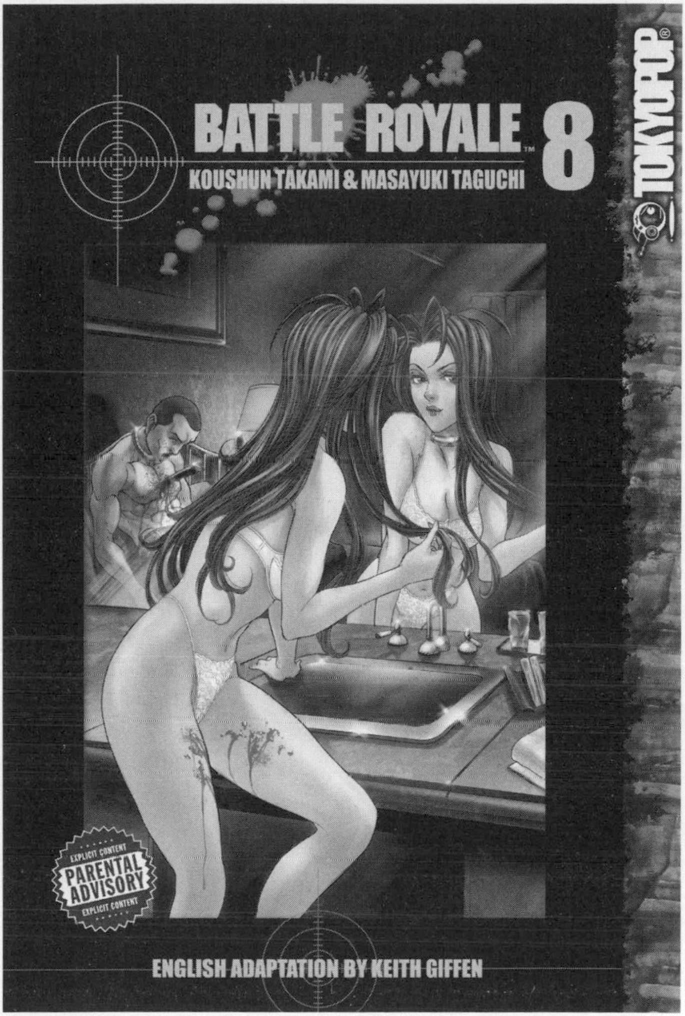
BATTLE ROYALE™ 8
KOUSHUN TAKAMI & MASAYUKI TAGUCHI
TOKYOPOP®
EXPLICIT CONTENT
PARENTAL ADVISORY
EXPLICIT CONTENT
ENGLISH ADAPTATION BY KEITH GIFFEN

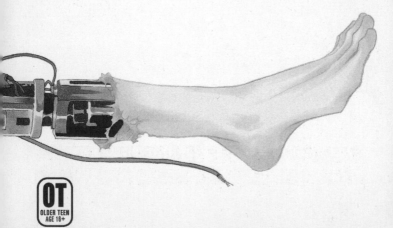

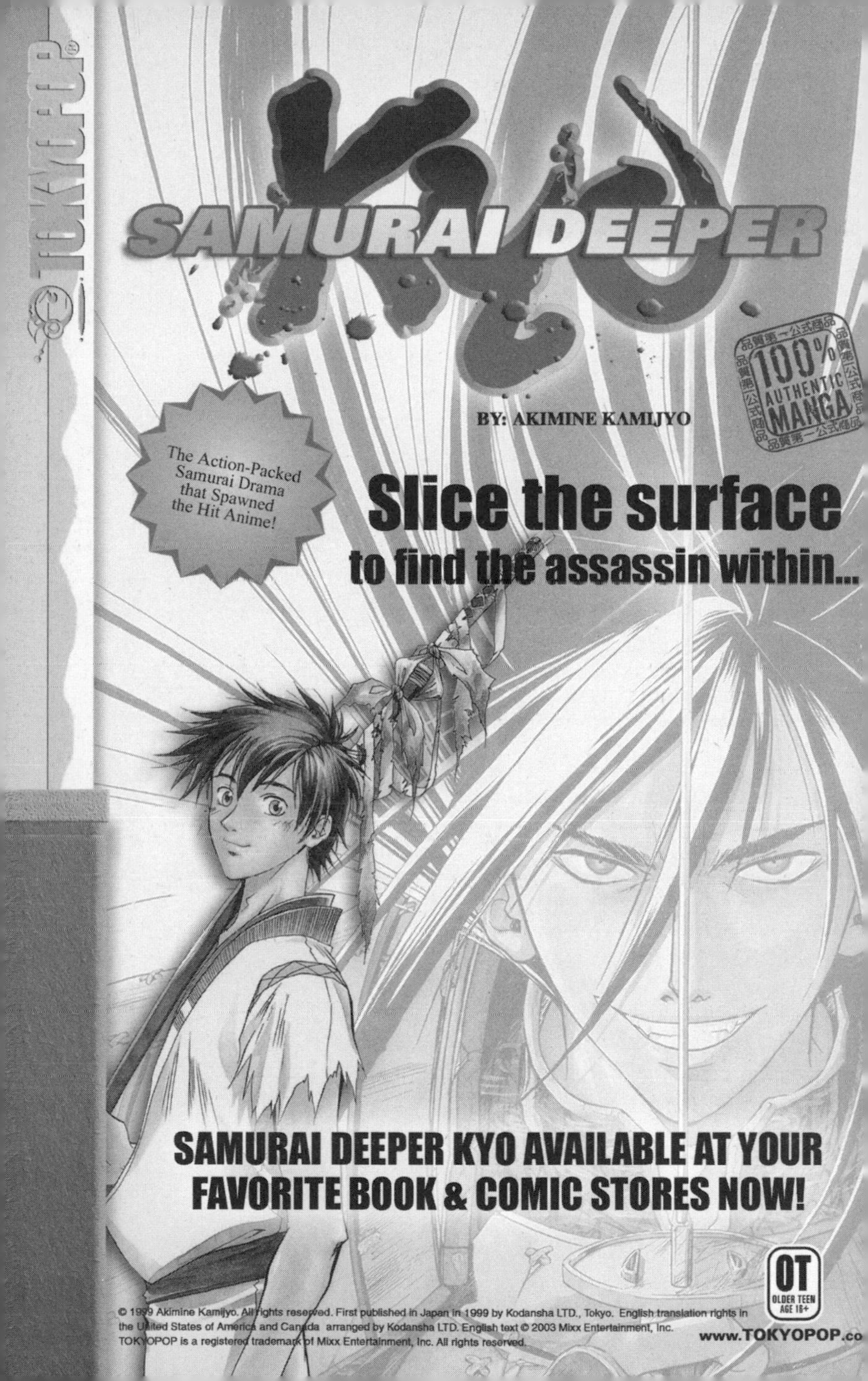
TOKYOPOP
SAMURAI DEEPER
KYO
100% AUTHENTIC MANGA
BY: AKIMINE KAMIJYO
The Action-Packed Samurai Drama that Spawned the Hit Anime!
Slice the surface
to find the assassin within...
SAMURAI DEEPER KYO AVAILABLE AT YOUR
FAVORITE BOOK & COMIC STORES NOW!
OT
OLDER TEEN AGE 16+
© 1999 Akimine Kamijyo. All rights reserved. First published in Japan in 1999 by Kodansha LTD., Tokyo. English translation rights in the United States of America and Canada arranged by Kodansha LTD. English text © 2003 Mixx Entertainment, Inc.
TOKYOPOP is a registered trademark of Mixx Entertainment, Inc. All rights reserved.
www.TOKYOPOP.co

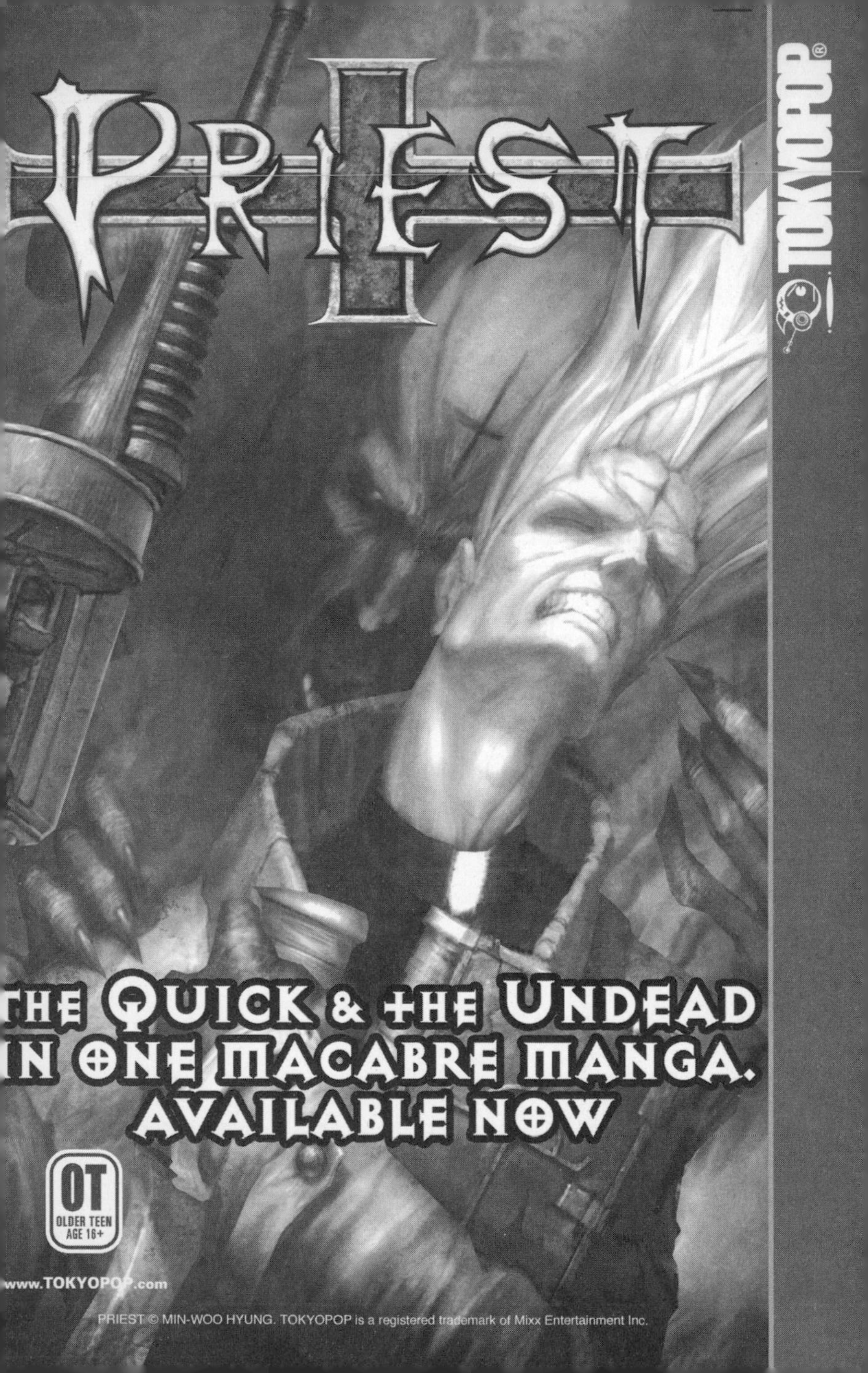
PRIEST
TOKYOPOP®
THE QUICK & THE UNDEAD
IN ONE MACABRE MANGA.
AVAILABLE NOW
OT
OLDER TEEN
AGE 16+
www.TOKYOPOP.com
PRIEST © MIN-WOO HYUNG. TOKYOPOP is a registered trademark of Mixx Entertainment Inc.

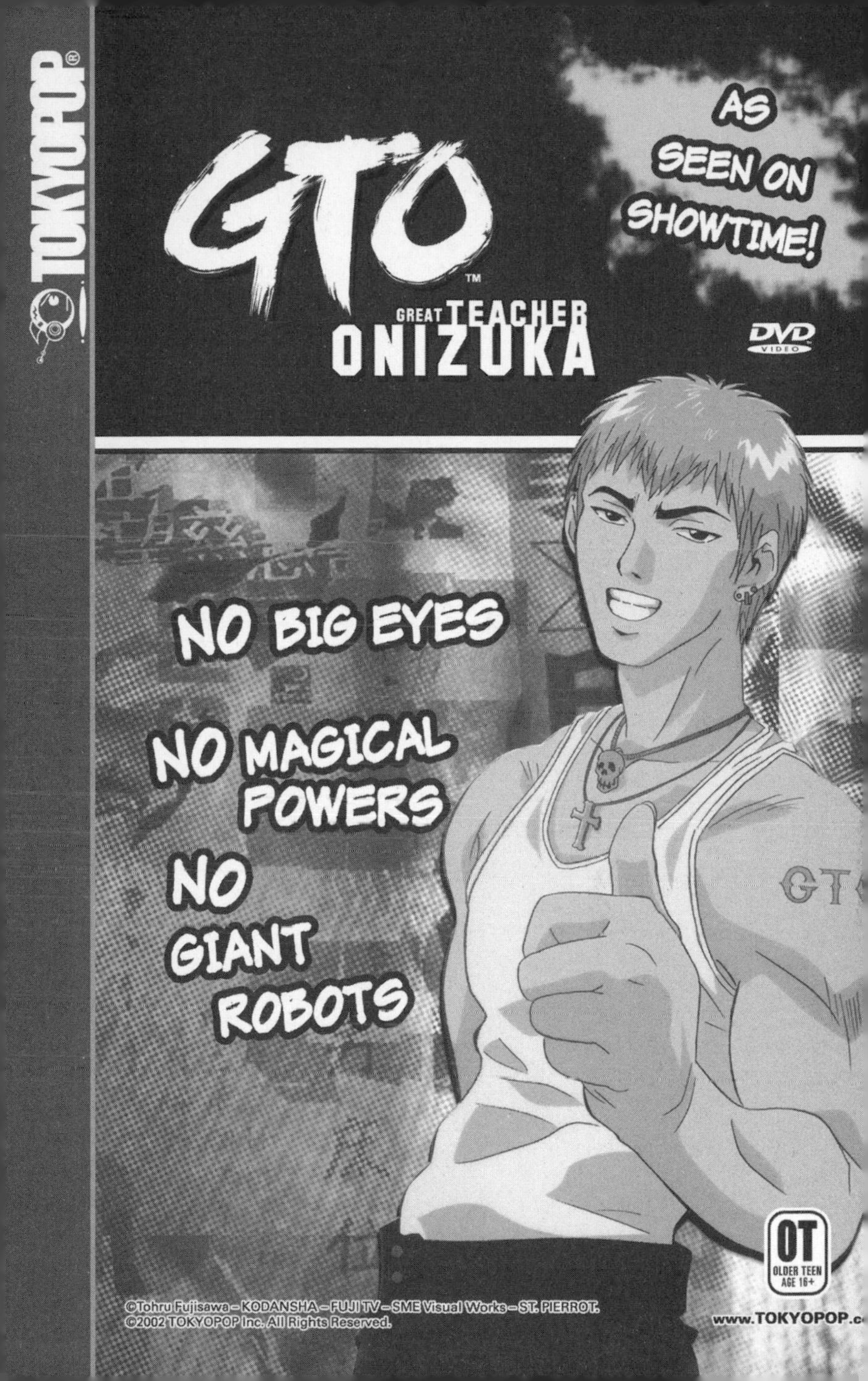
TOKYOPOP®
GTO™
GREAT TEACHER ONIZUKA
AS SEEN ON SHOWTIME!
DVD VIDEO
NO BIG EYES
NO MAGICAL POWERS
NO GIANT ROBOTS
GTO
OT OLDER TEEN AGE 16+
©Tohru Fujisawa - KODANSHA - FUJI TV - SME Visual Works - ST. PIERROT.
©2002 TOKYOPOP Inc. All Rights Reserved.
www.TOKYOPOP.c

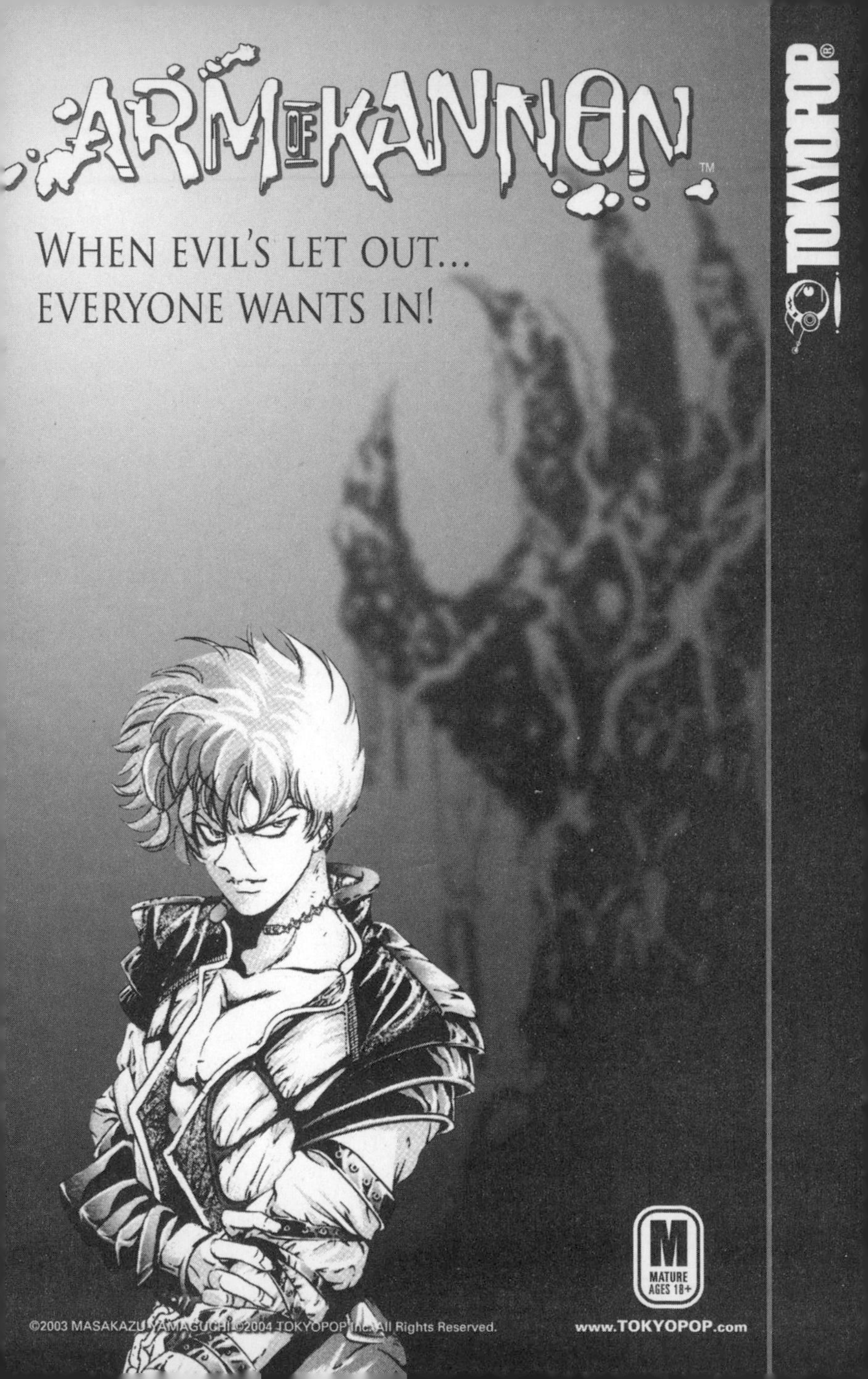
ARM OF KANNON™
WHEN EVIL'S LET OUT...
EVERYONE WANTS IN!
TOKYOPOP®
M
MATURE
AGES 18+
©2003 MASAKAZU YAMAGUCHI ©2004 TOKYOPOP Inc. All Rights Reserved.
www.TOKYOPOP.com

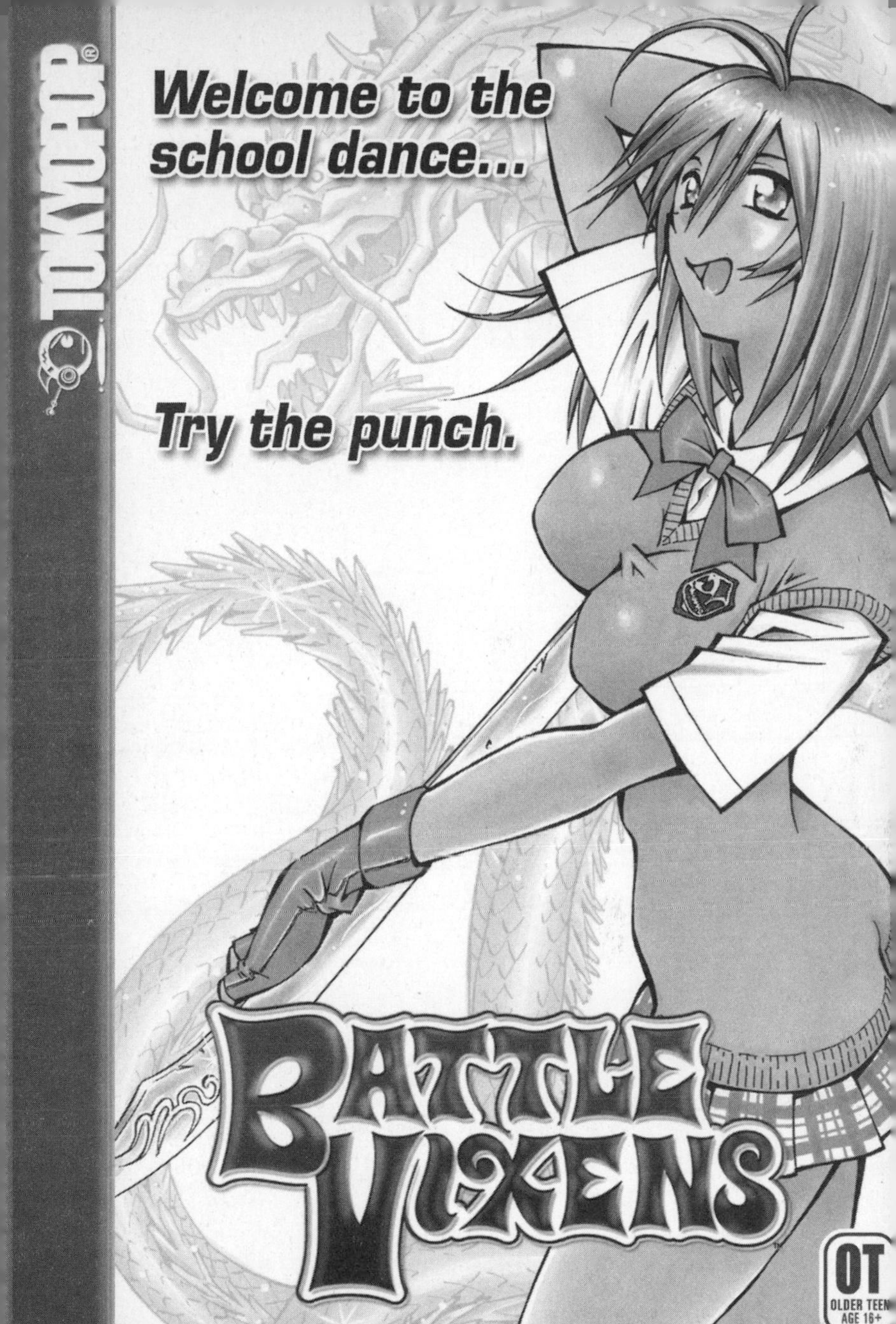
TOKYOPOP®
Welcome to the school dance...
Try the punch.
BATTLE VIXENS
OT
OLDER TEEN AGE 16+

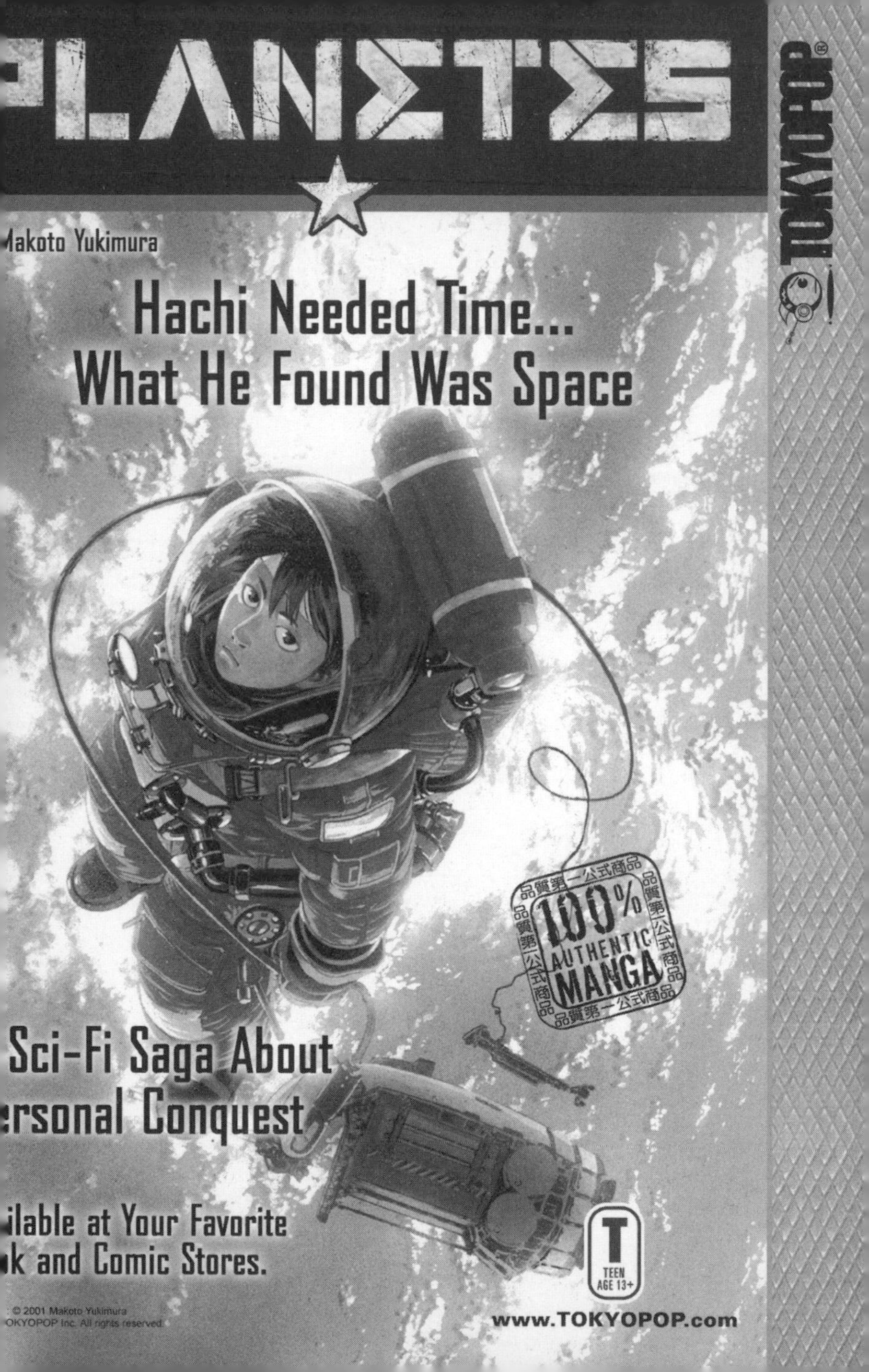
PLANETES
TOKYOPOP®
lakoto Yukimura
Hachi Needed Time...
What He Found Was Space
100% AUTHENTIC MANGA
Sci-Fi Saga About
ersonal Conquest
ilable at Your Favorite
k and Comic Stores.
T TEEN AGE 13+
© 2001 Makoto Yukimura
OKYOPOP Inc. All rights reserved.
www.TOKYOPOP.com

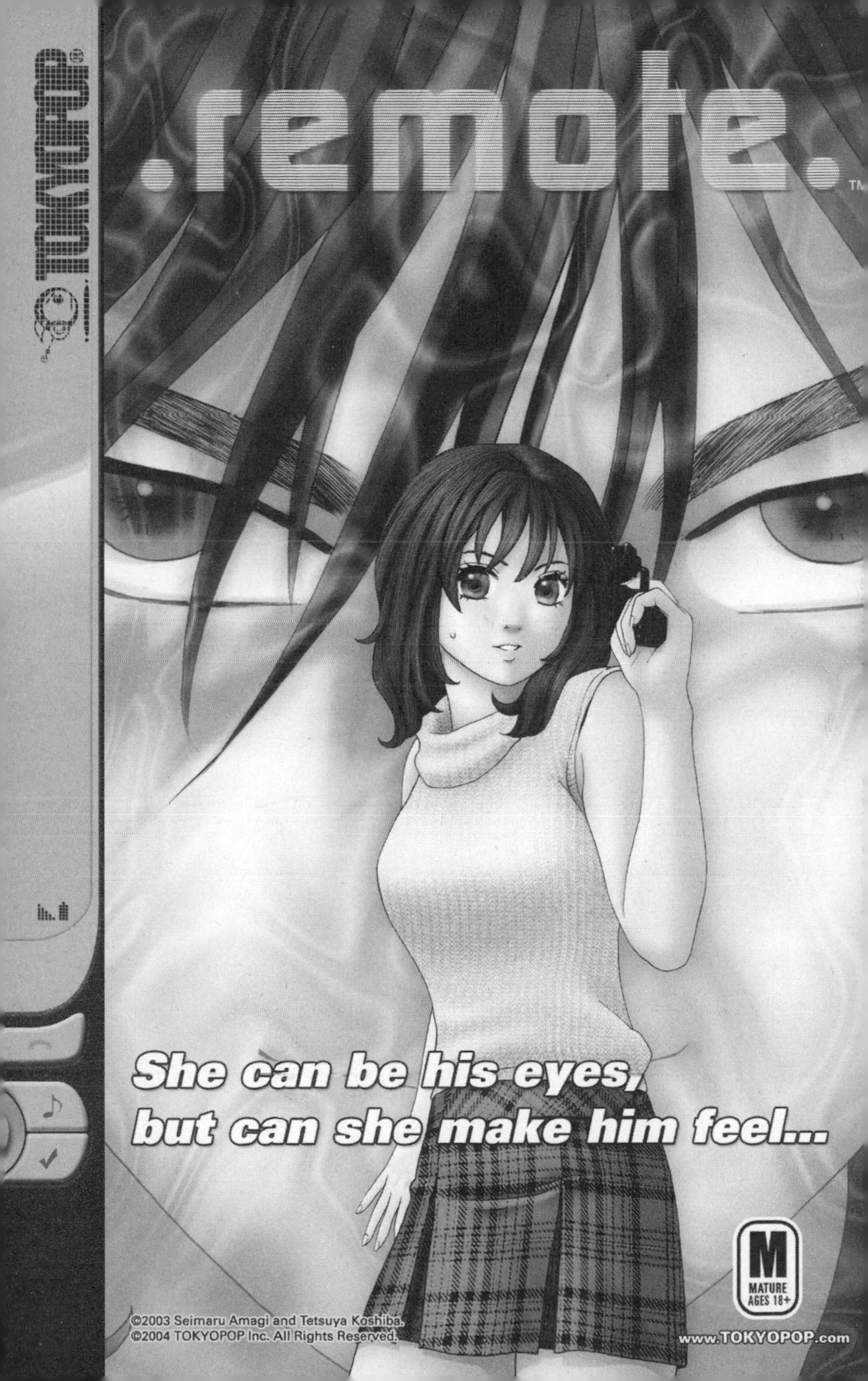
TOKYOPOP®
.remote.™
She can be his eyes,
but can she make him feel...
M
MATURE
AGES 18+
©2003 Seimaru Amagi and Tetsuya Koshiba.
©2004 TOKYOPOP Inc. All Rights Reserved.
www.TOKYOPOP.com

STOP!

This is the back of the book.
You wouldn't want to spoil a great ending!

This book is printed "manga-style," in the authentic Japanese right-to-left format. Since none of the artwork has been flipped or altered, readers get to experience the story just as the creator intended. You've been asking for it, so TOKYOPOP® delivered: authentic, hot-off-the-press, and far more fun!

DIRECTIONS

If this is your first time reading manga-style, here's a quick guide to help you understand how it works.

It's easy... just start in the top right panel and follow the numbers. Have fun, and look for more 100% authentic manga from TOKYOPOP®!